Sebastian Raedler
Kant and the Interests of Reason

Kantstudien-Ergänzungshefte

—
Im Auftrag der Kant-Gesellschaft
herausgegeben von
Manfred Baum, Bernd Dörflinger
und Heiner F. Klemme

Band 182

Sebastian Raedler

Kant and the Interests of Reason

DE GRUYTER

ISBN 978-3-11-055465-6
e-ISBN (PDF) 978-3-11-042322-8
e-ISBN (EPUB) 978-3-11-042334-1
ISSN 0340-6059

Library of Congress Cataloging-in-Publication Data
A CIP catalog record for this book has been applied for at the Library of Congress.

Bibliographic information published by the Deutsche Nationalbibliothek
The Deutsche Nationalbibliothek lists this publication in the Deutsche Nationalbibliografie; detailed bibliographic data are available on the Internet at http://dnb.dnb.de.

© 2017 Walter de Gruyter GmbH, Berlin/Boston
This volume is text- and page-identical with the hardback published in 2015.
Printing and binding: Hubert & Co. GmbH & Co. KG, Göttingen
♾ Printed on acid-free paper
Printed in Germany

www.degruyter.com

Contents

Foreword —— VII

Introduction —— 1

1 Humans as hybrids —— 6
Kant's conception of reason —— 7
Freedom and necessity —— 15
The problem of transcendental freedom —— 20
Conclusion —— 24

2 A brief exercise in transcendental idealism —— 26
The nature of necessity —— 26
The doctrine of ideas —— 36
The doctrine of practical knowledge —— 42
Conclusion —— 51

3 The moral law —— 53
What is the moral law? —— 53
Morality and the interests of reason —— 60
Conclusion —— 66

4 The fact of reason —— 68
The *Grundlegung* account —— 68
The transition to the fact of reason —— 79
The fact of reason —— 83
Conclusion —— 97

5 The will —— 101
The faculty of desire —— 101
Negative freedom —— 103
The highest maxim —— 109
The principle of self-love —— 116
Problems with Kant's theory of the will —— 121
Conclusion —— 142

6 Value —— 143
The predispositions of human nature —— 143
Kant's theory of value —— 146
Value and teleology —— 163
Conclusion —— 173

7 The highest good —— 175
The ambiguity in Kant's conception of the highest good —— 175
The juridical conception of the highest good —— 180
The maximal conception of the highest good —— 191
Conclusion —— 202

8 *Aufklärung* —— 204
The history of reason —— 204
Aufklärung —— 209
The possibility of progress —— 222
Conclusion —— 226

9 Social life —— 227
Human beings are destined for society —— 227
Entering civil society —— 236
Ethical community —— 249
The highest good as a social conception of the good life —— 254
Conclusion —— 257

10 Conclusion —— 258

Bibliography —— 261
Works by Kant —— 261
Secondary literature —— 262

Subject index —— 265

Index of names —— 274

Foreword

This is an unlikely book. Or so I have been told when I started writing it. Both friends and family members warned me that it would probably not work out: after all, I was about to start working in investment banking in London, a career not known for leaving much time for philosophical reflection. Trying to write a doctoral dissertation in practical philosophy in my free time, surely, would end in failure.

I am glad to say that it has not. Yet, in hindsight I clearly was too optimistic: when asked to map out a time line for this project, I confidently stated that it would be finished within two years. That was in 2008. Six years later, I finally submitted the completed draft. I have learnt a lot in the meantime: about Kant, about myself and about the charms and challenges of being locked into a long-term project. When I started writing this book, it was meant to contrast Kant's and Nietzsche's conception of the fulfilled human life—and my sympathies clearly lay with Nietzsche. Yet, the more I came to understand Kant's work, the more I became enthralled by its magnificent structure—and in the end Nietzsche simply dropped out of the picture. I hope this book does some justice to the unlikely beauty of Kant's thought that has kept me fascinated during the past six years.

This essay was submitted as a doctoral dissertation to the University of Cologne in Germany. I would like to thank Professor Dr. Wilfried Hinsch for supervising this project—and for his invaluable advice at crucial points during its realization. Furthermore, my thanks go to Sven Nyholm for his helpful comments on earlier drafts of the essay.

Lastly, I want to thank my mother, to whom this book is dedicated, for a lifetime of support.

London
December 2014

Introduction

The present work argues that we can only develop a proper grasp of Kant's practical philosophy if we appreciate the central role played in his thought by the notion of the interests of reason. While it is generally acknowledged that reason, for Kant, is not a purely instrumental faculty, but one endowed with its own essential interests, few commentators have attempted to explain how the notion of the interests of reason fits into Kant's overall account of the functioning of our rational faculties—and how it is linked to his wider philosophical project. The present work attempts to fill this gap.

More specifically, it will try to show that a proper understanding of Kant's conception of reason as an interested faculty allows us to make sense of the following key aspects of his practical thought, which must otherwise appear puzzling:

– *The fact of reason:* in his mature work, Kant maintains that we only have grounds for regarding ourselves as (transcendentally) free because of what he calls the "fact of reason"—that is, our awareness of being subject to the unconditional demands of morality. This makes the fact of reason the very foundation of Kant's practical philosophy. However, none of the commentators consulted in the preparation for this work offers a fully worked-out explanation of how Kant's fact-of-reason is to be understood. I argue that we can make sense of this notion if we appreciate how deeply it is rooted (and prepared for) in Kant's theoretical philosophy—and how the latter, in turn, is organized around the notion of reason's interest in achieving a systematically unified worldview. I try to show that once we trace these linkages, we can give a coherent account of Kant's fact-of-reason argument.
– *The highest good as the complete satisfaction of the interests of reason:* the highest good (the combination of virtue and happiness) is Kant's vision of the best possible state of affairs in the empirical world. Commentators have generally followed Beck in accepting the juridical conception of that notion, according to which the highest good is marked by the distribution of happiness according to virtue. Yet, if we accept the juridical conception of the highest good, Kant's claim that we have a duty to realize the highest good in the empirical world becomes all but unintelligible (for what could we possibly do to bring about the distribution of happiness according to virtue?). I will show that the juridical conception is rooted in a superseded ethical framework (the one Kant had operated with in *Kritik der Reinen Vernunft*)—and that it is inconsistent with his mature ethical theory. I argue that there are good reasons for rejecting the juridical conception in favor

of the maximal conception, according to which the highest good is the state of affairs in which the interests of reason in its practical application are completely satisfied.

In Chapter 1, we start our discussion by exploring Kant's conception of human beings as finite rational beings (that is, as hybrids composed of a physical body, on the one hand, and reason, on the other)—and his conception of reason, in particular. Kant conceives of reason as self-reflective and spontaneous thought, guided by its own essential interests. The most important of these is the interest in imposing systematic unity on our knowledge (in its theoretical application) and our actions (in its practical application). That is, reason, for Kant, is not a merely instrumental faculty (serving as a tool to satisfy whatever independent interests we have)—but is rather guided by its need to integrate every aspect of our life into a systematically unified whole.

The challenge for Kant at this point is to show how regarding our reason as guided by its own interests (and, hence, as spontaneous) is consistent with his conception of the world of our experience as governed by natural necessity. This question takes its most pressing form in the context of the practical use of reason. To put the issue in Kant's own terms: we have to explain how can we conceive of ourselves as transcendentally free—i.e. as able to be first causes of our actions—in spite of the fact that our actions are determined with necessity by the laws of nature.

Our discussion in Chapters 2 and 3 prepares the ground for Kant's answer to this question, which will be discussed in Chapter 4. Chapter 2 highlights three results of Kant's theoretical investigations that will prove crucial in our attempt to understand his solution to the problem of transcendental freedom: a) his account of the nature of necessity, according to which the necessity we encounter in the world of our experience is imposed by our own epistemic apparatus; b) his doctrine of ideas, according to which the correct use of reason involves the use of concepts to which nothing in the world of our experience corresponds—but which is nonetheless required to satisfy the interests of reason; and c) what I will call Kant's *doctrine of practical knowledge*. This last doctrine—which, I argue, is one of the central (if unobvious) results of Kant's major theoretical work, *Kritik der Reinen Vernunft*—states that if the truth-value of a given judgment (such as the one regarding our own transcendental freedom) cannot be settled on the basis of theoretical fact and if, furthermore, the truth of this judgment is linked to the essential interests of our practical reason, then we are entitled to accept the judgment as objectively true, in spite of the fact that we have no theoretical basis for doing so.

Chapter 3 explores Kant's notion of the moral law. The only way to account for the necessity with which the moral law commands, Kant holds, is to understand it as valid *a priori*, i.e. as the product of our pure practical reason. Thus, if we were to accept that the moral law is valid for us (a point to be established in Chapter 4), doing so would commit us to attributing a noumenal (and, hence, transcendentally free) will to ourselves. Such a noumenal will would, Kant argues, be free from the influence of any sensuous interest—and would, consequently, be necessarily guided by the interests of reason. We can thus understand the demands of the moral law, which present themselves as duties to our sensuously affected wills, as expressing the willing of our idealized pure wills—or, equivalently, as expressing the conditions under which the interests of our reason in its practical application would be fully satisfied.

On the basis of these preparatory discussions, Chapter 4 offers a reconstruction of Kant's fact-of-reason argument as his solution to the problem of transcendental freedom. Kant takes it as an uncontroversial aspect of our common moral experience that, when deciding on how to act, we find ourselves confronted with unconditional moral demands. (In fact, many moral skeptics do not dispute that we experience these demands—but rather that we have reason to take them seriously). Our reason's interest in systematic unity demands that all our experiences both as cognizers and as agents in the world be integrated into a systematically unified view of the world. Given that there is no theoretical fact of the matter as to whether the moral law is valid for us, the necessary practical interest we take in the moral law (i.e. the fact that we are confronted by its unconditional demand) entitles (and requires) us—given Kant's doctrine of practical knowledge —to ascribe objective validity to the moral law. Yet, the only way to account for the possibility of an unconditionally binding demand on us, Kant holds, is to regard it as the product of our own noumenal wills. Thus, to be able to integrate our experience of being subject to an unconditional moral demand, we have to attribute to ourselves noumenal existence as transcendentally free wills. That is, Kant argues, we are entitled (and required) to assume both the objective validity of the moral law and the objective reality of our own transcendental freedom.

With the objective reality of our free will thus established, Chapter 5 discusses Kant's theory of the will—and, in particular, his account of how our will can be guided by both our sensuous interests and the interests of our reason. In this context, I highlight the need to distinguish between the different determining grounds of the will (the incentive, the subjective determining ground and the objective determining ground)—as well as the different Kantian notions of freedom (transcendental freedom, negative freedom, moral freedom and external freedom). Furthermore, I argue that there are good grounds for rejecting the claim that, according to Kant's theory of the will, the moral value of our actions depends on our first-order maxims (*pace* Frierson) and that we cannot know our first-order maxims (*pace* Wood and O'Neill).

Chapter 6 focuses on Kant's theory of value. I argue that Kant's conceives of the objective good as that which satisfies the interests of reason. This focus on the interests of reason as the core of Kant's theory of value allows us to understand why for Kant our personality (i.e. our status as beings with transcendentally free wills) rather than our humanity (i.e. our ability to set ends for ourselves) is the ground for regarding ourselves as ends in ourselves (*pace* Korsgaard, Wood and Guyer) and as the final end of creation (i.e. that for the purpose of which the whole of the natural world exists). Furthermore, while most commentators accept Kant's claim that the good will is the only thing that has unconditional value, I argue that this assertion is misleading, given that his theory of value commits him to regarding our personality and the highest good as having unconditional value as well.

This discussion, in turn, prepares the ground for the argument in Chapter 7 that Kant's conception of the "highest good" (i.e. the best possible state of the empirical world) should be understood as combining the highest moral perfection with the greatest happiness (rather than as involving the distribution of happiness according to virtue, as Beck suggests). To make sense of Kant's contention that happiness forms part of the highest good, I argue, we have to understand it as consisting of the realization of our subjective ends (rather than the satisfaction of our desires, as suggested by Allison and Yovel). Lastly, I highlight how accepting the maximal conception of the highest good fatally undermines Kant's attempt to offer a moral proof for the objective reality of God.

The final two chapters are concerned with filling out the details of Kant's conception of the highest good. Chapter 8 discusses Kant's conception of enlightenment (*Aufklärung*) as the process by which we become increasingly aware of, and capable of acting in line with, the requirements for the proper use of both our technical-practical reason (i.e. our ability to realize our ends) and our moral-practical reason (i.e. our ability to choose good ends), thus coming closer to realizing the highest good in the empirical world. Introducing the notion of enlightenment allows us to make the important distinction between the two conceptions of the good human life Kant is operating with: on the one hand, the highest good as the ideal condition of the complete satisfaction of the interests of reason—and, on the other, our actual existence spent in the attempt to realize this ideal condition, overcoming the weakness of our imperfect wills and the temptation posed by our sensuous nature.

Lastly, Chapter 9 discusses how, for Kant, the realization of the highest good is possible only as the result of a collective effort. Kant holds that we require social interaction for the development of our talents (and, in particular, the correct use of our rational faculties), that we have to enter into a society governed by shared external laws to be able to make secure and effective use of our technical-practical reason in the pursuit of our ends and that satisfying our reason's interest in the systematic unity among the wills of all rational beings requires that we determine our wills on the basis of shared moral principles. As a consequence, we should understand Kant's notion of the highest good as offering an essentially social conception of the good human life.

1 Humans as hybrids

> "Zweifaches ich. Sofern ich leidend oder tätig bin, tierisch oder menschlich." [R 278, XV, 105]

The central structural element in Kant's anthropology is the hybrid character of human nature: on the one hand, man is part of physical nature, governed by natural necessity—on the other, he is endowed with reason, and thus in a position to regard himself as free. Much of Kant's practical philosophy is a meditation on the interaction between these two elements of human nature:

> Wir bemerken daher auch im Menschen zweierlei ganz verschiedenartige Teile, nämlich auf der einen Seite Sinnlichkeit und Verstand und auf der andern Vernunft und freien Willen, die sich sehr wesentlich von einander unterscheiden... Der Mensch muss für zwei ganz verschiedene Welten bestimmt sein, einmal für das Reich der Sinne und des Verstandes, also für diese Erdenwelt: dann aber auch noch für eine andere Welt, die wir nicht kennen, für ein Reich der Sitten. [SF, VII, 70; see also: MS, VI, 418; MAM, VIII, 116n][1]

For Kant, humans are physical beings, living as part of the empirical world, in which everything is perfectly determined by natural necessity [KrV, III, 374]. Every event in this world is caused by a previous state of affairs in combination with the laws of nature—and is, in turn, the cause of other events that follow in time. Everything that happens in the empirical world is part of an indefinite causal chain beyond anyone's control[2]. To be part of this world is to be passive: even living beings are only so many billiard balls made to move by external stimuli. When an animal leaps, snaps, or squeals, it does so because of certain de-

---

[1] "In Kantian terms, the rational and the non-rational differ not in degree or in form, but in kind; they are not two stages along a single scale, but two heterogeneous and mutually exclusive principles" [Yovel, 1989, 281]. The divide between reason and sensuous nature maps neatly onto a series of further key distinctions—active versus passive, formal versus material, objective versus idiosyncratic and noble versus base—which we will explore in the following chapters.

[2] "[J]ede Begebenheit, folglich auch jede Handlung, die in einem Zeitpunkte vorgeht, unter der Bedingung dessen, was in der vorhergehenden Zeit war, [ist] notwendig ... Da nun die vergangene Zeit nicht mehr in meiner Gewalt ist, so muss jede Handlung, die ich ausübe, durch bestimmende Gründe, die nicht in meiner Gewalt sind, notwendig sein, d. i. ich bin in dem Zeitpunkte, darin ich handle, niemals frei. Denn in jedem Zeitpunkte stehe ich doch immer unter der Notwendigkeit, durch das zum Handeln bestimmt zu sein, was nicht in meiner Gewalt ist, und die a parte priori unendliche Reihe der Begebenheiten, die ich immer nur nach einer schon vorherbestimmten Ordnung fortsetzen, nirgend von selbst anfangen würde, wäre eine stetige Naturkette, meine Kausalität also niemals Freiheit" [KpV, V, 94–5].

sires or feelings, reliably triggered by the physical conditions it finds itself in. Man is just such an animal, endowed with a physical body and subject to desires and urges. Like any other animal, he is a natural being whose actions are perfectly determined by natural necessity:

> Wenn wir alle Erscheinungen seiner Willkür bis auf den Grund erforschen könnten, so würde es keine einzige menschliche Handlung geben, die wir nicht mit Gewissheit vorhersagen und aus ihren vorhergehenden Bedingungen als notwendig erkennen könnten. In Ansehung dieses empirischen Charakters gibt es also keine Freiheit, und nach diesem können wir doch allein den Menschen betrachten, wenn wir lediglich beobachten und, wie es in der Anthropologie geschieht, von seinen Handlungen die bewegenden Ursachen physiologisch erforschen wollen. [KrV, III, 372]

Kant's conception of reason

Yet, human beings are different from other animals in that they are endowed with reason ("[Der Mensch ist ein] mit Vernunftfähigkeit begabtes Tier (*animal rationabile*)" [A, VII, 321; see also: KrV, IV, 452])[3]. To understand Kant's notion of reason we have to spend a moment to understand his conception of human thought more generally. First, human thought is *self-reflective*. Kant holds that, as rational beings, we are self-conscious—that is, in thinking and judging we experience ourselves as thinking and judging [KrV, III, 108; see also: A, VII, 127][4]. This self-consciousness distinguishes us from all other living beings: "Dass der Mensch in seiner Vorstellung das Ich haben kann, erhebt ihn unendlich über alle andere auf Erden lebende Wesen" [A, VII, 127].

---

3 As Kemp Smith points out, Kant's uses the term "reason" in different ways [2003, 2]. The two most important uses for our purposes are what I will call the narrow and the broad meaning of "reason". In the narrow sense, reason is contrasted with the understanding. The understanding is that aspect of our thought concerned with cognition of the external world, while reason is concerned with guiding our understanding in a way that makes the most complete use of the understanding possible [KrV, III, 427]. In the broad use of the term, reason refers to the entirety of our self-reflective thought, comprising both the understanding and reason in the narrow sense. In the following, "reason" will typically refer to reason in the narrow sense, unless otherwise specified.

4 "We cannot conceive or represent to ourselves an x as F without not only doing it, that is, consciously taking it as such, but without also in some sense 'knowing what one is doing'. This peculiar mode of cognitive self-awareness is what Kant terms 'apperception'. As such, it is not another thing that one does when one judges (a kind of second-order knowing that one is knowing); it is rather an inseparable component of the first-order activity itself" [Allison, 1990, 37].

Secondly, human thought is *spontaneous*. As rational beings we have to regard ourselves as free—both in our theoretical activity (i.e., in making judgments about what is the case in the world) and in our practical activity (i.e. in determining our actions). That is, we attribute to ourselves both freedom of judgment and of action (Kant calls the latter *transcendental freedom*, a term we will discuss in more detail below)—i.e. we do not see either our thinking or our actions as subject to deterministic forces. This is particularly obvious when it comes to our freedom of judgment. For the very notion of thinking to be coherent we have to regard our thought as self-guided, i.e. as not determined by natural necessity: "[Die] Idee der Freiheit als eines Vermögens absoluter Spontaneität [ist] nicht ein Bedürfnis, sondern, was deren Möglichkeit betrifft, ein analytischer Grundsatz der reinen spekulativen Vernunft" [KpV, V, 48][5].

To say that freedom is an analytic principle of reason is to say that we cannot reject it without this leading to contradiction. Thus, if we regarded our thought as unfree—as determined by external factors –, we would have lost all ground on which to ascribe truth to any of our judgments (including that regarding the unfreedom of our own thought). As Henrich puts it: "[D]ie Annahme der Urteilsfreiheit ist unvermeidbar, weil es ohne sie kein Denken gibt" [1975, 72; see also: Allison, 1996, 133]. Certainly, we cannot *prove* that our thought is not determined by natural forces. Yet, if we are to think at all, we have to do so under the assumption of our own freedom of judgment. As self-aware beings seeing themselves as required to ascribe freedom to their own thought, we regard our beliefs and our actions not as foisted onto us by external factors. Rather, we see ourselves as having the ability to reflect on them and decide, on reflection, whether to accept or reject them[6].

---

5 See Reflektion 4220: "Freiheit ist eigentlich nur die Selbsttätigkeit, deren man sich bewusst ist. Wenn man sich etwas beifallen lässt, so ist dieses ein Akt der Selbsttätigkeit, aber man ist sich hierbei nicht seiner Tätigkeit, sondern der Wirkung bewusst. Der Ausdruck: ich denke (dieses Objekt), zeigt schon an, dass ich in Ansehung der Vorstellung nicht leidend bin, dass sie mir zuzuschreiben sei, dass von mir selbst das Gegenteil abhänge" [XVII, 463; see also: SF, VII, 27]. The novelty of Kant's conception of reason as spontaneity is highlighted by Yovel: "Kant conceives of reason mainly as a spontaneous activity, not as a mere set of forms. This dynamic conception of reason is radically different from that of Plato and, indeed, breaks away from the whole classic view of the logos as fixed and independent, governing the mind and the world as a thing in itself" [1989, 12]. See also Henrich: "Im Gegensatz zu der *vis repraesentativa* Wolffs hat Kant die Vernunft als reine Aktuosität verstanden" [1973, 245].

6 This foundational thought of Kant's conception of reason is highlighted by Korsgaard: "The animal finds herself in a world that consists of things that are directly perceived as food or prey, as danger or predator, as potential mate, as child ... These normatively or practically loaded teleological perceptions serve as the grounds of the animal's actions—where the ground of an

The third important characteristic of human thought for Kant is that it is *discursive:* it works on the basis of concepts rather than through intuitions [KrV, III, 85]. Empirical concepts are rules for recognizing objects in the world around us on the basis of certain selective attributes, which abstract from the multitude of impressions provided by our senses [KrV, III, 136][7]. In this sense, our understanding is the faculty of rules [KrV, III, 131]. In thinking, we judge whether a given concept does or does not apply to a given object that we represent to ourselves [KrV, III, 86][8].

Yet, the understanding has an even more fundamental function, namely that of impressing its own order onto the material of our experience, the intuitions provided by the senses. Instead of merely deriving empirical concepts by abstracting from our experience, it structures these in a way that the inchoate chaos of our senses appears to us as orderly experience[9]. It does so through

---

action is a representation that causes the animal to do what she does ... We human beings ... are aware not only of our perceptions but also of the way in which they tend to operate on us ... I believe that this awareness is the source of reason ... Once the space of reflective awareness—reflective distance, as I like to call it—opens up between the potential ground of a belief or action and the belief or action itself, we must step across that distance, and so must be able to endorse the operation on that ground, before we can act or believe. What would have been the cause of our belief or action, had we still been operating under the control of instinctive or learned responses, now becomes something experienced as a consideration in favor of a certain belief or action instead, one we can endorse or reject" [2008, 31].

7 In this sense, it is the mark of the discursive mind that it goes from the general to the particular, while an intuitive mind would be one that has direct epistemic access to the specific content of our experience, without requiring any contributions from the senses: "Unser Verstand ist ein Vermögen der Begriffe, d. i. ein diskursiver Verstand, für den es freilich zufällig sein muss, welcherlei und wie sehr verschieden das Besondere sein mag, das ihm in der Natur gegeben werden und das unter seine Begriffe gebracht werden kann; so kann man sich auch einen intuitiven Verstand (negativ, nämlich bloß als nicht diskursiven) denken, welcher nicht vom Allgemeinen zum Besonderen und so zum Einzelnen (durch Begriffe) geht, und für welchen jene Zufälligkeit der Zusammenstimmung der Natur in ihren Produkten nach besondern Gesetzen zum Verstande nicht angetroffen wird, welche dem unsrigen es so schwer macht, das Mannigfaltige derselben zur Einheit des Erkenntnisses zu bringen" [KU, V, 406].

8 Only in the later *Kritik der Urteilskraft* will Kant distinguish between the understanding and a newly introduced faculty of judgment. For a discussion of this change in his epistemological theory, see note 54 in Chapter 6 below.

9 "Kant's idealism, as an idealism of epistemic conditions, is inseparable from his analysis of the discursive nature of human cognition ... [T]his analysis is based on three bedrock epistemological assumptions: (1) cognition of any kind requires that an object somehow be given (this applies even to the problematic intellectual or archetypal intuition); (2) since a finite mind like ours is receptive rather than creative, its intuition must be sensible, resting on an affection by objects; and (3) sensible intuition, of itself, is insufficient to yield cognition of objects and requires the cooperation of the spontaneity of the understanding" [Allison, 2004, 77].

the pure concepts of the understanding, which Kant calls the *categories*[10]. One category is that of causality: because of the structure impressed on empirical reality by our understanding, this reality presents itself in the forms of chains of cause and effect, rather than a mere "rhapsody of perceptions" [KrV, III, 144]. In this sense, the order we perceive in the world is not something existing in itself, but something we project onto it: "Es ist also der Verstand nicht bloß ein Vermögen, durch Vergleichung der Erscheinungen sich Regeln zu machen: er ist selbst die Gesetzgebung für die Natur, d. i. ohne Verstand würde es überall nicht Natur, d. i. synthetische Einheit des Mannigfaltigen der Erscheinungen nach Regeln, geben" [KrV, IV, 93]. Thus, on the Kantian picture of cognition, our senses are affected by the world around us, and the content of this sense-experience is structured by our understanding (by means of concepts) into the coherent, orderly experience we have of the world[11].

This is the importance of the Kantian notion of the discursive nature of our understanding: our thought does not generate its own material content[12]; rather, it orders the content given to it from external sources (our senses)[13]. The essential function of our mind is to impose order according to its own rules. Hence, for

---

10 We will discuss the Kantian notion of the categories as pure concepts of the understanding in more detail below.

11 "Allein die Verbindung (conjunctio) eines Mannigfaltigen überhaupt kann niemals durch Sinne in uns kommen und kann also auch nicht in der reinen Form der sinnlichen Anschauung zugleich mit enthalten sein; denn sie ist ein Akt der Spontaneität der Vorstellungskraft, und da man diese zum Unterschiede von der Sinnlichkeit Verstand nennen muss, so ist alle Verbindung ... eine Verstandeshandlung, die wir mit der allgemeinen Benennung Synthesis belegen würden, um dadurch zugleich bemerklich zu machen, dass wir uns nichts als im Objekt verbunden vorstellen können, ohne es vorher selbst verbunden zu haben, und unter allen Vorstellungen die Verbindung die einzige ist, die nicht durch Objekte gegeben, sondern nur vom Subjekt selbst verrichtet werden kann, weil sie ein Akt seiner Selbsttätigkeit ist" [KrV, III, 107].

12 "Nicht dadurch, dass ich bloß denke, erkenne ich irgend ein Objekt, sondern nur dadurch, dass ich eine gegebene Anschauung in Absicht auf die Einheit des Bewusstseins, darin alles Denken besteht, bestimme, kann ich irgend einen Gegenstand erkennen" [KrV, III, 267].

13 Kant insists that the only source for the content of our experience that our discursive understanding can avail itself of are the intuitions (*Anschauungen*) of our senses [KpV, V, 45], referring to our understanding as "unser diskursiver, der Bilder bedürftiger Verstand" [KU, V, 408]. In thus stressing the importance of the senses in cognition, Kant is opposing Leibniz' theory of knowledge. Kant argues that the senses make an independent, irreplaceable contribution to our epistemic access to the world—and do not, as Leibniz claims, offer the same knowledge the intellect has access to, only in a more muddled way [KrV, III, 220]. In Kant's model, the senses provide the matter, and the intellect the form—in a way that knowledge results from the contributions of two independent sources, neither of which could do without the other. Kant specifically rejects Leibniz' suggestion that the understanding has access to its own innate and pure intuitions ("angeborne reine Verstandesanschauungen" [A, VII, 141; see also: VT, VIII, 389]).

experience to be possible, we need the contribution of both our senses and our understanding, where the senses play a passive-receptive role (being affected by the world around us [KrV, III, 107]) and the understanding a spontaneous one (giving form to the content of our sense experience) [KrV, IV, 92][14].

As the understanding structures the intuitions of our senses, so reason structures the concepts of the understanding, in a way that unifies our experiences, turning them into experiences of a single, connected world [KrV, III, 253][15]. Reason, for Kant, is the ability to relate the particular to the general. In its merely *formal-logical* use, it operates in the form of syllogisms: the general rule is given and recognized to apply to a given particular item, in a way that properties about the item can be inferred (All men are mortal; Socrates is a man etc [KrV, III, 255]). In its *hypothetical* use—the one we will be mainly concerned with –, reason is confronted by a multiplicity of particular items and projects an overarching order into which they are embedded [KrV, III, 429][16]. Where the understanding by itself only offers us structured bits of experience, our reason guides its use to make possible the integration of these bits into a unified and coherent worldview, thus achieving "systematic unity in the use of our understanding" [KrV, III, 440][17]. That is, the principles of reason provide an *a priori* structure

---

14 Kemp Smith points out that Kant's analysis of consciousness radically breaks with a philosophical tradition that had treated "consciousness merely as a medium whereby the existent gets itself reported": "From the Kantian standpoint ... all awareness, no matter how rudimentary or apparently simple, is an act of judgment, and therefore involves the relational categories. Not passive contemplation but active judgment, not mere conception but synthetic interpretation, is the fundamental form, and the only form, in which our consciousness exists" [2003, xlvii; see also: Allison, 2004, 195].
15 More precisely, as Kemp Smith highlights, we should speak about reason as that aspect of our understanding that allows it to regulate itself: "Reason, Kant teaches [in the *Dialectic* of *Kritik der Reinen Vernunft*], is not a faculty separate from the understanding, and does not therefore produce any concept peculiar to itself. Reason is simply a name for the understanding in so far as it acts independently of sensibility, and seeks, by means of its pure forms, in abstraction, from all empirical limitations, to grasp the unconditioned" [2003, 478–9].
16 Confusingly, Kant refers to the *hypothetical* use of reason also as the *real* use of reason: "Es gibt von [der Vernunft] wie von dem Verstande einen bloß formalen, d. i. logischen Gebrauch, da die Vernunft von allem Inhalte der Erkenntnis abstrahiert, aber auch einen realen, da sie selbst den Ursprung gewisser Begriffe und Grundsätze enthält, die sie weder von den Sinnen, noch vom Verstande entlehnt" [KrV, III, 237]. The distinction between the logical and the real (or hypothetical) use of reason is highlighted by Beck: "[R]eason in its logical use is the faculty of drawing inferences and of systematizing knowledge, of finding a 'wherefore' for every 'therefore'; and ... in its real use it posits certain a priori synthetic propositions or principles which are supposed to state the unconditioned conditions for all that is found in experience" [1960, 75].
17 In fact, seeing everything that is particular as necessarily subsumed under general rules is, for Kant, the hallmark of rationality itself: "Und dies, dass alles unter dem Allgemeinen stehe

of our experience, which serves as the guideline for the understanding's exploration of the world of experience[18]. This is the most profound sense in which our knowledge, for Kant, is not passive-receptive, but active-creative. Before any actual experience, reason provides the understanding with a framework into which to organize its knowledge. Without this *a priori* order, Kant claims, no coherent use of our understanding, and therefore no empirical knowledge, would be possible [KrV, III, 432].

Thus, reason, as the faculty coordinating the activity of the understanding, is the ultimate source for the order in the world of our experience[19]. While reason supervises the understanding, it itself is not supervised by any other faculty. It is autonomous in the sense that it is required, and able, to supervise itself [KpV, V, 119]. This raises the question: How—and on the basis of what—does this auto-supervision take place? The answer is: on the basis of reason's own essential interests. Reason, for Kant, is as an interested faculty, in the sense that it has its own essential ends (*wesentliche Zwecke* [KrV, III, 542]), which it strives to achieve. In this sense, Kantian reason is, as Yovel puts it, an "erotic" faculty [1989, 9], aiming to satisfy its interests [KpV, V, 120], "inclinations" (*Hang* [KrV, III, 518]), "needs" (*Bedürfnis* [SDO, VIII, 136]) and "desires" (*Begierde* [KrV, III, 517]).

Kant defines an "interest" as the "principle that contains the conditions under which alone [a faculty's] exercise is being promoted" ("ein Prinzip, welches die Bedingung enthält, unter welcher allein die Ausübung desselben befördert

---

und in allgemeinen Regeln bestimmbar sei, ist eben das Prinzip der Rationalität oder der Notwendigkeit (*principium rationalitatis sive necessitatis*)" [Logik, IX, 120].

18 "Übersehen wir unsere Verstandeserkenntnisse in ihrem ganzen Umfange, so finden wir, dass dasjenige, was Vernunft ganz eigentümlich darüber verfügt und zu Stande zu bringen sucht, das Systematische der Erkenntnis sei, d. i. der Zusammenhang derselben aus einem Prinzip. Diese Vernunfteinheit setzt jederzeit eine Idee voraus, nämlich die von der Form eines Ganzen der Erkenntnis, welches vor der bestimmten Erkenntnis der Teile vorhergeht und die Bedingungen enthält, jedem Teile seine Stelle und Verhältnis zu den übrigen a priori zu bestimmen. Diese Idee postuliert demnach vollständige Einheit der Verstandeserkenntnis, wodurch diese nicht bloß ein zufälliges Aggregat, sondern ein nach notwendigen Gesetzen zusammenhängendes System wird. Man kann eigentlich nicht sagen, dass diese Idee ein Begriff vom Objekte sei, sondern von der durchgängigen Einheit dieser Begriffe, so fern dieselbe dem Verstande zur Regel dient. Dergleichen Vernunftbegriffe werden nicht aus der Natur geschöpft, vielmehr befragen wir die Natur nach diesen Ideen und halten unsere Erkenntnis für mangelhaft, so lange sie denselben nicht adäquat ist" [KrV, III, 428].

19 From the Kantian perspective, nature itself—i.e. the product of our creative-cognitive efforts—consequently forms a rule-governed whole: "Alles in der Natur, sowohl in der leblosen als auch in der belebten Welt, geschieht nach Regeln, ob wir gleich diese Regeln nicht immer kennen... Die ganze Natur überhaupt ist eigentlich nichts anders als ein Zusammenhang von Erscheinungen nach Regeln; und es gibt überall keine Regellosigkeit" [L, IX, 11].

wird" [KpV, V, 119])[20]. In this sense, the interests of reason are simply the conditions that allow for the most complete use of our highest mental faculty. One important interest of reason is that of *systematic unity*. Reason aims at the harmonious integration of everything that is particular into a systematic whole, in a way that eliminates any form of contradiction. Rules of reasoning that generate contradictions lead to defective thought. In this sense, it is an interest of reason to avoid contradiction—and to operate on the basis of principles that allow it to do so: "Vollständige zweckmäßige Einheit ist Vollkommenheit (schlechthin betrachtet)... Die größte systematische, folglich auch die zweckmäßige Einheit ist die Schule und selbst die Grundlage der Möglichkeit des größten Gebrauchs der Menschenvernunft. Die Idee derselben ist also mit dem Wesen unserer Vernunft unzertrennlich verbunden" [KrV, III, 456; see also: KrV, III, 432].

A second interest of reason is *completeness*—the ability to trace back any particular item of knowledge to its conditions, without any of the chains of conditions resulting in loose ends [KrV, III, 242]. For Kant, an attempt to give an explanation of a certain fact that arbitrarily stops at another fact without, in turn, giving an explanation for that fact as well is defective because of its incompleteness. It is only when we have provided a complete chain of explanation from the given fact to its unconditioned first condition that we have given a fully satisfactory (i.e. non-defective) explanation—that is, one that satisfies the demands of reason: "Nun ist es ein wesentliches Prinzip alles Gebrauchs unserer Vernunft, ihre Erkenntnis bis zum Bewusstsein ihrer Notwendigkeit zu treiben (denn ohne diese wäre sie nicht Erkenntnis der Vernunft)" [GMS, IV, 463][21].

Thus, reason is that dynamic and interested aspect of our thought that seeks to integrate everything that is individual and particular (sense impressions and items of knowledge in its theoretical use and principles of action in its practical

---

20 Yet, Kant also says that only finite rational beings have interests [GMS, IV, 413; KpV, V, 79]. So, we should perhaps say that while reason has essential ends, only our human reason, the rational faculty of us finite rational beings, has interests. However, for convenience's sake, I will use the terms "end of reason", "interest of reason" and "need of reason" synonymously.
21 "Denn das, was uns notwendig über die Grenze der Erfahrung und aller Erscheinungen hinaus zu gehen treibt, ist das Unbedingte, welches die Vernunft in den Dingen an sich selbst notwendig und mit allem Recht zu allem Bedingten und dadurch die Reihe der Bedingungen als vollendet verlangt" [KrV, III, 13; see also KrV, III, 243]. The problem that Kant focuses on in *Kritik der Reinen Vernunft* is precisely that, on the one hand, reason only finds itself satisfied when it has traced any conditional item of knowledge back to its unconditioned cause—but that, on the other hand, the nature of our cognitive faculties makes any knowledge of the unconditional impossible [GMS, IV, 463]. We will discuss this topic in more detail below.

use) into a complete and self-consistent system[22]: "Die Vernunft wird durch einen Hang ihrer Natur getrieben, über den Erfahrungsgebrauch hinaus zu gehen, sich in einem reinen Gebrauche und vermittelst bloßer Ideen zu den äußersten Grenzen aller Erkenntnis hinaus zu wagen und nur allererst in der Vollendung ihres Kreises, in einem für sich bestehenden systematischen Ganzen, Ruhe zu finden" [KrV, III, 518][23].

In doing so, reason is driven by nothing but its own essential interests. As an interested faculty, reason, in Kant's conception, is teleological, or end-directed, aiming at the attainment of its interests. As Yovel, one of the few writers to attach appropriate weight to the Kantian notion of the interests of reason, puts it: "Kant describes reason primarily as a system of interests. Its basic feature is teleological activity, pursuing its own 'essential ends' or immanent tasks ... [R]ational activity is a goal-setting activity, directed to the attainment of ends not given to it from without but set or projected by reason itself" [1989, 14][24]. In this sense "pure reason is in effect concerned with nothing but itself" ("Die reine Vernunft ist in der Tat mit nichts als sich selbst beschäftigt" [KrV, III, 448]): in its activities in both the theoretical and the practical field, it is guided by nothing but its own essential ends—and seeks nothing but to satisfy its own essential interests. In fact, the whole of Kant's philosophy can be understood as an exploration of the interests of reason ("Philosophie [ist] die Wissenschaft von der Beziehung aller Erkenntnis auf die wesentlichen Zwecke der menschlichen Vernunft" [KrV, III, 542])—and much of what Kant says must appear puzzling without an

---

22 In identifying systematic unity and completeness as central among the many interests, needs and demands of reason that Kant mentions in his texts, I follow Guyer: "[T]he two conceptions of unity I have characterized, completeness ... and systematicity..., should not be thought of as competing conceptions of the unity of reason but rather as, at least in the end, two aspects of the unity of reason, or two criteria both of which must be satisfied if any body of thought is ultimately to satisfy the claims of reason" [2000, 62].

23 See also: "Denn nicht allein, dass unsere Vernunft schon ein Bedürfnis fühlt, den Begriff des Uneingeschränkten dem Begriffe alles Eingeschränkten, mithin aller anderen Dinge zum Grunde zu legen; so geht dieses Bedürfnis auch auf die Voraussetzung des Daseins desselben, ohne welche sie sich von der Zufälligkeit der Existenz der Dinge in der Welt, am wenigsten aber von der Zweckmäßigkeit und Ordnung, die man in so bewunderungswürdigem Grade (im Kleinen, weil es uns nahe ist, noch mehr wie im Großen) allenthalben antrifft, gar keinen befriedigenden Grund angeben kann" [SDO, VIII, 137].

24 Brandt also notes the importance of the notion of the interests of reason: "Wenn diese Rekonstruktion der KrV von ihrem Ende und Endzweck her richtig ist, dann leitet sich die juridische Verfassung aus einem Rechtsanspruch des Interesses der Vernunft und der Moral her, und damit ist die Rechtlichkeit keine austauschbare Metapher, sondern eine normative Rede auf der Ebene der Moral und ihrer Voraussetzung" [2007, 336].

appreciation of how central the notion of the interests of reason is to his thinking[25].

Given that, for Kant, the principles of reason express the very conditions for the complete and non-stultifying use of our mental faculties [KrV, III, 432; see also: O'Neill, 1989, 38], he regards their validity as independent from any personal characteristics or preferences of any given individual[26]. This distinguishes them from our desires, which are idiosyncratic, in the sense that each human being has his own, at least partly non-overlapping, set of desires. The principles of reason are shared in that they are the same for all rational individuals. That is, they are, Kant holds, *objectively valid*[27].

Freedom and necessity

We have now explored Kant's conception of reason—and are in a position to consider the fundamental tension that marks Kant's vision of the human condition: on the one hand, human beings are natural beings with physical bodies, living in a world in which everything is perfectly determined by natural necessity. On the other hand, as rational beings they have to regard themselves as free both in their theoretical activity (that is, they attribute to themselves freedom of judgment) and in their practical activity (that is, they attribute to themselves transcendental freedom).

---

25 One could, for instance, easily be under the impression that Kant offers an ethics of disinterestedness. Yet, this would be to misunderstand him. As we will see below, the moral law—the law of reason—for him is the set of rules that allow us consistently to satisfy the interests of reason in its practical application. What he urges us to do is to give priority to the interests of reason —the interests of our proper self (see below)—over those of our physical nature. Thus, his moral theory is crucially built on the notion of the interests of reason, and in this sense not disinterested at all.

26 Kant uses the term "principle" to refer to rules under which reason operates and which it gives to itself [GMS, IV, 448]. As we have seen, reason essentially aims at the satisfaction of its own interests—and the principles of reason are the tools it employs for this purpose. In this sense, the principles of reason express the conditions under which the interests of reason are satisfied. Consequently, the principles of reason are valid *a priori* [L, IX, 110]—that is, their validity does not depend on anything given to us in experience, but rather on the interests of reason, which we are confronted with independently of the content of any particular experience.

27 "Also entspringt das Gesetz, anderer Glückseligkeit zu befördern, ... bloß daraus, dass *die Form der Allgemeinheit, die die Vernunft als Bedingung bedarf,* einer Maxime der Selbstliebe die objektive Gültigkeit eines Gesetzes zu geben, der Bestimmungsgrund des Willens wird" [KpV, V, 34, my emphasis; see also: KpV, V, 76].

How we can regard ourselves as free if we exist as part of a deterministic world? Or, put differently, what justifies us in attributing freedom to ourselves in spite of us being part of a world that is subject to natural necessity? The logical form of this problem recurs in many of Kant's investigations. It is the problem of certifying that the concepts we are using are well-grounded, that there is something in the world corresponding to them, rather than them being bogus concepts, which in spite of their grammatical correctness, refer to nothing at all. Solving this type of problem involves two steps: first, showing that the concept in question can be thought coherently and can be integrated into our general worldview without contradiction (this is what Kant calls establishing the concept's *logical possibility*) and, secondly, showing that we have grounds to believe that there is in fact some reality corresponding to it (establishing its *real possibility* [KrV, III, 17n])[28].

The concepts under investigation here are that of our freedom of judgment and that of our transcendental freedom. Let us start with the notion of freedom of judgment—i.e. our ability to guide our thought on the basis of the principles of reason, without our reason, in turn, being determined by external factors. To establish its *logical possibility*, we require a central piece of Kant's doctrine of transcendental idealism: the distinction between the phenomenal and the noumenal. As we have seen above, Kant holds that the world of our experience, located in time and space and ordered by laws of nature, is the creation of our own cognitive faculties. Time and space are not properties of objects in themselves,

---

[28] As Kant highlights in *Kritik der Urteilskraft*, the fact that we have to distinguish between logical and real possibility (or what we would call possibility and reality) is directly linked to the discursive nature of our understanding, i.e. the fact that a mere thought is just the empty form of a judgment—and that only when that form is given material content by the intuition of our senses can we say that the judgment is true: "[W]ären zu dieser ihrer Ausübung nicht zwei ganz heterogene Stücke, Verstand für Begriffe und sinnliche Anschauung für Objekte, die ihnen korrespondieren, erforderlich: so würde es keine solche Unterscheidung (zwischen dem Möglichen und Wirklichen) geben. Wäre nämlich unser Verstand anschauend, so hätte er keine Gegenstände als das Wirkliche. Begriffe (die bloß auf die Möglichkeit eines Gegenstandes gehen) und sinnliche Anschauungen (welche uns etwas geben, ohne es dadurch doch als Gegenstand erkennen zu lassen) würden beide wegfallen. Nun beruht aber alle unsere Unterscheidung des bloß Möglichen vom Wirklichen darauf, dass das erstere nur die Position der Vorstellung eines Dinges respektiv auf unsern Begriff und überhaupt das Vermögen zu denken, das letztere aber die Setzung des Dinges an sich selbst (außer diesem Begriffe) bedeutet. Also ist die Unterscheidung möglicher Dinge von wirklichen eine solche, die bloß subjektiv für den menschlichen Verstand gilt, da wir nämlich etwas immer noch in Gedanken haben können, ob es gleich nicht ist, oder etwas als gegeben uns vorstellen, ob wir gleich noch keinen Begriff davon haben" [KU, V, 401–2]. For further discussions on the Kantian distinction between logical and real possibility, see Beck [1960, 272] and Guyer [2000, 356].

but are instead the way our senses represent these objects to us [KrV, III, 16]. Similarly, causality is not a feature of the world as it is in itself, but part of the tool-set our understanding employs to synthesize the material provided by the senses into objects of our experience [KrV, IV, 93].

When we abstract, for any given experience, from all contributions made by our senses and our understanding, we are left with the notion of the object as it exists in itself—that is, that object x which the representation by our senses is a representation of [KrV, III, 209]. This is what Kant calls the "noumenon". The world of the noumena is not some mysterious, deeper reality, but merely the logical correlate of assuming that the structure of the world of our experience (i.e., that it is presented in time and space and operates according to the laws of causality) is imposed by our epistemic apparatus (our senses and our understanding), rather than being part of reality as it is in itself[29]. That is, to speak of the world of the noumena is merely to assume a particular perspective on the world of our experience—namely, to consider it insofar as it exists independently from the contribution made to it by our epistemic apparatus.

Crucially, we can have no experience of the world of the noumena—for all experience is given to us in the form of time and space and the world of the noumena is precisely the world as it exists independently from these forms of intuition. The world of the noumena is, in a term that we will discuss in more detail in Chapter 2 below, a mere idea of reason, a necessary assumption we have to make to be able to regard the structure of the empirical world as provided by our senses and our understanding[30]. Thus, the noumenon is a merely negative

---

29 "Sobald dieser Unterschied [zwischen Erscheinung und Ding an sich selbst] einmal gemacht ist, so folgt von selbst, dass man hinter den Erscheinungen doch noch etwas anderes, was nicht Erscheinung ist, nämlich die Dinge an sich, einräumen und annehmen müsse, ob wir gleich uns von selbst bescheiden, dass, da sie uns niemals bekannt werden können, sondern immer nur, wie sie uns affizieren, wir ihnen nicht näher treten und, was sie an sich sind, niemals wissen können" [GMS, IV, 451].

30 "Der Verstand begrenzt demnach die Sinnlichkeit, ohne darum sein eigenes Feld zu erweitern, und indem er jene warnt, dass sie sich nicht anmaße, auf Dinge an sich selbst zu gehen, sondern lediglich auf Erscheinungen, so denkt er sich einen Gegenstand an sich selbst, aber nur als transzendentales Objekt, das die Ursache der Erscheinung (mithin selbst nicht Erscheinung) ist und weder als Größe, noch als Realität, noch als Substanz etc. gedacht werden kann (weil diese Begriffe immer sinnliche Formen erfordern, in denen sie einen Gegenstand bestimmen) ... Wollen wir dieses Objekt Noumenon nennen, darum weil die Vorstellung von ihm nicht sinnlich ist, so steht dieses uns frei. Da wir aber keine von unseren Verstandesbegriffen darauf anwenden können, so bleibt diese Vorstellung doch für uns leer und dient zu nichts, als die Grenzen unserer sinnlichen Erkenntnis zu bezeichnen und einen Raum übrig zu lassen, den wir weder durch mögliche Erfahrung, noch durch den reinen Verstand ausfüllen können" [KrV, IV, 185].

notion, a mere residual that we cannot know anything about, given that we can only learn about the world through our epistemic apparatus—and this only acquaints us with representations of objects, not the objects as they are in themselves [KrV, IV, 166].

This distinction between the phenomenal (i.e. the world we are acquainted to through experience) and the noumenal opens the conceptual space for conceiving of our reason as noumenal—that is, as existing in itself outside the spatiotemporal realm (i.e. the world of the appearances). Thus, while we know we exist as natural beings, as part of the phenomenal world, in which all events are perfectly determined by natural necessity, Kant's transcendental idealism allows us to conceive of the possibility of our reason's noumenal activity[31]. In so far as we conceive of our reason as noumenal we can integrate without contradiction the notion of its spontaneity with that of our empirical existence being governed by natural necessity—i.e. we can explain the *logical* possibility of our freedom of judgment[32].

With the *logical* possibility of our freedom of judgment secured, establishing its *real* possibility (i.e. establishing that the concept really applies to us) is a small step, given the results of our earlier discussion of the spontaneity of reason: we found there that if we are to think at all—and think of ourselves as thinking—we have to regard our thought as free (i.e. as guided by its own interests, rather than as determined by natural necessity). That is, in reflecting on our own status as thinking beings, we have to ascribe freedom of judgment to ourselves.

---

[31] "Kant's task as a philosopher is to show how the thought of the I and its spontaneity can be reconciled with this naturalistic story ... Transcendental idealism, construed in terms of a contrast between two 'points of view' or 'ways of considering', as opposed to two 'worlds' or sets of entities, is the key to Kant's solution to this problem. It accomplishes this goal by providing a conceptual space in which the thought of freedom can be held alongside of the thought of nature, not by the positive assignment of freedom to an inaccessible noumenal world" [Allison, 1996, 128].

[32] The obvious question arising at this point is how the spontaneity of reason can interact with the determinism of the empirical world. As we will see below the same problem is replicated in Kant's account of the possibility of transcendental freedom. In that latter case, Kant holds that no explanation of the compossibility of freedom and necessity is possible: "[W]ie der Prädeterminism, nach welchem willkürliche Handlungen als Begebenheiten ihre bestimmende Gründe in der vorhergehenden Zeit haben (die mit dem, was sie in sich hält, nicht mehr in unserer Gewalt ist), mit der Freiheit, nach welcher die Handlung sowohl als ihr Gegenteil in dem Augenblicke des Geschehens in der Gewalt des Subjekts sein muss, zusammen bestehen könne: das ists, was man einsehen will und nie einsehen wird" [R, VI, 49n]. The similarity between these two problems in the theoretical and the practical spheres suggests that the same answer applies here.

Alle unsere und anderer Wesen Handlungen sind necessitiert, nur allein der Verstand und der Wille, sofern er durch Verstand bestimmt werden kann, ist frei und eine reine Selbsttätigkeit, die durch nichts anderes als sich selbst bestimmt ist. Ohne diese ursprüngliche und unwandelbare Spontaneität würden wir nichts a priori erkennen; denn wir wären zu allem bestimmt und unsere Gedanken selbst ständen unter empirischen Gesetzen. Das Vermögen, a priori zu denken und zu handeln, ist die einzige Bedingung der Möglichkeit aller anderen Erscheinungen. [R 5441, XVIII, 182]

Thus, as far as our freedom of judgment is concerned, the true challenge lies in establishing its logical possibility (i.e. determining how its possibility can be coherently thought, given natural necessity). Once the Kantian distinction of the phenomenal and the noumenal allows us to do so, we are committed to attributing noumenal activity to our own reason in order to be able to account for the possibility of thought at all: "Der Mensch... ist sich selbst freilich einesteils Phänomen, andernteils aber, nämlich in Ansehung gewisser Vermögen, ein bloß intelligibler Gegenstand, weil die Handlung desselben gar nicht zur Rezeptivität der Sinnlichkeit gezählt werden kann. Wir nennen diese Vermögen Verstand und Vernunft" [KrV, III, 371; see also: SF, VII, 27][33].

These reflections allow us to elucidate the relation between the Kantian distinctions of the higher and the lower faculties, on the one hand, and that of the

---

33 On reflection, we can see that this attribution of noumenal activity to our reason is not only a consequence of his theory of cognition, but even presupposed and required by it. For if the causal order governing the natural world is imposed by our reason—understood in the broad sense explained above –, reason cannot itself be subject to natural necessity, for that necessity itself is, properly understood, just a product of our reason's activity: "Wenn wir nämlich noch eines andern Blicks (der uns aber freilich gar nicht verliehen ist, sondern an dessen Statt wir nur den Vernunftbegriff haben), nämlich einer intellektuellen Anschauung desselben Subjekts, fähig wären, so würden wir doch inne werden, dass diese ganze Kette von Erscheinungen in Ansehung dessen, was nur immer das moralische Gesetz angehen kann, von der Spontaneität des Subjekts als Dinges an sich selbst abhängt, von deren Bestimmung sich gar keine physische Erklärung geben lässt" [KpV, V, 99]. That is, the very logic of Kant's transcendental idealism requires us to accept the notion of the noumenal activity of our reason. This is noted by Allison: "From a Kantian standpoint, the elimination of the I is not only pragmatically impossible (since the I must do the eliminating), but also incoherent on a deeper level, for the broadly mechanistic world in which the I is dissolved in the thoroughly naturalistic story is itself only for the I" [1996, 128; see also Prauss: 1982, 203]. Once we accept transcendental idealism, the skeptic's plausible-seeming claim that our reason is itself determined by the laws of nature must be analyzed into the incoherent notion that our reason is determined by laws which are themselves a product of the spontaneous activity of our reason. If, as transcendental idealism claims, natural necessity is a product of our reason, then the spontaneity of our reason is a condition of, and cannot be restricted by, natural necessity. Kant's doctrine of our noumenal existence as an idea of reason is an attempt to spell out how this is possible.

empirical and our pure use of our faculties, on the other (as in the notion of "pure reason"). Kant holds that both in cognition and in volition—i.e. in our theoretical and our practical activity—our reason, on the one hand, and our sensuous nature, on the other, make important contributions. That is, both cognition and volition involve a spontaneous-active and a receptive-passive element. The distinction between the higher and lower faculties coincides with this distinction of the active and the passive. Our lower faculty of cognition (*unteres Erkenntnisvermögen*) comprises the senses—i.e. the passive-receptive component of cognition—while the notion of the higher faculty of cognition (*oberes Erkenntnisvermögen*) refers to the spontaneous-active component [A, VII, 140–1; see also: KU, V, 196–7]. As we have just seen, we can only account for the spontaneity of our higher faculties insofar as we regard them as having noumenal existence—that is, insofar as we conceive them as existing free from the necessity governing empirical reality, i.e. as pure ("Die reine Vernunft, als ein bloß intelligibeles Vermögen, ist der Zeitform und mithin auch den Bedingungen der Zeitfolge nicht unterworfen" [KrV, III, 373]). Hence, we can only ascribe higher faculties (i.e. spontaneity) to ourselves insofar as we conceive them as pure—i.e. having noumenal existence.

The problem of transcendental freedom

As freedom of judgment refers to our reason's spontaneity in its theoretical application, transcendental freedom refers to its spontaneity in its practical application (i.e. in so far as it is concerned with determining our actions). Kant distinguishes between the notion of *transcendental* freedom and that of *practical* freedom. The latter refers to the experience we have of being able to choose our actions, without being determined to act by the desires and urges we happen to be confronted with [KrV, III, 363; see also: KrV, III, 521]. Yet, the fact that, in acting, we have the impression of being in charge of our actions does not prove that we are not subject to natural necessity. In fact, if all we had were the experience of feeling in control of our actions, we would—paradoxically—have to conclude that they are subject to natural necessity after all. For, as we have seen, any event in the spatiotemporal world—i.e. any experience we have, including our own thoughts and decisions to act, regarded as empirical events—is necessarily subject to the laws of causality, i.e. caused by an event coming before it in time[34]. While my action would still be a consequence of

---

34 "[E]s ist nichts in der Natur (als einem Sinnenwesen), wozu der in ihr selbst befindliche Bes-

my decision to act, this decision would, in turn, be "nature again", in Kant's term [KrV, III, 521], caused by the natural workings of my brain, in a way that a given decision of mine, far from disrupting the causal continuity of the empirical world, would just be an instance of its smooth working[35].

Transcendental freedom, on the other hand, is the notion of a freedom that starts causal chains from the beginning, without, in turn, being caused by any external factor ("[Transzendentale Freiheit ist] eine absolute Spontaneität der Ursachen, eine Reihe von Erscheinungen, die nach Naturgesetzen läuft, von selbst anzufangen" [KrV III, 310]). As such, it is *prima facie* inconsistent with natural necessity, for if a given action is considered an act of transcendental freedom, it would appear that it cannot also be continuous with the causally determined realm of the empirical world [KpV, V, 97]. Thus, we are confronted with two different kinds of causality: natural causality refers to a causal relationship in which each cause is itself an effect in the endless chain of causes and effects [KrV, III, 363], while transcendental freedom refers to a causal relationship in which the cause itself is uncaused, not itself the effect of a preceding cause. For this reason, we can have no experience of transcendental freedom: all experience is experience of appearances—and appearances, by their very nature, are subject to the laws of natural causality, in a way that whatever happens in the world of appearances is caused by another appearance. Consequently, we can have no experience of transcendental freedom [KrV, III, 369].

Yet, Kant holds that we nonetheless require the notion of transcendental freedom to arrive at a satisfactory view of the world—not only because of the practical interest we take in the notion (a point we will discuss in Chapter 4), but also for purely theoretical reasons: as we have seen above, completeness in the explanation of the world is a need of reason. That is, reason demands to know the conditions for every given conditioned state of affairs. Hence, reason is only satisfied with an explanation of the world if everything that is conditioned in our experience has been traced back to its unconditioned grounds. Yet, an explanation of the world based only on natural causality cannot offer such a complete explanation of the world. For a worldview only involving natu-

---

timmungsgrund nicht immer wiederum bedingt wäre; und dieses gilt nicht bloß von der Natur außer uns (der materiellen), sondern auch in uns (der denkenden): wohl zu verstehen, dass ich in mir nur das betrachte, was Natur ist" [KU, V, 435].

35 We will discuss Kant's notion of practical freedom—which Kant refers to as negative freedom in *Kritik der Praktischen Vernunft*—in more detail in Chapter 5 below. As we will see in that discussion, we are warranted in attributing objective reality to our practical freedom (i.e. our belief that it is up to us whether we choose a certain action or not) only if we have reason to consider ourselves transcendentally free [KrV, III, 363].

ral causality presents the world as consisting of a multitude of chains of cause and effect, without these being grounded in an unconditioned first cause. To achieve closure—and thus completeness—in our explanation of the world, Kant argues, we require a first cause that can be regarded as the unconditioned condition of the conditioned chains of cause and effect [KrV, III, 349]. That is, to achieve closure, we require the notion of transcendental freedom.

Consequently, a worldview that only allows for natural causality is deficient. Conceiving of the whole world merely as chains of cause and effect will not yield a complete explanation of nature, i.e. an explanation that meets rational standards. A complete description of the world has to involve both kinds of causality: natural causality and freedom. Without natural causality, we would have no experience at all, given that only the rule-governed regularity of natural causality makes experience possible [KrV, III, 168]. Yet, without the causality of freedom, the system of natural causality would remain unfinished, incomplete. Thus, transcendental freedom is a concept to which nothing in our experience corresponds—and which, nonetheless, we cannot do without[36].

As in the argument concerning our freedom of judgment, Kant's argument to establish the objective reality of our transcendental freedom breaks down into two parts: the first is concerned with establishing the *logical possibility* of transcendental freedom (i.e. showing how we can integrate the notion of transcendental freedom into our general view of the world—and, in particular, how we can make it consistent with the notion of natural necessity). The second is focused on establishing its *real possibility* (i.e. showing that we have grounds to hold that the notion applies to us). We will discuss the first part of the argument here. The second part of the argument, concerned with establishing the real possibility of our transcendental freedom, is considerably more complicated and drawn-out than was the case for the notion of our freedom of judgment—and we will spend the next three chapters discussing it.

The argument establishing the logical possibility of transcendental freedom is similar to that establishing the logical possibility of our freedom of judgment. As before, the main problem lies in showing how transcendental freedom can be thought to be consistent with natural necessity—and, as before, the tension between these two notions disappears once we take seriously Kant's distinction between the noumenal and the phenomenal: natural causality governs the realm of experience, that is, the appearances—yet, this does not mean that it governs the

---

[36] "[Die Philosophie] muss also wohl voraussetzen: dass kein wahrer Widerspruch zwischen Freiheit und Naturnotwendigkeit eben derselben menschlichen Handlungen angetroffen werde, denn sie kann eben so wenig den Begriff der Natur, als den der Freiheit aufgeben" [GMS, IV, 456].

whole of reality [KpV, V, 94]. Given that we know nothing about the world as it is in itself, we cannot exclude the possibility that transcendental freedom is realized in it. That is, while the peculiar functioning of our understanding leads us to experience the world as governed by natural necessity, this leaves open the possibility that transcendental freedom is real in the world as it is in itself [KrV, III, 377].

Applied to human beings as agents this means that while all our actions, considered as events in the empirical world, are necessarily determined by events preceding them in time (in a way that, insofar as we exist in the empirical world, we are not free [KrV, III, 372; see also: KpV, V, 97]), this still leaves open the possibility that we are free insofar as we have noumenal existence. It is important to note that Kant does not intend to establish the reality (real possibility) of our transcendental freedom with this argument. Rather, his argument merely aims at establishing its logical possibility—i.e., the point that, given his transcendental idealism, there is no logical inconsistency involved in holding, on the one hand, that empirical reality is governed by natural necessity and that, on the other, we are transcendentally free [KrV, III, 377; see also KpV, V, 97–8].

This leaves us with the problem of securing the real possibility of transcendental freedom. It is tempting to believe that we can deduce it from the real possibility of our freedom of judgment, which we have already ascertained. That is, we could try to argue that our ability to determine our actions on the basis of the interests of reason and without these actions being determined by forces outside our control can be established as a corollary of the fact that, in thinking, we have to regard our thought as free. Henrich argues that Kant seriously considered arguments of this type (he cites Reflektion 5441 [XVIII, 182–3] as an example), but that he came to recognize that, unlike in the case of freedom of judgment, no contradiction arises if we think our actions as determined by natural necessity: "Das Denken des Ich geschieht zwar aus Spontaneität, aber es entsteht kein Widerspruch, wenn man annimmt, dass der transzendentale Grund [unseres] Handelns nicht Freiheit ist" [1973, 247][37]—and that, consequently, he abandoned this line of argument by the time he wrote *Kritik der Praktischen Vernunft*[38].

---

37 As a textual basis for imputing this argument to Kant, Henrich offers the rather obscure Reflektion 5442 ("Logische Freiheit in Ansehung alles dessen, was zufällige Prädikate sind. Alle Zufälligkeit am Subjekt ist objektive Freiheit, das Gegenteil zu denken. Wenn der Gedanke auch zur Tat zureicht, auch subjektive Freiheit. Transzendentale Freiheit ist die völlige Zufälligkeit der Handlungen. Es ist logische Freiheit in Vernunfthandlungen, aber nicht transzendentale" [XVIII, 183]) without explaining how this passage is related to his conclusion. I contend that it is not obvious how—and that—it is. More helpful appears Kant's assertion in *Religion* [R, VI, 26n] that there is no logical contradiction involved in conceiving a rational being as

The argument Kant finally settled on to ground the objective reality (or real possibility) of our transcendental freedom is perhaps the single most controversial element of his practical philosophy. He claims that we can establish the objective reality of our transcendental freedom on the basis of our consciousness of the moral law as making authoritative demands on us: "[W]äre nicht das moralische Gesetz in unserer Vernunft eher deutlich gedacht, so würden wir uns niemals berechtigt halten, so etwas, als Freiheit ist (ob diese gleich sich nicht widerspricht), anzunehmen" [KpV, V, 4]. Kant calls this awareness of the authoritativeness of the moral law *a fact of reason*. Both the notion of the fact of reason and the argument he offers as its justification are as obscure as they are controversial—and we will spend some time trying to make sense of them in the next chapters.

Conclusion

Kant conceives of reason as our highest mental faculty, in the sense that while all other faculties are guided, in their use, by other faculties, reason guides itself—and thus ultimately the use of all other faculties—on the basis of its own essential interests. Kant focuses on two interests of reason in particular, namely its interests in systematic unity and in completeness.

As rational beings, we see ourselves as endowed with spontaneous thought (i.e. thought guided by the principles—and, hence, interests—of reason) and with transcendental freedom (i.e., the ability to act in a way that is not determined by natural necessity). This leads to the fundamental tension marking Kant's conception of human nature: on the one hand, man exists as part of the empirical world, marked by natural necessity—and, on the other, he regards himself as free to judge and to act in a self-guided manner. We can account for the logical possibility of our freedom of judgment and our transcendental freedom, Kant holds, by regarding our reason as having noumenal activity, i.e. as operating outside the world of our experience. Yet, this leaves us with the task

---

not being endowed with pure practical reason (i.e. able to determine its behavior on the basis of the demands of reason alone), for as we will see below, being endowed with pure practical reason is, for Kant, a necessary and sufficient condition for transcendental freedom.

38 This point is overlooked by Rawls when he writes (in the German translation for the anthology by Ameriks & Sturma): "Für Kant besteht kein wesentlicher Unterschied zwischen der Freiheit des Willens und der des Denkens. Wenn unser mathematisches und theoretisches Denken frei ist, wie sich dies in freien Urteilen zeigt, so auch unsere reine praktische Vernunft, wie sich dies in freien praktischen Urteilen zeigt" [2004, 51–2].

of establishing the real possibility of these two notions (i.e. the task of showing that we have grounds for holding that they really apply to us). This argument is straightforward in the case of the notion of freedom of judgment, given that if we are to think of ourselves as thinking at all, we cannot do so without presupposing our own freedom of judgment. That is, freedom of judgment is the condition of the possibility of thought. This means that as long as we do not want to forfeit the conception of ourselves as thinking, we are logically constrained to ascribe freedom of judgment to ourselves. The argument establishing the real possibility of transcendental freedom is considerably more complicated. In the next chapter, we will turn to the aspects of Kant's doctrine of transcendental idealism that underpin his attempt to construct such an argument.

2 A brief exercise in transcendental idealism

The previous chapter has left us with the task of investigating Kant's solution to the problem of the real possibility of transcendental freedom. However, trying to make sense of that solution—and of the foundations of his practical philosophy, more generally—without reading it in the context of his theoretical philosophy is a hazardous and unrewarding enterprise. The current chapter lays out the main elements of Kant's transcendental idealism, which will serve as a basis for our account of Kant's practical philosophy—and, in particular his solution to the problem of transcendental freedom, which we will discuss in Chapter 4. This interpretative strategy will help us to remove much of the mystery surrounding the foundations of Kant's practical philosophy.

There are three aspects of Kant's transcendental idealism that will be of relevance for us: Kant's account of the nature of necessity, his doctrine of the ideas of reason (according to which the correct use of reason involves the application of concepts to which nothing in the world of our experience corresponds—but which is nonetheless required to satisfy the interests of reason) and his doctrine of practical knowledge (according to which we are entitled and required to accept the objective validity of a judgment in which we take a necessary practical interest, even if its truth value is not settled by theoretical fact).

The nature of necessity

The starting point of Kant's theoretical investigations is the question of how we can account for the possibility of necessity. More precisely, it is the question of how non-tautological judgments can be necessarily true—as, for instance, in the identification of causal relations, in which the cause is understood to be necessarily followed by its effect. In addressing the issue, Kant responds to a challenge posed by David Hume, who had claimed that causality, far from involving necessary relations, was merely based on mental habits. The statement "A causes B" should, Hume contended, be understood to mean "When we witness A, we expect B to happen, because that's what has typically happened in the past", rather than "When A is present, B follows by necessity". On this interpretation of causality, if I release a ball in mid-air and expect it to fall, I am not describing a necessary consequence of my action, but am merely making a conjecture based on my past experience. Consequently, on Hume's account, the notion of necessary causal relations is chimerical—and we have no right to ascribe objective reality to it [KpV, V, 51]. All we can ever get to in the ambit of causal relations is the subjective necessity to expect sequences of events observed in the past to repeat themselves.

To understand Kant's reply to this challenge, we have to appreciate two distinctions that are central to his argument: that between analytic and synthetic judgments—and that between *a priori* and *a posteriori* judgments. An analytic judgment is one that elucidates the content of one of the concepts contained in it. For instance, "A bachelor is an unmarried man" is an analytic judgment. Analytic judgments are tautologies—and, as such, necessarily true [L, IX, 111]. One way to think of synthetic judgments is simply to think of them as judgments that are not analytic. These are judgments about what is or is not the case in the world, rather than mere elucidations of the concepts contained in them[1].

The second distinction is that between *a priori* and *a posteriori* judgments. *A posteriori* judgments are those that depend for their truth on the contingent content of our experience. For instance, the judgment "There is a glass of milk on the table" is true if there is, in fact, a glass of milk on the table—and is false if there is not. *A priori* judgments are those that are necessarily and universally true, independently of any facts presented to us in our experience: "Wird ... ein Urteil in strenger Allgemeinheit gedacht, d. i. so, dass gar keine Ausnahme als möglich verstattet wird, so ist es nicht von der Erfahrung abgeleitet, sondern schlechterdings *a priori* gültig" [KrV, III, 29]. Again, a tautology is an example of *a priori* truths.

There are some points of contact between these distinctions: all analytic judgments are *a priori* truths—and all *a posteriori* judgments are synthetic (for in depending for their truth on the content of our experience, they must contain more than the mere elucidation of concepts). From this, it follows that there can be no analytic *a posteriori* judgments. This leaves the class of the synthetic *a priori* judgments—i.e., judgments that say something about the world (rather than just clarifying concepts) and are nonetheless necessarily true.

---

1 For a discussion of the difficulties surrounding Kant's distinction between analytic and synthetic judgments, see Quine [1953]. See also Hinsch [1986, 71]: "Um entscheiden zu können, ob ein bestimmtes Urteil der Subjekt-Prädikat-Form analytisch oder synthetisch ist, müssen wir wissen, welche Prädikate zur Bedeutung des verwendeten Subjektbegriffs gehören. Dies ist unproblematisch festzustellen, solange wir es mit Begriffen zu tun haben, deren Bedeutung definitorisch festgelegt ist... Dieses Verfahren ist aber auf einen sehr kleinen Bereich von Begriffen eingeschränkt. Es kann nur angewendet werden, wenn die Bedeutung eines Begriffs durch die Angabe seiner Definition stipulativ festgesetzt worden ist, und dies ist bei den wenigsten Begriffen der Fall. In der Regel verfügen wir über keine vollständige Kenntnis der Bedeutung eines Begriffs, und zwar deshalb nicht, weil wir über keine vollständige Kenntnis der Objekte, die unter einen Begriff fallen, verfügen" [1986, 71].

We can understand Hume's position as built on the claim that there are no synthetic *a priori* judgments. His argument then runs as follows: a causal judgment is a synthetic one, for it describes what is happening in the world, rather than just being concerned with the elucidation of concepts. We obtain all the information we have about what is the case in the world through our experience. Yet, all experience is contingent. That is, we have no way of experiencing necessary relations—for all we know everything we experience might have been otherwise. Thus, only logical truths (tautologies) are necessary truths, as far as we know[2]. Yet, for something to be an *a priori* judgment it has to be a necessary truth. Hence, there can be no synthetic *a priori* judgments—and all a judgment concerning the content of our experience can aspire to is a high subjective degree of probability, based on past experience, but not necessity.

Kant argues against Hume that causal judgments in fact describe necessary relations. Yet, he agrees with Hume that mere experience is not a sufficient ground for the ascription of necessity [KrV, III, 103]. That is, for judgments to be necessary truths they have to be valid *a priori*. Consequently, for judgments about the world of our experience to be true, they have to be synthetic *a priori* truths. Thus, for his repost to Hume to be successful, Kant has to show that, contrary to Hume's contention, synthetic *a priori* judgments are possible.

Kant's argument crucially depends on his theory of cognition, which we have started to outline in the previous chapter—and, more specifically, on his claim that both our senses and our understanding impose their own form on the content of our experience. Once this is granted, Kant holds, it follows that there are certain formal properties that characterize all possible experience, simply because these are the structures imposed on our experience by the functioning of our epistemic apparatus. Consequently, we would not be able to have any experience of a given event if the experience were not structured in this way. We can, Kant holds, identify as synthetic *a priori* truths the judgments describing these necessary structural features of our experience. That is, Kant's answer to Hume's challenge is that synthetic *a priori* judgments are possible because they describe the conditions of the possibility of all experience. Put differently, we know that any given experience will necessarily have certain characteristics because only these characteristics make it possible for it to be an experience of ours in the first place.

---

2 There is an ambiguity in this argument between the notion that something is a necessary truth and the notion that we know something to be a necessary truth. This ambiguity is an interesting one, for something might be a necessary truth without us being able to know that it is. Strictly speaking, the relevant point we should understand Hume's argument to be aiming at is to establish is that we cannot know whether something is a necessary truth.

> Die Ordnung und Regelmäßigkeit also an den Erscheinungen, die wir Natur nennen, bringen wir selbst hinein und würden sie auch nicht darin finden können, hätten wir sie nicht oder die Natur unseres Gemüts ursprünglich hineingelegt. Denn diese Natureinheit soll eine notwendige d. i. a priori gewisse, Einheit der Verknüpfung der Erscheinungen sein. Wie sollten wir aber wohl a priori eine synthetische Einheit auf die Bahn bringen können, wären nicht in den ursprünglichen Erkenntnisquellen unseres Gemüts subjektive Gründe solcher Einheit a priori enthalten, und wären diese subjektiven Bedingungen nicht zugleich objektiv gültig, indem sie die Gründe der Möglichkeit sind, überhaupt ein Objekt in der Erfahrung zu erkennen. [KrV, IV, 92]

What are the necessary structural features Kant has in mind? The first important *a priori* elements of our experience are space and time. Space, Kant argues, cannot be an empirical notion, for we cannot conceive of any experience of the world around us that is not embedded in space. That is, the fact that our experience of the external world is situated in space is a necessary feature of our experience. Thus, space is the condition of the possibility of any experience of the world around us. As such, it is an *a priori* element of our experience of the world. Yet, space is not something that we think (i.e., not a concept of the understanding), but is an intuition (something given to us by our senses). We can infer this, Kant holds, from the fact that we can, through investigations into the properties of space, arrive at (necessary *a priori*) geometrical truths, which are not contained in the concept of space (and if space were a concept of the understanding, the only necessary truths that could be derived from it would be analytic truths, that is, those contained in the concept of space itself) [KrV, III, 53][3]. Thus, Kant holds, space is the *a priori* form of all intuitions given to us by our senses. It is the form our senses impose on any experience we have of the external world. That is, space is not, on Kant's analysis, a feature of the world as it is in itself, but rather a feature of the world as it appears when filtered through our senses. Other beings with a different epistemic make-up might, for all we know, experience the world in a non-spatial manner [KrV, III, 55]. For us, however, space is a necessary feature of the world of our experience, as it is only in space that our senses can present that experience to us. That is, the judgment that our experience of the world around us will be situated in space is, Kant holds, a synthetic *a priori* truth. It is a truth about the world of our experience (i.e. not a mere tautology), which, nonetheless, holds with necessity [KrV, III, 54].

Similarly, time is, Kant argues, a pure form of our intuition. As in the case of space, we cannot conceive of any experience that is not located in time. That is,

---

[3] For a critique of the crucial Kantian notion of something being "contained in a concept", see Quine [1953].

time is not a contingent, empirical feature of our experience, but a necessary representation [KrV, III, 57]. Furthermore, in exploring our experience, we can identify certain necessary *a priori* features of time (for instance, that it has only one dimension and that several different times cannot coincide), which, Kant holds, cannot be deduced from a mere analysis of the concept of time. As in the case of the argument concerning space, this shows that time is an intuition, not a concept of the understanding. Time, like space, is a pure form of our intuition, an *a priori* form imposed on all experience by our senses—and the judgment that all experience is situated in time is a synthetic *a priori* truth [KrV, III, 60][4].

Thus, space and time are the *a priori* forms imposed on our experience of the world by our senses[5]. Hence, they are empirically real (that is, they are objective features of the world of our experience), but transcendentally unreal (they are not features of the things as they are in themselves, i.e. of the things as they are independently of our experience of them)[6]. Yet, space and time are not the only formal *a priori* features of our experience. Like our senses, our understanding also imposes characteristic features on our experience, which on reflection we can identify as necessary properties of that experience. As we have seen above, the understanding, on Kant's account, is discursive—that is, it cannot generate its own intuitions, but rather synthesizes the intuitions delivered by our senses into the coherent whole that is our experience. The understanding fulfills this function on the basis of the categories—that is, rules that combine and structure the material of our senses: "[D]ie Kategorien... sind... Regeln für einen Verstand, dessen ganzes Vermögen im Denken besteht, d. i. in der Handlung, die Synthesis des Mannigfaltigen, welches ihm anderweitig in der Anschauung gegeben worden, zur Einheit der Apperzeption zu bringen, der also für sich gar nichts erkennt, sondern nur den Stoff zum Erkenntnis, die Anschauung, die ihm durchs Objekt gegeben werden muss, verbindet und ordnet" [KrV, III, 116]. Given that they determine the structure into which the material of our experience is or-

---

4 For an extended discussion of Kant's claim that space and time are pure forms of our intuition rather than concepts of the understanding, see Hinsch [1986, 88–96].
5 "Unsere Welterkenntnis wird zur Binnenerkenntnis des menschlichen Subjekts, denn dadurch, dass Raum und Zeit zu unseren Anschauungsformen werden, ist die erkennbare Welt dem menschlichen Subjekt einverleibt" [Brandt, 2007, 244].
6 Kant takes it as a confirmation of his transcendental idealism that it can account for the nature of space and time, a feature of our experience which, in his view, must confound other theories, which are forced to treat them either as things in themselves (which, as such, have many inconvenient properties that are difficult to account for, such as their infinity) or mere empirical features of our experience (which, Kant holds, would make it difficult to account for the necessary nature of geometrical truths) [KrV, III, 63].

dered[7], the categories—like space and time—are necessary conditions for the possibility of experience[8]. If we are to have any experience at all, this experience will necessarily conform to the categories. Any judgment concerning the conformity of our experience to the form of the categories will be a synthetic *a priori* judgment—and, consequently, necessarily true[9].

Kant identifies twelve categories[10], of which the most important for our purposes is that of causality, which concerns the temporal relation of possible objects of experience. In our experience, structured by the category of causality, every event is caused by a preceding event—and is, in turn, the cause of later events [KrV, III, 369]. There can be no exception to this causal ordering, as being part of the continuum of cause and effect is a necessary condition for something to be a possible experience of ours. Consequently, the whole world

---

[7] That is, all structure that we perceive in the world of our experience is, Kant holds, the product of the spontaneity of our pure understanding. The intuitions of senses, Kant insists, are given to us piecemeal and in an unconnected manner—and it is only due to the operations of our understanding that we experience them as part of an integrated whole: "Wir [können] uns nichts als im Objekt verbunden vorstellen..., ohne es vorher selbst verbunden zu haben, und unter allen Vorstellungen [ist] die Verbindung die einzige..., die nicht durch Objekte gegeben, sondern nur vom Subjekte selbst verrichtet werden kann, weil sie ein Akt seiner Selbsttätigkeit ist" [KrV, III, 103].

[8] "Die transzendentale Deduktion aller Begriffe a priori [also der Kategorien] hat also ein Prinzip, worauf die ganze Nachforschung gerichtet werden muss, nämlich dieses: dass sie als Bedingungen a priori der Möglichkeit der Erfahrung erkannt werden müssen (es sei der Anschauung, die in ihr angetroffen wird, oder des Denkens). Begriffe, die den objektiven Grund der Möglichkeit der Erfahrung abgeben, sind eben darum notwendig" [KrV, IV, 74; see also: KrV, III, 175].

[9] The argument for establishing the categories as the conditions of the possibility of experience that Kant actually presents in the *Kritik der Reinen Vernunft* is considerably more complex. Yet, for our purposes this summary will be sufficient. For a more detailed outline of Kant's argument see Kemp Smith [2003, 284] and Allison [2004, 159].

[10] Why twelve? Kant's argument is based on his claim that the reason we can judge in an empirical context, i.e., to analyze the content of our experience, at all is that the forms of judgment of our understanding conform to the principles that have made synthesis of our experience possible. That is, we can only analyze (i.e., take apart) that which we have previously synthesized (i.e., put together): "Man wird hier leicht gewahr, ... dass die ... Analysis, die [das Gegenteil der Synthesis] zu sein scheint, sie doch jederzeit voraussetze; denn wo der Verstand vorher nichts verbunden hat, da kanh er auch nichts auflösen, weil es nur durch ihn als verbunden der Vorstellungskraft hat gegeben werden können" [KrV, III, 107]. Thus, Kant argues the principles underlying the processes of synthesis that generate our experience must correspond to the logical functions of judgment ("Auf solche Weise entspringen gerade so viel reine Verstandesbegriffe, welche a priori auf Gegenstände der Anschauung überhaupt gehen, als es in der vorigen Tafel logische Funktionen in allen möglichen Urteilen gab" [KrV, III, 92])—and he has, earlier in his argument, identified twelve logical functions of judgment [KrV, III, 87].

of our experience is governed by the law of causality—not because this causality is a feature of the world as it is in itself, but because our understanding necessarily imposes a causal order on our experience [KrV, III, 368].

Thus, everything in the world of our experience happens according to the laws of nature ("Die ganze Natur überhaupt ist eigentlich nichts anders als ein Zusammenhang von Erscheinungen nach Regeln; und es gibt überall keine Regellosigkeit" [L, IX, 11]). Yet, the lawlike character of our experience is not a feature of the world as it is in itself, but the product of the operation of our understanding, the faculty of rules—and hence based on the categories: "Kategorien sind Begriffe, welche den Erscheinungen, mithin der Natur als dem Inbegriffe aller Erscheinungen... Gesetze a priori vorschreiben" [KrV, III, 126][11]. Consequently, the laws of nature hold only from the viewpoint of the cognizing subject [KrV, III, 127].

This gives us a first understanding of the important Kantian notion of a law. A law, for Kant, is a rule with the following characteristics:
a. It is valid *a priori* (and hence necessarily and universally valid) [KpV, V, 26];
b. It makes the orderly integration of the individual items of our experience into a unified whole possible [KpV, V, 28]; and
c. It stems from the spontaneous activity of our reason ("Die Vernunft [ist diejenige], aus der allein alle Regel, die Notwendigkeit enthalten soll, entspringen kann" [KpV, V, 20]).

All order and all normativity is, Kant insists, the product of our own structuring activity, not a feature of brute nature[12]. In particular, causality is, for Kant, always law-governed causality, for it is the product of the rule-based activity of our higher faculties [KpV, V, 89; see also: KrV, III, 366].

Before concluding this section, we should highlight two important points about Kant's argument establishing space and time as well as the categories as synthetic *a priori* features of our experience. The first of these is the important

---

[11] Yet, Kant insists that this does not mean that we can deduce all natural laws simply by investigating our understanding: "Besondere Gesetze, weil sie empirisch bestimmte Erscheinungen betreffen, können davon nicht vollständig abgeleitet werden, ob sie gleich alle insgesamt unter jenen stehen. Es muss Erfahrung dazu kommen, um die letztere überhaupt kennen zu lernen; von Erfahrung aber überhaupt und dem, was als ein Gegenstand derselben erkannt werden kann, geben allein jene Gesetze a priori die Belehrung" [KrV, III, 127].
[12] "Kant's basic principle [is] that the representation of unity requires a synthetic activity and cannot be passively received through sensibility" [Allison, 2004, 195]. Kant himself writes in a 1794 letter to Beck: "Die Zusammensetzung können wir nicht als gegeben wahrnehmen, sondern wir müssen sie selbst machen: wir müssen zusammensetzen, wenn wir uns etwas als zusammengesetzt vorstellen sollen (selbst den Raum und die Zeit)" [XI, 515].

role played by non-conscious mental activity in Kant's picture of cognition. The reason for our ability to think correctly (i.e., make correct judgments) is that the form of our judgments corresponds to the structure of empirical reality. That is, the relation of the concepts in our judgments corresponds to the relation of the objects of our experience in the empirical world. This is possible because our judgments use the same logical forms that are involved in the synthesizing activity of the understanding that imposes structure on the world of our experience in the first place[13]. Thus, Kant says, we can understand the world because we ourselves have structured it—and we would not be able to understand it had we not done so:

> [Wir können] uns nichts als im Objekt verbunden vorstellen..., ohne es vorher selbst verbunden zu haben, und unter allen Vorstellungen [ist] die Verbindung die einzige..., die nicht durch Objekte gegeben, sondern nur vom Subjekt selbst verrichtet werden kann, weil sie ein Akt seiner Selbsttätigkeit ist. Man wird hier leicht gewahr, dass diese Handlung ursprünglich einig und für alle Verbindung gleichgeltend sein müsse, und dass die Auflösung, Analysis, die ihr Gegenteil zu sein scheint, sie doch jederzeit voraussetze; denn wo der Verstand vorher nichts verbunden hat, da kann er auch nichts auflösen, weil es nur durch ihn als verbunden der Vorstellungskraft hat gegeben werden können. [KrV, III, 107]

Yet, we are obviously not aware of conducting the synthesis of the intuitions into the coherent film of our experience. This operation of the understanding, Kant holds, is something that we cannot have any experience of, because it alone is what makes experience possible ("Nun ist zwar sehr einleuchtend, dass ich dasjenige, was ich voraussetzen muss, um überhaupt ein Objekt zu erkennen, nicht selbst als Objekt erkennen könne" [KrV, IV, 250]).

That is, the synthetic processes, the pure spontaneous activity that underlies the whole of empirical reality (and our own self-consciousness) is not experienced, but merely imputed: we have to postulate it as a necessary condition for the possibility of experience. As Kemp Smith puts it: "Mental processes, in so far as they are generative of experience, must fall outside the field of consciousness, and as activities dynamically created cannot be of the nature of ideas. They are not subconscious ideas, but non-conscious processes. They are not submerged content of experience, but its conditioning grounds" [2003,

---

[13] This point is highlighted by Hill: "For Kant, the operation of synthesis involves taking the syntactical forms of the language of thought and projecting them into our sensations so that sensations appear to us as possessing fact-structure, a structure isomorphic with the structure of judgment. This allows judgments to map onto empirical facts making representation of empirical fact possible... It was precisely this inter-connectedness of object, reference, and syntax that enabled Kant to argue that syntactical structure must be presupposed if there is to be empirical awareness of objects qua objects" [2003, 176–7].

273][14]. That is, at the basis of the possibility of consciousness, on Kant's account, lies a dark ground that we cannot hope to penetrate any further[15]. Or, as he puts it in a different context, when—in our analysis—we get to the fundamental powers of our mind, all explanation ends [KpV, V, 46].

The second important point to highlight is the method Kant employs in his operation to establish the validity of synthetic *a priori* judgments. As we have seen above, he grants Hume the premise that we can have no experience of necessity [KpV, V, 12]. He also grants him the premise that we have no special faculty for detecting *a priori* truths. Yet, he still holds that it is possible for us to become aware of necessary truths through reflection. As we have seen, his argument works by taking ordinary experience and identifying the conditions without which this experience would not be possible. This allows Kant to hold that if we are to have any experience at all, it will necessarily conform to these conditions of its possibility. Kant calls this form of argument a *transcendental deduction*. A deduction, in general, is an argument establishing the objective validity of a claim [KpV, V, 46], while a transcendental deduction is an argument establishing the objective validity of a claim concerned with the necessary conditions for the possibility of experience: "Die transzendentale Deduktion aller Begriffe a priori hat also ein Prinzip, worauf die ganze Nachforschung gerichtet werden muss, nämlich dieses: dass sie als Bedingungen a priori der Möglichkeit der Erfahrung erkannt werden müssen (es sei der Anschauung, die in ihr angetroffen wird, oder des Denkens). Begriffe, die den objektiven Grund der Möglichkeit der Erfahrung abgeben, sind eben darum notwendig" [KrV, III, 105][16].

---

14 Yet, in a different passage Kemp Smith himself professes some uncertainty as to whether it is correct to call these non-conscious processes "'mental" at all [2003, 277].

15 This distinguishes Kant's analysis of consciousness from a philosophical tradition that had operated on the assumption that the mind is fully transparent to itself: "Leibniz's contention that the mind is conscious of its fundamental activities, and that it is by reflection upon them that it gains all ultimate a priori concepts, is [no] longer tenable in view of the conclusions established in the objective deduction. Mental processes, in so far as they are generative of experience, must fall outside the field of consciousness..." [Kemp Smith, 2003, 273]. For a further distinguishing trait of Kant's conception of consciousness—namely, that it involves active judgment, not passive contemplation—see note 14 in Chapter 1 above.

16 Hinsch holds that the transcendental deduction should be understood as serving a more extended purpose, namely not only that of grounding the objective validity of the categories as the conditions for the possibility of a unified experience, but also that of establishing the claim that we are justified in regarding all our impressions of the world as being part of one unified experience in the first place: "In [der Transzendentalen Deduktion] unternimmt Kant den Versuch, im Rückgang auf allgemeine und notwendige Strukturmerkmale menschlicher Wirklichkeitserkenntnis zu zeigen, dass alle Wahrnehmungen eines Subjekts *notwendigerweise* in *einer* Erfah-

The transcendental deduction is embedded in the larger philosophical project that we have already touched upon above, namely that of certifying that the concepts we are using are well-grounded—and that we are warranted in assuming that there is something in the world corresponding to them, thus establishing our right to use these concepts. At the beginning of his discussion of the transcendental deduction of the categories, Kant distinguishes two questions we can ask concerning concepts: the first demands an exposition of the content (i.e. meaning) of a given concept, while the second asks for a proof that we can legitimately use it. These two questions are that of the *quid facti* (the question concerning the content of the concept) and that of the *quid juris* (concerning our right to apply that concept [KrV, III, 99][17]). They correspond roughly to the tasks of establishing the logical and the real possibility of concepts that we have encountered in our discussion of freedom in the previous chapter[18]. The transcendental deduction of the notion of causality is an answer to the second question: it is an argument seeking to establish that we can legitimately apply the concept of causality in the context of our lives. For empirical concepts, Kant holds, no such extravagant arguments are necessary: all we need is an empirical deduction, i.e., a pointing out the thing in our experience that the concept corresponds to [KrV, III, 100]. Yet, where the content of the concept in question is not met with in our experience (because it is itself the condition of the possibility of experience), we require an argument that shows that the concept can be legitimately employed. That is the role played by the transcendental deduction.

Before moving to the next section, let us summarize the results of our discussion: On Kant's account, the necessity we encounter in the world of our ex-

---

rung vereinigt gedacht werden und eben darum als Wahrnehmungen einer einzigen Wirklichkeit zu betrachten sind" [1986, 3]. Furthermore, Hinsch argues that Kant's argument on the first of these points (i.e. his argument seeking to ground the objective validity of the categories) requires, as its premise, our awareness of the unity of space and time as an *a priori* fact—and that, once this is granted, it implies that Kant's argument only succeeds in establishing the objective validity of one of the categories, namely that of quantity [1986, 104].
17 Beck calls these two different projects the metaphysical deduction and the transcendental deduction, respectively: "The metaphysical deduction is distinguished from the transcendental deduction... The metaphysical deduction is Kant's effort to discover what the categories are; the transcendental deduction is his effort to show that they are valid." [1960, 109]
18 More precisely, answering the question of the *quid facti* is only one part of the exercise of establishing the logical possibility of a concept—for in addition to specifying the content of the thought expressed by the concept, establishing its logical possibility also requires showing that the content of the concept can be integrated in our general worldview without generating inconsistencies.

perience is imposed by our own epistemic apparatus. Judgments describing these necessary features of our experience are necessary truths—and yet are synthetic judgments (i.e. they do more than merely clarify the content of the concepts contained in them). In making these synthetic *a priori* judgments, we are not saying anything about the material content of our experience, but only about the form that experience will necessarily take [KrV, III, 180]. All necessity we find in the world around us can be accounted for by the *a priori* elements of our cognition—that is, by something contributed by the cognizing subject itself. While we can have *a priori* knowledge, this does not mean we have a special sense to detect *a priori* truths. Rather, we can identify the *a priori* elements of our cognition by reflecting on the necessary features of our experience—and thus by distinguishing the aspects of that experience that we receive from the outside from those that are contributed by our own faculties[19].

The doctrine of ideas

As we have seen, the concepts and the judgments of the understanding taken by themselves merely express possible thoughts[20]. It is only when the concepts contained in the judgment are given material content—that is, only when we have confirmation that there is something corresponding to these concepts in reality—that we can say that the concepts have *real possibility* and that the judgment is true. The central case for a concept being given material content is that of the empirical judgment, in which case the content is provided by the intuitions of our senses. Given this content, the merely logical possibility of our thought is turned into the real possibility of a true judgment: "Denn dass der Begriff vor der Wahrnehmung vorhergeht, bedeutet dessen bloße Möglichkeit; die Wahrnehmung aber, die den Stoff zum Begriff hergibt, ist der einzige Charakter der Wirklichkeit" [KrV, III, 189]. A mere thought is thus turned into cognition of the

---

19 Kant gives a pithy summary of the logic underlying his notion of the *a priori* when he writes that: "[Wir erkennen] von den Dingen nur das a priori…, was wir selbst in sie legen" [KrV, III, 13]. Wood states, in some more detail: "It is important that on Kant's theory, what is a priori is produced by our faculties, not given to them, whether through sensation or otherwise. This means that for Kant, a priori cognition is utterly different from innate cognition, whose existence Kant emphatically denies… What is a priori,… we ourselves produce through the exercise of our faculties" [Wood, 1999, 59].

20 "Könnte dem Begriffe eine korrespondierende Anschauung gar nicht gegeben werden, so wäre er ein Gedanke der Form nach, aber ohne allen Gegenstand und durch ihn gar keine Erkenntnis von irgend einem Dinge möglich, weil es, so viel ich wüsste, nichts gäbe, noch geben könnte, worauf mein Gedanke angewandt werden könne" [KrV, III, 117].

world. Thus, Kant insists that our discursive understanding requires intuitions to move from thoughts to cognition—and that our senses are the only source of intuitions available to us [KrV, III, 118][21].

This position of Kant's amounts to a restriction of the sphere of possible facts—and to a corresponding restriction of the class of true factual statements. For if there are concepts that allow for the expression of possible thoughts but to which no possible sensuous experience corresponds (such as the concepts of God, immortality or transcendental freedom), these cannot be used to form true factual judgments—in a way that we cannot make any true factual statements concerning either the existence of God or the reality of transcendental freedom.

Yet, while Kant holds that there are concepts that cannot be used to generate true statements of fact, he does not deny that these concepts are useful. He highlights three legitimate ways of employing non-empirical concepts, i.e. those that cannot be given material content through the input of our senses. The first is, as we have already seen, the use of concepts referring to the non-empirical conditions of our experience (as certified by transcendental deductions). The second is the regulative use of concepts for the purpose of integrating the individual items of knowledge into a structured whole. Kant calls concepts used in this way the *ideas of reason* in its theoretical application. An idea of reason for Kant is a necessary assumption made by our reason—and warranted not by its being backed up by empirical evidence, but rather by its being required to satisfy the interests of our reason. We find nothing in the world corresponding to these ideas and cannot have any experience of their content [KU, V, 342]. Rather, accepting them is an act of taking-for-certain (*Für-wahr-halten*), warranted by "subjective requirements for the use of our reason" [SDO, VIII, 137]. That is, ideas do not involve claims of existence—but are merely useful fictions: "Vernunftbegriffe sind [...] bloße Ideen und haben freilich keinen Gegenstand in irgend einer Erfahrung, aber bezeichnen darum doch nicht gedichtete und zugleich dabei für möglich angenommene Gegenstände. Sie sind bloß problematisch gedacht, um in Beziehung auf sie (als heuristische Fiktionen) regulative Prinzipien des systematischen Verstandesgebrauchs im Felde der Erfahrung zu gründen" [KrV, III, 503]. As Kant highlights in this passage, ideas are fictions—but not arbitrarily invented

---

21 That is, Kant excludes the possibility of intellectual (i.e., non-sensuous) intuition [VT, VIII, 389], a point that will be of importance in Chapter 4 where we will discuss the charge that Kant's grounding of the moral law involves a form of intuitionism.

ones ("erdichtet"). Rather, they are pressed upon us by the very nature of our reason ("durch die Natur der Vernunft selbst aufgegeben" [KrV, III, 254])[22].

One example of an idea of reason in its theoretical application is the notion of the world as a whole (i.e. the entirety of all appearances) [KrV, III, 254]. The world as a whole is not something that we ever come to experience—that is, our senses will never provide us with any intuitions corresponding to that concept. The notion has a merely regulative use: it guides us in our efforts of gathering knowledge about the world. The notion of the world as a whole is a blueprint that allows us to organize individual bits of information into a coherent framework [KrV, III, 428]. All we ever come to experience are individual bits of sensual input. The notion of an ordered world of which they form part is not part of that experience, but one provided by our reason as a tool to organize our knowledge. The idea of the world of our experience as a whole is thus a merely regulative principle of reason, required to integrate our experiences into a structured whole. This is one of the meanings of Kant's claim that reason is architectonical [KrV, III, 329]: using the ideas as tools, reason specifies an order in which we organize our knowledge about the world *a priori*, before all experience, and based purely on its need for the systematic unity of all knowledge [KrV, III, 428].

What holds for the idea of the world of our experience as a whole is true for the ideas of reason in its theoretical application more generally: they are assumptions that ground the system of our knowledge, allowing us to locate every individual experience in a coherent worldview. In this sense, Kant calls an idea of reason a *focus imaginarius*, an imagined focus point outside the field of our experience, which provides us with guidance in our attempt to systematize our knowledge about the world, thus making possible the most extensive and coherent use of the concepts of our understanding [KrV, III, 428][23]. It is

---

22 Kant insists on using the term "idea" with a very specific, technical meaning—and sharply distinguishes it from the loose sense of the term in which it designates any kind of thought or mental representation: "[Kant] urges upon all true lovers of philosophy the imperative need of rescuing from misuse a term so indispensable to mark a distinction more vital than any other to the very existence of the philosophical disciplines" [Kemp Smith, 2003, 449]. Kemp Smith points out that Kant substitutes the term *Vorstellung* for Descartes' and Locke's use of the term *idea*, to preserve the proper meaning of that latter term. We can fail to appreciate the import of some of Kant's statements if we understand "idea" in a loose sense. On Kant's account of the origin of the ideas, see Kemp Smith [2003, 478 and 558–561], Beck [1960, 264–65] and Shell [1980, 47n].

23 As with any non-empirical concept, Kant sees the need to offer a deduction of the ideas, i.e. an argument establishing our right to make use of these concepts: "Die Ideen der reinen Vernunft verstatten zwar keine Deduktion von der Art, als die Kategorien; sollen sie aber im mindesten einige, wenn auch nur unbestimmte, objektive Gültigkeit haben und nicht bloß leere Ge-

important to bear in mind, however, that an idea in its theoretical use is a mere regulative principle: it is not used to make any claims of existence [KrV, III, 449], but is a merely "subjective law of housekeeping with the inventory of our understanding" ("ein subjektives Gesetz der Haushaltung mit dem Vorrat unseres Verstandes" [KrV, III, 241]).

Before continuing our discussion of the different types of legitimate use of non-empirical concepts, we will take a moment to explore one of the ideas of reason Kant principally focuses on: the idea of God. Kant is unambiguous that the notion of God is a mere postulate, a mere creation of ours to give coherence and structure to our view of the world—in short, an idea of reason [KrV, III, 451][24]. In its theoretical use, the idea of God allows for the satisfaction of reason's need for completeness. To achieve a completely unified vision of the world, reason requires us to trace every contingent item of knowledge back to its unconditional cause ("[D]er eigentümliche Grundsatz der Vernunft überhaupt (im logischen Gebrauche) [ist]... zu dem bedingten Erkenntnisse des Verstandes das Unbedingte zu finden, womit die Einheit desselben vollendet wird" [KrV, III, 242]). Yet, given that we experience the events in the empirical world as chains of causes and ef-

---

dankendinge (*entia rationis ratiocinantis*) vorstellen, so muss durchaus eine Deduktion derselben möglich sein" [KrV, III, 442]. This deduction consists in showing, he argues, that no coherent use of the faculty of the understanding would be possible without the employment of the ideas of reason: "Wenn man nun zeigen kann, dass, obgleich die ... transzendentalen Ideen direkt auf keinen ihnen korrespondierenden Gegenstand und dessen Bestimmung bezogen werden, dennoch alle Regeln des empirischen Gebrauchs der Vernunft unter Voraussetzung eines solchen Gegenstandes in der Idee auf systematische Einheit führen und die Erfahrungserkenntnis jederzeit erweitern, niemals aber derselben zuwider sein können: so ist es eine notwendige Maxime der Vernunft, nach dergleichen Ideen zu verfahren. Und dieses ist die transzendentale Deduktion aller Ideen der spekulativen Vernunft, nicht als konstitutiver Prinzipien der Erweiterung unserer Erkenntnis über mehr Gegenstände, als Erfahrung geben kann, sondern als regulativer Prinzipien der systematischen Einheit des Mannigfaltigen der empirischen Erkenntnis überhaupt, welche dadurch in ihren eigenen Grenzen mehr angebaut und berichtigt wird, als es ohne solche Ideen, durch den bloßen Gebrauch der Verstandesgrundsätze, geschehen könnte" [KrV, III, 443].

24 See also: "Religionspflicht [als] 'Erkenntnis aller unserer Pflichten als... göttlicher Gebote'... ist nicht das Bewusstsein einer Pflicht gegen Gott. Denn da *diese Idee* ganz aus unserer eigenen Vernunft hervorgeht und von uns, es sei in theoretischer Absicht, um sich die Zweckmäßigkeit im Weltganzen zu erklären, oder auch um zur Triebfeder in unserem Verhalten zu dienen, selbst gemacht wird, so haben wir hierbei nicht ein gegebenes Wesen vor uns, gegen welches uns Verpflichtung obläge" [MS, VI, 443–4; my emphasis]. Kant also refers to the notion of God as "[eine] Idee..., welche [die Vernunft] sich selber macht [MS, VI, 487; see also MS, VI, 241], "[ein] Begriff..., welchen uns selbst zu machen die praktische reine Vernunft nötigt" [VT, VIII, 399n] and, in his handwritten notes, as "ein ideales Wesen, was sich die Vernunft selbst schafft" [XXI, 48].

fects and that, hence, every cause of a given event is, in turn, the effect of some preceding cause, in a way that the empirical world presents itself as an aggregate of endless chains of cause and effect, we can never meet with such an unconditional cause in our experience. Consequently, Kant holds, to satisfy its need for closure, reason requires us to see the world *as if* at the beginning of these chains of cause and effect lay a first unconditioned cause. In Kant's words, reason sees itself required to assume the unconditional cause of the totality of conditions, God [KrV, III, 452][25].

Yet, the notion of God as an idea of theoretical reason is a merely problematic, or regulative, notion: in assuming the idea of God, we are not making an existential claim, but only give a certain structure to our inquiry into, and way of seeing, the world that allows for our worldview to form a coherent and unified whole (which it would not be if all it consisted of were countless chains of cause and effect)[26]. The great risk in the theoretical use of the ideas, Kant insists, is to misunderstand their status, by taking the judgments in which they are employed as making existential claims. When committing this mistake—and falling for what he terms the "transcendental illusion" [KrV, III, 345]—we understand something that is merely a tool to keep order in our use of reason, a mere regulative principle, as an assertion about what kind of entities exist in the world. That is, we ascribe objective reality to something that is based on a merely subjective requirement of thought ("Man kann allen Schein darin setzen: dass die subjektive Bedingung des Denkens für die Erkenntnis des Objekts gehalten wird" [KrV, III, 247])[27]. This is the case, for instance, if we misunderstand the idea of God not as

---

[25] Thus, Kant's argument for the notion of God as a necessary idea of reason in its theoretical use bears strong similarities to his argument for transcendental freedom as a necessary idea of reason (see Chapter 1 above).

[26] "Das Ideal des höchsten Wesens ist nach diesen Betrachtungen nichts anders, als ein regulatives Prinzip der Vernunft, alle Verbindung in der Welt so anzusehen, als ob sie aus einer allgenugsamen notwendigen Ursache entspränge, um darauf die Regel einer systematischen und nach allgemeinen Gesetzen notwendigen Einheit in der Erklärung derselben zu gründen, und ist nicht eine Behauptung einer an sich notwendigen Existenz" [KrV, III, 412–3].

[27] "The conditions of all judgment are the categories, but out where experience cannot reach they are mere Ideas, rules, or maxims for the employment of our reason. Unchecked by experience, they inevitably appear to be objective truths of the highest kind, since no experience can ever refute them" [Beck, 1960, 239–40]. See also Kemp Smith: "The Idea is a mere fiction, necessary for comprehending the limited, not a reality that can be asserted, even hypothetically, as given along with the limited. Nonetheless, owing to a natural transcendental illusion, the mind inevitably tends to hypostatize it, and so generates the object of rational theology" [2003, 524].

an ordering principle required for achieving a coherent worldview, but as asserting the objective existence of God [KrV, III, 413][28].

Misunderstanding the ideas of reason as making existential claims results in reason entangling itself in contradictions [KrV, III, 460]. One of the purposes of the *Kritik der Reinen Vernunft* is to remove these contradictions by highlighting their source, namely the misunderstanding of the theoretical ideas of reason as making constitutive claims, rather than functioning as regulative principles —and thus to help us to satisfy reason's need of a unified and self-consistent view of the world [KrV, III, 492]. Crucially, there is no external authority that could help reason to untangle and remove the contradictions. Reason is reliant only on its own ability for self-critique to understand their origin and on self-discipline to regulate itself in a way that allows us to avoid them [KrV, III, 484]. In this sense, Kant's *Kritik* is precisely to be understood as a self-critique of reason.

This highlights the core of Kant's doctrine of ideas: *there is nothing reason can find orientation in but itself*. Everything we find outside ourselves, empirical reality, owes its structure to reason's spontaneity—and that which transcends this reality we can know nothing about, in a way that it does not offer any guidance either. In this sense, the question posed in the title of his 1786 essay "Was heißt: Sich im Denken Orientieren?" is central to Kant's philosophical project. Kant's answer, in brief, is that reason has only itself—and, more specifically, the requirements for its own coherent use—to guide itself. That is, reason can find orientation only in its own essential interests: "Nun aber tritt das Recht des Bedürfnisses der Vernunft ein, als eines subjektiven Grundes etwas vorauszusetzen und anzunehmen, was sie durch objektive Gründe zu wissen sich nicht anmaßen darf; und folglich sich im Denken, im unermesslichen und für uns mit dicker Nacht erfüllten Raume des Übersinnlichen, lediglich durch ihr eigenes Bedürfnis zu orientieren" [SDO, VIII, 137].

That is, the *Richtmaß* of reason [KrV, III, 384], our compass in thinking [SDO, VIII, 142], is not some external standard of truth (for the standard of any truth, according to transcendental idealism, is reason itself [KrV, III, 432]), but reason's own interests. In this sense, reason for Kant is autonomous: the only uncompromised use of reason is the one in which the principles of its use are not forced upon it from the outside, but based on its own subjective requirements—that is, principles given to reason by reason itself: "Freiheit im Denken [bedeutet] die Unterwerfung der Vernunft unter keine andere Gesetze als: die sie sich selbst gibt; und ihr Gegenteil ist die Maxime eines gesetzlosen Gebrauchs der Vernunft"

---

28 This, Kant holds, is the error committed, for instance, in Descartes' proof of the existence of God [SDO, VIII, 137n].

[SDO, VIII, 145]. Any use of reason in which reason is subjected to rules and guidelines other than those based on its own interests, Kant holds, is corrosive, and ultimately self-destructive. The only proper use of reason is a free use of reason—that is, the one in which the use of reason is guided by principles based on reason's own interests.

The doctrine of practical knowledge

With our account of the Kantian notion of the ideas of reason in place, we can now return to our discussion of the legitimate use of non-empirical concepts. I have said above that there are three classes of concepts that Kant holds we can legitimately use even though they cannot be given material content through the intuitions of our senses. We have already discussed two of these: the concepts referring to the conditions of the possibility of our experience and the ideas of reason in their theoretical employment (i.e., in so far as they are needed to facilitate the most complete use of our understanding). The remaining class of non-empirical concepts, for which Kant sees a legitimate use, is that of concepts backed by *practical interests*. He first introduces the notion of concepts backed by practical interests in *Kritik der Reinen Vernunft*. However, at this stage he does not provide a full explanation of what he understands the relevant interests to be. In the context of his discussion of the transcendental deduction of the categories, he writes:

> Wir können uns keinen Gegenstand denken, ohne durch Kategorien; wir können keinen gedachten Gegenstand erkennen, ohne durch Anschauungen, die jenen Begriffen entsprechen. Nun sind alle unsere Anschauungen sinnlich, und diese Erkenntnis, so fern der Gegenstand derselben gegeben ist, ist empirisch. Empirische Erkenntnis aber ist Erfahrung. Folglich ist uns keine Erkenntnis a priori möglich, als lediglich von Gegenständen möglicher Erfahrung... Damit man sich nicht voreiliger Weise an den besorglichen nachtheiligen Folgen dieses Satzes stoße, will ich nur in Erinnerung bringen, dass die Kategorien im Denken durch die Bedingungen unserer sinnlichen Anschauung nicht eingeschränkt sind, sondern ein unbegrenztes Feld haben, und nur das Erkennen dessen, was wir uns denken, das Bestimmen des Objekts, Anschauung bedürfe; wo beim Mangel der letzteren der Gedanke vom Objekte übrigens noch immer seine wahren und nützlichen Folgen auf den Vernunftgebrauch des Subjekts haben kann, *der sich aber, weil er nicht immer auf die Bestimmung des Objekts, mithin aufs Erkenntnis, sondern auch auf die des Subjekts und dessen Wollen gerichtet ist*, hier noch nicht vortragen lässt. [KrV, III, 128; my emphasis]

In this paragraph, Kant condenses the movement of thought that we have gone through in the previous pages: we can only have theoretical knowledge of facts where our concepts are backed by the intuition of our senses. Yet, the sphere of concepts that we can think is considerably larger than the sphere of thoughts whose reality is backed by such intuitions. The concepts that are not certified as corresponding to empirical reality in this way can nonetheless still have their proper uses. However—and this is the new thought—these uses do not necessarily have to arise in a theoretical context (i.e., in the context of gaining knowledge about the world), but can equally present themselves in a practical context (i.e., in the context of our acting in the world). How this can be the case, though, Kant does not yet discuss at this point.

Similarly, in the introduction of the same work, Kant highlights how his theoretical inquiries show the impossibility of gaining theoretical knowledge about an object if that knowledge is not backed by intuitions from our senses—and yet hints that the metaphysical (i.e. non-empirical) concepts, such as that of our own transcendental freedom, which have thus been declared unfit to be objects of possible theoretical knowledge, might nonetheless be given reality through "practical data", leading to "practical knowledge":

> Nun bleibt uns immer noch übrig, nachdem der spekulativen Vernunft alles Fortkommen in diesem Felde des Übersinnlichen abgesprochen worden, zu versuchen, ob sich nicht in ihrer praktischen Erkenntnis Data finden, jenen transzendenten Vernunftbegriff des Unbedingten zu bestimmen und auf solche Weise dem Wunsche der Metaphysik gemäß über die Grenze aller möglichen Erfahrung hinaus mit unserem, aber nur in praktischer Absicht möglichen Erkenntnisse a priori zu gelangen. Und bei einem solchen Verfahren hat uns die spekulative Vernunft zu solcher Erweiterung immer doch wenigstens Platz verschafft, wenn sie ihn gleich leer lassen musste, und es bleibt uns also noch unbenommen, ja wir sind gar dazu durch sie aufgefordert, ihn durch praktische Data derselben, wenn wir können, auszufüllen. [KrV, III, 14]

Thus, far from banning the use of metaphysical concepts, Kant suggests his theoretical inquiries have "created the space" for these concepts to be used in their proper practical context, backed by "practical data". Yet, again he does little to elucidate what these practical data are[29].

---

[29] A similar passage occurs a few pages later, where Kant writes: "Einen Gegenstand erkennen, dazu wird erfordert, dass ich seine Möglichkeit (es sei nach dem Zeugnis der Erfahrung aus seiner Wirklichkeit, oder a priori durch Vernunft) beweisen könne. Aber denken kann ich, was ich will, wenn ich mir nur nicht selbst widerspreche, d. i. wenn mein Begriff nur ein möglicher Gedanke ist, ob ich zwar dafür nicht stehen kann, ob im Inbegriffe aller Möglichkeiten diesem auch ein Objekt korrespondiere oder nicht. Um einem solchen Begriffe aber objektive Gültigkeit (reale Möglichkeit, denn die erstere war bloß die logische) beizulegen, dazu wird etwas mehr erfordert. Dieses Mehrere aber braucht eben nicht in theoretischen Erkenntnisquellen gesucht zu werden, es kann auch in praktischen liegen" [KrV, III, 17n]. Kant also mentions—but does not elucidate— the term "practical knowledge" in [KrV, III, 8]. In *Kritik der Urteilskraft*, he distinguishes between

The basic idea behind the notion of concepts being backed by practical needs—which Kant also refers to as the *ideas of practical reason* [KrV, III, 254] —is that for our practical orientation in the world (i.e. our predicament as beings confronted with the need to act in the world), we require concepts to which our senses do not deliver corresponding intuitions. An important example of such a concept is that of transcendental freedom. As we have seen above, we can have no experience of transcendental freedom. Yet, as rational agents we have to ascribe transcendental freedom to ourselves—that is, we have to regard our actions not as caused by natural necessity, but as starting new causal chains in the empirical world (a claim that we will discuss in more detail in the next two chapters). Hence, the notion of our own transcendental freedom is a concept that is not backed by any empirical data, nor is it a condition of the possibility of experience—yet, we are nonetheless justified, Kant holds, in making use of the concept to satisfy the interests we have in a practical context, i.e. insofar as we are agents that have to act in the world[30].

Kant's main point concerning the notion of our right to use concepts backed by practical interests is that the restriction of the sphere of the empirical facts leaves many questions that are relevant for practical purposes (such as: are we free?) undetermined by the facts available to theoretical inquiry. Yet, he holds, if there is a judgment in which we take a necessary practical interest but which is not determined by theoretical facts, we are entitled to accept its objective validity simply on the basis of our practical interests. In other words, if a matter cannot be settled with reference to the facts, but if settling it is required to make sense of our role as agents, we are entitled to act *as if* it were settled. I will call this position of Kant's, which, as we will see, will be critical for our understanding of the foundations of his practical philosophy, his *doctrine of practical knowledge*.

Kant provides the clearest statement of the doctrine of practical knowledge in *Kritik der Praktischen Vernunft:*

> [W]enn reine Vernunft für sich praktisch sein kann...so ist es doch immer nur eine und dieselbe Vernunft, die, es sei in theoretischer oder praktischer Absicht, nach Prinzipien a priori urteilt, und da ist es klar, dass, wenn ihr Vermögen in der ersteren gleich nicht zulangt,

---

theoretical and practical facts, but again without laying down criteria for identifying the latter: "Alle Tatsachen gehören entweder zum Naturbegriff, der seine Realität an den vor allen Naturbegriffen gegebenen (oder zu geben möglichen) Gegenständen der Sinne beweiset; oder zum Freiheitsbegriffe, der seine Realität durch die Kausalität der Vernunft in Ansehung gewisser durch sie möglichen Wirkungen in der Sinnenwelt, die sie im moralischen Gesetze unwiderleglich postuliert, hinreichend dartut" [KU, V, 475].
30 We will explore Kant's justification for this claim in Chapter 4 below.

gewisse Sätze behauptend festzusetzen, indessen dass sie ihr auch eben nicht widersprechen, eben diese Sätze, so bald sie unabtrennlich zum praktischen Interesse der reinen Vernunft gehören, zwar als ein ihr fremdes Angebot, das nicht auf ihrem Boden erwachsen, aber doch hinreichend beglaubigt ist, annehmen und sie mit allem, was sie als spekulative Vernunft in ihrer Macht hat, zu vergleichen und zu verknüpfen suchen müsse; doch sich bescheidend, dass dieses nicht ihre Einsichten, aber doch Erweiterungen ihres Gebrauchs in irgend einer anderen, nämlich praktischen, Absicht sind... In der Verbindung also der reinen spekulativen mit der reinen praktischen Vernunft zu einem Erkenntnisse führt die letztere das Primat, vorausgesetzt nämlich, dass diese Verbindung nicht etwa zufällig und beliebig, sondern a priori auf der Vernunft selbst gegründet, mithin notwendig sei. Denn es würde ohne diese Unterordnung ein Widerstreit der Vernunft mit ihr selbst entstehen. [KpV, V, 121][31]

This passage states the doctrine of practical knowledge we have just discussed: if a given judgment cannot be determined by means of theoretical inquiry ("wenn ihr Vermögen in [theoretischer Absicht] gleich nicht zulangt... gewisse Sätze behauptend festzusetzen"), but we take a practical interest in the truth of that judgment ("so bald sie unabtrennlich zum praktischen Interesse der reinen Vernunft gehören"), then we are entitled to treat the judgment in question as if it were true ("diese Sätze... als... hinreichend beglaubigt... annehmen und sie mit allem, was sie als spekulative Vernunft in ihrer Macht hat... zu verknüpfen")[32]. In addition to

---

31 For a further, yet less complete, statement of the doctrine of practical knowledge occurs in Kant's lectures on logic: „Zwischen der Erwerbung einer Erkenntnis durch Erfahrung (a posteriori) und durch die Vernunft (a priori) gibt es kein Mittleres. Aber zwischen der Erkenntnis eines Objekts und der bloßen Voraussetzung der Möglichkeit desselben gibt es ein Mittleres, nämlich einen empirischen oder einen Vernunftgrund, die letztere anzunehmen in Beziehung auf eine notwendige Erweiterung des Feldes möglicher Objekte über diejenige, deren Erkenntnis uns möglich ist. Diese Notwendigkeit findet nur in Ansehung dessen statt, dass das Objekt als praktisch und durch Vernunft praktisch notwendig erkannt wird, denn zum Behuf der bloßen Erweiterung der theoretischen Erkenntnis etwas anzunehmen, ist jederzeit zufällig... Dieses ist eine subjektive Notwendigkeit, die Realität des Objekts um der notwendigen Willensbestimmung halber anzunehmen... Dies ist der casus extraordinarius, ohne welchen die praktische Vernunft sich nicht in Ansehung ihres notwendigen Zwecks erhalten kann, und es kommt ihr hier favor necessitatis zu statten in ihrem eigenen Urteil. Sie kann kein Objekt logisch erwerben, sondern sich nur allein dem widersetzen, was sie im Gebrauch dieser Idee, die ihr praktisch angehört, hindert. Dieser Glaube ist die Notwendigkeit, die objektive Realität eines Begriffs... d. i. die Möglichkeit seines Gegenstandes, als a priori notwendigen Objekts der Willkür anzunehmen... Der Vernunftglaube... ist bloß eine Voraussetzung der Vernunft in subjektiver, aber absolut-notwendiger praktischer Absicht" [L, IX, 67n; see also: MS, VI, 354; KU, V, 471n].

32 Yovel is among the few commentators to give a clear statement of the doctrine of practical knowledge: "These criteria justify the assertion of propositions which transcend the limits of the theoretical domains under the following conditions: (a) they fulfill a 'pure need' of reason; (b) they are taken not as scientific judgments but only as 'postulates' which make the realization of morality possible" [1989, 91n]. See also: "The primacy of practical reason... is ... a methodological

this basic outline of the doctrine of practical knowledge, the passage makes the following important points:
- First, the doctrine is justified with reference to the notion of the *unity of reason*. According to this latter notion, the distinction between the theoretical and the practical application of reason notwithstanding, reason is always "one and the same" ("immer nur eine und dieselbe Vernunft"). A corollary of this position is that, given its interest in systematic unity, reason has to integrate the experience that we have in our theoretical and our practical activity into one coherent worldview[33] in order to avoid self-contradiction ("Denn es würde... ein Widerstreit der Vernunft mit ihr selbst entstehen")[34]. Hence, if our practical reason requires us to accept the truth of a given judgment in order for us to be able to make sense of our predicament as agents in the world, we have to integrate the judgment in question into our theoretical picture of the world in order to avoid a contradiction of reason with itself: "The impact of Kant's insistence on the unity of reason is to make clear that it is impossible rationally to accept some proposition (from a practical point of view) but at the same time to reject it (from a theoretical point of view)" [Willaschek, 2010, 177].
- Secondly, Kant insists that the doctrine of practical knowledge only finds application if the judgment in question is linked to an essential interest of practical reason ("... diese Sätze, so bald sie unabtrennlich zum praktischen Interesse der reinen Vernunft gehören..."). Where the interest in question is a sensuous, rather than a rational interest, we are not justified in accepting the judgment as objectively valid: "[S]o fern praktische Vernunft als patholo-

---

principle... 'You may rationally believe in a cognitive proposition that cannot be decided cognitively, if and only if this belief is necessary for moral action in a concrete situation that you face' [1989, 269; see also: Beck, 1960, 27–8; Willaschek, 2010, 168–169]. The viability of the Kantian doctrine of practical knowledge is linked to the four characteristics of reason that we have discussed in Chapter 1: its self-reflectivity, its discursiveness, its autonomy and its interestedness. As discursive, reason is not confronted with a pre-fabricated order in our worldview, but has to construct this order itself. As self-reflective, it can choose the rules used to generate this order on the basis of reflection. As interested and autonomous, it can—and has to—choose these rules on the basis of its own interests, rather than by reference to some external standard.

33 Regarding our reason's need to integrate the experiences we have in our theoretical and our practical activity into one coherent whole, Kant writes: "[Wir haben die] Erwartung, es vielleicht dereinst bis zur Einsicht der Einheit des ganzen reinen Vernunftvermögens (des theoretischen sowohl als praktischen) bringen und alles aus einem Prinzip ableiten zu können; welches das unvermeidliche Bedürfnis der menschlichen Vernunft ist, die nur in einer vollständig systematischen Einheit ihrer Erkenntnisse völlige Zufriedenheit findet" [KpV, V, 91].
34 See also [KU, V, 471n].

gisch bedingt, d. i. das Interesse der Neigungen unter dem sinnlichen Prinzip der Glückseligkeit bloß verwaltend, zum Grunde gelegt würde, so ließe sich diese Zumutung an die spekulative Vernunft gar nicht tun" [KpV, V, 120][35]. This is consistent with our discussion of the role played by the notion of the unity of reason: the doctrine of practical knowledge is grounded in the need of reason to satisfy all its interests without conflict between them—hence, it simply does not apply in cases in which no interest of reason is involved (i.e. in cases in which we are confronted with a merely sensuous interest)[36].

- Thirdly, while Kant holds that we have to regard judgments backed by practical data as objectively valid[37], he also insists that doing so does not aug-

---

[35] Kant uses the terms "sensuous" and "pathological" as synonymous, employing both to refer to that which is related to our physical, rather than our rational, nature [KpV, V, 75].

[36] Kant discusses this difference between the roles played by sensuous and rational interests in the context of the doctrine of practical knowledge in more detail in a later passage in *Kritik der Praktischen Vernunft:* "Im deutschen Museum, Febr. 1787, findet sich eine Abhandlung von einem sehr feinen und hellen Kopfe, dem sel. Wizenmann, dessen früher Tod zu bedauern ist, darin er die Befugnis, aus einem Bedürfnisse auf die objektive Realität des Gegenstandes desselben zu schließen, bestreitet und seinen Gegenstand durch das Beispiel eines Verliebten erläutert, der, indem er sich in eine Idee von Schönheit, welche bloß sein Hirngespinst ist, vernarrt hätte, schließen wollte, dass ein solches Objekt wirklich wo existiere. Ich gebe ihm hierin vollkommen Recht in allen Fällen, wo das Bedürfnis auf Neigung gegründet ist, die nicht einmal notwendig für den, der damit angefochten ist, die Existenz ihres Objekts postulieren kann, viel weniger eine für jedermann gültige Forderung enthält und daher ein bloß subjektiver Grund der Wünsche ist. Hier aber ist es ein Vernunftbedürfnis, aus einem objektiven Bestimmungsgrunde des Willens, nämlich dem moralischen Gesetze, entspringend, welches jedes vernünftige Wesen notwendig verbindet, also zur Voraussetzung der ihm angemessenen Bedingungen in der Natur a priori berechtigt und die letztern von dem vollständigen praktischen Gebrauche der Vernunft unzertrennlich macht" [KpV, V, 143]. An important distinction, which Kant does not make in this passage, between the example given by Wizenmann and the cases in which the doctrine of practical knowledge finds legitimate application is that the empirical existence of a given object of our desire is a matter that is determined by theoretical fact, while the doctrine only applies where the truth-value of a judgment cannot be determined by theoretical means. Hence, at the very least the enamoured person in Wizenmann's example would have to provide an explanation of how the alleged fact of the existence of the beloved object can be integrated into a coherent and unified worldview, while Kant has already provided such an explanation. For a discussion of the Wizenmann passage, see Beck [1960, 254] and Willaschek [2010, 169]. We discuss the distinction between rational and sensuous interests in more detail in Chapter 5 below.

[37] Kant does not emphasize the fact that the judgments backed by practical data have objective validity for us in the passage we are discussing—but he does so in the next passage quoted in the text as well as in the preface of *Kritik der Praktischen Vernunft:* "Hier ist nun ein in Vergleichung mit der spekulativen Vernunft bloß subjektiver Grund des Fürwahrhaltens, der doch einer

ment our theoretical knowledge of the world ("... dass dieses nicht ihre Einsichten, aber doch Erweiterungen ihres Gebrauchs in irgend einer anderen, nämlich praktischen, Absicht sind"). As he puts it later in the same work: "Diese Postulate sind nicht theoretische Dogmata, sondern Voraussetzungen in notwendig praktischer Rücksicht, erweitern also zwar nicht das spekulative Erkenntnis, geben aber den Ideen der spekulativen Vernunft im Allgemeinen (vermittelst ihrer Beziehung aufs Praktische) objektive Realität und berechtigen sie zu Begriffen, deren Möglichkeit auch nur zu behaupten sie sich sonst nicht anmaßen könnte" [KpV, V, 132][38]. That is, while the concepts backed by practical data have reality for us, the resulting knowledge is only valid "from a practical point of view" ("in praktischer Rücksicht" [GMS, IV, 448]): we learn nothing about how the world really is, but only about what kind of assumptions we are entitled to make for the purpose of fulfilling our role as agents in a way that is consistent with the interests of our reason[39].

---

eben so reinen, aber praktischen Vernunft objektiv gültig ist, dadurch den Ideen... objektive Reälität und Befugnis, ja subjektive Notwendigkeit (Bedürfnis der reinen Vernunft) sie anzunehmen verschafft wird, ohne dass dadurch doch die Vernunft im theoretischen Erkenntnisse erweitert, sondern nur die Möglichkeit, die vorher nur Problem war, hier Assertion wird, gegeben und so der praktische Gebrauch der Vernunft mit den Elementen des theoretischen verknüpft wird" [KpV, V, 4–5; see also: KU, V, 456; R, VI, 5 and ED, VIII, 333]. While the logic governing practical beliefs differs from that governing theoretical knowledge, Kant insists that the degree of certainty we have in each of these cases is comparable: "[D]ieses Fürwahrhalten [steht] dem Grade nach keinem Wissen [nach], ob es gleich der Art nach davon völlig unterschieden ist" [SDO, VIII, 141]. Yovel comments: "[B]y the term scientific Kant does not understand a certain kind of knowledge, but a certain epistemic status, i.e. apodictic validity and certainty, that can be obtained by all the rationally founded disciplines, ethics and metaphysics no less than physics and mathematics" [1989, 230–1].

38 Kant defines a postulate as a theoretical proposition that cannot be given objective reality by means of theoretical enquiry, but only on the basis of practical knowledge: "[Unter einem] Postulat der reinen praktischen Vernunft [verstehe ich] einen theoretischen, als solchen aber nicht erweislichen Satz..., so fern er einem a priori unbedingt geltenden praktischen Gesetze unzertrennlich anhängt" [KpV, V, 122]. The validity of the postulates is based on the interests of our practical reason ("Ein Bedürfnis der reinen Vernunft in ihrem spekulativen Gebrauche führt nur auf Hypothesen, das der reinen praktischen Vernunft aber zu Postulaten" [KpV, V, 142]). Kant calls the epistemic attitude of accepting the objective validity of the postulates "rational faith": "Glaube... ist die moralische Denkungsart der Vernunft im Fürwahrhalten desjenigen, was für das theoretische Erkenntnis unzugänglich ist" [KU, V, 471; see also: SDO, VIII, 141]. For a discussion of the notion of the postulates in the secondary literature, see Beck [1960, 251–55].

39 Kant writes that, concerning the practical use of the ideas, "die Realität der Begriffe [wird] hinreichend gesichert, ohne gleichwohl durch diesen Zuwachs die mindeste Erweiterung des Er-

– Lastly, it is worth re-iterating that, according to the doctrine of practical knowledge, we are warranted in accepting the objective validity of a judgment backed by practical data only if the truth-value of the judgment in question cannot be determined on the basis of theoretical data[40]—and, hence, if doing so does not create a contradiction with our theoretical knowledge of the world ("gewisse Sätze behauptend festzusetzen, indessen dass sie ihr auch eben nicht widersprechen")[41]. This requirement for the proper application of the doctrine of practical knowledge is of particular interest

---

kenntnisses nach theoretischen Grundsätzen zu bewirken" [KpV, V, 136; see also KpV, V, 5]. Yet, he also states that theoretical reason is warranted in accepting the real possibility (i.e. reality) of the ideas in question: "[Für die theoretische Vernunft] sonst problematische (bloß denkbare) Begriffe [werden] jetzt assertorisch für solche erklärt [...], denen wirklich Objekte zukommen, weil praktische Vernunft die Existenz derselben zur Möglichkeit ihres und zwar praktisch schlechthin notwendigen Objekts, des höchsten Guts, unvermeidlich bedarf, und die theoretische dadurch berechtigt wird, sie vorauszusetzen" [KpV, V, 134]. This commits Kant to the rather delicate position that theoretical reason can accept the objective reality of the concepts in question (on the basis of the practical argument), without this, though, leading to any extension of our theoretical knowledge.

40 Other passages in which Kant discusses the requirement that the truth-value of the judgments in question has to be undeterminable from a theoretical point of view include [KrV, III, 16], [KrV, III, 187], [KpV, V, 4], [KU, V, 397], [SDO, VIII, 137] and [L, IX, 67]. This condition is discussed in detail by Willaschek [2010, 168].

41 This insight makes Kant's suggestion problematic that there is a hierarchy between the theoretical and the practical application of our reason—and that practical reason enjoys primacy in this hierarchy ("In der Verbindung also der reinen spekulativen mit der reinen praktischen Vernunft zu einem Erkenntnisse führt die letztere das Primat" [KpV, V, 121]). For according to Kant's own statement of his doctrine of practical knowledge, this practical knowledge—i.e. the acceptance of judgments on the basis of practical data in the sense discussed in the text—is possible only where there are gaps in our theoretical knowledge. As Kant himself insists, in cases where, in the determination of the truth-value of a given judgment, theoretical data are in conflict with our necessary practical interests, it is the former that prevail: "Gesetzt nun, die Moral setze notwendig Freiheit (im strengsten Sinne) als Eigenschaft unseres Willens voraus... die spekulative Vernunft aber hätte bewiesen, dass diese sich gar nicht denken lasse: so muss notwendig jene Voraussetzung, nämlich die moralische, derjenigen weichen, deren Gegenteil einen offenbaren Widerspruch enthält, folglich Freiheit und mit ihr Sittlichkeit... dem Naturmechanismus den Platz einräumen" [KrV, III, 18; see also: KU, V, 446]. This position sits uncomfortably with his assertion about the primacy of practical reason. That said, the notion of the primacy of practical reason can be given an unproblematic interpretation if it is understood not as the notion that in case of conflict the interests of practical reason take precedence, but as the position that it "is not in knowledge but in action that the ultimate metaphysical interest of reason will find its adequate expression or even satisfaction" [Yovel, 1989, 289–90]. Yovel continues this passage by noting correctly that: "... In [the] transformation of the metaphysical interest from a means of absolute knowledge into a principle of will, Kant sees the apex of the critique of reason" [1989, 289–90].

for us, given that Kant himself fails to heed it in a later application of his doctrine, as we will discuss in Chapter 7.

An appreciation of the doctrine of practical knowledge enables us to understand the double movement of the *Kritik der Reinen Vernunft:* in the first—negative—move, Kant restricts the sphere of the facts, that is, of that which is accepted as empirical facts in good standing, banning everything which is not related to an object of possible experience from this sphere. In the second—positive—move, he allows that the content of some concepts has reality (i.e. real possibility) for us because these concepts are required for practical purposes, even though their reality is not grounded in empirical fact (i.e., they do not correspond to any possible sense impression)[42]. Thus, it is not the fervor of the skeptic, with which Kant is operating, but the cleanliness of the scientist: his aim is not to dissuade us from holding beliefs that cannot be backed by experience, but rather to make us aware that the logic governing these beliefs (and the possible justification we can give for holding them) is different from that governing beliefs based on empirical facts[43]:

---

[42] In this sense epistemic modesty, the restriction and exact delineation of the boundaries of possible knowledge, is an important theme of *Kritik der Reinen Vernunft*—not only because it removes the pretense of knowledge where knowledge is impossible ("Der größte und vielleicht einzige Nutzen aller Philosophie der reinen Vernunft ist also wohl nur negativ: da sie nämlich nicht als Organ zur Erweiterung, sondern als Disziplin zur Grenzbestimmung dient und, anstatt Wahrheit zu entdecken, nur das stille Verdienst hat, Irrtümer zu verhüten" [KrV, III, 517]), but also because only an attitude of epistemic modesty opens the conceptual space for practical knowledge ("Ich musste also das Wissen aufheben, um zum Glauben Platz zu bekommen, und der Dogmatismus der Metaphysik, d. i. das Vorurteil, in ihr ohne Kritik der reinen Vernunft fortzukommen, ist die wahre Quelle alles der Moralität widerstreitenden Unglaubens" [KrV, III, 19]).
[43] While we have raised doubts about the notion of the primacy of practical reason, there is clearly a sense in which Kant's philosophical work aims at cutting back the pretense of theoretical knowledge in favor of our practical interests. This point is highlighted in the following passage: "Weil gleichwohl die menschliche Vernunft immer noch nach Freiheit strebt: so muss, wenn sie einmal die Fesseln zerbricht, ihr erster Gebrauch einer lange entwöhnten Freiheit in Missbrauch und vermessenes Zutrauen auf Unabhängigkeit ihres Vermögens von aller Einschränkung ausarten, in eine Überredung von der Alleinherrschaft der spekulativen Vernunft, die nichts annimmt, als was sich durch objektive Gründe und dogmatische Überzeugung rechtfertigen kann, alles übrige aber kühn wegleugnet" [SDO, VIII, 146]. The doctrine of practical knowledge is precisely Kant's antidote against the autarchy of speculative reason that he castigates in this passage.

This point is a crucial difference between Kant's philosophical project and that of Wittgenstein in the *Tractatus*, which—like Kant's *Kritik der Reinen Vernunft*—tries to show that there is a correspondence between the structure of our thought, on the one hand, and the structure of empirical reality, on the other. While Kant's guiding thought in this venture is, as we have seen, to

[E]ine Kritik, welche die [Erfahrungsgrenze] einschränkt, [ist] so fern zwar negativ, aber, indem sie dadurch zugleich ein Hindernis, welches den [reinen praktischen Vernunftgebrauch] einschränkt, oder gar zu vernichten droht, aufhebt, in der Tat von positivem und sehr wichtigem Nutzen, so bald man überzeugt wird, dass es einen schlechterdings notwendigen praktischen Gebrauch der reinen Vernunft (den moralischen) gebe, in welchem sie sich unvermeidlich über die Grenzen der Sinnlichkeit erweitert, dazu sie zwar von der spekulativen keiner Beihilfe bedarf, dennoch aber wider ihre Gegenwirkung gesichert sein muss, um nicht in Widerspruch mit sich selbst zu geraten. [KrV, III, 16; see also R, VI, 69 n]

We should emphasize that all we have done so far is to discuss the logic underlying the doctrine of practical knowledge. We do not yet know what the practical interests are which, according to the doctrine, ground the objective reality of practical judgments. To answer this question, we have to wait until Chapter 4, in which we will analyze the application of the doctrine of practical knowledge in Kant's argument to establish the objective reality of our transcendental freedom. Before embarking on that venture, though, we first have to explore, in the next chapter, his conception of the moral law in more detail.

Conclusion

We have come to the end of our survey of the elements of transcendental idealism that will be of relevance in understanding Kant's practical philosophy—and his solution to the problem of the real possibility of transcendental freedom, in particular. We have focused on two main points. First, Kant holds that we can account for the necessary laws of nature if we understand them as *a priori* elements of our cognitive processes—that is, as features imposed on our experience by the cognizing subject, rather than as features of the world as it is in itself. A *priori* knowledge is possible not because we can boast of a special faculty to de-

---

preserve the possibility of a non-empirical—and, especially, practical—use of concepts, Wittgenstein denies the legitimacy of a non-empirical use of language: "The right method of philosophy would be this. To say nothing except what can be said, i.e. the propositions of natural science" (Tractatus, 6.53). This motivates the famous last line of the Tractatus: "Whereof one cannot speak, thereof one must be silent" (Tracatatus, 7). Kant appears to address this conclusion directly when he writes some 130 years earlier in the *Kritik der Reinen Vernunft:* "[W]enn der Empirismus in Ansehung der Ideen (wie es mehrenteils geschieht) selbst dogmatisch wird und dasjenige dreist verneint, was über der Sphäre seiner anschauenden Erkenntnisse ist, so fällt er selbst in den Fehler der Unbescheidenheit, der hier um desto tadelbarer ist, weil dadurch dem praktischen Interesse der Vernunft ein unersetzlicher Nachtheil verursacht wird" [KrV, III, 327].

tect *a priori* truths, but rather because we can, through reflection, identify certain elements of our cognitive processes as necessary conditions of the possibility of experience. We have to understand these, Kant maintains, as imposed by the functioning of our epistemic apparatus. In particular, we can only account for the possibility of *a priori* laws if we regard them as the products of our pure understanding, i.e. as the product of the noumenal activity of our understanding.

A second focus for Kant's theoretical investigations is the question concerning the conditions under which we can legitimately make use of a given concept. One legitimate use of concepts is their employment to describe facts in the world. Yet, Kant holds that only those concepts for which our senses provide corresponding material content are grounded in this way. He identifies three cases in which we can legitimately use non-empirical concepts, namely those involving concepts describing the conditions of the possibility of experience, concepts expressing assumptions necessary for the proper use of our understanding (ideas of reason in its theoretical employment) and concepts required to make sense of our conditions as agents (ideas of reason in its practical employment).

3 The moral law

As we have seen in Chapter 1, a key concern of Kant's practical philosophy is to establish the real possibility of transcendental freedom—i.e. to show that we are justified in considering ourselves as transcendentally free (that is, as first causes of our actions, rather than these being determined by natural necessity). In Chapter 2, we have explored two important results from Kant's theoretical work—his conception of necessity and his doctrine of practical knowledge –, which will help us to understand his solution to the problem of the real possibility of transcendental freedom. Before we discuss the latter, however, we require one last preparatory step: we need to develop a good grasp of Kant's conception of morality, which, as we will see, is central to the argument with which he aims to establish the objective reality of our transcendental freedom.

Like Kant's reflections on transcendental freedom, his investigations into the nature of morality have two aims. The first is to elucidate the notion of the moral law—i.e., to clarify what we mean when we speak about the moral law. The second is to show that this law is valid for us—not only as the correct standard for judging our actions (or, in Kant's term, the *principle of adjudication*), but also as a possible determining ground of our actions (the *principle of execution*) [E, 1924, 44]. That is, Kant's inquiry is structured around the two questions of the *quid facti* (the question concerning the content of the concept) and that of the *quid juris* (concerning our right to apply that concept), i.e. the two questions about the logical and the real possibility of the notion of morality. In the present chapter, we focus on Kant's answer to the first question, i.e. the one concerned with the content of the notion of morality. His answer to the second question—that about the validity of the moral law for us, which is, as we will see, closely linked to his solution of the problem of the real possibility of transcendental freedom—will be discussed in the next chapter.

What is the moral law?

In the first part of his argument, Kant is concerned with the question of what we mean when we speak about morality—and how this notion can be integrated without contradiction into our general worldview (i.e., how the possibility of morality can be thought consistently). That is, in the terminology that we have used above, in this first part of his enquiry he is concerned with the *logical*, not the *real*, possibility of the notion of morality.

In considering the content of the notion of morality, Kant starts with what he takes to be our everyday understanding of that notion. He sees the following to be the generally accepted features of our common moral experience:

1. Morality confronts us with a command regarding the principles guiding our action. That is, the proper object of morality are not feelings or actions themselves, but the principles on which we act [KpV, V, 45][1];
2. The moral law provides us with the standard of rightness for our principles of action (it is the *principle of adjudication*, in the sense explained above) [KpV, V, 64];
3. The moral command has motivational pull. Our knowledge of what is our moral duty can (though not always does) lead us to act. That is, the moral law can be the *principle of execution* of our actions [KpV, V, 30];
4. The moral law commands with unconditional necessity—that is, it is not dependent for its validity on us having any particular empirical interests [GMS, IV, 389];
5. The moral command is universally valid: it is directed at, and valid for, all rational agents in the same way [KpV, V, 32].

As in his theoretical investigations, Kant aims to provide an account that explains how these features of our everyday moral experience are possible[2]. As before, Kant is particularly focused on the notions of necessity and universality. While in his earlier work, the challenge was to explain how necessity and universality are possible in the context of cognition, his task is now to give an account of their possibility in the ambit of practice (i.e. our experience of the world insofar as we find ourselves confronted with the need to act in it). This is the crucial link between the deduction of the categories in *Kritik der Reinen Vernunft* and his account of the categorical imperative in his ethical writings.

An important result of the earlier investigations was that the universally valid and necessary are features of the *a priori*. Consequently, Kant holds that if there is such a thing as the moral law, commanding with necessity and universality, we must regard it as an *a priori* law—and cannot account for it merely as an empirical rule [KpV, V, 26]. We can easily see why this should be so: the moral law would be a mere empirical rule if the hold it has over us were due to the pun-

---

[1] Kant calls these principles on which we act "maxims", a notion we will discuss in more detail in Chapter 5 below.
[2] This similarity is noted by Beck, who points out that in both cases Kant "begins with a problem presented by ordinary experience to philosophical analysis, and he reaches his conclusion by attempting to demonstrate that only one principle or theory is capable of rendering the problematic experience intelligible" [Beck, 1960, 111].

ishment we expect in the case of non-compliance or the rewards we are promised in the case of compliance. Consequently, to the degree that we happen to be indifferent towards punishment or rewards the moral law would not bind us. Yet, that would mean that its command is not unconditionally valid. Hence, insofar as the moral law is universally and necessarily valid, it cannot be an empirical rule. Rather—as we have learnt in Chapter 2—to account for the possibility of a rule that is necessarily valid for us, we have to regard it as valid *a priori* [KpV, V, 32][3].

Our earlier discussion has also taught us that, according to Kant, we can only account for *a priori* laws as the products of our own pure faculties (that is, of our higher faculties conceived as having noumenal existence). In discussing his theory of cognition, Kant had argued that we have to regard *a priori* laws as imposed by our pure understanding. As we have seen above, pure understanding is not a faculty that we can have any experience of—but is rather postulated as the ground of the possibility of all experience. That is, in addition to the empirical understanding of which we are aware, we have to attribute to ourselves a pure understanding the activity of which makes the world of our experience possible in the first place.

To understand the implications of this result for the current discussion, we have to give an outline of Kant's theory of the will (we will discuss this topic in more detail in Chapter 5 below): Our will, for Kant, is our ability to determine our actions on the basis of maxims—i.e. rules of actions—that we are free to adopt or to reject on the basis of reflection. Our maxims typically specify a desired outcome of our actions, some object of our desires the mental representation of which is linked to a feeling of pleasure. To the degree that we experience our will as free (i.e. as not determined by natural necessity), we regard our will as guided by practical reason, that is, as self-reflective, spontaneous thought applied to the determination of our action [GMS, IV, 412]. Thus, in Kant's theory of volition we again find the dual contribution of our lower (i.e. passive-receptive) and our higher (i.e. active-spontaneous) faculties that also marked his theory of cognition: our sensual nature is affected by some desire and our active will has to determine whether to adopt the object of this desire into its maxim.

---

[3] "For Kant, there are two marks of a priori knowledge: necessity and universality; and these marks apply to practical as well as to theoretical knowledge. (a) Necessity here means practical necessity. That is, what is required by the principles of pure practical reason... (b) As for universality, this means that the requirements in question hold for all reasonable and rational persons in virtue of their nature as such persons, independently of any particular conditions of inclinations and circumstances that mark off one reasonable and rational person from another" [Rawls, 2000, 247].

Kant holds that just as we can only account for the possibility of *a priori* laws in the context of cognition by regarding them as imposed by our pure understanding, we can only account for the possibility of a practical *a priori* law—that is, a law whose command applies with necessity and universality—as imposed by our own pure faculty of volition [KU, V, 196–7; see also: KpV, V, 22][4]. That is, if we are to explain the possibility of a practical law that is valid *a priori*, we have to attribute a noumenal dimension to our practical reason. In addition to our empirical will, we have to regard ourselves as endowed with pure practical reason (that is, reason which is perfectly unaffected by any physical desires or inclinations, but rather guided exclusively by its own proper interests[5])—and have to conceive of this pure will as legislating the moral law to us. Kant himself highlights this parallel between his epistemology and his moral theory when he writes:

> Wir können uns reiner praktischer Gesetze bewusst werden, eben so wie wir uns reiner theoretischer Grundsätze bewusst sind, indem wir auf die Notwendigkeit, womit sie uns die Vernunft vorschreibt, und auf Absonderung aller empirischen Bedingungen, dazu uns jene hinweiset, Acht haben. Der Begriff eines reinen Willens entspringt aus den ersteren, wie das Bewusstsein eines reinen Verstandes aus dem letzteren. [KpV, V, 30]

Hence, only by treating the moral law as imposed by our own pure practical reason, in the same way in which the natural laws are imposed on the structure of our experience by our pure understanding—that is, by treating the moral law as something generated *a priori* within the subject, rather than given to it from the outside—can we account for its features of necessity and universality.

In both the theoretical and the practical context (i.e., in the context of cognizing the world and of acting in it), Kant argues, we could easily be led to believe that the phenomenon in question—cognition in the theoretical field, volition in the practical field—can be accounted for within an empirical framework alone. Yet, in both cases reflection on the element of necessity leads us to postulate the presence of a purely rational, *a priori* element. That is, in both cases close examination of our experience—and, in particular, the el-

---

4 "[Kant's] theoretical philosophy provided the clue to his concept of the source of law. In his theoretical philosophy, reason is the source of the law of nature; the laws of nature are not passively recorded but are conditions we place upon experience as criteria of its objective significance... [I]f the source of the objective necessity of the theoretical laws of nature lies in us as rational beings, it is easy to see how Kant could also locate the source of moral law in autonomous reason and guarantee its objective necessity at the same time" [Beck, 1960, 124; see also: Timmermann, 2010, 87].

5 For a discussion on Kant's notion of the interests of reason see Chapter 1 above.

ement of necessity we discover in it—reveals that it is made up of two very different elements: on the one hand, the material content of our experience (the manifold of our intuitions in the theoretical case; and our desires and impulses in the practical case), which is contingent and accidental; on the other hand, the rational element that is necessary as well as being universally and objectively valid (the conditions of the possibility of experience in the theoretical case; and the moral law in the practical case). In both the fields of theory and of practice, Kant argues, we will only be able properly to understand our experience if we are mindful of the *a priori* contribution made by our rational faculties:

> Erkenntnis kann auf zweierlei Art auf ihren Gegenstand bezogen werden, entweder diesen und seinen Begriff (der anderweitig gegeben werden muss) bloß zu bestimmen, oder ihn auch wirklich zu machen. Die erste ist theoretische, die andere praktische Erkenntnis der Vernunft. Von beiden muss der reine Teil, so viel oder so wenig er auch enthalten mag, nämlich derjenige, darin Vernunft gänzlich a priori ihr Objekt bestimmt, vorher allein vorgetragen werden und dasjenige, was aus anderen Quellen kommt, damit nicht vermengt werden. [KrV, III, 8; see also KpV, V, 163]

Like pure understanding, pure practical reason is not something we can have any experience of. Rather, it is a mere idea, something that we have to attribute to ourselves in order to be able to give an account of our condition as agents subject to a necessary law. While our empirical will is subject not only to the distorting influences of our desires and impulses, but also to the laws of nature, we have to conceive of pure practical reason as noumenal, i.e. as existing outside the spatiotemporal realm, unencumbered by the influence of our physical nature. This noumenal will is an ideal vision of our own fallible, sensuously affected will[6]. Independent from the laws of causality, we have to conceive of the nou-

---

6 "Es ist niemand, selbst der ärgste Bösewicht, wenn er nur sonst Vernunft zu brauchen gewohnt ist, der nicht, wenn man ihm Beispiele der Redlichkeit in Absichten, der Standhaftigkeit in Befolgung guter Maximen, der Teilnehmung und des allgemeinen Wohlwollens... vorlegt, nicht wünsche, dass er auch so gesinnt sein möchte. Er kann es aber nur wegen seiner Neigungen und Antriebe nicht wohl in sich zu Stande bringen, wobei er dennoch zugleich wünscht, von solchen ihm selbst lästigen Neigungen frei zu sein. Er beweiset hierdurch also, dass er mit einem Willen, der von Antrieben der Sinnlichkeit frei ist, sich in Gedanken in eine ganz andere Ordnung der Dinge versetze, als die seiner Begierden im Felde der Sinnlichkeit, weil er von jenem Wunsche keine Vergnügung der Begierden, mithin keinen für irgend eine seiner wirklichen oder sonst erdenklichen Neigungen befriedigenden Zustand (denn dadurch würde selbst die Idee, welche ihm den Wunsch ablockt, ihre Vorzüglichkeit einbüßen), sondern nur einen größeren inneren Wert seiner Person erwarten kann. Diese bessere Person glaubt er aber zu sein, wenn er sich in den Standpunkt eines Gliedes der Verstandeswelt versetzt, dazu die Idee

menal will as transcendentally free (that is, in acting, it starts causal chains, rather than itself being caused to act): it is pure activity, freed of everything about us that is passive-receptive[7].

Kant holds that we have to conceive of our transcendentally free will as governed by the law of freedom, i.e. a law that it imposes on itself. The ground for this claim is the following: a will, for Kant, is a type of causality. Given that causality is a concept of the understanding and the understanding is the faculty of rules, any form of causality is necessarily law-governed (see Chapter 1). As we have seen above, Kant recognizes only two types of causality—natural causality and freedom. Each is governed by its particular law: the causal law, in one case, and the law of freedom, in the other [GMS, IV, 387]. While the causal law is imposed on the object from the outside, we have to conceive of the law of freedom as given by the free will to itself, independently of all empirical determination [GMS, IV, 447][8]. As noumenal, our pure will would not be subject to the laws of nature, given that the laws of nature only govern the empirical realm (i.e., are the structures we impose on our experience to make it orderly). Hence, we have to conceive of our noumenal will, our pure practical reason, as subject to the law of freedom. That is, to account for the possibility of the moral law as commanding with unconditional necessity, we have to conceive of it as the law that our noumenal will imposes on itself.

A completely pure will, i.e. one not affected by any sensuous desire, would invariably and infallibly follow the law of freedom, for while our sensuously affected—and, hence, impure—empirical will is marked by a conflict between our desires and the demands of morality, there is, in the pure will, no conflict and no incentive to diverge from the moral law ("Als bloßen Gliedes der Verstandeswelt

---

der Freiheit, d. i. Unabhängigkeit von bestimmenden Ursachen der Sinnenwelt, ihn unwillkürlich nötigt" [GMS, IV, 454–5].

7 In *Metaphysik der Sitten*, Kant attempts to clarify this distinction between our fallible empirical will, on the one hand, and the ideal conception of our will as noumenally free, on the other, by referring to them with different terms—*Willkür* and *Wille*, respectively: "Das Begehrungsvermögen nach Begriffen, sofern der Bestimmungsgrund desselben zur Handlung in ihm selbst, nicht in dem Objekte angetroffen wird, heißt ein Vermögen nach Belieben zu tun oder zu lassen. Sofern es mit dem Bewusstsein des Vermögens seiner Handlung zur Hervorbringung des Objekts verbunden ist, heißt es Willkür... Der Wille ist ... das Begehrungsvermögen, nicht sowohl (wie die Willkür) in Beziehung auf die Handlung, als vielmehr auf den Bestimmungsgrund der Willkür zur Handlung betrachtet, und hat selber vor sich eigentlich keinen Bestimmungsgrund, sondern ist, sofern sie die Willkür bestimmen kann, die praktische Vernunft selbst" [MS, VI, 213; see also: MS, VI, 226]. However, as Allison notes "Kant's formulations of the Wille–Willkür distinction are hardly models of philosophical lucidity" [1990, 134; see also: Beck, 1960, 191n].
8 See Allison [1990, 203] for a detailed discussion of this argument.

würden also alle meine Handlungen dem Prinzip der Autonomie des reinen Willens vollkommen gemäß sein" [GMS, IV, 453; see also: KpV, V, 32])[9]. Thus, it is only for our empirical will that following the moral law requires effort. And only to this struggling, impure will, the moral law presents itself in the form of an imperative—i.e. a demand that it can (and often does) fail to obey [GMS, IV, 449][10].

Kant's argument so far implies that a transcendentally free will and a will under the moral law is the same thing (that is, a will is transcendentally free if and only if it is subject to the moral laws [KpV, V, 29; GMS, IV, 447]). This is what Allison calls Kant's *Reciprocity Thesis* [1990, 201; see also: Henrich, 1975,

---

9 This point is missed by Guyer who writes: "There is... a fatal flaw in Kant's argument. A free will is not logically or analytically compelled to act only on moral rather than material considerations, but rather must do so only if it is to maintain or preserve its freedom. There is no logical contradiction in freely choosing to give in to inclination or even to undercut the possibility of subsequent free actions... The connection between the freedom of the will and the categorical imperative is thus not logical, but substantive. A free will is logically free to destroy its own freedom but a free will that does not will to do so needs to abide by the moral law" [Guyer, 2000, 56]. Guyer here confuses two different conceptions of the will: the will of a finite rational being as it exists in the empirical world, on the one hand, and the ideal conception of our noumenal (and, hence, transcendentally free) will, on the other. Kant refers to the will under both these conceptions as free, but the conceptions of freedom in each of these cases are not the same: a noumenal will—not subject to natural laws and not affected by sensuous desire—has only one determining ground, namely its own essential interests as codified in the law of freedom (see our argument in the text below). Hence, this will knows no conflict of interests—and necessarily follows the law of freedom. We are warranted in regarding our empirical will as free, on the other hand, only because we have to regard it as the appearance of our noumenal will in the empirical world (for reasons we will discuss in Chapter 4). The problem with Guyer's argument is that he inadvertently switches between these two conceptions of a free will. When Kant holds that, in Guyer's words, a free will is "analytically compelled to act only on moral rather than material considerations" he is speaking about our noumenal will (for given that this is the ideal conception of will not affected by sensuous interests, it is by definition not confronted by any material considerations). Yet, when Kant asserts that, in Guyer's words, a "free will is logically free to destroy its own freedom", given that there is "no logical contradiction in freely choosing to give in to inclination", this is said with reference to our empirical will. Guyer fails to note that the term "free will" has different referents in both cases. That is to say, the "fatal flaw" he mentions resides not in Kant's argument, but in his own interpretation.

10 "Rational personality as lawgiving expressed an 'is' which is ipso facto an 'ought' for partially rational beings. The law and its imperative and the conditions necessary to obedience to it have a common source which Kant's predecessors never found... The doctrine of autonomy was anticipated only by Rousseau, for only Rousseau saw the essential connection between law and freedom, while others in the eighteenth century saw law only as a restriction on freedom... With Rousseau, Kant can... say that obedience to a law that one has himself prescribed is the only real freedom" [Beck, 1960, 199–200].

90]. Let us see how the Reciprocity Thesis follows from what we have said so far. First, if a will is subject to the moral law, it has to be transcendentally free. For in order to be able to account for the moral law's unconditional validity, we have to regard it as valid *a priori*. Yet, *a priori* laws are only possible as the products of our pure faculties, which for Kant means our faculties insofar as they have noumenal existence. Thus, practical *a priori* laws are only possible as the product of pure practical reason, i.e., our will insofar as it has noumenal existence. Hence, if a will is subject to the moral law, then it has noumenal existence. Yet, a noumenal will is transcendentally free. Hence, if a will is subject to the moral law, then it is transcendentally free.

Secondly, Kant also holds that if a will is transcendentally free, then it is subject to the moral law. As we have seen above, even if a will is transcendentally free, as a kind of causality, it must still be governed by a law. Yet, a transcendentally free will is not subject to the laws of nature. Given that, for Kant, there are only two kinds of causality—natural causality and freedom –, it follows that the will in question must be subject to the law of freedom. Yet, the law of freedom is the moral law. Hence, if a will is transcendentally free, then it is subject to the moral law.

Morality and the interests of reason

Kant holds that in order to be able to account for the moral law as unconditional, we have to regard it as the law our noumenal will imposes on itself. This raises the question: on the basis of what does this self-legislation take place? The answer is based on the notion of reason as an interested faculty, which we have encountered in Chapter 1 above. According to Kant's conception of reason, reason guides itself not by external standards, but on the basis of its own essential interests alone (i.e. those principles that allow for its complete and self-consistent use). Consequently, just as in the case of reason in its theoretical application, we have to regard our pure practical reason as guiding itself on the basis of its own essential interests: "[W]o es auf Sittlichkeit ankommt, muss... reine praktische Vernunft ihr eigenes Interesse ganz allein besorgen" [KpV, V, 118][11].

---

11 See also: "Der [moralische Wille] muss also von allem Gegenstande so fern abstrahieren, dass dieser gar keinen Einfluss auf den Willen habe, damit praktische Vernunft (Wille) nicht fremdes Interesse bloß administriere, sondern bloß ihr eigenes gebietendes Ansehen als oberste Gesetzgebung beweise" [GMS, IV, 441]. Kant explains that the "moral interest" ("das moralische Interesse") is "ein reines sinnenfreies Interesse der bloßen praktischen Vernunft" [KpV, V, 79]. Given that we have to regard our noumenal will as our "proper self" (see Chapter 4), Kant

This is the core of Kant's conception of morality: the moral law is an expression of the interests of our reason[12]. It is not a demand made on us by the nature of things or the command of God, but expresses the requirements of the proper use of our practical reason ("Das moralische Gesetz [ist die] formale Vernunftbedingung des Gebrauchs unserer Freiheit" [KU, V, 450]). In this sense, the moral law is an idea of reason [R, VI, 59n]: just as in the sphere of theory the ideas of reason impose an *a priori* order on our cognitions, thereby making a complete and non-contradictory use of our understanding possible, the moral law expresses the *a priori* norm that allows for a non-contradictory and non-stultifying use of our will ("[Das moralische] Prinzip... ist die einzige Bedingung, unter der ein Wille niemals mit sich selbst im Widerstreite sein kann" [GMS, IV, 437; see also: KrV, III, 239]). It is not an arbitrary self-imposed norm, but expresses the conditions under which the use of our will is consistent with the interests of reason[13].

---

holds that we have to conceive of the moral interest as our highest interest ("dass es überall kein höheres Interesse geben kann" [GMS, IV, 449]).

12 "Kant's essential claim is that... in addition to the familiar panoply of empirical determining grounds [of the will], there is also a non-empirical determining ground, a 'pure interest'" [Allison, 1998, 98; see also: Ameriks, 2005, 279].

13 This "appreciative" reading of Kant's conception of morality is suggested by Ameriks, who aims at showing that the Kantian notion of autonomy is consistent with value realism. In particular, he cautions that we should not misunderstand Kant's notion of self-legislation as involving the choice of arbitrary rules: "The idea of self-legislation here is not that reason literally does something, as a person might cross a street. The idea is simply that the nature of reason itself primarily determines—as a matter of essence—what the basic goals are for reason. In theoretical contexts, this is no more mysterious than saying that consistency and the working out of implications is not only assisted but also demanded by reason itself—which of course leaves open the empirical issues of whether particular rational beings will assert consistent sentences... This is nothing like the willful autonomy 'of me' in the 'me generation' sense of our times" [2005, 279–80]. This position receives support from Kant's own clarifications of what he means by "making a rule for ourselves" in his 1796 essay "Von einem neuerdings erhobenen vornehmen Ton in der Philosophie": "Aus dem moralischen Gesetz, welches uns unsere eigene Vernunft mit Autorität vorschreibt, nicht aus der Theorie der Natur der Dinge an sich selbst geht nun der Begriff von Gott hervor, welchen uns selbst zu machen die praktische reine Vernunft nötigt.... Es ist für sich selbst klar: das ein Begriff, der aus unserer Vernunft hervorgehen muss, von uns selbst gemacht sein müsse" [VIII, 399n]. That is, Kant himself suggests that we can read the notion of "making a rule for ourselves" as equivalent to that of accepting a rule as generated required by the nature of our own reason ("aus unserer Vernunft hervorgehen muss").

The appreciative reading of Kant's conception of morality stands in conflict with the "constructivist" reading, according to which Kant holds that valid moral principles are the product of our reflective activity. As Rawls, the main proponent of the constructivist reading on Kant's theory, puts it, "Kant's idea of autonomy requires that there exists no moral order prior and independent of those conceptions that determine the form of the procedure that specifies the content of the duties of justice of virtue" [2000, 236–7]. Rawls is very cautious in his statement—but I take him to mean that whether or not a given moral judgment is objectively valid is a function of whether it is the product of a correct procedure of reasoning. Other commentators advocating the constructivist reading are less circumspect in their statements than Rawls is. Yovel, for instance, who refers to the constructivist interpretation as the "constitution theory of rationality", attributes to Kant the view that "[n]o set of universal norms is rational in itself, except as it is constituted by the subject and can be recognized by him as such. And correspondingly, we become rational not by complying with a system of pre-established norms, but by setting up the norms with which we comply. In this way, the very status of rationality is not ready-made but constituted, depending on the spontaneous activity of the ego" [1989, 13; see also: O'Neill, 1989, 21]. More clearly than Rawls, Yovel states that the principles of reason are not "pre-established norms", but rather the product of our spontaneous activity. Consequently, Yovel holds that "reason should not be equated with some latent, pure and final paradigm that awaits explication once and for all" [1989, 24]).

Both the constructivist and the appreciative reading of Kant's moral theory agree that moral truths are not a feature of the world as it is independently of our reason, but only appear from the viewpoint of reason—and are, more specifically, generated by our own reason. However, they disagree on how this "generated by our reason" is to be understood: according to the appreciative interpretation, moral principles express the interests of reason—and, hence, the immutable requirements for the proper use of our rational faculties in their practical application –, while according to the constructivist reading the moral principles are generated by us in the process of making use of our reason. That is, the difference between these two interpretations of Kant's moral theory lies in whether moral principles are determined by the nature of our reason (and only have to be discovered or "appreciated" by us)—or whether they are generated by us in the process of making use of our reason.

There are two problems with the constructivist reading of Kant's theory. First, the suggestion that moral principles are generated by us in the process of making use of our reason is profoundly at odds with Kant's conception of moral principles as "immutable" [KpV, V, 107; see also: GMS, IV, 451] and "unchanging" [KrV, III, 547; see also: ED, VIII, 339]. Attempts to deal with Kant's assertions about the immutable nature of the moral order at times leads proponents of the constructivist reading to spectacular contradictions. Yovel, for instance, before asserting in the quote above that reason should not be seen to be aiming at a final paradigm, writes that, according to Kant, philosophy aims at "finally [actualizing] the latent paradigm of reason in full" [1989, 9; see also: 1989, 18]. The second problem with the constructivist reading is that if we assert that moral principles are objectively valid only if they result from a process of correct reasoning, this in effect just pushes back the issue by one step, for we now have to ask what grounds the validity of these rules that determine whether we have reasoned correctly. It might well be that, at this stage, the defender of the constructivist reading has to take refuge in the appreciative camp, declaring that the rules that allow for correct reasoning are those that allow for a satisfaction of the interests of reason.

Both these problems of the constructivist account—in combination with the fact that the constructivist reading, taken at face value, is inconsistent with the interpretation of Kant's moral theory developed in the text—should lead us to reject the constructivist reading.

Insofar as it aims at nothing but the satisfaction of its own essential interests, reason is concerned with nothing but itself ("Die reine Vernunft ist in der Tat mit nichts als sich selbst beschäftigt" KrV, III, 448])—and the moral law is best understood as an expression of this relation of our practical reason to itself ("Hier... ist vom objektiv-praktischen Gesetze die Rede, *mithin von dem Verhältnisse eines Willens zu sich selbst*" [GMS, IV, 427; my emphasis]).

As in the case of reason in its theoretical application, the relevant interests of reason are the interests in *systematic unity* and *completeness*. The interest of our practical reason in systematic unity is the interest in a use of the will that ensures that all our principles of willing can be integrated into a harmonious, mutually supportive whole, free of self-contradiction[14]. A non-contradictory use of the will involves choosing one's maxims in a way that they can form part of a consistent set[15]. Crucially, the self-contradiction to be avoided in order for us to satisfy practical reason's interest in unity is not merely the one among the different principles of the same will—but the one among the principles of the wills of different rational beings. That is, Kant holds that a fundamental need of ours remains unmet as long as the principles of willing on which the naturally uncoordinated rational beings act leave open the possibility of unlaw-

---

However, there is nonetheless a kernel of truth in the constructivists' case: for Kant insists that the proper ways of to use our reason are not imprinted in our minds, but have to be arrived at through reflection on our current ways of thinking and through a critique of our reasoning. This opens the possibility of understanding the constructivist reading not so much as an ontological account of moral principles (i.e. telling us what moral principles really are), but a heuristic device (i.e. telling us what we have to do to discover them). We will discuss Kant's notion of the requirements for our discerning the correct moral principles in more detail in Chapter 8.

14 "[M]orality does not constrain our purposes except by requiring them to be systematic—that, of course, means that each agent's purposes, both known and as yet unknown, must be able to constitute such a systematic sum and that all agents' purposes, again both known and as yet unknown, must be able to constitute such a sum. Morality sets us no more specific purpose than that all purposes be able to constitute a sum—or a unity of reason" [Guyer, 2000, 85–6; see also: Wood, 1999, 164; Pogge, in: Höffe, 2000, 191].

15 Arendt points out the link between the role of consistency in Kant's theoretical and his practical work: "[T]he rule of consistency... This axiom, which for Socrates was 'logical'... as well as 'ethical' (It is better to be at odds with multitudes than, being one, to be at odds with yourself, namely, to contradict yourself), became with Aristotle the first principle of thinking, but of thinking only. However, with Kant it became again part of ethics... It is, again, the same general rule that determines both thinking and acting" [1992, 37]. See also Henrich: "Zwischen Kants Konzeption der Verstandesfunktionen und seiner Formel des Kategorischen Imperativs besteht eine auffällige Analogie. Das Böse ist daran zu erkennen, dass es eine vernünftige Allgemeinheit im Handeln ausschließt und den Willen in einen Widerspruch mit sich selbst bringt... Der kategorische Imperativ scheint nur eine besondere Weise zu sein, in der sich die allgemeine vernünftige Forderung nach Einheit realisiert" [1973, 240; see also: Guyer, 2000, 115].

ful conflict between their wills. This is what happens in a world in which everyone follows his own urge for happiness. The resulting actions are uncoordinated and therefore mutually disruptive: "[D]a sonst ein allgemeines Naturgesetz alles einstimmig macht, so würde hier, wenn man der Maxime die Allgemeinheit eines Gesetzes geben wollte, grade das äußerste Widerspiel der Einstimmung, der ärgste Widerstreit und die gänzliche Vernichtung der Maxime selbst und ihrer Absicht erfolgen. Denn der Wille Aller hat alsdann nicht ein und dasselbe Objekt, sondern ein jeder hat das seinige (sein eigenes Wohlbefinden)" [KpV, V, 28]. This is what Kant, following Hobbes, calls the *ethical state of nature:* a condition in which there is no common reference point on the basis of which the different wills can coordinate their activity—and, hence, a condition which is marked by permanent latent conflict [MS, VI, 312]. In such a state of uncoordinated willing, Kant holds, our practical reason's interest in systematic unity of our practical reason must remain frustrated[16].

The moral law offers the objective reference point that is lacking in the ethical state of nature. It demands that each rational agent choose his maxims in a way that makes the harmony among the wills of all rational agents possible, in the same way in which the laws of nature make possible the harmonious integration of all events in the empirical world into one coherent whole. Kant himself notes this analogy when he writes: "Weil die Allgemeinheit des Gesetzes, wonach Wirkungen geschehen, dasjenige ausmacht, was eigentlich Natur im allgemeinsten Verstande (der Form nach), d. i. das Dasein der Dinge, heißt, so fern es nach allgemeinen Gesetzen bestimmt ist, so könnte der allgemeine Imperativ der Pflicht auch so lauten: handle so, als ob die Maxime deiner Handlung durch deinen Willen zum allgemeinen Naturgesetze werden sollte" [GMS, IV, 421][17]. In the

---

[16] See Chapter 9 for a more detailed discussion of Kant's notion of the ethical state of nature.
[17] This is one of the ironies in Kant's philosophy: while the natural determinism of Newtonian physics presents itself as one of the main obstacles to explaining the possibility of freedom, Kant's conception of the proper use of our freedom, namely that of achieving order among naturally uncoordinated agents on the basis of the moral law, is clearly inspired by Newton's conception of a world governed by natural laws: "So kann ich mir nach der Analogie mit dem Gesetze der Gleichheit der Wirkung und Gegenwirkung in der wechselseitigen Anziehung und Abstoßung der Körper unter einander auch die Gemeinschaft der Glieder eines gemeinen Wesens nach Regeln des Rechts denken" [KU, V, 464; see also: MS, VI, 232 and P, IV, 357n]. This analogy is noted by Brandt (who quotes Schlegel: "Kants Moral geht hervor aus einem Wunsch, für die sittliche Welt ein Gesetz zu finden, das so allgemein wäre wie das Newtonische Attraktionsgesetz in der physischen Welt" [2007, 233n]). Saner explores the influence of Newton's mechanics on Kant's thought more generally: "The ground of Kant's character is... inexorably molded by the rigor of natural laws, so to speak. Having absorbed the formalism of those laws, he spreads it

ideal condition in which all rational agents follow the moral law they stop being one the obstacle of the other's will. They form a system—or, as Kant calls it, a *realm of ends*—in which their willing is perfectly consistent and in which, hence, their practical reason's interest in systematic unity is completely satisfied [GMS, IV, 433].

Second, there is reason's interest in completeness—or well-groundedness. In reason's theoretical application, this interest pushes us to search for an unconditional ground of the contingent experiences we encounter in the world of the appearances. To satisfy this interest, we had to postulate a first uncaused cause to ground the multitude of chains of cause and effect that make up the empirical world (see Chapter 1). Similarly, in the field of practice, we are confronted with a multitude of individual desires and inclinations, which force themselves onto us. It is only the moral law, Kant claims, that establishes an unconditional objective value, thus grounding the value of all our other objects of desire. Kant's theory of value is a complex matter, which we will discuss in more detail in Chapter 6 below. For our purposes here, it is sufficient to note that the moral law establishes rational nature as an unconditional value, in so far as it is the condition of the possibility of all objective value [KU, V, 443]. This notion is expressed in the second formulation of the categorical imperative: act in a way that you treat every rational being as an end in itself as well as a means [GMS, IV, 429]. By establishing rational nature—and hence our ability to choose our own ends freely—as a necessary end, an end that all our actions are required to be respectful of, the moral law grounds the unconditional value of our willing in general, turning a set of unconnected desires into a complete system of willing. Kant himself highlights the parallel between the role of the unconditional in the theoretical and practical employment of reason in *Grundlegung*: "Der spekulative Gebrauch der Vernunft in Ansehung der Natur führt auf absolute Notwendigkeit irgend einer obersten Ursache der Welt; der praktische Gebrauch der Vernunft in Absicht auf die Freiheit führt auch auf absolute Notwendigkeit, aber nur der Gesetze der Handlungen eines vernünftigen Wesens als eines solchen" [GMS, IV, 463].

We have now delineated the Kantian conception of morality as grounded in the notion of reason as an interested faculty. A corollary of this position is that our duties are based on the interests of reason. I will call this the *Grounding Thesis*. It follows directly from what we have said so far: the moral law, for Kant, is an expression of the interests of our reason. It is the principle that would guide our will if it were perfectly free, i.e. determined only by its own interests, and not

---

all over his thinking and does not shrink from its consistency" [Saner, 1973, 33; see also: Beck, 1960, 159n].

affected by the distorting influence of our physical nature. Yet, because we are sensuous beings, these principles, which would be freely willed by perfectly rational beings, present themselves to us in the form of obligations [GMS, IV, 449]. Thus, what appears as an obligation to our sensuously affected will is, for Kant, the expression of the interests of our reason. Consequently, all duties are based on the interests of reason[18].

Conclusion

We now have an outline of the Kantian notion of the moral law. The moral law is the formal principle we impose on our will, in a way that our willing becomes consistent with the interests of our reason in its practical employment. As in the theoretical case, this order is not something we receive from an external source, but is generated by reason itself ("Die Vernunft... macht sich mit völliger Spontaneität eine eigene Ordnung nach Ideen" [KrV, III, 372]). As in Kant's theory of cognition, we can only account for the necessity with which the moral law presents itself to us if we understand the moral law to be grounded in a pure —i.e. non-empirical—faculty of willing. That is, in order to understand the possibility of the moral law we have to ascribe to ourselves a noumenal will—i.e., a will that exists as a thing-in-itself outside the spatiotemporal realm, free from the influence of our sensuous nature and guided only by the interests of our practical reason in perfectly systematically unified and complete willing, i.e. willing on the basis of a well-grounded system of principles that allow for the perfect

---

[18] To my knowledge, Kant never makes this corollary of his moral theory explicit. Yet, it is implied in many of his remarks. One example is the following passage in *Metaphysik der Sitten:* "Mit dem Zwecke der Menschheit in unserer eigenen Person ist also auch *der Vernunftwille, mithin die Pflicht* verbunden, sich um die Menschheit durch Kultur überhaupt verdient zu machen" [MS, VI, 392]. This statement implies that for something to be a duty is for it to be *Vernunftwille*. The latter is Kant's term of the willing of the perfectly rational, i.e. pure, will. As we have seen above, such a will would be precisely the one that is exclusively guided by the interests of reason. Hence, a duty is the requirement to act in a way in which a will would be acting if it were guided only by the interests of reason. This is precisely the content of the Grounding Thesis, as proposed here. A further example can be found in *Grundlegung:* "Denn dieses Sollen ist eigentlich ein Wollen, das unter der Bedingung für jedes vernünftige Wesen gilt, wenn die Vernunft bei ihm ohne Hindernisse praktisch wäre; für Wesen, die wie wir noch durch Sinnlichkeit als Triebfedern anderer Art affiziert werden, bei denen es nicht immer geschieht, was die Vernunft für sich allein tun würde, heißt jene Notwendigkeit der Handlung nur ein Sollen" [GMS, IV, 449]. Again, the Grounding Thesis follows if we accept that the pure will (i.e. the will in which "reason is practical without any obstacles") determines itself on the basis of the interests of reason.

harmony of all rational wills. This ideal vision of ourselves as noumenally free wills is a central element of Kant's moral theory. The moral phenomenon, as understood by Kant, is the restriction of the interests of our empirical self—that is, the self and the interests that we can experience directly—on the basis of this idea of our higher existence as pure reason[19]: "[M]an muss gestehen,... dass diesen Urteilen insgeheim die Idee von einer andern und viel würdigern Absicht ihrer Existenz zum Grunde liege, zu welcher und nicht der Glückseligkeit die Vernunft ganz eigentlich bestimmt sei, und welcher darum als oberster Bedingung die Privatabsicht des Menschen größtenteils nachstehen muss" [GMS, IV, 396; see also: Beck, 1960, 123].

It is important to note that Kant's argument up to this point was purely analytical: all he has done so far is to explore the content of the notion of morality—and the conceptual commitments that come with the attempt to integrate it into our general view of the world. In other words, so far we have been concerned only with the *logical* possibility of the notion of morality. In the next chapter, we will focus on Kant's attempt to establish the *real* possibility of the moral law, i.e. to show that the moral law has objective validity for us.

---

19 That is, Kant's moral theory is based on the distinction between two fundamentally different sets of interests that come into play when we determine our actions. On the one hand, there is the urge to satisfy our different physical needs and idiosyncratic plans. On the other, there is the interest we have in the proper, non-contradictory, non-stultifying use of our will. Thus, his moral theory is based on the distinction between material interests and the interests of reason. We will further explore this distinction in Chapter 6 below.

4 The fact of reason

We have now explored Kant's answer to the question of the *quid facti* of the notion of the moral law (i.e., the question concerning the content of this concept). This leaves us with the task of understanding his answer to the second question, that of the *quid juris*—i.e., the question of whether the concept has objective reality for us. Kant's final (and rather surprising) answer to that question is our consciousness of the moral law is a self-validating fact of reason. In our attempt to make sense of this claim, we will trace the development of Kant's position on the question of the *quid juris*, starting with his attempt to offer a deduction of the moral law in *Grundlegung*. As we will see, his final position on this issue will allow us to answer the question that we started out with in Chapter 1, namely that concerning the real possibility of our transcendental freedom.

The *Grundlegung* account

The argument Kant offers in *Kritik der Praktischen Vernunft* for the claim that our consciousness of the moral law is a fact of reason is notoriously obscure. Unfortunately for the reader (and luckily for those offering exegesis), the argument it replaces—namely, the deduction of the moral law in the third part of *Grundlegung*—is hardly any clearer[1]. Henrich calls Kant's argument in the *Grundlegung* "well laid-out and yet impenetrable" [1975, 110], while Allison holds that it is "one of the most enigmatic of the Kantian texts" [1990, 214]. We will briefly review Kant's argument, try to identify the source of its obscurity—and explore why Kant ultimately came to replace it with the argument presented in *Kritik der Praktischen Vernunft*[2].

The first two parts of the *Grundlegung* are, Kant says, merely analytical—that is, merely concerned with determining the content of the notion of the moral law [GMS, IV, 445]. This leaves open the question whether the moral law is really valid for us—or whether morality is a mere "figment of the brain" [GMS, IV, 445]. The third part of *Grundlegung* aims to address this question by offering a justification for the claim that the moral law really has validity for us.

---

[1] Henrich discusses Kant's earlier attempts to ground the validity of the moral law in his essay "Der Begriff der sittlichen Einsicht und Kants Lehre vom Faktum der Vernunft", [Henrich, 1973]
[2] The following discussion is strongly influenced by Henrichs' essay "Die Deduktion des Sittengesetzes" [1975].

At the beginning of the third part of *Grundlegung*, Kant lays out his program for what follows: he wants, he says, to make "intelligible the possibility of a categorical imperative" [GMS, IV, 447][3]. He intends to do this by offering a deduction of the notion of transcendental freedom (i.e., showing that we are justified in regarding ourselves as transcendentally free) and infer from this, by way of the Reciprocity Thesis, according to which a free will and a will under moral laws is one and the same thing (see Chapter 3 above), the validity of the moral law for us. That is, he aims to offer an argument grounding the validity of the moral law on the basis of the notion of freedom.

Yet, Kant's task does not end there. Although he does not highlight this at the beginning of the argument, it will turn out that once he has established the objective reality of the moral law for us, there are further questions that have to be answered before the real possibility of the moral law can be said to have been established. First, Kant holds that we are not only aware of the demands of the moral law, but can also be moved to act by this awareness (in a way that the moral law can function as a principle of execution, in the sense explained in Chapter 3). A full explanation of the real possibility of the moral law would show how awareness of the moral demands on us can be a sufficient motive for action. Secondly, the moral law is, on Kant's analysis, not merely one of many possible determining factors of our will, but has overriding character—that is, where its commands are in conflict with other interests of ours, it is supposed to take precedence. An argument purported to establish the real possibility of the moral law will have to explain why this should be the case.

Let us see how Kant goes about implementing this program. In the first step of his argument, he explores the conditions under which we can legitimately regard our will as free. He writes:

> Ich sage nun: Ein jedes Wesen, das nicht anders als unter der Idee der Freiheit handeln kann, ist eben darum in praktischer Rücksicht wirklich frei, d. i. es gelten für dasselbe alle Gesetze, die mit der Freiheit unzertrennlich verbunden sind, eben so als ob sein Wille auch an sich selbst und in der theoretischen Philosophie gültig für frei erklärt würde. [GMS, IV, 448]

---

3 In an earlier passage, Kant has clarified the difference between the moral law and the categorical imperative, which we have also already touched upon in the previous chapter: a perfectly rational will would have no other determining ground than its own law (i.e. the moral law)—and would hence necessarily act in a way that is consistent with that law. For such a will, the moral law would simply be an expression of its own essential interests. Yet, to our will, which is subject to the influence of desires and inclinations, the moral law presents itself as a command—as something that makes an unconditional demand on us, without us, though, necessarily conforming to that demand in our actions. That is, the moral law presents itself to finite rational beings in the form of a categorical imperative [GMS, IV, 449].

In this paragraph, Kant in effect lowers the hurdle that has to be cleared in order for a deduction of freedom to be successful. He asserts (without argument) that he will not be required to give a theoretical proof of our freedom, but that it is sufficient for a deduction of freedom to show that, in acting, it is necessary for us to accept the idea of our own freedom—i.e. to ascribe freedom to ourselves. If this is the case, then we are really free—even if only "from a practical point of view".

These more lenient conditions of success for an argument establishing the reality of our freedom would be very helpful indeed, for—as we have seen above—Kant holds that a theoretical proof of our transcendental freedom is impossible. Given this latter position, just basing our view of the world on the facts available from a theoretical perspective must lead us to consider the notion of our own freedom as a mere thought—one that is not inconsistent with our theoretical view of the world, but which nonetheless can never be shown to be true (i.e. to have real possibility). Yet, Kant claims in the *Grundlegung* passage quoted above that, insofar as we are agents—that is, have a will –, we are aware of additional data that simply are not available from a purely theoretical point of view and that if, on the basis of this additional information, we have ground to accept the idea of freedom, we are entitled to ascribe freedom to ourselves just as if we had shown ourselves to be free from a theoretical perspective. As he puts it in an accompanying footnote: this allows us to liberate ourselves from the burden that afflicts the theoretical argument [GMS, IV, 448n].

Critics have claimed that Kant's contention that all that is required for a deduction of freedom is to show that it is practically necessary to accept the idea of our own freedom is nothing but an unfounded assertion [Allison, 1990, 217]. Yet, our discussion of Kant's transcendental idealism helps us to understand the logic governing his position. As we have seen above, his critical position in *Kritik der Reinen Vernunft* was not aimed at eliminating the class of judgments that could not be given empirical backing, but rather at distinguishing carefully between different ways in which judgments could be shown to be valid for us. In particular, that earlier work has prepared the ground for the position that a certain judgment whose truth could not be determined from a purely theoretical perspective could still be valid for us if its validity was required to make sense of our condition as agents. This is what we have called Kant's doctrine of practical knowledge. We will discuss his application of that doctrine in more detail below. For now, we can content ourselves with noting that what appears as a blunt claim in *Grundlegung* is a position that is well-grounded in Kant's critical project of identifying the different sources of validity of judgments.

However, even if this is granted, all we have done so far is to establish a hypothetical statement: if we can show that it is necessary for us to act under the idea of freedom, then we would be able to ascribe freedom to ourselves, which in turn, by means of the Reciprocity Thesis, would allow us to establish the validity of the moral law for us. Yet, how can we show that it is necessary for us to act under the idea of freedom, as Kant puts it? This question is addressed in the next step of his argument:

> Nun behaupte ich: dass wir jedem vernünftigen Wesen, das einen Willen hat, notwendig auch die Idee der Freiheit leihen müssen, unter der es allein handle. Denn in einem solchen Wesen denken wir uns eine Vernunft, die praktisch ist, d. i. Kausalität in Ansehung ihrer Objekte hat. Nun kann man sich unmöglich eine Vernunft denken, die mit ihrem eigenen Bewusstsein in Ansehung ihrer Urteile anderwärts her eine Lenkung empfinge, denn alsdann würde das Subjekt nicht seiner Vernunft, sondern einem Antriebe die Bestimmung der Urteilskraft zuschreiben. Sie muss sich selbst als Urheberin ihrer Prinzipien ansehen unabhängig von fremden Einflüssen, folglich muss sie als praktische Vernunft, oder als Wille eines vernünftigen Wesens von ihr selbst als frei angesehen werden; d. i. der Wille desselben kann nur unter der Idee der Freiheit ein eigener Wille sein und muss also in praktischer Absicht allen vernünftigen Wesen beigelegt werden. [GMS, IV, 448]

The first sentence of this passage immediately addresses the issue at hand by laying down the condition under which someone can be said to be acting "under the idea of freedom" (i.e., acting in a way that necessarily involves his accepting the notion of his own freedom). This condition is merely that the being in question has to be a rational being with a will. Kant is here trying to establish a parallel between this freedom of judgment in the theoretical context and transcendental freedom in the practical context: just as reason in its theoretical application (that is, in judging) has to regard itself as guided by its own principles, so does reason in its practical application (that is, in determining our actions).

If we accept this reasoning by parallel, then we arrive at another hypothetical: if we can be shown to be rational beings with a will (or, more precisely, rational beings whose actions are determined by reason) then we are entitled to regard (and, in fact, are committed to regarding) our will as determined by the principles of reason—and, hence, are entitled to regard ourselves as free. Put differently, if we have grounds to regard ourselves as rational beings with a will, we are thereby committed to regarding ourselves as having to act under the idea of freedom (just as, in the theoretical case, we have to think under the idea of our freedom of judgment). By the first premise of Kant's argument, we could thus be shown to be free from a practical point of view, in the sense discussed above.

The problem with this argument is that its conclusion is useless. For we have, rather carelessly, stumbled into a circular argument. To see why this is

so, let us grant that we have established the truth of the premise that we are rational beings with a will. The line of reasoning then runs as follows:
1. We are rational beings with a will—that is, we are beings whose actions can be determined by the principles of reason in its practical application (by assumption);
2. If we are rational beings with a will, then we have to act under the idea of freedom (Kant's premise, as discussed above);
3. Hence—by 1. and 2.—we have to act under the idea of freedom;
4. If we have to act under the idea of freedom, then we are—for all practical purposes—really free, and, in particular, the laws of freedom apply to us just as if we were shown to be free from a theoretical point of view (the doctrine of practical knowledge);
5. Hence—by 3. and 4.—we are really free and the laws of freedom apply to us;
6. If we are free then we are subject to the moral law (the Reciprocity Thesis);
7. Hence—by 5. and 6.—we are subject to the moral law.

This argument establishes that if our will is governed by the principles of reason in its practical application then we are subject to the moral law. Given, however, that for Kant the moral law and the principle of reason in its practical application are the same thing, the argument is circular: it infers as a conclusion that which has been fed into it as a premise.

Kant himself notes this circularity: "Es scheint also, als setzten wir in der Idee der Freiheit eigentlich das moralische Gesetz, nämlich das Prinzip der Autonomie des Willens selbst, nur voraus und könnten seine Realität und objektive Notwendigkeit nicht für sich beweisen" [GMS, IV, 449]. Although Kant's diagnosis of a circularity has led to much head-scratching among commentators[4], it is a perfectly accurate analysis of the situation: in regarding ourselves as rational beings with a will, in the sense explained above, we in effect regard ourselves as beings whose actions are determined by the principles of reason. That is, we only regard ourselves as free because we see our will as determined by the prin-

---

4 An example is Paton who writes: "In plain fact, [Kant's] objection totally misrepresents his argument. He never argued from the categorical imperative to freedom, but at least professed, however mistakenly, to establish the presupposition of freedom by an insight into the nature of self-conscious reason quite independently of moral considerations. Perhaps when he came to the objection he was beginning to see dimly that the presupposition of freedom of the will did really rest on moral considerations; but it is surely unusual for a man to answer the sound argument which he has failed to put and to overlook the fact that this answer is irrelevant to the unsound argument which alone he has explicitly stated" [1948, 225].

ciples of practical reason. It is not very fruitful to try to infer from this that the principles of practical reason determine our actions.

As Kant himself realizes, we need to understand the program, which he has laid out at the beginning, to aim not merely at inferring the validity of the moral law from a notion of freedom—but rather at inferring it from a notion of freedom that does not already itself presuppose the validity of the moral law. The argument in its present form fails to meet this requirement, for it already starts out with a moralized—or thick—notion of the will (i.e., a notion of a will under moral laws). Consequently, Kant concludes, we need an independent, non-moral ground for ascribing freedom to ourselves if the notion of our freedom is to serve as a premise in the argument establishing the validity of the moral law.

Kant immediately proceeds to identify such a non-moral starting point for his argument: even the man of the most common understanding, he claims, makes—if only darkly—the distinction which is central to his, Kant's, own transcendental idealism, namely that between the world of appearances and the noumenal realm: "[Der gemeinste Verstand ist], wie bekannt, sehr geneigt..., hinter den Gegenständen der Sinne noch immer etwas Unsichtbares, für sich selbst Tätiges zu erwarten, [verdirbt] es aber wiederum dadurch..., dass er dieses Unsichtbare sich bald wiederum versinnlicht, d. i. zum Gegenstande der Anschauung machen will" [GMS, IV, 452]. On the basis of this distinction, Kant holds, every rational being regards his reason as belonging to the intelligible (i.e., noumenal) realm, in a way that makes it possible for it to account for its own freedom of judgment:

> Um [der Spontaneität der Vernunft willen] muss ein vernünftiges Wesen sich selbst als Intelligenz (also nicht von Seiten seiner untern Kräfte), nicht als zur Sinnen-, sondern zur Verstandeswelt gehörig, ansehen; mithin hat es zwei Standpunkte, daraus es sich selbst betrachten und Gesetze des Gebrauchs seiner Kräfte, folglich aller seiner Handlungen erkennen kann, einmal, so fern es zur Sinnenwelt gehört, unter Naturgesetzen (Heteronomie), zweitens, als zur intelligibelen Welt gehörig, unter Gesetzen, die, von der Natur unabhängig, nicht empirisch, sondern bloß in der Vernunft gegründet sind. [GMS, IV, 452][5]

---

5 Allison [1990, 222] points out that this passage is reminiscent of a passage in *Kritik der Reinen Vernunft:* „Allein der Mensch, der die ganze Natur sonst lediglich nur durch Sinne kennt, erkennt sich selbst auch durch bloße Apperzeption und zwar in Handlungen und inneren Bestimmungen, die er gar nicht zum Eindrucke der Sinne zählen kann, und ist sich selbst freilich eines Teils Phänomen, anderen Teils aber, nämlich in Ansehung gewisser Vermögen, ein bloß intelligibeler Gegenstand, weil die Handlung desselben gar nicht zur Rezeptivität der Sinnlichkeit gezählt werden kann. Wir nennen diese Vermögen Verstand und Vernunft; vornehmlich wird die letztere ganz eigentlich und vorzüglicher Weise von allen empirisch bedingten Kräften unterschieden, da sie ihre Gegenstände bloß nach Ideen erwägt und den Verstand darnach bestimmt,

This need to regard our reason as part of the noumenal realm, Kant holds, is the non-moral premise that we need in order for our quest to establish the objective validity of our transcendental freedom to succeed.

To make sense of the resulting argument, we have to understand Kant as taking our awareness of having a will as his starting point—with this will taken in a thin (i.e. non-moral) sense of our being able to act on maxims (i.e, to determine our actions on the basis of rules [GMS, IV, 412] that allow us to us set ends for ourselves [GMS, IV, 427]). That is, while Kant never specifies which notion of the will he is operating with in this context, it is reasonable to assume that his argument no longer starts from the thick, moral notion of the will that led to the problem of circularity above—but rather from the thin, non-moral notion of the will that he had set out earlier in the text. The argument then takes the following form:

1. As agents, we are aware of having a will, i.e. to be able to determine our actions on the basis of rules;
2. Our will is practical reason ("Da zur Ableitung der Handlungen von Gesetzen Vernunft erfordert wird, so ist der Wille nichts anders als praktische Vernunft" [GMS, IV, 412]);
3. Hence, we are endowed with practical reason (from 1 and 2);
4. If we are endowed with reason, we have to regard this reason as spontaneous—i.e. we have to ascribe freedom of judgment to ourselves ("[Vernunft] muss sich selbst als Urheberin ihrer Prinzipien ansehen unabhängig von fremden Einflüssen" [GMS, IV, 448]);
5. Hence, we have to regard our practical reason as spontaneous (from 3 and 4);
6. We can only account for the spontaneity of our reason if we regard it as noumenal ("Um [der Spontaneität der Vernunft willen] muss ein vernünftiges Wesen sich selbst als Intelligenz..., nicht als zur Sinnen-, sondern zur Verstandeswelt gehörig, ansehen" [GMS, IV, 452]);
7. Hence, we have to regard our reason as noumenal (from 5 and 6);
8. Hence, we have to regard our will as noumenal—and, consequently, as transcendentally free (from 2 and 7).

Given that we cannot use our reason without regarding its activity as noumenal, the use of our will—that is, reason insofar as it determines our action—commits us to the idea of our will as noumenal and, hence, as transcendentally free.

---

der denn von seinen (zwar auch reinen) Begriffen einen empirischen Gebrauch macht" [KrV, III, 371].

Given the doctrine of practical knowledge, we are entitled to regard our freedom as having objective reality, just as if it were shown to be real by means of a theoretical argument. By the Reciprocity Thesis, we can then infer the validity of the moral law for us [GMS, IV, 452]. Thus, Kant claims, we have managed to break the circle that threatened our argument [GMS, IV, 453].

To understand Kant's argument properly, we have to appreciate the idealistic dimension of the ascription of freedom it involves. As we have seen above, we can have no theoretical knowledge of our own transcendental freedom. This freedom is a mere idea. Yet, what Kant claims to have established now is that we naturally and necessarily adopt this idea when confronted with the need to act in the world[6] ("naturally", because even the most simple-minded person operates with this idea, in his view; "necessarily", because without it we cannot develop a coherent view of our own ability to determine our actions through reason). Kant tries his best to convince us of the innocence of this assumption: it is not the case, he claims, that we attribute to ourselves another kind of existence. Rather, the idea of our noumenal existence is merely the ideal conception of our will as free from the influence of any external factor.

> Der Begriff einer Verstandeswelt ist also nur ein Standpunkt, den die Vernunft sich genötigt sieht, außer den Erscheinungen zu nehmen, um sich selbst als praktisch zu denken, welches, wenn die Einflüsse der Sinnlichkeit für den Menschen bestimmend wären, nicht möglich sein würde, welches aber doch notwendig ist, wofern ihm nicht das Bewusstsein seiner selbst als Intelligenz, mithin als vernünftige und durch Vernunft tätige, d. i. frei wirkende, Ursache abgesprochen werden soll. [GMS, IV, 458; see also GMS, IV, 462]

This is the position Kant has prepared in *Kritik der Reinen Vernunft:* the facts about the world are not the only ground for making legitimate judgments. Rather, in addition to being backed by facts our judgments can legitimately be grounded by "subjective requirements of thought". Our interest in having a self-consistent and well-organized view of the world requires that we make certain assumptions about the world and ourselves that are not backed by any facts about the world. This is true in particular, Kant holds, when it comes to finding a

---

[6] "Freiheit aber ist eine bloße Idee, deren objektive Realität auf keine Weise nach Naturgesetzen, mithin auch nicht in irgend einer möglichen Erfahrung dargetan werden kann, die also darum, weil ihr selbst niemals nach irgend einer Analogie ein Beispiel untergelegt werden mag, niemals begriffen, oder auch nur eingesehen werden kann. Sie gilt nur als notwendige Voraussetzung der Vernunft in einem Wesen, das sich eines Willens, d. i. eines vom bloßen Begehrungsvermögen noch verschiedenen Vermögens, (nämlich sich zum Handeln als Intelligenz, mithin nach Gesetzen der Vernunft unabhängig von Naturinstinkten zu bestimmen) bewusst zu sein glaubt" [GMS, IV, 459].

way to integrate our experience as agents (i.e. our awareness of having a will) into our view of the world. Thus, in speaking about the two standpoints—the one of regarding ourselves as sensuous beings in a world of natural necessity and the one of regarding ourselves as transcendentally free—Kant is not referring to different forms of existence, but rather of different ways we have to think about ourselves in order to integrate our complete experience of the world into a coherent whole. These are distinct ways in which we have to conceive of ourselves in order to do justice to the different ways in which we experience the world[7].

Yet, in spite of its idealistic character, the ascription of freedom that results from Kant's argument is as robust, he holds, as if it had been established from a theoretical perspective. As we have phrased it above: if we have to act under the idea of freedom, then we are—for all practical purposes—really free and the laws of freedom apply to us just as if we had been shown to be free from a theoretical point of view. Or, as Kant puts it in a later passage in *Grundlegung*, reason's need to regard itself as spontaneous grounds our rightful claim (*Rechtsanspruch*) to apply the concept of freedom to ourselves: "Der Rechtsanspruch aber selbst der gemeinen Menschenvernunft auf Freiheit des Willens gründet sich auf das Bewusstsein und die zugestandene Voraussetzung der Unabhängigkeit der Vernunft von bloß subjektiv bestimmenden Ursachen, die insgesamt das ausmachen, was bloß zur Empfindung, mithin unter die allgemeine Benennung der Sinnlichkeit gehört" [GMS, IV, 457].

Kant can now proceed to answer the remaining questions we have laid out at the beginning of this section. The first regards the overriding character of the categorical imperative. As free intelligences and as sensuous beings we have different sets of interests, which raises the question which of these prevails in the case on conflict. Kant's response to this question is premised on his claim that we have to regard our noumenal will as our "proper self" (*eigentliches Selbst* [GMS, IV, 457])[8]. He offers two arguments for this claim. First, the noumenal

---

[7] A crucial point underlying Kant's argument, highlighted in our discussion of the doctrine of practical knowledge in Chapter 2, is that if it could be shown from a theoretical perspective that it is impossible for us to have noumenal existence, then that would settle the matter—and our interest in regarding ourselves this way would have to remain frustrated. Yet, Kant's theoretical argument has shown this question to be undetermined by fact, in a way that leaves the space for us to accept the judgment about our own noumenal existence on the basis of our practical interests.

[8] This identification of our noumenal will as our proper self is prepared for in *Kritik der Reinen Vernunft*, where Kant emphasizes that an implication of his epistemology is that we can have no experience of our proper self: for given that all our thoughts are events in time and that all events in time are, by definition, mere appearances, our thoughts themselves are mere appear-

will is our will as it is in itself, while our empirical will is a mere appearance—and "reason necessarily subordinates that which is merely an appearance to the thing as it is in itself" [GMS, IV, 461]. Secondly, as noumenal wills we are active and autonomous, while existing as appearances we are passive and determined in our actions by the laws of nature. That is, only in regarding ourselves as having noumenal existence are we really in charge of our own actions and our own lives [GMS, IV, 451]. Thus, insofar as we regard ourselves as active and able to determine our own actions, we have to regard our own noumenal will—marked by spontaneity and autonomy—as our proper self. Ironically, though, the caveat of the idealistic character of Kant's account continues to apply: our proper self, the person that we are in ourselves, is a mere idea, a mere assumption[9], while that self that we have experience of—our empirical self—is merely an appearance[10].

With this distinction between our empirical and our proper (noumenal) self in place, Kant can give an explanation of the overriding character of the categorical imperative: our desires and inclinations are the interests of ourselves only insofar as we are appearances, while the *Vernunftinteressen*, our interests in so far as we are spontaneous reason, are the interests of our proper self. The latter, Kant holds, as the essential interests of our proper self, have greater value for us —and hence should prevail in the case of conflict [GMS, IV, 450][11].

---

ances. Consequently, in being aware of our thoughts, we do not experience ourselves as we are in ourselves, but rather only experience ourselves as appearances: "[I]ch habe... keine Erkenntnis von mir, wie ich bin, sondern bloß, wie ich mir selbst erscheine" [KrV, III, 123; see also: GMS, IV, 451; KpV, V, 6; KU, V, 435]. Thus, his theoretical investigations show that we have no direct knowledge of ourselves as we are in ourselves, leaving open the question concerning our proper identity, which is then to be answered by means of the practical argument establishing our noumenal will as our proper self.

9 "[Der Mensch muss] über diese aus lauter Erscheinungen zusammengesetzte Beschaffenheit seines eigenen Subjekts noch etwas anderes zum Grunde Liegendes, nämlich sein Ich, so wie es an sich selbst beschaffen sein mag, annehmen und sich also in Absicht auf die bloße Wahrnehmung und Empfänglichkeit der Empfindungen zur Sinnenwelt, in Ansehung dessen aber, was in ihm reine Tätigkeit sein mag, (dessen, was gar nicht durch Affizierung der Sinne, sondern unmittelbar zum Bewusstsein gelangt) sich zur intellektuellen Welt zählen..., die er doch nicht weiter kennt" [GMS, IV, 451].

10 This dualism of Kant's account of the self is brought out in his description of the criminal, who in spite of his misdeeds treasures the ideal conception of himself as a better person, free of the urges and desires that afflict his empirical self [GMS, IV, 454–5].

11 Schönecker & Wood point out that Kant's assumptions of the purely phenomenal character of our inclinations might not be consistent with the tenets of his transcendental idealism: "Der gravierendste Mangel der Deduktion liegt in der Art und Weise, wie Kant seine von ihm selbst eingeführte Unterscheidung zwischen Ding an sich und Erscheinung benutzt. Damit sind

The second question Kant still has to address is the one concerning the way in which the demands of reason can move us to act. Kant's short answer is that it is inexplicable. As we have seen above, he identifies morality as a peculiar form of causality, namely one in which the cause is not another event in the empirical world (another appearance), but rather an idea of pure reason. However, he holds, we can only explain events governed by the laws of nature: "Da diese aber kein Verhältnis der Ursache zur Wirkung, als zwischen zwei Gegenständen der Erfahrung an die Hand geben kann, hier aber reine Vernunft durch bloße Ideen (die gar keinen Gegenstand für Erfahrung abgeben) die Ursache von einer Wirkung, die freilich in der Erfahrung liegt, sein soll, so ist die Erklärung, wie und warum uns die Allgemeinheit der Maxime als Gesetzes, mithin die Sittlichkeit interessiere, uns Menschen gänzlich unmöglich" [GMS, IV, 460][12]. All we can say is that the imperative does not leave us indifferent, that we take an interest in its demands. The basis for that interest is what Kant calls a "moral feeling", i.e., the ability of the moral demand to trigger an emotional response, which then functions as an incentive to act—just as other feelings and desires do[13]. That is, moral action is possible because of "an ability of reason to inspire a feeling of pleasure in the completion of our duty" [GMS, IV, 460]. Yet, Kant maintains, it still remains impossible for us to explain how the idea of the moral law—a mere thought—can inspire this feeling.

> Um das zu wollen, wozu die Vernunft allein dem sinnlich-affizierten vernünftigen Wesen das Sollen vorschreibt, dazu gehört freilich ein Vermögen der Vernunft, ein Gefühl der Lust oder

---

nicht (numerisch) verschiedene Welten gemeint, sondern Standpunkte oder Betrachtungsweisen. Eine und dieselbe Sache kann als Ding an sich oder als Erscheinung charakterisiert werden… Neigungen müssen verstanden werden als etwas, das wie andere Entitäten auch zugleich als Ding an sich und als Erscheinung existiert, wenn sie auch nur als Erscheinungen erfahrbar sind. Kant aber unterstellt in einem quasi trivialplatonischen Sinne, Neigungen hätten nicht nur in epistemologischer, sondern auch in ontologischer Hinsicht einen ganz anderen Status als Dinge an sich" [2002, 203].

12 Yet, Kant points out that our understanding of the possibility of natural causality is not any more advanced than our understanding of the possibility of transcendental freedom: "Dasjenige also in der Frage über die Freiheit des Willens, was die spekulative Vernunft von jeher in so große Verlegenheit gesetzt hat, ist eigentlich nur transzendental und geht lediglich darauf, ob ein Vermögen angenommen werden müsse, eine Reihe von sukzessiven Dingen oder Zuständen von selbst anzufangen. Wie ein solches möglich sei, ist nicht eben so notwendig beantworten zu können, da wir uns eben sowohl bei der Kausalität nach Naturgesetzen damit begnügen müssen, a priori zu erkennen, dass eine solche vorausgesetzt werden müsse, ob wir gleich die Möglichkeit, wie durch ein gewisses Dasein das Dasein eines andern gesetzt werde, auf keine Weise begreifen und uns desfalls lediglich an die Erfahrung halten müssen" [KrV, III, 310].

13 For a more detailed discussion of Kant's notion of moral feeling, see Chapter 5 below.

> des Wohlgefallens an der Erfüllung der Pflicht einzuflößen, mithin eine Kausalität derselben, die Sinnlichkeit ihren Prinzipien gemäß zu bestimmen. Es ist aber gänzlich unmöglich, einzusehen, d. i. a priori begreiflich zu machen, wie ein bloßer Gedanke, der selbst nichts Sinnliches in sich enthält, eine Empfindung der Lust oder Unlust hervorbringe. [GMS, IV, 460]

This is the account of the real possibility of the moral law offered in *Grundlegung*. According to this account, we have to accept the hypothesis of the spontaneity of our own reason to explain our ability to think. Yet, against the backdrop of a world of natural necessity, this requires us to regard the activity of our reason as noumenal—i.e. not as part of the empirical world. This leads us to conceive of our will *qua* practical reason as noumenal and, hence, as transcendentally free—if only from a practical point of view. Regarding our will as transcendentally free commits us to conceiving it as governed by the laws of freedom, i.e. the moral law. In regarding ourselves as having noumenal existence, we see ourselves not only as passive beings in the world of appearances, but also as things-in-themselves, guided in our actions by the laws imposed by our own spontaneous self. In spite of the fact that it is a mere projection, we have, Kant holds, to regard our noumenal will as our "proper self", as it is only because of it that we can conceive of ourselves as actively determining our own actions. The thought of the interests of our higher self has the power to affect our emotions, in a way that can translate into action. Yet, this power of the thought of the moral law to move us to action is a brute fact not amenable to further elucidation.

The transition to the fact of reason

Why did Kant, in his later work, shift away from the argument he offered in *Grundlegung*? Most likely he discovered a profound confusion in the construction of his argument. To understand the problem it helps to make use of Henrich's distinction between a strong and a weak form of deduction [1975, 82]. In the strong form, the validity of that which one is aiming to deduce is not assumed, but rather established in the course of the argument. In the weak form, on the other hand, that which is to be deduced is assumed to be valid from the outset—and the purpose of the deduction is merely to show how we can account for its possibility. As Henrich points out, this latter procedure is used by Kant in the *Prolegomena*, where he offers a weak deduction of the categories, which before he had established by means of a strong deduction in *Kritik der Reinen Vernunft*.

As we have seen, the starting point of Kant's argument in the third part of *Grundlegung* is our awareness of having a will as a "practical datum", i.e. information that is not available from the theoretical, but only from the practical perspective (that is, only insofar as we find ourselves confronted with the need to act in the world). Yet, to be successful in his aim to deduce the validity of the moral law from merely non-moral premises and, hence, to avoid the danger of circularity that had ensnared his first attempt to develop his argument, this awareness has to be awareness of a will in a thin, non-moral sense—i.e., merely as an ability to determine our actions on the basis of maxims to pursue the ends that we have as sensuous beings, without any suggestion that we can be moved to action by moral considerations (for this is the conclusion that we are hoping to reach).

One problem with Kant's argument, which we have already noted above is that he never properly distinguishes the problematic, thick notion of a will that led him to abort his first attempt of a deduction and the thin, non-moral notion that he is supposedly operating with now. This lack of conceptual precision opens Kant's argument to the danger of sliding between the required and the problematic sense in which we can be said to be aware of having a will. This is precisely what seems to be happening when Kant summarizes his argument in a later part of *Grundlegung*, where he writes:

> Freiheit... gilt nur als notwendige Voraussetzung der Vernunft in einem Wesen, das sich eines Willens, d. i. eines vom bloßen Begehrungsvermögen noch verschiedenen Vermögens, (nämlich sich zum Handeln als Intelligenz, mithin nach Gesetzen der Vernunft unabhängig von Naturinstinkten zu bestimmen) bewusst zu sein glaubt. [GMS, IV, 459]

Here Kant says that freedom is a necessary presupposition in a being that sees itself as having a will in the sense of being able to determine its actions "according to the laws of reason". Yet, given that the "law of reason", for Kant, is the moral law, it appears that Kant is again taking a thick—rather than a thin, non-moral—notion of a will as the starting point of his argument[14]. That is,

---

[14] A similar passage occurs two pages later, where Kant writes: "Diese Freiheit des Willens vorauszusetzen, ist auch nicht allein (ohne in Widerspruch mit dem Prinzip der Naturnotwendigkeit in der Verknüpfung der Erscheinungen der Sinnenwelt zu geraten) ganz wohl möglich (wie die spekulative Philosophie zeigen kann), sondern auch sie praktisch, d. i. in der Idee, allen seinen willkürlichen Handlungen als Bedingung unterzulegen, ist einem vernünftigen Wesen, das sich seiner Kausalität durch Vernunft, mithin eines Willens (der von Begierden unterschieden ist) bewusst ist, ohne weitere Bedingung notwendig" [GMS, IV, 461]. Again, the reason for regarding our will as free is said to be the fact that we are aware of our ability to determine our will on the basis of the principles of reason.

while Kant appears to be giving a summary of his argument, he has in fact modified it by re-introducing the discarded premise of our awareness of a will in the thick, moral sense. As Henrich puts it:

> Erst nachdem der Anschein stark genug geworden war, die Voraussetzung des Willens ergebe sich aus der Zweiweltenlehre, wird vom Willen so gesprochen, dass eine neue Frage sich erheben müsste—eben die Frage nach dem Ursprung des Bewusstseins vom Willen in den elementaren sittlichen Vernunftsprinzipien. Da die 'Grundlegung' auf sie gar keine Antwort geben könnte, ohne ihre Deduktionsversprechen grundlegend zu modifizieren und auf die schwache Legitimationsform der Sittlichkeit ausdrücklich zurückzunehmen, macht sie das Zugeständnis, durch das sich der Charakter der von ihr geleisteten Deduktion überhaupt erst bestimmen lässt, am Schluss und in der irreführenden Verkleidung eines Resumés. [1975, 93]

The slide back from the thin, non-moral to the thick conception of the will is likely not only due to imprecise terminology, but also to a real philosophical problem that Kant was grappling with. For, as we have highlighted in Chapter 1 above, during his work on establishing the validity of the moral law, he became increasingly aware of—and concerned about—the fact that we can conceive of a rational being that is aware of having a will in the thin, non-moral sense (i.e. in the sense of being able to determine its actions on the basis of maxims), without though being aware of any moral constraints on its actions. As Kant puts it in *Religion*:

> [E]s folgt daraus, dass ein Wesen Vernunft hat, gar nicht, dass diese ein Vermögen enthalte, die Willkür unbedingt durch die bloße Vorstellung der Qualifikation ihrer Maximen zur allgemeinen Gesetzgebung zu bestimmen und also für sich selbst praktisch zu sein: wenigstens so viel wir einsehen können. Das allervernünftigste Weltwesen könnte doch immer gewisser Triebfedern, die ihm von Objekten der Neigung herkommen, bedürfen, um seine Willkür zu bestimmen; hiezu aber die vernünftigste Überlegung, sowohl was die größte Summe der Triebfedern, als auch die Mittel, den dadurch bestimmten Zweck zu erreichen, betrifft, anwenden: ohne auch nur die Möglichkeit von so etwas, als das moralische, schlechthin gebietende Gesetz ist, welches sich als selbst und zwar höchste Triebfeder ankündigt, zu ahnen. [R, VI, 26n][15]

---

[15] This passage undermines O'Neill's claim that for Kant „there are and can be no merely instrumental reasoners" [1989, 73]. For Kant here acknowledges the logical possibility of a being that makes merely technical-practical use of its rational faculties—i.e. is not capable of making moral-practical use of these. Yet, to make technical-practical use of our reason is to make instrumental use of it. Hence, in this passage Kant discusses a being that is a merely instrumental reasoner, contrary to O'Neill's suggestion that Kant does not acknowledge this possibility. Kant also points to the possibility of a being endowed merely with instrumental reason in *Kritik der Urteilskraft*: „Wären dagegen auch vernünftige Wesen, deren Vernunft aber den Wert des Daseins der Dinge nur im Verhältnisse der Natur zu ihnen (ihrem Wohlbefinden) zu setzen, nicht aber sich einen solchen ursprünglich (in der Freiheit) selbst zu verschaffen im Stande wäre: so

That is, while *Grundlegung*, at its most ambitious, aims to deduce the validity of the moral law from the premise of our awareness of a will in a thin, non-moral sense, Kant's later writings suggest that he seriously doubted the viability of such a deduction. It is not impossible that he was already aware of these concerns, even if only dimly, during the time of writing *Grundlegung*. This would explain why a slide between the two conceptions of the will must have been tempting for him. For if the validity of these concerns is accepted, grounding the deduction of the moral law on the thin, non-moral conception of the will must appear hopeless.

Thus, Kant's argument in *Grundlegung* appears stuck between two unappetizing options: either he bases his argument on the non-moral premise demanded by the logic of his initial programme outline, which, though, seems unable to get him to the desired conclusion; or he bases it on a premise which already comes with a moral charge and which, consequently, allows him to reach the intended conclusion easily, but which does so only at the price of circularity. Kant's response to this problem, it appears, is not to address the problem—but rather to slide, intentionally or not, between the different notions of a will.

To the extent that Kant's final statement of his position in *Grundlegung* is built around the notion of the will in a thick sense, we can understand Kant's argument as a weak—not a strong—deduction: its reference to our noumenal existence explains how we can coherently think the possibility of a spontaneous will guided by the principles of reason, but it still requires that the awareness of such a will—a will subject to the moral law—be given independently. Yet, no independent argument establishing that we have this awareness is forthcoming in *Grundlegung*. As Henrich puts it, while Kant aims to offer a deduction of the moral law from purely non-moral premises, the argument he actually provides includes a hidden moral premise, namely that of a will under the moral law[16].

Kant himself never explained why he abandoned his attempts to derive the validity of the moral law from purely non-moral premises—and we do not know whether in re-reading his attempts in *Grundlegung* he came to realize the confusion in his argument. The fact is, though, that by the time of writing *Kritik der*

---

wären zwar (relative) Zwecke in der Welt, aber kein (absoluter) Endzweck, weil das Dasein solcher vernünftigen Wesen doch immer zwecklos sein würde" [KU, V, 449].

16 "Die 'Grundlegung' hat wirklich ihr Beweisversprechen am Ende und de facto auf eine Deduktion nach schwächerer Form zurückgenommen, die nicht ohne eine Prämisse geführt werden kann, die aus dem sittlichen Bewusstsein selber kommt. Dass diese Prämisse aber im Bewusstsein der Verbindlichkeit selber ihren Grund hat, konnte Kant unmöglich auch nur andeuten oder implizit einräumen" [Henrich, 1975, 91].

Praktischen Vernunft, which appeared three years after the publication of *Grundlegung*, he had abandoned the earlier strategy—and instead based his argument explicitly on the moral premise that had only been admitted implicitly into his argument in the earlier work.

The fact of reason

The finely layered argument aiming to establish the validity of the moral law presented in *Grundlegung* is replaced, in *Kritik der Praktischen Vernunft*, by a mere assertion—we are aware of the moral law as an *a priori* fact of reason: "Man kann das Bewusstsein dieses Grundgesetzes ein Faktum der Vernunft nennen, weil man es nicht aus vorhergehenden Datis der Vernunft, z. B. dem Bewusstsein der Freiheit (denn dieses ist uns nicht vorher gegeben), herausvernünfteln kann, sondern weil es sich für sich selbst uns aufdringt als synthetischer Satz a priori, der auf keiner, weder reinen noch empirischen, Anschauung gegründet ist" [KpV, V, 31]. There are a further seven passages in *Kritik der Praktischen Vernunft* that mention the fact of reason [Rawls, 2000, 255][17], but they give little further illumination. Kant merely adds that it is only through our consciousness of the moral law that our own freedom is revealed to us and that the latter is the "keystone of the whole architecture of the system of pure reason" [KpV, V, 3]. That is to say, Kant hardly gives us any guidance on how to understand his notion of the fact of reason—yet, strongly emphasizes its importance.

This position has led to puzzlement among commentators. Some even see it as inconsistent with the principles of Kant's critical philosophy. Karl Ameriks, for instance, regards Kant's embrace of the notion of the fact of reason as a "'regression' to dogmatism" [2005, 213]—and claims that "only some technical peculiarities of his system prevent the labeling of his position as fundamentally intuitionistic" [2005, 184]. Prauss calls Kant's argument in *Kritik der Praktischen Vernunft* an "act of desperation" ("Verzweiflungstat" [1982, 67]) and a "failure of a unique, almost quaint character" [1982, 231]. Others choose to mention the fact of reason as little as possible, in spite of the fact that it constitutes the foundation of Kant's mature moral philosophy. In *Creating the Kingdom of Ends* [1996], Christine Korsgaard refers to the fact of reason a mere four times on 440 pages, without ever discussing the notion in detail. Similarly, Allen

---

17 Beck [1960, 167] and Rawls [2000, 258] point out that there is some ambiguity about what Kant's term of the 'fact of reason' refers to: sometimes it refers to our consciousness of the moral law, sometimes to the moral law itself. There is general agreement among all commentators, however, that the consciousness of the moral law is the correct referent of the term.

Wood dedicates a single line to it in his work on *Kant's Ethical Thought* [1999]. Others still restate Kant's rather obscure assertions on the topic as if no further explanation were required. Frierson, for instance, writes that: "Kant asserts on the basis of practical reason that one is free. Although this postulate is called mere 'belief' or 'faith', it is absolutely certain from the standpoint of practical reason" [2003, 100], without offering any further elucidation as to why we should regard an assertion "on the basis of practical reason" to be "absolutely certain"— almost as if the matter had already been sufficiently clarified[18].

Taken by itself, the position Kant adopts in *Kritik der Praktischen Vernunft* indeed seems surprising. However, the long preparation that has taken us through the relevant aspects of Kant's transcendental idealism as well as his attempts at the deduction of the moral law in *Grundlegung* allows us to trace the logic underlying Kant's position. The starting point of this reconstructed argument is the claim that, as agents, we are confronted with the demands of the moral law[19]. In deciding on how to act, Kant holds, we experience these demands as unconditionally obliging for us, regardless of which empirical interests we happen to have: "Also ist es das moralische Gesetz, dessen wir uns unmittelbar bewusst werden (so bald wir uns Maximen des Willens entwerfen), welches

---

18 Beck and Allison both attempt defenses of Kant's position. However, while Beck's short discussion [1960, 166–170] offers some helpful observations about Kant's argument (by pointing out, for instance, that the starting point of the argument is Kant's claim that in acting we see ourselves confronted with a moral demand, as discussed in the text below), it is nonetheless shrouded in obscurity and fails to take into consideration crucial aspects of Kant's position, such as his notion of the interests of reason and his doctrine of practical knowledge. These are also ignored in Allison's *Kant's Theory of Freedom*, in which the discussion of the fact-of-reason argument—which starts with a critique of Beck's interpretation—introduces some germane points (noting, for example, the structural similarities between Kant's discussion of space and time in *Kritik der Reinen Vernunft* and his discussion of the fact of reason in *Kritik der Praktischen Vernunft*) but then descends into something that comes very close to impenetrability, with Allison excusing the terseness of his comments with the remark that the "present study is not intended as a study of Kant's moral theory per se" [1990, 238]. Kleingeld discusses some further interpretations of Kant's argument [2010, 61–2]. However, she herself falls into the trap of attributing to the Kant of *Kritik der Praktischen Vernunft* the view that awareness of a will in a thin (i.e. non-moral) sense is sufficient to establish the real possibility of our transcendental freedom ("When [agents] conceive of themselves as acting on reasons, they conceive of their will as a causality on the basis of reason and 'independent from empirical conditions'" [2010, 68]), in effect making Kant revert back to the position of *Grundlegung*—even though he had come to reject this position by the time he wrote *Kritik der Praktischen Vernunft*, as discussed in the text above. Consequently, not a single complete and satisfactory account of Kant's fact-of-reason argument is to be found in the secondary literature surveyed for this work.
19 Beck: "The 'moral judgment of every man' is the true starting point of the Kantian moral philosophy" [1960, 164].

sich uns zuerst darbietet und, indem die Vernunft jenes als einen durch keine sinnliche Bedingungen zu überwiegenden, ja davon gänzlich unabhängigen Bestimmungsgrund darstellt, gerade auf den Begriff der Freiheit führt". [KpV, V, 29; see also: VT, VIII, 402]

Kant takes it as an uncontroversial feature of our experience as agents that, in deliberating on our actions, we are confronted with unconditional moral demands[20]. This assumption is accepted by many skeptics of morality, including Nietzsche. They take issue not with the claim that we are aware of moral demands—but rather with the claim that we should take them seriously[21]. These skeptics hold that in spite of the apparent authority with which the moral law appeals to us, properly understood it is an entirely empirical phenomenon, a tool of social control perhaps or an expression of enlightened self-interest. That is, they try to convince us that what we regarded as objective necessity is, properly considered, mere subjective necessity [KpV, V, 12][22].

Crucially, Kant holds that this common moral experience not only involves our being aware of the demands of the moral law—but also our awareness of being able to *act on it*. This is the upshot of Kant's important thought experiment of the person facing the choice between giving false evidence against an innocent man or being sent to the gallows.

> Setzet, dass jemand von seiner wollüstigen Neigung vorgibt, sie sei, wenn ihm der beliebte Gegenstand und die Gelegenheit dazu vorkämen, für ihn ganz unwiderstehlich: ob, wenn ein Galgen vor dem Hause, da er diese Gelegenheit trifft, aufgerichtet wäre, um ihn sogleich nach genossener Wollust daran zu knüpfen, er alsdann nicht seine Neigung bezwingen würde. Man darf nicht lange raten, was er antworten würde. Fragt ihn aber, ob, wenn sein Fürst ihm

---

20 "Die Regel der Urteilskraft unter Gesetzen der reinen praktischen Vernunft ist diese: Frage dich selbst, ob die Handlung, die du vorhast, wenn sie nach einem Gesetze der Natur, von der du selbst ein Teil wärest, geschehen sollte, sie du wohl als durch deinen Willen möglich ansehen könntest. *Nach dieser Regel beurteilt in der Tat jedermann Handlungen*, ob sie sittlich gut oder böse sind" [KpV, V, 69, my emphasis]. Kant frequently highlights that even rule-breakers do acknowledge the validity of the law—and would obey, if only their desires did not get into the way [e.g., GMS, IV, 454–5].

21 Beck makes the helpful distinction between "the undisputed fact (that we are conscious of a moral law)" and "the disputed fact (that there is a law that can come only from pure practical reason)" [1960, 168]. The challenge Kant is facing in his argument is to make the transition from the first to the second fact. Yet, the crucial point is that the first of these—namely, the fact that we are aware of unconditional moral demands—is taken to be uncontroversial. See also Allison [1990, 234].

22 Thus, from Kant's perspective, skepticism about morality is relevantly similar to Hume's skepticism about natural laws we have encountered in Chapter 2: it tries to deflate the claim about the presence of a necessary element in our experience by analyzing it as something merely empirical.

> unter Androhung derselben unverzögerten Todesstrafe zumutete, ein falsches Zeugnis wider einen ehrlichen Mann, den er gerne unter scheinbaren Vorwänden verderben möchte, abzulegen, ob er da, so groß auch seine Liebe zum Leben sein mag, sie wohl zu überwinden für möglich halte. Ob er es tun würde, oder nicht, wird er vielleicht sich nicht getrauen zu versichern; dass es ihm aber möglich sei, muss er ohne Bedenken einräumen [KpV, V, 30].

That is, while we might often fail to act on the demands of the moral law, we nonetheless, Kant contends, never doubt our ability to do so.

Once this starting point of our awareness of the moral law in the wide sense (that is, including our awareness of being able to act on its demands) has been established, the question arises: how can we account for this awareness? Or, put differently: how can it coherently be integrated into our general view of ourselves and our place in the world? Here the results from our previous discussions find their application. Kant's analysis of the moral law has shown that we can conceive of the possibility of our being subject to an unconditional practical law only if this law is regarded as an *a priori* law given to us by ourselves *qua* noumenal will (see Chapter 3 above). That is, Kant holds that to take our ordinary moral experience of finding ourselves confronted with an unconditional demand at face value, rather than to explain it away as the skeptic does, we have to attribute to ourselves a noumenal will, that is, pure practical reason[23].

At this point, Kant's argument makes use of the doctrine of practical knowledge, which was first foreshadowed in *Kritik der Reinen Vernunft* and first put to use in *Grundlegung*. As we have seen in Chapter 2 above, the doctrine of practical knowledge holds that if there is a judgment the truth of which cannot be settled by the facts available from a theoretical perspective and if, furthermore, we have a strong practical interest in the judgment being true, then we can—and have to —regard the truth of the judgment as established from a practical point of view. That is, the judgment is objectively valid for us and the concepts included in it can be regarded as having objective reality.

---

[23] "Ordinary consciousness... starts from the assumption of the absolute validity of the moral law... [T]he consciousness of the law is discovered on examination to be explicable, even as a possibility, only on the assumption that it is due to the autonomous activity of a noumenal being. By its existence it proves the conditions through which alone it is explicable. Its mere existence suffices to prove that its validity is objective in a deeper and truer sense than the principles of understanding. The notion of freedom, and therefore all the connected Ideas of pure Reason, gain noumenal reality as the conditions of a moral consciousness which is incapable of explanation as illusory or even phenomenal. Since the consciousness of the moral law is thus noumenally grounded, it has a validity with which nothing in the phenomenal world can possibly compare. It is the one form in which noumenal reality directly discloses itself to the human mind" [Kemp Smith, 2003, 573].

In *Grundlegung*, Kant held that a being that cannot but act under the idea of freedom is, for all practical purposes, really free (as long as the facts that are available from a theoretical perspective do not rule out the possibility of its freedom). The crucial (if only implicit) shift between *Grundlegung* and *Kritik der Praktischen Vernunft* is that Kant no longer applies the doctrine of practical knowledge to the notion of freedom, as he did in *Grundlegung*, but now applies it to our awareness of the moral law: we are aware of the demands made on us by the moral law and are faced with the task of accounting for the possibility of this awareness (i. e. integrate it into our general worldview). The only way to account for the necessity with which the moral law presents its demands to us is to regard it as an *a priori* law legislated by our own noumenal self. Yet, there is, from a theoretical point of view, simply no fact of the matter of whether we really exist as noumena and whether the moral law really is valid for us. Given the doctrine of the practical data, however, and the fact that we have a strong practical interest in the matter (as we find ourselves faced with an undeniable demand made on us as agents by the moral law), we can (and have to) determine the matter on the basis of these practical interests. In strict parallel with the premise in *Grundlegung*, we can say: for beings such as ourselves, who cannot but act under the idea of being subject to the moral law—i.e., who, in acting, see themselves confronted with the demands of morality –, the moral law is objectively valid, just as if its validity had been established from a theoretical point of view. Using the Reciprocity Thesis, Kant can then deduce the real possibility of transcendental freedom [KpV, V, 47]: in order to make sense of the demands that the moral law makes on us, we have to regard ourselves as transcendentally free and, hence, ascribe noumenal existence to ourselves[24].

In analyzing the argument, the first thing to focus on is the shift in the question Kant is trying to answer. He no longer aims to produce an argument establishing that the moral law is valid for us. Rather, he starts from the claim that we are aware of the unconditional demands of morality—and asks how can we ac-

---

[24] The fact-of-reason argument—i.e. the position that our being aware of the demands of the moral law is an *a priori* fact of reason, which grounds the objective validity of our transcendental freedom—is Kant's settled view for the remainder of his philosophical work. In *Religion*, for instance, he writes: "Wäre dieses Gesetz nicht in uns gegeben, wir würden es als ein solches durch keine Vernunft herausklügeln, oder der Willkür anschwatzen: und doch ist dieses Gesetz das einzige, was uns der Unabhängigkeit unsrer Willkür von der Bestimmung durch alle andern Triebfedern (unsrer Freiheit) und hiermit zugleich der Zurechnungsfähigkeit aller Handlungen bewusst macht" [R, VI, 26n]. Similarly, in *Metaphysik der Sitten* he asserts: "[D]er Begriff der Freiheit [ist] keiner theoretischen Deduktion seiner Möglichkeit fähig... und [kann] nur aus dem praktischen Gesetze der Vernunft (dem kategorischen Imperativ), als einem Fakt derselben, geschlossen werden" [MS, VI, 252; see also: MS, VI, 239; KU, V, 403; KU, V, 475].

count for the possibility of these unconditional demands. That is, in *Kritik der Praktischen Vernunft* the moral law is something that we find ourselves confronted with before any argument begins. In this it resembles the notions of space and time in Kant's theoretical inquiries. In both cases, we are facing a brute datum, simply given to us in experience and which stands in no need to be proved or inferred [KpV, V, 31][25]. In both cases, furthermore, this datum is invested with an element of necessity. In the case of space and time, we cannot conceive any empirical experience that does not present itself to us as embedded in space and time. That is, all empirical experience is necessarily given to us in space and in time. The moral law makes a demand on us that is unconditional—i.e. is necessarily valid for us regardless of our other interests. In both cases, Kant holds, we can only account for the element of necessity by regarding the data in question as *a priori* facts of our experience. This does not mean that we have some special faculty to apprehend *a priori* facts. Rather, we find in our experience of the world (which we are confronted with either as cognizers or as agents) features, which we recognize, on reflection, as involving an element of necessity. Regarding them as *a priori* facts, Kant holds, is the only way we have to account for this necessity[26].

---

25 This parallel is noted by Brandt: "Wir müssen beides als Faktum des Bewusstseins hinnehmen, die Form unserer Sinnlichkeit, nämlich Raum und Zeit, und die Form unserer praktischen Vernunft, nämlich das Freiheitsgesetz" [2007, 310; see also: Hinsch, 1986, 100; Yovel, 1989, 234; Allison, 1990, 235]. Kemp Smith, on the other hand, compares the role of the moral law in the practical argument to that of possible experience in the theoretical argument: "The moral law... exercises, in the process of its transcendental proof, a function which exactly corresponds to that which is discharged by possible experience in [*Kritik der Reinen Vernunft*]. Our consciousness of the moral law is, like sense-experience, a given fact. It is de facto, and cannot be deduced from anything more ultimate than itself. But as given, it enables us to deduce its transcendental conditions" [2003, 572]. This is unconvincing, given that the practical argument is aimed at giving an account of our consciousness of the moral law as an *a priori* fact, while clearly no such status is claimed for possible experience in the theoretical argument.

26 Kant himself highlights the parallel between the role of the moral law, on the one hand, and that of space and time, on the other, in Reflexion 7201: "Die Möglichkeit [von reiner praktischer Vernunft] kann [man] *a priori* nicht einsehen, weil es das Verhältnis eines Realgrundes zur Folge betrifft, also muss etwas gegeben sein, was lediglich aus ihr entspringen kann; und aus der Wirklichkeit kann auf die Möglichkeit geschlossen werden. Die moralische Gesetze sind von der Art, und dieses muss so bewiesen werden, wie wir die Vorstellungen von Raum und Zeit als Vorstellungen a priori bewiesen, nur mit dem Unterschiede, dass diese Anschauungen jene aber bloße Vernunftbegriffe betrifft" [XIX, 274]. This is noted by Brandt [2007, 355], but missed by Prauss who writes: "Kant [muss] das Moralgesetz nicht nur als Faktum, sondern auch noch als ‚apriorisches Faktum' ansetzen... [Aber: der Transzendentalphilosophie] zufolge nämlich darf gerade Apriorisches doch immer nur genau soweit in Anspruch genommen werden, als es sich auch deduzieren oder ableiten lässt. Danach aber läuft jene Inanspruchnahme eines Moralgesetzes, das

This is the explanation of Kant's claim that the consciousness of the moral law is an *a priori* fact, a claim that has brought about much puzzlement among commentators. Our examination of the notion should make clear that, as in the case of time and space, this does not mean that we have the power to apprehend super-sensible facts. Rather, it means that, in Kant's view, the only way to account for the unconditional necessity with which the demands of the moral law confront us—that is, the only way to integrate the moral experience into a coherent view of the world and our place in it—is to regard our consciousness of the moral law as an *a priori* fact of reason.

Thus, in *Kritik der Praktischen Vernunft*, our awareness of the moral law is presented as something that is in no need to be inferred, but is a mere datum in our experience as agents. Hence, Kant's argument takes the form of a weak deduction in the sense highlighted above (i.e. it aims to account for the possibility of something that has been independently given)[27]. However, as Henrich points out, the fact that an argument is a weak deduction is consistent with it having legitimizing force[28]. By showing how we can account for the possibility of the moral law by integrating it into our general worldview, the argument undermines the skeptic's claim that the notion of an objectively valid moral law is

---

einerseits etwas Apriorisches, doch andererseits etwas Unabgeleitetes, nämlich ein bloßes Faktum sein soll, dann geradezu auf ein Unding hinaus" [1982, 68].

27 This is inconsistent with Kant's own assertion that no deduction of the moral law is possible [KpV, V, 47]. Yet, as Kemp Smith argues, there are good reasons to discount this assertion: "Kant does... assert that the moral law requires no deduction... Yet, in the very same section he argues that the deduction of freedom from the moral law is a credential of the latter, and is a sufficient substitute for all a priori justification. According to the first statement we have an immediate consciousness of the validity of the moral law; according to the second statement the moral law proves itself indirectly, by serving as a principle for the deduction of freedom. The second form of statement alone harmonizes with the argument developed in the third section of [*Grundlegung*], and more correctly expresses the intention of Kant's central argument in [*Kritik der Praktischen Vernunft*]" [2003, 572; see also: Beck, 1960, 172].

28 "Ist nun die Erkenntnis zuvor nur bekannt, nicht aber glaubwürdig, so gewinnt sie durch den Ursprungsnachweis auch eine Legitimation. Sowohl in der starken als auch in der schwachen Deduktionsform lassen sich somit Erkenntnisse verteidigen, so dass es also möglich wäre, die eine wie die andere bei der ‚Festsetzung' des Prinzips der Moralität [...] zu gebrauchen. Jede Deduktion aber, ob sie nun die deduzierte Erkenntnis verteidigt oder ob sie, wie in den Prolegomena, deren Ursprung nur um der Verteidigung anderer Erkenntnisse willen sucht, muss zum deduzierten Prinzip aus einer Untersuchung der inneren Konstitution der Vernunft überleiten" [Henrich, 1972, 82; also see: Henrich, 1972, 100].

inconsistent with a scientific view of the world—and that, hence, it should be rejected[29].

In this sense, the moral law receives coherentist support from the weak deduction offered in Kritik der Praktischen Vernunft[30]. This again makes the argument of that work similar to the deduction of space in Kritik der Reinen Vernunft, where Kant is partly concerned with countering the doctrine of idealism, according to which the notion that space is a "mere illusion" [KrV, III, 191]. In both cases—that of space in the theoretical field and that of the awareness of the moral law in the practical—the skeptic accepts that something is given to us in experience, but doubts its objective reality. Against this skeptical position, Kant offers his deductions, aiming to show how we can account for the objective reality of the experience in question[31].

Kant argues that the notion of the objective reality of the moral law receives further legitimization from the fact that it allows us to establish the objective reality of our transcendental freedom. This notion is required for the grounding of the whole of his transcendental idealism, for—as we have discussed in Chapter 1

---

29 We should remember that one of Kant's aims in Kritik der Reinen Vernunft is to establish the basis for a fully scientific view of the world—i.e. a view that does not involve self-contradictions or assertions for which no justification can be given. His transcendental idealism is the basis that he proposes for this venture. By showing how the moral law can be accounted for within this framework, thus, Kant shows how this notion is consistent with a scientific view of the world.

30 This point is made by Rawls: "I believe that by the time of the second Critique, Kant has developed not only a constructivist conception of practical reason but a coherentist account of how it can be authenticated. This is the significance of his doctrine of the fact of reason and of his abandoning his hitherto vain search for a so-called deduction of the moral law" [2000, 268].

31 In this context, it is notable that the suggestion that the moral law could be a "chimerical idea", which was still present in Grundlegung [GMS, VI, 445], has disappeared in Kritik der Praktischen Vernunft. This is fully consistent with the reconstruction of Kant's argument as based on the doctrine of practical knowledge: for to speak of an illusion only makes sense where there is an underlying reality and underlying fact of the matter that could falsify the content of our consciousness. So, for instance, if I see a stick in the water as bent this can only be an illusion if the fact of the matter is that the stick is straight. Yet, a crucial point in Kant's argument is precisely that there is no fact to the matter of our being subject to the moral law (and to our being transcendentally free) that is independent of our consciousness of this being the case. As we have seen above, establishing the objective reality of the notions that we are subject to the moral law and that we are transcendentally free from a practical point of view crucially presupposes that there are no theoretical facts settling the matter. Kant's transcendental idealism has restricted the sphere of possible facts in a way that judgments on both these points remain undetermined from a theoretical point of view. This creates the space that can be filled with practical convictions. Yet, because there is no underlying fact that is distinct from these convictions, the suggestion that the convictions could be mere illusions loses its basis.

above—without the possibility of freedom no complete explanation of the world is possible [KrV, III, 363; see also KpV, V, 48]. From a theoretical viewpoint, all we could do was to assume the possibility of transcendental freedom as a regulative idea. Now, however, on the basis of the moral law as a fact of reason, we have given objective reality to the concept of freedom, even if only from a practical point of view, and have thus grounded the "keystone of the whole architecture of the system of pure reason" [KpV, V, 3][32]. Thus, Kant holds, if any further justification were required for accepting the validity of the moral law, it would be provided by the fact that doing so allows us to establish the objective reality of the notion of our transcendental freedom that, in his view, no worldview satisfying rational standards can do without:

> Diese Art von Creditiv des moralischen Gesetzes, da es selbst als ein Prinzip der Deduktion der Freiheit als einer Kausalität der reinen Vernunft aufgestellt wird, ist, da die theoretische Vernunft wenigstens die Möglichkeit einer Freiheit anzunehmen genötigt war, zur Ergänzung eines Bedürfnisses derselben statt aller Rechtfertigung a priori völlig hinreichend. Denn das moralische Gesetz beweiset seine Realität dadurch auch für die Kritik der spekulativen Vernunft genugtuend, dass es einer bloß negativ gedachten Kausalität, deren Möglichkeit jener unbegreiflich und dennoch sie anzunehmen nötig war, positive Bestimmung... hinzufügt und so der Vernunft, die mit ihren Ideen, wenn sie spekulativ verfahren wollte, immer überschwänglich wurde, zum ersten Mal objektive, obgleich nur praktische Realität zu geben vermag. [KpV, V, 48][33]

---

32 Kant highlights the foundational role played by the argument grounding the objective reality of our transcendental freedom in his 1796 essay *Von einem Neuerdings Erhobenen Vornehmen Ton in der Philosophie:* "Hier ist nun das, was Archimedes bedurfte, aber nicht fand: ein fester Punkt, woran die Vernunft ihren Hebel ansetzen kann, und zwar, ohne ihn weder an die gegenwärtige, noch eine künftige Welt, sondern bloß an ihre innere Idee der Freiheit, die durch das unerschütterliche moralische Gesetz als sichere Grundlage darliegt, anzulegen, um den menschlichen Willen selbst beim Widerstande der ganzen Natur durch ihre Grundsätze zu bewegen" [VT, VIII, 403].

33 The grounding of the objective validity of the ideas of reason from a practical point of view is already foreshadowed in *Kritik der Reinen Vernunft*, where Kant writes: „Indessen muss es doch irgendwo einen Quell von positiven Erkenntnissen geben, welche ins Gebiet der reinen Vernunft gehören, und die vielleicht nur durch Missverstand zu Irrtümern Anlass geben, in der Tat aber das Ziel der Beeiferung der Vernunft ausmachen. Denn welcher Ursache sollte sonst wohl die nicht zu dämpfende Begierde, durchaus über die Grenze der Erfahrung hinaus irgendwo festen Fuß zu fassen, zuzuschreiben sein? Sie ahndet Gegenstände, die ein großes Interesse für sie bei sich führen. Sie tritt den Weg der bloßen Spekulation an, um sich ihnen zu nähern; aber diese fliehen vor ihr. Vermutlich wird auf dem einzigen Wege, der ihr noch übrig ist, *nämlich dem des praktischen Gebrauchs*, besseres Glück für sie zu hoffen sein" [KrV, III, 517; my emphasis].

As in *Grundlegung*, we have to be careful not to overlook the idealistic character of Kant's argument. In spite of the fact that Kant's argument aims to establish the objective reality of our transcendental freedom, this freedom continues to be a mere idea of reason—albeit one that has objective reality for us: "Denn in der Tat versetzt uns das moralische Gesetz *der Idee nach* in eine Natur, in welcher reine Vernunft, wenn sie mit dem ihr angemessenen physischen Vermögen begleitet wäre, das höchste Gut hervorbringen würde, und bestimmt unseren Willen die Form der Sinnenwelt, als einem Ganzen vernünftiger Wesen, zu erteilen" [KpV, V, 43, my emphasis]. The only experience we have of ourselves is as sensuous beings in the empirical realm. It is only to give a coherent account of our condition as agents and, in particular, as agents confronted with the unconditional demands of the moral law, that we are entitled—and required—to regard the idea of our own transcendental freedom as having objective reality for us.

As in *Grundlegung*, Kant links the notion of our noumenal will with that of a higher more dignified existence ("[Das moralische Gesetz eröffnet uns] eine Aussicht in eine höhere, unveränderliche Ordnung der Dinge, in der wir schon jetzt sind" [KpV, V, 107]). In both works, our noumenal existence is presented as an idealized vision of ourselves as pure rational activity. Thus, while the term of the "proper self", which Kant had used in *Grundlegung*, does not recur, the thought underlying this expression continues to be present[34].

Another important aspect of Kant's argument that we have to appreciate is the role played by the doctrine of practical knowledge. As we have seen above, in *Kritik der Reinen Vernunft* Kant holds that the empty space left by theory could be filled by "practical knowledge". He hinted that concepts could be given objective reality for us on the basis not of the intuitions of the senses, but rather by "practical data". In that work, Kant left open what these practical data were. His argument in *Kritik der Praktischen Vernunft* now elucidates this notion: the datum that we are confronted with in our experience as agents, but not from a theoretical perspective, is our awareness of being confronted with the unconditional demands of the moral law[35].

---

[34] This position is maintained throughout his mature work, in which Kant holds that it is only insofar as we attribute a noumenal will—and, hence, transcendental freedom—to ourselves that we are entitled (and required) to regard ourselves as having dignity and as being ends in ourselves [MS, VI, 434–5; see also: Chapter 6]. The identification of our noumenal will with our "true self" is recognized by Ameriks [2005, 279].

[35] "Die Bestimmung der Kausalität der Wesen in der Sinnenwelt als einer solchen konnte niemals unbedingt sein, und dennoch muss es zu aller Reihe der Bedingungen notwendig etwas Unbedingtes, mithin auch eine sich gänzlich von selbst bestimmende Kausalität geben. Daher war die Idee der Freiheit als eines Vermögens absoluter Spontaneität nicht ein Bedürfnis, son-

Our reconstruction of Kant's argument of the fact of reason reveals the deep significance of his transcendental idealism for his practical philosophy[36]: the critical program in his theoretical philosophy has considerably reduced the set of respectable judgments (by tightening the conditions for a concept to count as having objective reality). As a consequence, many judgments, which express possible thoughts, can no longer be legitimately asserted within a purely theoretical context. Yet—and that is the crucial point—Kant does not insist that these judgments are therefore useless. Rather, he acknowledges that many of these (such as the ones concerning our own freedom and the validity of the moral law) matter deeply to us, even if they cannot be shown to be true from a purely theoretical point of view.

As we have seen, his doctrine of practical knowledge is the position that if the truth-value of a given judgment cannot be settled by merely theoretical considerations, and if, furthermore, necessary practical interests constrain us to take that judgment to be true and if, lastly, taking the judgment to be true does not result in any contradictions in our worldview, then it is, for all practical purposes, not only legitimate but even necessary for us to accept the judgment as true— and, hence, the concepts contained in it as having objective reality ("[D]ie Möglichkeit, die vorher nur Problem war, [wird] hier Assertion" [KpV, V, 4]). In this sense, Kant claims that he had to restrict theory to create space for faith [KrV, III, 19]—where faith is understood very broadly as the commitments we have from the perspective of the agent: "Es gibt also ein unbegrenztes, aber auch unzugängliches Feld für unser gesamtes Erkenntnisvermögen, nämlich das Feld des Übersinnlichen... ein Feld, welches wir zwar zum Behuf des theoretischen sowohl als praktischen Gebrauchs der Vernunft mit Ideen besetzen müssen, denen wir aber in Beziehung auf die Gesetze aus dem Freiheitsbegriffe keine andere als praktische Realität verschaffen können, wodurch demnach

---

dern, was deren Möglichkeit betrifft, ein analytischer Grundsatz der reinen spekulativen Vernunft. Allein [ist] es schlechterdings unmöglich... , ihr gemäß ein Beispiel in irgend einer Erfahrung zu geben, weil unter den Ursachen der Dinge als Erscheinungen keine Bestimmung der Kausalität, die schlechterdings unbedingt wäre, angetroffen werden kann... Ich konnte aber diesen Gedanken nicht realisieren, d. i. ihn nicht in Erkenntnis eines so handelnden Wesens auch nur bloß seiner Möglichkeit nach verwandeln. *Diesen leeren Platz füllt nun reine praktische Vernunft durch ein bestimmtes Gesetz der Kausalität in einer intelligibelen Welt (durch Freiheit), nämlich das moralische Gesetz, aus*" [KpV, V, 48–49; my emphasis].

36 This casts doubt on the viability of Rawls' project of offering a Kantian theory of justice that is freed from a grounding in Kant's transcendental idealism: "The problem is this: to develop a viable Kantian conception of justice the force and content of Kant's doctrine must be detached from its background in transcendental idealism and given a procedural interpretation by means of the construction of the original position" [1977, 165].

unser theoretisches Erkenntnis nicht im Mindesten zu dem Übersinnlichen erweitert wird" [KU, V, 175][37].

After clarifying these aspects of Kant's argument in *Kritik der Praktischen Vernunft*, we should take a moment to address the doubts that have been voiced about this argument. We have already discussed the first of these, namely the suggestion that the very notion of an *a priori* fact is unintelligible. Our discussion of this point partly addresses the second charge, namely that the notion of an *a priori* fact introduces an element of intuitionism into Kant's theory. For this would apply only if Kant's argument involved the claim that we have a special faculty for apprehending *a priori* truths. Yet, as we have seen, there is no suggestion to this effect in Kant's text. Rather, he takes our ordinary moral experience as a given—and develops a view of ourselves as agents that allows us to account for the salient feature of our practical experience. While Kant's argument does involve the immediate presence of moral demands in our consciousness, its status as a "fact of reason" is not secured by an act of intuition [KpV, V, 31], but by a process of reflection. It is, as Beck puts it, "a fact known reflexively, not intuitively" [1965, 210].

Yet, this answer opens the path for another charge, namely that Kant leaves the starting point of his argument, our consciousness of a necessary law, unexplained[38]. This charge, however, misses the point of Kant's argument. He is just as little concerned with explaining *why* we are aware of the demands of the moral law in his practical argument as he is concerned with explaining *why* we experience the world as structured by natural causality or embedded in

---

[37] Kant himself emphasizes the importance of being familiar with his preparatory work in *Kritik der Reinen Vernunft* for a correct understanding of his argument in *Kritik der Praktischen Vernunft* in the foreword of that latter work: "[Es ist wichtig,] die Idee des Ganzen richtig zu fassen und aus derselben alle jene Teile in ihrer wechselseitigen Beziehung auf einander vermittelst der Ableitung derselben von dem Begriffe jenes Ganzen in einem reinen Vernunftvermögen ins Auge zu fassen. Diese Prüfung und Gewährleistung ist nur durch die innigste Bekanntschaft mit dem System [also dem philosophischen System Kants] möglich, und die, welche in Ansehung der ersteren Nachforschung [in der *Kritik der Reinen Vernunft*] verdrossen gewesen, also diese Bekanntschaft zu erwerben nicht der Mühe wert geachtet haben, gelangen nicht zur zweiten Stufe, nämlich der Übersicht, welche eine synthetische Wiederkehr zu demjenigen ist, was vorher analytisch gegeben worden, und es ist kein Wunder, wenn sie allerwärts Inkonsequenzen finden, obgleich die Lücken, die diese vermuten lassen, nicht im System selbst, sondern bloß in ihrem eigenen unzusammenhängenden Gedankengange anzutreffen sind" [KpV, V, 10].
[38] As Fichte puts it: "Des kategorischen Imperatives ist man nach Kant sich doch wohl bewusst? Was ist denn dies nun für ein Bewusstsein? Diese Frage vergaß Kant sich vorzulegen, wie er nirgends die Grundlage aller Philosophie behandelte" [quoted in Brandt, 2007, 355].

space and time in his theoretical investigations[39]. He is explicit about the fact that no such explanation is possible—either in the practical case ("Wie nun dieses Bewusstsein der moralischen Gesetze oder, welches einerlei ist, das der Freiheit möglich sei, lässt sich nicht weiter erklären, nur die Zulässigkeit derselben in der theoretischen Kritik gar wohl verteidigen" [KpV, V, 46]) or the theoretical[40]. What we are confronted with here is a sheer given, a brute datum. These are features of our existence that we find present as soon as we become aware of ourselves. All we can do is to give an account of these features of our experience of the world and of ourselves in a way that makes them fit into a self-consistent, complete worldview, i.e. a worldview that satisfies rational standards. The moral skeptic could reply that he is not aware of the moral law, just as the theoretical skeptic could claim that he, in fact, does not perceive the world as embedded in space and time. Kant would have nothing to say in reply. For his argument is merely aimed at allowing us to account for a feature of our common experience (space and time in the theoretical field, the moral law in the practical field). He tries to help us to understand the implication of our shared moral consciousness, which he takes as a given—his aim is not to force such a moral consciousness onto us.

A further worry is that voiced by Karl Ameriks who sees Kant's argument as a step back into dogmatism [2005, 192]. In reply to this charge we should note that while Kant's position in *Kritik der Praktischen Vernunft* is a step back from his position in *Grundlegung* (in that the project of providing a strong deduction of the moral law is given up), it is nonetheless well grounded in his critical theory, better perhaps than the argument in *Grundlegung*. For only in *Kritik der Praktischen Vernunft* does Kant offer a full-fledged and coherent (if cryptic) application of his doctrine of practical knowledge, which allows one of the most profound

---

[39] This is noted by Brandt: "Wer eine andere, durch keine Einflüsterungen verdorbene Person fragt, warum sie nicht einfach lügt und sich so aus einer beklemmenden Lage hilft, gleicht jemandem, der eine andere Person fragt, warum sie Gegenstände in Raum und Zeit erkennt. Die gefragte Peson ist perplex und kann nicht antworten, es sei denn, ihr stehe in einer Metaebene das Instrument der kritischen Philosophie zur Verfügung, die umständlich und kompliziert die Nichtbeantwortbarkeit der beiden Fragen demonstrieren kann. Teufeln ist dieses Faktum des Bewusstseins so wenig zu übermitteln, wie man Wesen, die keine Raum- und Zeitanschauung haben, telefonisch von deren nicht-diskursiver Qualität berichten können: ‚Raum und Zeit sind folgendermaßen beschaffen'..." [2007, 355].

[40] "Von der Eigentümlichkeit unsers Verstandes aber, nur vermittelst der Kategorien und nur gerade durch diese Art und Zahl derselben Einheit der Apperzeption a priori zu Stande zu bringen, lässt sich eben so wenig ferner ein Grund angeben, als warum wir gerade diese und keine andere Funktionen zu Urteilen haben, oder warum Zeit und Raum die einzigen Formen unserer möglichen Anschauung sind" [KrV, III, 116].

aspects of his transcendental idealism to come into play—namely, the possibility of ascribing objective reality to concepts on the basis of practical interests. As we have seen, far from being an *ad hoc* contraption, this argument has been prepared for since the inception of Kant's transcendental idealism in *Kritik der Reinen Vernunft*. Thus, far from constituting a move away from his transcendental idealism, the argument in *Kritik der Praktischen Vernunft* makes full use of the possibilities opened up by that doctrine.

However, the observation that the tone of *Kritik der Praktischen Vernunft* is more dogmatic than that in *Kritik der Reinen Vernunft* [Vaihinger, 2007, 652] is nonetheless correct. Yet, the preceding discussion suggests that this might have to do less with a change in the author's position—and more with the nature of the topic: in *Kritik der Reinen Vernunft*, Kant is concerned with restricting the field of possible knowledge, cutting back our pretense to know what cannot be known. In *Kritik der Praktischen Vernunft*, on the other hand, the resulting empty space is filled with something that is not knowledge, but serves—for all practical purposes—as a substitute. That is, it is due to the role *Kritik der Praktischen Vernunft* plays in Kant's wider philosophical project that the tone in that work is assertive where that of *Kritik der Reinen Vernunft* was critical.

Yet, it is important not to mistake the assertive tone of *Kritik der Praktischen Vernunft* for dogmatism. Dogmatism, for Kant, is the assertion of judgments that have not be checked by criticism [KrV, III, 31]. It is the assumption of truths without addressing the question of the 'quid juris?'—i.e. the question concerning our right to accept the truth of the judgment in question. Yet, in the current case that question has been posed—and answered: because from a theoretical point of view, the validity of the moral law (and the objective reality of our own transcendental freedom) cannot be established and its impossibility cannot be proved and, furthermore, because we are confronted with the awareness of the unconditional demands of the moral law when considering how to act, we are entitled, on the strength of the doctrine of practical knowledge, to accept the objective validity of the moral law for us (and to infer the reality of our own transcendental freedom from this).

Before concluding, we should note two implications of our results so far. First, with the objective reality of the moral law for us now established, we are in a position to make sense of Kant's dictum that "from ought follows can", i.e. the claim that if we have a duty to do x then it must be possible for us to do x ("Er urteilt also, dass er etwas kann, darum weil er sich bewusst ist, dass er es soll" [KpV, V, 30]). Like the doctrine of practical knowledge, this dictum is grounded in Kant's notion of the unity of reason: given that both the laws of nature and the moral law are, according to Kant's transcendental idealism, legislated by our reason, reason would be contradicting itself if the moral law imposed duties on us which it would be impossible to discharge [KU, V, 471n]. For in that case reason (in the form of the moral law) would demand something of us which reason itself (in the form of the laws of nature) would make impossible for us to do. Thus, in order to ensure that our worldview is free of contradictions (and, hence, consistent with reason's interest in systematic unity), we have to assume that if we have a duty to do x, then it is possible to do x.

Secondly, our interpretation of Kant's notion of the fact-of-reason allows us to elucidate the relation between the arguments offered in *Grundlegung* and *Kritik der Praktischen Vernunft*. There has been some debate about whether Kant's position in the latter work constitutes a "great reversal", as Ameriks has claimed [2005, 192], or involves an argument that was in essence already present in *Grundlegung*, as asserted by Henrich [1975, 88]. Our analysis suggests that this difference in interpretation is due to the gap between the argument Kant *claims to* offer in *Grundlegung* and the argument that he in fact *does* offer. If we look at Kant's planned program for that work (to offer a deduction of the moral law from the notion of freedom), then his position in *Kritik der Praktischen Vernunft* (where he offers a deduction of our freedom from the notion of the moral law) must appear to be a dramatic reversal. If, however, we consider the central step in the argument that he does in fact offer in *Grundlegung*—namely, one from the implicit assumption of a will subject to the moral law to our transcendental freedom –, the continuity with the argument structure in *Kritik der Praktischen Vernunft* becomes apparent[41]. In fact, we can speculate, as we have in fact done, about whether Kant's argument in the latter work has its form in part because he became clearer on the argument he had in fact offered in *Grundlegung*.

Conclusion

Kant's argument concerning the moral law has a double purpose: to elucidate the notion of the moral law (an answer to the question of the 'quid facti')— and to offer an argument to show that this law applies to us (an answer to the

---

41 Henrich: "[D]as Programm der zweiten Kritik [entfaltet sich] im wesentlichen in Übereinstimmung mit dem Argument, das Kants ‚Grundlegung' im wesentlichen gegeben hat, wenn auch im Gegensatz zu der Selbstdarstellung, die in ihr dominant ist. Die zweite Kritik lässt nur noch eine Deduktion der Freiheit zu. Die des sittlichen Bewusstseins schließt sie ausdrücklich aus, eben deshalb, weil sie keinen hinreichenden Ansatz in einer von sittlichen Überzeugungen gänzlich unabhängigen Kritik des Subjekts finden kann... Sobald diese Unterscheidung ausdrücklich gemacht war, musste auch das Theorem vom Sittengesetz als einem ‚Faktum der Vernunft' formuliert werden" [1975, 99].

question of the 'quid juris'). In discussing the first question regarding the content of the notion of the moral law, Kant claims that part of our common understanding of that notion is that the moral law makes unconditional demands on us, i.e., demands that are valid regardless of any idiosyncratic interests or desires we might happen to have. Building on his results in *Kritik der Reinen Vernunft*, Kant holds that the only way to account for the possibility of the unconditional demands made on us by the moral law is to regard the law as valid *a priori*—that is, as imposed on us by our own pure faculties (where "pure faculty", for Kant, has the specific technical meaning of a non-empirical faculty of the mind). Thus, in order to show how a necessary practical law is possible, we have to regard ourselves as having noumenal existence—i.e., we have to accept an idealized vision of ourselves as pure practical reason, unencumbered by the demands of our sensuous nature and guiding ourselves purely on the basis of the interests of reason.

In trying to establish the validity of the moral law for us, Kant makes use of his doctrine of practical knowledge, according to which we are entitled (and required) to accept the objective reality of a concept if the question regarding its reality can neither be established nor disproven from a theoretical perspective and if we have a necessary practical interest in accepting it. In *Grundlegung*, he holds that the validity of the concept of our own transcendental freedom can be established in this way. He argues that we are aware of guiding our actions on the basis of our reason—and in doing so, have to regard our reason as guided by its own principles, i.e. as free. Given the doctrine of practical knowledge in combination with the fact that our freedom can neither be established nor disproven from a theoretical perspective, this means that our freedom has objective reality for us, if only from a practical perspective. To account for the possibility of our freedom, we have to regard our will as having noumenal existence and, consequently, as being governed by the law of freedom, i.e. the moral law.

The problem with this argument is that it does not deliver on its promise to establish the validity of the moral law from purely non-moral premises. On scrutiny, it emerges that the argument is built on a hidden moral premise, namely that we have to conceive of our will as guided by the laws of reason. Yet, for Kant the laws of reason *are* the moral law. Thus, the conclusion, which the argument in *Grundlegung* was set to establish, has effectively been smuggled into the argument as a premise.

In *Kritik der Praktischen Vernunft*, Kant builds his argument on an explicitly moral premise—namely, that it is part of our common experience as agents that, in acting, we are aware of the unconditional demands made on us by the moral law. Reflection on this awareness leads us to recognize that the only coherent way to account for its possibility is to regard the moral demands as issued by our pure reason, that is, by our own will conceived as noumenally free. Given the doctrine of practical knowledge, this entitles and requires us to regard our own freedom as objectively real. While this argument is no longer a strong deduction (i.e. an argument aiming to establish the objective validity of the moral law from non-moral premises), it nonetheless confers legitimacy on the notion by showing how the fact of the moral law's validity for us forms part of a coherent vision of ourselves as agents in a deterministic world.

These results are doubtless more modest than Kant's readers, and perhaps even Kant himself, would have hoped for. Yet, Kant came to believe that this was the best that could be achieved. The philosopher's stone—the explanation of how the moral law can motivate us—is not to be found[42]. All we can do is start from the fact that the moral law seems to have the power to move us to action and give an account of our condition as agents that allows us to account for the possibility of this fact. Indeed, it is, for Kant, only because of our being subject to the moral imperative that we have grounds to ascribe transcendental freedom to ourselves—and thus conceive of ourselves as free agents rather than merely parts of a world governed by natural necessity[43].

---

[42] Rosen seems to disagree on this point, suggesting that once we come to regard the moral law as self-imposed we thereby establish a sufficient reason to follow it: "Once a rational being has decided to impose a law on himself... he does not need additional reasons for obeying such a law. The reasons he has for choosing to impose the law on himself are ipso facto reasons for obeying it. Choosing to impose a law on oneself entails choosing to obey it... The principle of autonomy is therefore unconditional because it rests ultimately on the law of non-contradiction, which, like all rules of logic, is unconditionally valid, as both a theoretical and practical norm, for all rational beings" [Rosen, 1993, 61; see also: Allison, 1990, 237]. According to this argument, Kant would have discovered the philosopher's stone after all, despite his own avowals of the modesty of his results, by showing that a common sense understanding of morality, on reflection, commits us to regarding the moral law as self-imposed, in a way that not following it would involve self-contradiction. The problem with this argument is that the self-imposition of the moral law is a merely postulated act, committed by our (equally postulated) pure will, while the decision to follow it is one we have to make as agents in the empirical realm. Thus, for Rosen's argument to work we have to show that we, as empirical agents, have reason to identify with the idealized vision of ourselves as noumenal wills. Yet, Kant's argument is built on the premise that the only ground for our attributing a noumenal will to ourselves is our consciousness of the demands the moral law makes on us. Hence, we cannot, within the context of this argument, use the identity of our empirical self and ourselves as noumenal will to establish that we have reason to follow the moral law without running into the kind of circularity that plagued Kant's argument in *Grundlegung*.

[43] Henrich: "Das Subjekt der Gedanken könnte auch der Materie entstammen. Das sittliche Selbst aber kann sich nur aus Freiheit verstehen, obschon es seine Freiheit theoretisch niemals erkennen wird. Erst im Praktischen gewinnt das Ich ein Verhältnis zum intelligiblen Grunde

seines Seins... Das sittliche Subjekt kann nur sein, was es ist, indem es an die Möglichkeit glaubt, dem einsichtigen Anspruch zu entsprechen. Diese Gewissheit ist in der bekannten Formel ‚Du kannst, denn Du sollst' ausgesprochen... Die Folgerung ist keine theoretische Konsequenz, sondern die Explikation der sittlichen Einsicht durch sie selbst... Es ist der Standpunkt von Hutcheson, die Skepsis in Beziehung auf eine theoretische Grundlegung der Ethik, den sie nun auf einer höheren Stufe wiederholt" [1973, 248].

5 The will

In the previous chapter, we have explored Kant's solution to the problem we started out with in Chapter 1—namely, that of the real possibility of our transcendental freedom. We are now in a position to understand how we can assert that we are endowed with a transcendentally free will in spite of the fact that we live as part of a world governed by natural necessity. With the objective reality of our transcendental freedom thus established, we can turn to Kant's theory of the will. Kant emphasizes that the fact that we are transcendentally free does not mean that our actions are necessarily guided by the moral law. Rather, as finite rational beings—i.e. as beings endowed both with reason and sensuous nature— we find ourselves confronted with two different sets of interests when determining of our actions: our reason's interests (as codified in the moral law) and the interests we have as sensuous beings in the satisfaction of our desires. Consequently, Kant's theory of the will, as his theory of cognition, is marked by the interplay between that which is rational and that which is sensuous. In the present chapter, we will explore this interplay in detail.

The faculty of desire

Kant defines desire (*Begierde*) as the possible determination of our actions on the basis of a feeling of pleasure that is linked to the mental representation of a possible object or state of affairs[1]. He calls the faculty of desire (*Begehrungsvermögen*) a being's ability to make itself, by means of such a mental representation, the cause of the realization of the object: "Das Begehrungsvermögen ist das Vermögen [eines Wesens], durch seine Vorstellungen Ursache von der Wirklichkeit der Gegenstände dieser Vorstellungen zu sein" [KpV, V, 9; see also: MS, VI, 211]. The connative factor in this picture, i.e. the element triggering the

---

[1] "Man kann die Lust, welche mit dem Begehren (des Gegenstandes, dessen Vorstellung das Gefühl so affiziert) notwendig verbunden ist, praktische Lust nennen... Was... die praktische Lust betrifft, so wird die Bestimmung des Begehrungsvermögens, vor welcher diese Lust als Ursache notwendig vorhergehen muss, im engen Verstande Begierde, die habituelle Begierde aber Neigung heißen" [MS, VI, 212; see also A, VII, 251]. Wood comments: "To desire an object (or state of affairs) [according to Kant] is to have a representation of it accompanied by a feeling of pleasure... In the case of empirical desire, the feeling of pleasure comes about through the way the representation of the object affects our susceptibility to feeling, and the feeling is called an 'impulse' (*Antrieb*)" [1999, 50].

action, is the feeling of pleasure that accompanies the mental representation [MS, VI, 399].

Thus, the faculty of desire is a kind of cause: we experience pleasure envisaging an object or state of affairs and—guided by this mental representation—bring it about. This causality is distinguished from mechanical causality (the one involved, say, when one billiard ball hits another one and causes it to move) by the element of mental mediation: our actions are brought about by a mental representation, while no such representation plays a role in the case of the billiard ball. In this sense, the faculty of desire is a teleological—i.e. aim-directed—cause. It is guided by a preconception of its effects, in a way that mechanical causes are not [KU, V, 172; see also: MS, VI, 21].

For Kant, this causality mediated by mental mediation is the distinguishing trait of living beings [KpV, V, 9]. Thus, we share the faculty of desire with animals: our actions and theirs do not come about because we are being pushed by external forces, as is the case of unanimated objects. The stimulus that is external in the latter case is internalized: a desired object or state of affairs is the object of a mental representation—and this representation, in combination with a feeling of pleasure, leads to action[2]. Let us call this the *first internalization*.

This process of internalization does not necessarily mean that the resulting action is any freer or more self-determined than the movement of the billiard ball. Animals, Kant holds, are driven to action by their desires with the same necessity as the ball is being moved by the external shock. Their faculty of desire is "pathologically determined" [KrV, III, 521]—that is to say, physical impulses, like hunger, thirst, etc., linked to the feeling of pleasure and displeasure, in combination with the mental representation of the desired object or state of affairs are being translated directly into action, without the mind which experiences the mental representation having any influence on the process. Animals' actions thus involve mental representation, but are nonetheless direct consequences

---

2 Kant contrasts his position that all living beings—human beings as well as animals—act on the basis of mental representations with Descartes' view of animals as mechanical automata: "[A]us der ähnlichen Wirkungsart der Tiere (wovon wir den Grund nicht unmittelbar wahrnehmen können), mit der des Menschen (dessen wir uns unmittelbar bewusst sind) verglichen, können wir ganz richtig nach der Analogie schließen, dass die Tiere auch nach Vorstellungen handeln (nicht, wie Cartesius will, Maschinen sind) und ungeachtet ihrer spezifischen Verschiedenheit doch der Gattung nach (als lebende Wesen) mit dem Menschen einerlei sind" [KU, V, 464n]. On this point, see [Beck, 1960, 91] and [Wood, 1999, 234].

of physical impulses[3]. The resulting actions merely happen to the body in question—they are not actions in the proper sense.

Negative freedom

However, as finite *rational* beings[4], we—unlike animals—experience our faculty of desire as guided by conscious thought [KU, V, 172; see also: KpV, 58–9]. As we have seen in Chapter 1 above, conscious thought is, for Kant, rule-governed. Consequently, he sees rational beings not as acting directly on the representation of desired objects, but on the representation of rules [GMS, IV, 412; see also: KpV, V, 60]. This is Kant's definition of a will: it is the ability to guide one's faculty of desire according to the rules of thought, i.e. concepts ("Das Begehrungsvermögen, sofern es nur durch Begriffe… bestimmbar ist, würde der Wille sein", [KU, V, 220]). Kant calls the rules on the basis of which we act maxims. A maxim is "the subjective principle of our volition" [GMS, IV, 400]: it specifies an action that we are intending to perform in a given situation to achieve a given end. Crucially, in acting we experience ourselves as choosing the maxims for ourselves (they are "sich selbst auferlegte Regeln" [GMS, IV, 438; see also: MS, VI, 225]), rather than have them forced upon us by natural forces[5].

---

[3] "Die tierische Handlung ist ein *arbitrium brutum* und nicht *liberum*, weil sie durch Stimulus necessitiert werden kann… Die Tiere werden per Stimulus necessitiert. So muss ein Hund essen, wenn ihn hungert und er was vor sich hat; der Mensch kann sich aber in demselbigen Fall enthalten." [E, 1924, 34]

[4] Yovel points out that our status as *finite* rational beings in Kant's philosophical system is directly linked to his hybrid anthropology, discussed in Chapter 1 above: "Kant's radical split between reason and nature [is] a derivative of the duality of spontaneity and receptivity. This duality is the most fundamental principle of the critical system… The split between spontaneity and receptivity expresses the finitude of man, his being a 'limited rational being'. As such, man is no *intellectus archetypus*, but is bound by sense-perceptions in knowledge and by natural appetites and desires in action" [1989, 298–9]. Kant himself describes our finitude thus: "Eingeschränktheit der Natur eines Wesens… da die subjektive Beschaffenheit seiner Willkür mit dem objektiven Gesetze einer praktischen Vernunft nicht von selbst übereinstimmt" [KpV, V, 79]. For further discussion of Kant's conception of humans as finite rational beings, see [O'Neill, 1989, 72–77].

[5] Kantian maxims play a role not only in the practical context—i.e. in the context of determining our actions—, but are rules for the self-guided use of our reason more generally: "Ich nenne alle subjektive Grundsätze, die nicht von der Beschaffenheit des Objekts, sondern dem Interesse der Vernunft in Ansehung einer gewissen möglichen Vollkommenheit der Erkenntnis dieses Objekts hergenommen sind, Maximen der Vernunft" [KrV, III, 440]. See also: "Die Vernunfteinheit ist die Einheit des Systems, und diese systematische Einheit dient der Vernunft nicht objektiv zu

Thus, unlike in the case of animals, the mere presence of a desire, no matter how strong, does not necessarily lead to action [MS, VI, 226]. As agents, Kant holds, we experience ourselves as able to step back from our desires, reflect on the actions that would help us to satisfy them and decide whether or not to incorporate the satisfaction of a given desire as an end into our maxims. This is what Allison calls Kant's *Incorporation Thesis* [1990, 36][6]. Kant himself puts it thus:

> Die Freiheit der Willkür ist von der ganz eigentümlichen Beschaffenheit, dass sie durch keine Triebfeder zu einer Handlung bestimmt werden kann, als nur sofern der Mensch sie in seine Maxime aufgenommen hat (es sich zur allgemeinen Regel gemacht hat, nach der er sich verhalten will); so allein kann eine Triebfeder, welche sie auch sei, mit der absoluten Spontaneität der Willkür (der Freiheit) zusammen bestehen. [R, VI, 23][7]

Let us call this the *second internalization:* in comparison with the case of the animal and its *arbitrium brutum* (i.e., the faculty of desire that is determined directly by physical desires), human beings make a further part of the action their own. An animal, Kant holds, acts on the representation of a desired object or state of affairs, but the action is nonetheless determined by forces outside its own control, namely by the causal chains that lead it to feel hunger, thirst etc. For human beings, the desires our action aims at satisfying continue to be provided by our physical nature. However, they do not directly lead to action. Rather, we see the decision on whether or not to act on a given desire as lying with us: "Das Begehrungsvermögen nach Begriffen, sofern der Bestimmungsgrund desselben zur Handlung in ihm selbst, nicht in dem Objekte angetroffen wird,

---

einem Grundsatze, um sie über die Gegenstände, sondern subjektiv als Maxime, um sie über alles mögliche empirische Erkenntnis der Gegenstände zu verbreiten" [KrV, III, 448].

6 Allison: "[T]his account of spontaneity has a parallel in the theoretical sphere, where Kant contrasts the spontaneity of the understanding with the receptivity of sense... The main point is that the reception of sensible data is no more capable of accounting for cognition than being sensibly affected is sufficient to account for rational choice... In both domains... we might say that the mind is 'undetermined by the data', and that complete determination requires a contribution on the part of the subject. In the cognitive domain, this contribution (the act of spontaneity) amounts to a determination of the object, whereas in the practical domain it is a matter of self-determination" [1996, 132–3].

7 It remains unclear what the difference is, for Kant, between adopting a maxim and acting (on the maxim). He suggests that these are not the same thing when he writes that „zwischen der Maxime und der Tat ist noch ein großer Zwischenraum" [R VI, 46] and highlights the problem of weakness of will, i.e. a situation in which we adopt a maxim, but then fail to act on it [R, VI, 29]. Yet, he offers, to my knowledge, no account of what else is required, according to his theory of action, for the adoption of a maxim to translate into action.

heißt ein Vermögen nach Belieben zu tun oder zu lassen" [MS, VI, 213; see also: KpV, V, 98; R, VI, 49n][8]. In comparison with animals, we see ourselves as having "reflective distance" [Korsgaard, 2008, 32] to our desires: their mere presence does not push us to action; rather, in order for us to act on them we have to endorse them, have to *decide* to act on them[9].

Reason and the reflective distance it makes possible allow for a first degree of freedom, "negative freedom" in Kant's term, the freedom not to be necessitated by nature in our actions, but rather to enjoy self-determination: "Die Freiheit der Willkür ist jene Unabhängigkeit ihrer Bestimmung durch sinnliche Antriebe; dies ist der negative Begriff derselben. Der positive ist: das Vermögen der reinen Vernunft für sich selbst praktisch zu sein" [MS, VI, 213–4]. This notion of negative freedom is the same as that of practical freedom we have encountered in Chapter 1: it is the ability to guide our actions on the basis of consciously chosen rules[10], rather than being determined in our actions by our desires[11]. Conse-

---

8 "The Incorporation Thesis of itself entails that desires do not come with pre-assigned weights. On the contrary, it is the value placed on a desire or inclination by an agent that gives it its 'motivational force', its status as a reason to act" Alison [1996, 113].

9 As Allison highlights, this implies that even in the case of an action aimed to satisfy a physical desire there is an element of spontaneity on the part of the subject: "[E]ven in the case of desire-based actions, a rational agent is not regarded as being determined in a quasi-mechanistic fashion by the strongest desire (roughly the Leibniz-Hume model). On the contrary, to the extent to which such actions are taken as genuine expressions of agency and, therefore, as imputable, they are thought to involve an act of spontaneity on the part of the agent, through which the inclination or desire is deemed or taken as an appropriate basis of action" [1990, 39; see also: Prauss, 1982, 15]. Consequently, negative freedom presupposes transcendental freedom, without which it would collapse into merely psychological freedom, as discussed in the text below.

10 In *Kritik der Reinen Vernunft*, Kant argued that the application of rules requires the faculty of judgment to determine whether a given particular meets the criteria specified in the rule (for if we had a another rule fulfilling this role, this would give rise to an infinite regress [KrV, III, 131–2; see also: TP, VIII, 275]). For the case of maxims, this suggests that we require practical judgment to determine in which cases a given generic maxim finds application. "[A]s rules dictating action types rather than particular actions, maxims, like concepts, are general with respect to the number of possible items (actions) falling under them. Accordingly, there are always (in principle), at least, a number of distinct ways in which an agent can act upon a maxim... This indeterminacy leaves scope for practical judgment, both in deciding whether action on the maxim is appropriate in given circumstances and in determining how best to carry out the general policy in a particular situation" [Allison, 1990, 90; see also: Yovel, 1989, 220n]. However, Beck points out that Kant does not specifically discuss practical judgment [1960, 128]. For more discussion of the important (if implicit) notion of practical judgment, see O'Neill [1989, 160].

quently, it is a kind of freedom that we can have experience of (i.e., in acting we experience ourselves as able to choose whether or not to act in a given way [KrV, III, 521])[12]. However, while we experience ourselves as being free to choose our own action, this experience does not preclude the possibility that our choice is itself subject to causal necessity (see Chapter 1). As we have explored in the previous chapter, it is only because we have an independent reason to assume the objective reality of our transcendental freedom—in the form of our awareness of the moral law as an *a priori* fact of reason –, that we are entitled, when reflecting on our status as agents, to attribute objective reality to our transcendental freedom[13]. That is, we are warranted in regarding our decisions on how to act as themselves starting causal chains, without them being, in turn, causally determined[14].

Given that a maxim we choose not only specifies the action we intend to perform, but also the end we aim to achieve, being free to choose our own maxims

---

[11] Compare Kant's definition of the notion of practical freedom in *Kritik der Reinen Vernunft* ("Die Freiheit im praktischen Verstande ist die Unabhängigkeit der Willkür von der Nötigung durch Antriebe der Sinnlichkeit" [KrV, III, 363]) with that of the notion of negative freedom in *Metaphysik der Sitten* cited in the text above ("Die Freiheit der Willkür ist jene Unabhängigkeit ihrer Bestimmung durch sinnliche Antriebe; dies ist der negative Begriff derselben. Der positive ist: das Vermögen der reinen Vernunft für sich selbst praktisch zu sein" [MS, VI, 213–4]).

[12] Thus, according to Kant we can have experience of our practical freedom, but not of our transcendental freedom. This confuses Sala, who, not distinguishing carefully between the two different conceptions of freedom, believes that Kant is contradicting himself on this point: "[Laut der KpV kann] ‚keine Erfahrung'... das Vermögen der Freiheit beweisen. Im Kanon-Hauptstück der KrV dagegen hieß es zweimal, dass 'praktische Freiheit durch Erfahrung bewiesen werden kann'" [2004, 127].

[13] This is noted by Beck: "Kant is insistent, in both [*Kritik der Reinen Vernunft* and *Kritik der Praktischen Vernunft*], on the necessity of transcendental freedom if practical freedom is to be real" [1960, 189–90].

[14] In discussing Kant's conceptions of freedom, we should bear in mind that our transcendental freedom is not a theoretical fact about the world, but only established from the practical point of view. From a theoretical standpoint—that is, when seeing man as a natural being in a deterministic world—we have to conclude that all human actions are predetermined and, therefore, not free [KpV, V, 94]. From a practical perspective, however,—that is, as agents seeing themselves confronted with the demands of the moral law—we are entitled to regard ourselves as free to decide on how to act. As I have argued in Chapter 2 above, Kant's theoretical philosophy should be understood to involve the project of constructing a logic of justification for statements backed not by theoretical, but by practical data (i.e. data available only from our perspective as agents). Only on the basis of this preparatory work can we make sense of his reference to the "practical point of view".

means being free to choose our own ends (*Zweck*)[15]. Crucially, it is only because of our reflective distance that there is such a thing as an end—for an end, Kant holds, is always the product of freedom, i.e. freely chosen: "[Niemand kann] einen Zweck haben..., ohne sich den Gegenstand seiner Willkür selbst zum Zweck zu machen, so ist es ein Akt der Freiheit des handelnden Subjekts, nicht eine Wirkung der Natur irgend einen Zweck der Handlungen zu haben" [MS, VI, 385]. In this sense, I can be forced to commit a certain act, but never to adopt a certain end [MS, VI, 381]. Animals, which, according to Kant, are causally necessitated to act, do not have ends [MS, VI, 392]. Only beings endowed with reason are capable of setting ends [GMS, IV, 437]. Reason can, thus, be regarded as the faculty of ends [KpV, V, 59][16]. This is a crucial point for understanding Kant's practical philosophy: there would be no ends in the world if it were not for rational willing. Ends only exist from the perspective of the rational will.

Furthermore, choosing a maxim involves determining the best available means to achieving our ends. Kant calls our ability to do so by means of self-reflective thought the technical-practical use of our practical reason [KU, V, 172][17].

---

15 Kant defines an end as the mental representation of an object or state of affairs which because of this mental representation gets realized in the world through the agency of a rational being ("[D]ie vorgestellte Wirkung, deren Vorstellung zugleich der Bestimmungsgrund der verständigen wirkenden Ursache zu ihrer Hervorbringung ist, heißt Zweck" [KU, V, 426; see also: MS, VI, 381]. In this sense, the rational will is teleological—i.e. aim-directed—causality: unlike in the case of mechanical causality, the process of willing starts with the mental representation of an intended effect, with that mental representation then leading to the realization of the effect in the world. Kant also refers to the end as the material content of our maxim [KpV, V, 21], as contrasted with its formal properties. Furthermore, the notion of an end is linked, for Kant, to that of pleasure. An end is an object in whose possession or realization we take pleasure: "Zweck ist jederzeit der Gegenstand einer Zuneigung, das ist, einer unmittelbaren Begierde zum Besitz einer Sache vermittelst seiner Handlung" [R, VI, 6n]. As we will explore in more detail in Chapter 6 below, Kant distinguishes between two kinds of interest—and, hence, two kinds of pleasure: namely, that linked to our sensual nature and that linked to our rational nature. Consequently, he distinguishes between two kinds of end, depending on whether its adoption its motivated by a sensual or a rational interest of ours.

16 In fact, there are two related senses in which reason is the faculty of ends. On the one hand, reason has its own essential ends, which, as an interested faculty, it aims to realize (in a way that, as we have highlighted in Chapter 1 above, we can say that reason is ultimately concerned only with itself, i.e. with the realization of its own ends). On the other hand, reason is the faculty of ends in the sense discussed in the text above, i.e. the faculty that allows us to choose our own ends freely.

17 Kant highlights the link between the technical-practical and the theoretical use of our reason: it is because of our theoretical knowledge of the world, our insight into the causal relations governing it, that we are in a position to determine effective means to bring about the desired end [KU, V, 173].

By allowing us to choose our actions in a way that makes them appropriate means for our end, our practical reason in its technical-practical use helps us to impose order on our behaviour. There is thus a parallel between the maxims of action in Kant's theory of the will and the rules of the understanding in his epistemology. Both serve to impose order on the naturally uncoordinated material content provided by our sensuous nature. Just as the rules of the understanding synthesize the intuitions of our senses into the coherent whole of the experience that we are conscious of, our maxims allow for an orderly pursuit of the satisfaction of our desires: "[In der technisch-praktischen Anwendung braucht] die Vernunft die Einheit der Maximen überhaupt, welche dem moralischen Gesetze eigen ist, bloß dazu…, um in die Triebfedern der Neigung unter dem Namen Glückseligkeit Einheit der Maximen, die ihnen sonst nicht zukommen kann, hinein zu bringen" [R, VI, 37; see also: KrV, III, 520; Wood, 1999, 56])[18].

We should note that even at the stage of negative freedom, feelings continue to play an important part in the determination of our action[19]. The feeling of pleasure linked to the representation of a certain possible object or state of affairs is the incentive (*Triebfeder*) for us to adopt the end of creating or obtaining it: "Alle Bestimmung der Willkür aber geht von der Vorstellung der möglichen Handlung durch das Gefühl der Lust oder Unlust, an ihr oder ihrer Wirkung ein Interesse zu nehmen, zur Tat" [MS, VI, 399][20]. That is, while we see ourselves as free to choose whether or not to incorporate a certain end into our maxims, our will remains linked to our sensuous nature in that the incentive to do so is provided by a feeling of pleasure linked to the mental representation of the end. In this sense, our will, while not determined in its choices by our sensuous desires, is still affected by them [MS, VI, 213].

---

18 Kant emphasizes a further parallel between the theoretical and the practical use of reason: in both cases, he holds, there is a merely instrumental use of reason (i.e. one in which it is used as an instrument for ends that are not its own—namely, the merely logical use in the theoretical sphere and the technical-practical one in the practical sphere)—and one in which it pursues its own interests (the hypothetical use of reason in the theoretical sphere, as discussed in Chapter 1 above, and reason's ability to guide itself on the basis of the moral law in the practical sphere). This is noted by Beck: "In addition to its real use in discovering or formulating the moral law, practical reason also has a merely logical use in the derivation of rules of actions either from the moral law or, in the case of prudence, from human desires and the laws of nature" [1960, 203; see also: O'Neill, 1989, 117].
19 This is recognized in Beck [1960, 223] and Wood [1999, 53].
20 In this sense, Kant calls the pleasure we take in the realization of the object of our will the "condition of the possibility of the determination of our will" ("Ein solches Verhältnis aber zum Subjekt heißt die Lust an der Wirklichkeit eines Gegenstandes. Also müsste diese als Bedingung der Möglichkeit der Bestimmung der Willkür vorausgesetzt werden" [KpV, V, 21]).

Thus, in his theory of the will, Kant is operating with the same hybrid anthropology that marks his theory of cognition: in both cases, the rule-guided spontaneity of our higher faculties imposes order on the raw material content provided by our senses. Hence, just as both our understanding and our senses are necessary for cognition, so both practical reason, as the source of our maxims, and our sensuous nature as the basis of our feelings are necessary for action[21]. Without practical reason, our actions would be mere mechanically caused events in the natural world, while without the emotional component of feelings, the rules we construe by means of self-reflective thought would not move us to action[22].

The highest maxim

The main challenge for Kant at this point is to explain what determines the choice of our maxims. The reason this is problematic is that we can give no explanation of freedom: for if we identified some event in the empirical world that caused our choice of maxim, we would have to regard the choice as governed by natural necessity—and, hence, as not free [R, VI, 25]. Conversely, if we regarded our choice—at least from the practical point of view[23]—as not determined by anything, it would just appear to be random. It would not be freedom, but mere chaos.

To be able to regard our maxims as freely chosen, Kant holds, we have to conceive them as determined by a highest maxim (*oberste Maxime*, [R, VI 31]), or *Gesinnung* [R, VI, 25][24], chosen by ourselves *qua* free intelligence, i.e. our nou-

---

21 "Kants Ansicht, dass die Beziehung des Objekts zum Begehrungsvermögen nur die der Lust oder Unlust sein kann, stellt offenbar das Pendant zu seiner Ansicht in der Erkenntnislehre dar, der zufolge die einzige Erkenntnishandlung, durch die ein Objekt dem Subjekt erkenntnismäßig gegeben werden kann, für uns Menschen die sinnliche Anschauung ist" [Sala, 2004, 88].

22 This parallel with Kant's theoretical philosophy is noted by Beck: "Kant says explicitly that there must be an object of desire if there is to be action at all... Content (object of desire) without form is blind impulse; form without object of desire is practically ineffective—this is as true of Kant's ethics as the corresponding sentence in the first *Critique* is of his theory of knowledge" [1960, 96].

23 This caveat is important, given that from a theoretical point of view, for any given event, being part of the continuum of cause and effect is a necessary condition for it to be part of the world of our experience.

24 Kant also refers to the highest maxim as "the first ground for adopting our maxims" [R, VI, 22], the "highest ground of all our maxims" [R, VI, 46], the "subjective principle of the use of our freedom" [R, VI, 21] and "the inner principle of our maxims" [R, VI, 22].

menal self[25]. Unlike the choice of the first-order maxims that determine our actions, the choice of this highest maxim is thus a mere postulate, i.e. an idea of reason[26]: "Von den freien Handlungen als solchen den Zeitursprung (gleich als von Naturwirkungen) zu suchen, ist [...] ein Widerspruch; mithin auch von der moralischen Beschaffenheit des Menschen, sofern sie als zufällig betrachtet wird, weil diese den Grund des Gebrauchs der Freiheit bedeutet, welcher [...] lediglich in Vernunftvorstellungen gesucht werden muss" [R, VI, 40][27].

That is, the choice of our highest maxim is not one we make as empirical agents in the world of our experience (who, after all, has any awareness of having chosen a highest maxim?)—but rather one that we attribute to our noumenal self. In consequence, Kant says about the choice of the highest maxim that it is "an intelligible deed"[28], that it is free[29] (i.e., not causally determined), that it takes place outside time[30] and that we can never be certain what our highest

---

[25] Kant only introduces the notion of the highest maxim in *Religion*. However, Allison argues that "[a]lthough Kant first explicates this conception [of a highest maxim or *Gesinnung*] in *Religion within the Limits of Reason Alone*..., it is already at work in the *Critique of Practical Reason* and is a key ingredient in his later account of virtue in *The Doctrine of Virtue* as well" [1990, 136].

[26] Much of the criticism that has been leveled against Kant's notion of the highest maxim is marred by a failure to understand the Kantian doctrine of the ideas of reason (for examples for such criticism, see the discussion in Allison [1990, 138–9]). These critics treat the highest maxim not as a regulative thought construct, but as something that has objective existence— and thus commit precisely the mistake of hypostatization of the ideas of reason that Kant had identified as the source of metaphysical error in *Kritik der Reinen Vernunft* [KrV, III, 460]. Even Yovel, who attributes much attention to Kant's notion of the ideas of reason, appears to misunderstand the status of the highest maxim as merely imputed when he writes: "The tie between the fundamental maxim and its particular expressions is one not of determination but of logical implication, requiring the free subject to draw this implication and implement it" [1989, 52–3]. Given that Kant is very clear about the fact that we can never know what our highest maxim is ([R, VI, 77; see also our discussion in the text below), the suggestion that we can somehow logically infer our first-order maxims from it is clearly mistaken.

[27] "[The choice of the highest maxim] is timeless or intelligible, not in the sense that it must be regarded as occurring in some timeless noumenal world but rather in the sense that it is not to be viewed as performed at a specific point in one's moral development... In effect, the assumption of such a propensity functions as a postulate of morally practical reason; something that must be presupposed both as a condition of the possibility of evil and... of the possibility of the attainment of virtue" [Allison, 1990, 154].

[28] "Jene ist intelligibele Tat, bloß durch Vernunft ohne alle Zeitbedingung erkennbar" [R, VI, 31].

[29] "Sie selbst aber muss auch durch freie Willkür angenommen worden sein, denn sonst könnte sie nicht zugerechnet werden" [R, VI, 25].

[30] "Die eine oder die andere Gesinnung als angeborne Beschaffenheit von Natur haben, bedeutet hier auch nicht, dass sie von dem Menschen, der sie hegt, gar nicht erworben, d. i. er nicht Urheber sei; sondern dass sie nur nicht in der Zeit erworben sei" [R, VI, 25].

maxim actually is³¹. That is, in our attempt to integrate that which is inexplicable (namely, how the free choice of maxims is possible) into a coherent and complete worldview, we have to accept the idea of the timeless choice by our noumenal self of a fundamental maxim that regulates the choice of our actual first-order maxims³². Only in this way, Kant holds, can we explain the possibility of free choice in a world of natural necessity³³.

There are, Kant thinks, only two principles that can serve as our highest maxim: the moral law and the principle of self-love. The reason for this is that according to Kant's conception of human nature, we only have two different sets of interests, namely the interests of our reason (as expressed in the moral law), on the one hand, and our sensuous desires and inclinations, on the other. The choice of the highest maxim is the decision of which of these sets of interests are to take precedence in the case of conflict [R, VI, 36].

Thus, for Kant our highest maxim is a mere thought construct we require to make sense of our condition as agents. In acting, we have to regard our actions as determined by maxims—and the choice of these maxims, in turn, as determined by a non-temporal, i.e. noumenal, and therefore merely posited, character (*Gesinnung*), which leads us to make either the moral law or the principle of self-love (i.e. of the satisfaction of our physical desires) the highest determinant of our actions—and thus to give either our interests as sensuous beings or our interests as rational beings precedence in situations in which they are in conflict³⁴.

We can call the case in which the moral law is the main determining ground of our action—i.e., where it is our highest maxim to follow the moral law—the *third internalization*. For in that case, the individual not only is brought to act

---

31 "[Er kann] von seiner wirklichen Gesinnung durch unmittelbares Bewusstsein gar keinen sichern und bestimmten Begriff bekommen, sondern ihn nur aus seinem wirklich geführten Lebenswandel abnehmen" [R, VI, 77].
32 The notion of the highest maxim enables us, furthermore, to conceive of our different actions not as unrelated events, but as part of a coherent life project. As with the ideas of reason in its theoretical application, the idea of the highest maxim allows us to regard that which we experience as separate (our individual experiences in the realm of cognition, our individual decisions on how to act in the realm of practice) as integrated into a unified whole.
33 "Kant's conception of Gesinnung... reflects his partial agreement with a tradition in moral psychology that stretches at least back to Aristotle and that includes, in addition to Leibniz and Hume, contemporary thinkers who insist that moral responsibility presupposes that actions be connected with the character of the agent... Kant breaks with this tradition... [in] his insistence that... an agent's Gesinnung is itself somehow chosen" [Allison, 1990, 137].
34 On the role of the highest maxim in Kant's theory of action, see Korsgaard [1996, 166–7] and Allison [1996, 116].

by means of a mental representation rather than external pushes and pulls (the first internalization) and has, through his reason, practical-technical control over the way in which he satisfies his desires (i.e., reflective distance, the second internalization), but his reason's own interests—that is, the interests of his "proper self" (see Chapter 4 above)—are now the prime determining factor of his actions (the third internalization). To have adopted the moral law as one's highest maxim is, in Kant's term, to have developed a *good will* [KpV, V, 79][35].

The crucial step between the second and the third internalization is that at the second, merely practical-technical stage, reason is in charge of choosing which desires to satisfy and how to satisfy them—yet, the standard that governs this choice (i.e. that which makes that certain options are judged to be more attractive than others) is provided by the pleasure linked to the mental representation of the various options, and thus is given to reason from the outside. In this sense, reason at the technical-practical stage is a mere servant to our physical desires [R, VI, 45]. Only at the third stage is reason in control of every step in the process of determining our action, in that the interests of reason itself, as codified in the moral law, become the highest criterion of choice in the determination of our actions. Given that, for Kant, we have to regard reason as our "proper self", only at this point do our actions cease to be ultimately determined by external factors and become fully our own.

However, even at this highest point of freedom Kant insists, our actions continue to be triggered by feelings: "Um das zu wollen, wozu die Vernunft allein dem sinnlich-affizierten vernünftigen Wesen das Sollen vorschreibt, dazu gehört freilich ein Vermögen der Vernunft, ein Gefühl der Lust oder des Wohlgefallens an der Erfüllung der Pflicht einzuflößen, mithin eine Kausalität derselben, die Sinnlichkeit ihren Prinzipien gemäß zu bestimmen" [GMS, IV, 460; see also KpV, V, 23; MS, VI, 399][36]. Kant calls this emotional component of the moral ac-

---

35 To have developed a good will is to be a good person ("[N]ur wenn der Mensch die für das moralische Gesetz in ihn gelegte Triebfeder in seine Maxime aufgenommen hat, wird er ein guter Mensch... genannt" [R, VI, 45])—and, hence, to have moral worth. O'Neill correctly notes that the question of moral worth is central to Kant's ethical project: "Kant is primarily concerned with judgments of moral worth... [This is easily forgotten] perhaps because he speaks of the Categorical Imperative as a test of duty, while we often tend to think of duty as confined to the outward aspects of action" [1989, 86]. See our discussion of this point in note 40 in Chapter 6 below.
36 Both Beck and Wood point out that the role played by moral feeling in Kant's practical philosophy is often overlooked by commentators: "It is hard to know whether the desiccated picture of Kant's personality as that of a *reiner Verstandesmensch* has led people to ignore his positive theory of the moral feeling or whether a caricature of his ethics as otherwordly has created the false picture of the man; but the two conceptions usually go together, and they are both wrong" [Beck, 1960, 223]. Wood comments: "Pure reason can determine the will because it is also a

tion the moral feeling, or respect (*Achtung*)[37]. He defines moral feeling as "the susceptibility to pleasure or pain merely from the consciousness of the fact that our actions are consistent with or contrary to the law of duty" [MS, VI, 399][38]. He holds that it is only because of the presence of a moral feeling that we are able to act morally, i.e. to adopt a maxim because doing so is demanded by the moral law: "[Das moralische Gefühl]... dient nicht zu Beurteilung der Handlungen, oder wohl gar zur Gründung des objektiven Sittengesetzes selbst, sondern bloß zur Triebfeder, um dieses in sich zur Maxime zu machen" [KpV, V, 76][39].

---

source of desire. The big mistake is to think that Kant regards moral truths (or our belief about them), as bringing about action in a way that is entirely distinct from (and even precludes) desire" [1999, 53n; see also: Guyer, 2010, 142; Schönecker, 2013, 32].

[37] Beck is mistaken when he claims that "in the Metaphysics [of Morals] moral feeling is not equated with respect, while in the Critique [of Practical Reason] it is" [1960, 225]. Rather, the sensuous precondition for moral action, which Kant calls *Achtung* in *Grundlegung*, *Kritik der Praktischen Vernunft* und *Religion*, he labels moral feeling (*moralisches Gefühl*) in *Metaphysik der Sitten*. In that latter work, he details four aesthetic preconditions for our awareness of moral duty [MS, VI, 399]: moral feeling, conscience, love of humanity (*Menschenliebe*) and self-respect (*Achtung für sich selbst*). Beck most likely is misled by the fact that Kant discusses the notion of self-respect under the title "respect", falsely suggesting that "moral feeling" and "respect" are two different notions (see also [MS, VI, 464]: "Die Achtung vor dem Gesetze, welche subjektiv als moralisches Gefühl bezeichnet wird, ist mit dem Bewusstsein seiner Pflicht einerlei."). In spite of this mistake, Beck offers a valuable discussion of the differences between Kant's notion of respect in *Kritik der Praktischen Vernunft* and his notion of moral feeling in *Metaphysik der Sitten*, noting, for instance, that "[in second Critique, Kant] thinks of pathological feeling as the material cause of moral feeling... in the *Metaphysics of Morals*, this relationship is neglected" [1960, 225]. For a discussion of the difference between Kant's use of the notion of respect in *Grundlegung* and *Kritik der Praktischen Vernunft*, see Allison [1990, 123].

[38] This casts doubts on Schönecker's suggestion that "the moral predispositions [i.e. moral feelings] are not merely the sensuous basis that allows us to be motivated by the moral law, but are the basis for us to comprehend the moral law as the [categorical imperative] at all" [2013, 29]. For if Kant defines the moral feeling as the ability to experience pleasure or pain as a function of our awareness that our action are or are not consistent with the moral law, as he does in the passage quoted in the text, this implies that our awareness of the moral law precedes our moral feeling. As a consequence, it is hard to see how the moral feeling could function as that which enables us to achieve awareness of the moral law in the first place, as Schönecker claims it does. The passage in [KpV, V, 75] referenced in the next paragraph in the text above poses a similar problem for Schönecker's suggestion.

[39] However, there are other passages in which Kant asserts that the moral feeling is not the determining ground of our will. In *Kritik der Praktischen Vernunft*, for instance, he writes: "Die Vernunft bestimmt in einem praktischen Gesetze unmittelbar den Willen, nicht vermittelst eines dazwischen kommenden Gefühls der Lust und Unlust, selbst nicht an diesem Gesetze" [KpV, V, 25; see also: KpV, V, 116]. Similarly, in *Kritik der Urteilskraft* he asserts: "[Die konstitutiven Prin-

Unlike the feeling linked to sensuous desire, Kant holds, *Achtung* is a feeling that we have to regard as not stemming from our physical nature, but as generated by our awareness of the demands of reason on us [KpV, V, 75; see also: KU, V, 178; MS, VI, 399][40]. That is, *Achtung* is, *qua* feeling, part of our passive side—and yet, Kant thinks, active in that it is generated by our own spontaneous reason:

---

zipien *a priori* für das Begehrungsvermögen enthält] die Vernunft, welche ohne Vermittelung irgend einer Lust, woher sie auch komme, praktisch ist" [KU, V, 196]. It appears impossible to make these statements consistent with Kant's assertions that we require the moral feeling as an incentive to act morally ("Achtung fürs moralische Gesetz ist also die einzige und zugleich unbezweifelte moralische Triebfeder" [KpV, V, 78]). This contradiction is noted by Beck [1960, 223n]. Wood, on the other hand, argues that these passages are in fact consistent with the central role attributed to feeling by Kant's theory of the will: "The feeling of respect is not so much a cause of the will's determination as a necessary by-product of this determination in a being whose will is finite, natural, and thus susceptible to feeling" [1999, 53]. Yet, this is inconsistent with Wood's own insistence that "pure reason can determine the will because it is a source of desire" [1999, 53n].

The contradiction in Kant's statements on the role of moral feeling in the determination of moral action is likely to be the result of the fact that Kant is pursuing two different goals: on the one hand, he wants to say that the moral feeling explains how our awareness of moral demands can lead us to action; yet, on the other, he also wants to present moral action as something pure, not dependent on our sensuous nature. The best way to deal with the contradiction is to understand Kant's assertions about the possibility of moral action without any involvement of feeling as overstatements of his (legitimate) point that moral feeling is different from pathological feeling in that it is not triggered by sensuous desire, but rather by an idea of reason ("Allein wenn Achtung gleich ein Gefühl ist, so ist es doch kein durch Einfluss empfangenes, sondern durch einen Vernunftbegriff selbstgewirktes Gefühl und daher von allen Gefühlen der ersteren Art, die sich auf Neigung oder Furcht bringen lassen, spezifisch unterschieden" [GMS, IV, 401n; see also: KpV, V, 75])—and that, in particular, moral action is not to be understood as triggered by the sensuous pleasure we take in being virtuous [VT, VIII, 395n; see also: MS, VI, 378]. Under the resulting interpretation, moral feeling would still be the incentive for moral action; yet, moral action would nonetheless be special in that it would be the only kind of action in which *pathological* feeling does not function as an incentive.

40 Kant holds, furthermore, that *Achtung* is the only feeling of whose presence we can have *a priori* knowledge: "Also ist Achtung fürs moralische Gesetz ein Gefühl, welches durch einen intellektuellen Grund gewirkt wird, und dieses Gefühl ist das einzige, welches wir völlig a priori erkennen, und dessen Notwendigkeit wir einsehen können" [KpV, V, 73]. We can make sense of this claim by considering that we know that we can act on the basis of moral demands (because of the fact of reason) and that all action requires feeling as an incentive. It follows that we can know *a priori* of the presence of a moral feeling that makes moral action possible for us. Kant himself puts the argument for his claim slightly differently: "[A]lle Neigung und jeder sinnliche Antrieb ist auf Gefühl gegründet, und die negative Wirkung aufs Gefühl (durch den Abbruch, der den Neigungen geschieht) ist selbst Gefühl. Folglich können wir a priori einsehen, dass das moralische Gesetz als Bestimmungsgrund des Willens dadurch, dass es allen unseren Neigungen Eintrag tut, ein Gefühl bewirken müsse, welches Schmerz genannt werden kann, und

> Hier geht kein Gefühl im Subjekt vorher, das auf Moralität gestimmt wäre. Denn das ist unmöglich, weil alles Gefühl sinnlich ist; die Triebfeder der sittlichen Gesinnung aber muss von aller sinnlichen Bedingung frei sein. Vielmehr ist das sinnliche Gefühl, was allen unseren Neigungen zum Grunde liegt, zwar die Bedingung derjenigen Empfindung, die wir Achtung nennen, aber die Ursache der Bestimmung desselben liegt in der reinen praktischen Vernunft, und diese Empfindung kann daher ihres Ursprunges wegen nicht pathologisch, sondern muss praktisch gewirkt heißen. [KpV, V, 75]

Kant's notion of respect is the core of his answer to one of the key problems that his ethical work sets out to solve, namely the question of how the moral law could not only be the standard for the evaluation of an action (the principle of adjudication), but also move us to action (i.e. be the principle of execution) [E, 1924, 53; see also: Allison, 1990, 68][41]. His answer is that all action requires an emotional trigger—and this trigger, in the case of moral action, is the feeling of respect, i.e. a feeling *sui generis*, generated by an idea of reason (namely, that of the moral law) [Schönecker & Wood, 2002, 81][42]. Yet, Kant holds that we can give no further explanation of how reason can inspire a feeling that leads us to act ("Es ist... gänzlich unmöglich, einzusehen, d. i. a priori begreiflich zu machen, wie ein bloßer Gedanke, der selbst nichts Sinnliches in sich enthält, eine Empfindung der Lust oder Unlust hervorbringe" [GMS, IV, 460])[43].

---

hier haben wir nun den ersten, vielleicht auch einzigen Fall, da wir aus Begriffen a priori das Verhältnis eines Erkenntnisses (hier ist es einer reinen praktischen Vernunft) zum Gefühl der Lust oder Unlust bestimmen konnten" [KpV, V, 72–3].

41 At the time of *Eine Vorlesung über Ethik* and *Kritik der Reinen Vernunft*, Kant believed he needed the idea of God to explain how moral demands could move us to act: "Es scheint also Gott Obligator der moralischen Gesetze zu sein. In der Exekution muss... ein drittes Wesen sein, das da nötigt, dasjenige zu tun, was moralisch gut ist" [E, 1924, 48; see also: KrV, III, 527]. This position is given up with the introduction of the notion of autonomy in *Grundlegung*. See Chapter 7 for a more detailed discussion of this shift in Kant's position.

42 Henrich points out that we can understand Kant's account of the possibility of moral action as a modification of Wolffian ethics (according to which moral action aims at realizing the good which can be cognized by theoretical reason) in the light of Hutcheson's criticism that theoretical insights by themselves are incapable of moving us to action. The crucial step in Kant's argument, as Henrich emphasizes, is to conceive of reason as an interested faculty, rather than merely as a faculty of logical inferences [1973, 237–8]. This new conception of reason as guided by its own interests allows Kant to merge the rationalists' account of morality as grounded in reason with the insight of the moral sense philosophers that we need to presuppose the presence of an interest to explain how we can be moved to action. This point is also noted by Brandt: "Kant lässt ... das moralische Gefühl das Erzeugnis des Gesetzes der reinen praktischen Vernunft sein... So werden die rationalistische Idee des Guten und das empiristische Moralgefühl in modifizierter Weise in die eigene Systematik integriert und als mögliche Gegeninstanzen aufgehoben [2007, 360; see also: Beck, 1960, 223; Wood, 1999, 46; O'Neill, 2004, 111].

43 We will discuss an ambiguity in Kant's use of the term "respect" in Chapter 6 below.

Before continuing our discussion, we should note that an implication of our results so far is that there are, in Kant's theory of action, two kinds of determining factors of our maxims—regardless of whether it is morally inspired or not: on the one hand, the emotional incentive to adopt the maxim, i.e. the feeling of pleasure linked to the mental representation of the action or the desired object (or *Achtung* in the case of the moral action); on the other hand, the highest maxim, i.e. a high-level rule guiding us in our choice on which incentive to adopt into our maxims. We will discuss the relation between them in more detail below.

The principle of self-love

We have discussed the moral law as the first option of the choice of our highest maxim. The second option is the principle of self-love—that is, the maxim of satisfying our desires and inclinations [KpV, V, 74]. A will that has made the principle of self-love its highest maxim is evil (*böse*) [R, VI, 21][44]. At the basis of the Kant's explanation of the possibility of evil lies his observation that the human being is not yet fully rational, but rather an *animal rationable,* an animal endowed with a talent for reason ("mit Vernunftfähigkeit begabtes Tier" [VII, 321]). Our rational faculties are still weak, shaky and entangled with our physical nature: our desires and inclinations are, Kant says, like strings tying down our will, making it unable to choose [KU, V, 432]. Thus, Kant holds, evil does not stem from the inherent badness of our physical desires (which, on the contrary, have to be considered a force for good, as they push us to take the steps necessary for our preservation as natural beings ([MAM, VIII, 116, see also: R, VI, 58]) or our lack of awareness of what the moral law demands of us [R, VI, 46], but a corruption of our will: our rational faculty, still in the process of development, has not yet fully emancipated itself from the influence of our physical nature[45]. In acting, Kant claims, we feel a constant inclination to accept non-moral motives as determining grounds of our action.

> Nun finden wir aber unsere Natur als sinnlicher Wesen so beschaffen, dass die Materie des Begehrungsvermögens (Gegenstände der Neigung, es sei der Hoffnung oder Furcht) sich zuerst aufdringt, und unser pathologisch bestimmbares Selbst, ob es gleich durch seine Maximen zur allgemeinen Gesetzgebung ganz untauglich ist, dennoch, gleich als ob es unser

---

44 The justification for this claim will be discussed in the text below.
45 We will discuss the notion that our rational faculties are still in the process of development in more detail in Chapter 8 below.

ganzes Selbst ausmachte, seine Ansprüche vorher und als die ersten und ursprünglichen geltend zu machen bestrebt sei. Man kann diesen Hang, sich selbst nach den subjektiven Bestimmungsgründen seiner Willkür zum objektiven Bestimmungsgrunde des Willens überhaupt zu machen, die Selbstliebe nennen, welche, wenn sie sich gesetzgebend und zum unbedingten praktischen Prinzip macht, Eigendünkel heißen kann. [KpV, V, 74; see also: KpV, V, 128][46]

In reflecting on our choice of action under the influence of our desires, our weak will re- and mis-interprets the demands of reason—and convinces itself that certain immoral courses of action, suggested by our desires, are permissible after all [GMS, IV, 405]. Thus, while some desires are like sudden assaults on our will (Kant calls these "affects", [A, VII, 252]), others silently nudge and tempt the will towards making exceptions for ourselves from the demand of the moral law. Kant calls these later desires "passions"[47]. They have, he holds, a particularly corrupting influence on our will, given that their presence—unlike that of the affects—is compatible with apparently detached reflection, which, though, under their influence, degenerates into an intentional misinterpretation of the demands of the moral law (Kant calls the resulting corrupted process of moral reflection "vernünfteln" [A, VII, 265]).

Under the influence of the passions, we lose control over ourselves [R 1025, XV, 459]. Our "proper self"—reason—is only apparently in charge, while it actually remains in the role of a servant to our inclinations. While, Kant believes, we never lose our respect for the moral law, we delude ourselves about our true motives, engage in bogus arguments to convince ourselves that our behaviour is consistent with the demands of morality[48]—and end up acting *as if* our highest maxim aimed at the pursuit of self-love (i.e., the satisfaction of our physical desires). Thus, for Kant there is a lie at the basis of every immorality—in the sense

---

46 For the difference between the Kantian notions of *Selbstliebe* and *Eigendünkel*, see Sala [2004, 165–6] and Engstrom [2010, 101–16].
47 "Leidenschaft... ist die zur bleibenden Neigung gewordene sinnliche Begierde (z.B. der Hass im Gegensatz des Zorns). Die Ruhe, mit der ihr nachgegangen wird, lässt Überlegung zu und verstattet dem Gemüt sich darüber Grundsätze zu machen und so, wenn die Neigung auf das Gesetzwidrige fällt, über sie zu brüten, sie tief zu wurzeln und das Böse dadurch (als vorsätzlich) in seine Maxime aufzunehmen; welches alsdann ein qualifiziertes Böse, d. i. ein wahres Laster, ist" [MS, VI, 408].
48 "Diese angeborne Schuld..., welche so genannt wird, weil sie sich so früh, als sich nur immer der Gebrauch der Freiheit im Menschen äußert, wahrnehmen lässt... hat zu ihrem Charakter eine gewisse Tücke des menschlichen Herzens (dolus malus), sich wegen seiner eigenen guten oder bösen Gesinnungen selbst zu betrügen, und, wenn nur die Handlungen das Böse nicht zur Folge haben, was sie nach ihren Maximen wohl haben könnten, sich seiner Gesinnung wegen nicht zu beunruhigen, sondern vielmehr vor dem Gesetze gerechtfertigt zu halten" [R, VI, 38].

that we deceive ourselves about our true motives for action [R, VI, 42; see also: TP, VIII, 270].

Our corrupted will loses its autonomy—and ends up under the control of our dumb physical nature, a condition which Kant calls heteronomy: "Wenn daher... das Objekt einer Begierde... in das praktische Gesetz als Bedingung der Möglichkeit desselben hineinkommt, so wird daraus Heteronomie der Willkür, nämlich Abhängigkeit vom Naturgesetze, irgend einem Antriebe oder Neigung zu folgen, und der Wille gibt sich nicht selbst das Gesetz, sondern nur die Vorschrift zur vernünftigen Befolgung pathologischer Gesetze" [KpV, V, 33; see also: GMS, IV, 444]. Our physical nature, however, does not provide any principles that could serve as a basis for the coherent use of our rational faculties. For our passions do not provide rules ("Die Neigungen sind nur Gegner der Grundsätze überhaupt (sie mögen gut oder böse sein)" [R, VI, 57n])—they merely push for exceptions to the rules set by the moral law [GMS, IV, 424]. The discipline that our reason requires—and the only sort that it is capable of—is self-discipline: the control by principles it gives to itself. Yet, where passions have undermined reason's ability for self-discipline, the use of our reason becomes lawless[49]. It is no longer effectively constrained by the laws of reason (i.e., those principles that allow for the satisfaction of reason's interests). In this condition, Kant holds, a human being becomes "the most dreadful of things" [E, 1924, 153]. He is unable to live in peace with other individuals (given that, for Kant, only the moral law allows for the peaceful coordination of naturally uncoordinated wills). He has castrated his own freedom, by making the coherent and unified use of his practical reason impossible, which alone allows him to become master over himself.

We should note how being unfree in the sense of having self-love as our highest maxim is consistent with two different, more basic, kinds of freedom. First, the fact that we choose self-love as our highest maxim does not undermine our claim to *transcendental freedom* (i.e. our status as bearers of a noumenal will). For even in this case, we continue to see ourselves confronted with moral demands—and, hence, (on the strength of the fact-of-reason argument) have grounds to attribute transcendental freedom to ourselves. Secondly, our choosing self-love as our highest maxim does also not affect our *negative freedom* (i.e. the freedom of adopting certain desires as incentives when choosing our maxims). The influence of passions does not consist in somehow determin-

---

[49] "Drittens bedeutet auch Freiheit im Denken die Unterwerfung der Vernunft unter keine andere Gesetze, als: die sie sich selbst gibt; und ihr Gegenteil ist die Maxime eines gesetzlosen Gebrauchs der Vernunft" [SDO, VIII, 145].

ing our actions in a way that bypasses our maxims[50]. Rather, they corrupt the process by which we determine our maxims. In this sense, we still act on maxims that we choose for ourselves (passions don't change anything about this), but the maxims we choose are not always consistent with the moral law (due to the influence of the passions).

To avoid confusion on this point, we should distinguish three different conceptions of freedom that are central to Kant's practical philosophy, even though Kant himself is not always careful to highlight the differences between them[51]:
- Transcendental freedom—our idealistic-fictional status as noumenal wills, subject to self-imposed laws. Kant also refers to transcendental freedom as "positive freedom" [e.g., MS, VI, 213–4]—and to our transcendentally free will as our moral personality (see Chapter 6 below);
- Negative freedom—our ability to guide our actions on the basis of reflectively endorsed principles of action[52];

---

50 However, Kant seems to accept that this can happen on occasions [R, VI, 29]. On Kant's notion of the weakness of will, see note 7 above as well as Wood [1999, 52]. Note also the discussion about the normative interpretation of Kant's notion of action on maxims below.
51 Sometimes commentators follow Kant's habit of carelessly referring to "freedom" without clarifying which conception of the term they have in mind. When, for instance, Beck writes that "*Willkür* may or may not be free, according to the kind of law it puts into the maxim" [1960, 178], this statement is false if we understand him to be referring to negative freedom, but true if we understand him as referring to moral freedom.
52 As we have highlighted in our discussion above, the notion of negative freedom is the same as that of practical freedom, which we have discussed in Chapter 1. The notion of negative or practical freedom is distinguished from that of comparative freedom [KpV, V, 96], which Kant also refers to as psychological freedom [KpV, V, 97]—and which we can think of as negative freedom in the absence of transcendental freedom. That is, if we were living in a world in which we had the impression of being able to decide on our actions, while we were in fact subject to natural necessity and had no grounds for attributing transcendental freedom to ourselves, we would only enjoy comparative freedom: "So mögen [die bestimmenden Vorstellungen unseres Willens] immer innerlich sein, sie mögen psychologische und nicht mechanische Kausalität haben, d. i. durch Vorstellungen und nicht durch körperliche Bewegung Handlung hervorbringen, so sind es immer Bestimmungsgründe der Kausalität eines Wesens, so fern sein Dasein in der Zeit bestimmbar ist, mithin unter notwendig machenden Bedingungen der vergangenen Zeit, die also, wenn das Subjekt handeln soll, nicht mehr in seiner Gewalt sind, die also zwar psychologische Freiheit (wenn man ja dieses Wort von einer bloß inneren Verkettung der Vorstellungen der Seele brauchen will), aber doch Naturnotwendigkeit bei sich führen, mithin keine transzendentale Freiheit übrig lassen, welche als Unabhängigkeit von allem Empirischen und also von der Natur überhaupt gedacht werden muss" [KpV, V, 96–7]. This would be, in Kant's words, merely the freedom of a spatula [KpV, V, 97] or a puppet [KpV, V, 101]. Comparative freedom is linked with the first, negative freedom with second and moral freedom with the third internal-

- Moral freedom—the ideal condition in which we adopt the moral law as our highest maxim, i.e. have developed a good will[53].

Confusing transcendental and moral freedom is tempting, given that both are forms of autonomy (i.e. concern a condition in which we ourselves determine the principles on which we act)[54]. Yet, we can keep them apart by noting that our transcendental freedom is a given, a status we know we have thanks to the fact of reason. It is not something we can lose—and not something that requires any effort on our part. Moral freedom, on the other hand—that is, the condition in which the moral law has become the highest determining ground of our will—is not a given, but rather a goal, one in fact that we can never be certain of having fully attained and which we consequently have to keep striving towards. The development of a good will requires constant effort and struggle on our part, in our attempt to resist and overcome the temptation posed by our sensuous de-

---

ization, as discussed in the text, with negative and moral freedom both requiring transcendental freedom as the condition of their possibility.

53 As we will see in Chapter 9, there is a further conception of freedom which plays an important role in Kant's practical philosophy, namely that of *external freedom*. Kant defines external freedom as our ability to act without being subject to the coercive influence of the wills of others. However, given that external freedom—unlike the other conceptions of freedom we discuss here—is important for his political philosophy, rather than his ethics in the narrow sense (as concerned with the correct principles of action), we do not discuss it here.

54 Commentators are not always careful to distinguish between the notions of personality (i.e. our transcendental freedom) and that of a good will. Guyer, for instance, writes that "moral personality as the unified exercise of freedom is analogous to the unity of apperception itself as the product of the exercise of our cognitive spontaneity, and is maximally pleasing as answering what is our most fundamental need of all, our need for unity itself" [2000, 115]. Yet, the "unified exercise of freedom" that answers "our need for unity" is not personality (which is rather the very freedom whose unified exercise confronts us as a task), but the good will: only once we have brought our freedom fully under rational control, exercising it according to the laws of reason—that is, only once we have achieved a good will—are we at the stage of the "unified exercise of freedom" that Guyer mentions. Another example of a commentator blurring the line between the notions of personality and the good will is Ricken, who writes: "Nur dann kann ein Wesen als 'Zweck an sich selbst' gedacht werden, wenn sein Wille 'jederzeit zugleich als gesetzgebend betrachtet' wird. Diese Formulierungen sind offensichtlich so zu verstehen, dass ein vernünftiges Wesen nur dann Zweck an sich selbst ist, wenn seine Maximen der Forderung der Formel des allgemeinen Gesetzes entsprechen" [Höfffe ed., 2000, 246]. Ricken here mistakenly equates our status as autonomous, i.e. self-legislating, beings (i.e. our personality) with a condition in which our maxims correspond to the demands of the moral law (i.e. a good will). As a consequence, he claims that we are only ends-in-ourselves if we act morally (i.e. have developed a good will), a claim that is clearly at odds with Kant's project. We will discuss this point in more detail in Chapter 6 below.

sires (see Chapter 8 below). We can think of our moral personality (i.e. our transcendental freedom) as a talent for the good will (i.e., our moral freedom): only because we are transcendentally free do we have the capacity to guide ourselves on the basis of the essential interests of reason, as codified in the moral law. In this sense, the talent for moral freedom is given to us—but the result, our actual good will, has to be the product of our own effort[55].

This distinction between the different Kantian conceptions of freedom allows us to see how we can be accountable for our deeds even if we have not achieved the highest level of freedom, moral freedom—i.e. the stage at which our will fully guides itself on the basis of the interests of reason. For, given our transcendental freedom, this unfreedom is still the product of our choice, namely the choice of self-love as our highest maxim (even if, as we have seen, that choice is a mere idea, a mere assumption)[56]. In this sense, this unfreedom, for Kant, is always chosen [R, VI, 21][57]. Or, more properly speaking, it is brought about by a lack of self-discipline, our inability to heed the demands made on us by our proper self and to make appropriate use of our freedom.

Problems with Kant's theory of the will

We have now explored Kant's theory of the will. In the process, I have tried to present it in as coherent a form as possible. However, it is undeniable that Kant's theory suffers from ambiguities, gaps and inconsistencies. In the following, we will take a closer look at these.
– The first problem in Kant's theory of the will is linked to his notion of the technical-practical use of reason. Kant holds that choosing our maxims

---

[55] Given the centrality of the notion of the good will as the highest level of moral development of which we are capable as individuals, it is astonishing to find Wood suggesting that this notion does not play an important role in "Kant's developed philosophical theory of moral duties" [1999, 20]. While Wood might be right that the concept does not feature prominently in the derivation of specific duties, it is nonetheless of central importance in the intellectual framework within which this derivation takes place, as our discussion in Chapters 6 and 7 will highlight.
[56] Kant himself highlights the link between transcendental freedom and moral accountability: "Die transzendentale Idee der Freiheit macht zwar bei weitem nicht den ganzen Inhalt des psychologischen Begriffs dieses Namens aus, welcher großen Teils empirisch ist, sondern nur den der absoluten Spontaneität der Handlung als den eigentlichen Grund der Imputabilität derselben" [KrV, III, 310].
[57] "[Handlung aus Neigung] so hatte Kant sich grundsätzlich verdeutlicht, [kann] keinesfalls einfach als Fremdbestimmung durch Neigung erfolgen, sondern nur als Selbstbestimmung des Subjekts zu solcher Fremdbestimmung" [Prauss, 1982, 15].

not only involves the ability to determine the appropriate means for the achievement of our ends, but that we also regard ourselves as rationally constrained to do so [GMS, IV, 414]. That is, in choosing our maxims we see ourselves confronted with what Kant calls a hypothetical imperative[58], i.e. the demand to use the most efficient and effective means to bring about our chosen end, in a way that choosing means that are ineffective in bringing about the desired end would be irrational. Kant himself suggests that explaining the real possibility of this rational constraint on the choice of our actions is straightforward:

> [W]ie ein Imperativ der Geschicklichkeit möglich sei, bedarf wohl keiner besondern Erörterung. Wer den Zweck will, will (so fern die Vernunft auf seine Handlungen entscheidenden Einfluss hat) auch das dazu unentbehrlich notwendige Mittel, das in seiner Gewalt ist. Dieser Satz ist, was das Wollen betrifft, analytisch; denn in dem Wollen eines Objekts als meiner Wirkung wird schon meine Kausalität als handelnde Ursache, d. i. der Gebrauch der Mittel, gedacht, und der Imperativ zieht den Begriff notwendiger Handlungen zu diesem Zwecke schon aus dem Begriff eines Wollens dieses Zwecks heraus. [GMS, IV, 417]

That is, Kant holds that the validity of the hypothetical imperative follows analytically from the concept of rational willing. This, however, is not convincing: like the categorical imperative, the hypothetical imperative involves the notion that we are confronted, in the process of determining our actions, with a demand of our reason that, Kant holds, is necessarily and universally—and hence *a priori* —valid for us ("Alle Imperativen werden durch ein Sollen ausgedrückt und zeigen dadurch das Verhältnis eines objektiven Gesetzes der Vernunft zu einem Willen an, der seiner subjektiven Beschaffenheit nach dadurch nicht notwendig bestimmt wird [GMS, IV, 413])[59]. While our wanting the means to a certain end is contingent on our wanting the end, the demand that if we want the end, we have to adopt the means required to achieve that end is *necessarily* valid for any rational being. If we fail to choose the necessary means to our ends, we

---

58 To be precise, in *Grundlegung*, Kant distinguishes between two kinds of hypothetical imperative: problematic-practical ones (the ones commanding that we take the means to our ends, whatever those ends may be) and the assertoric-practical ones (the ones commanding that we that take the appropriate means to achieve our own happiness [GMS, IV, 415]; on Kant's conception of happiness, see Chapter 7 below).

59 This is highlighted by Wood, who writes: "[T]hose who find nothing problematic about instrumental rationality should recognize that they cannot consistently object to the idea of a categorical imperative on the ground that it is supposed to be universally valid, necessary and *a priori* or that it is supposed to move the will independently of empirical desires, for those properties already belong to hypothetical imperatives" [1999, 65].

fall foul of the standards of rationality, regardless of which contingent ends we are striving to achieve.

Yet, as we have seen in the previous sections, Kant's critical standards demand that we offer a deduction for any non-empirical concept that we wish to employ to ensure that it has real possibility. Thus, if we posit—as Kant does—that, in the process of choosing the maxims determining our actions, we are confronted with objectively valid constraints, we have to show how such constraints are possible—that is, how they can be consistently incorporated into our world view (i.e., establish their logical possibility) and what grounds we have to accept their objective validity (i.e. establish their real possibility). Merely claiming that the existence of the rational constraints involved in the hypothetical imperative follows tautologically from the concept of willing does not meet these demanding standards.

While we can, in the present context, not aim to offer the missing deduction of the hypothetical imperative, our interpretation of Kant's philosophy as organized around the notion of reason as an interested faculty allows us to see which form such a grounding of the possibility of hypothetical imperative would take. As we have argued above, duties—and rational demands on us more generally—are grounded in the interests of reason. Reason, for Kant, is a teleological faculty in that it strives towards the satisfaction of its own interests. Yet, in order to be able to achieve this satisfaction, it must will itself as effective in its striving. That is, Kant's very conception of reason as an interested faculty implies a meta-interest of reason in its own effectiveness—or, as Kant puts it in *Religion:* "[Es ist] eine von den unvermeidlichen Einschränkungen des Menschen und seines (vielleicht auch aller andern Weltwesen) praktischen Vernunftvermögens, sich bei allen Handlungen nach dem Erfolg aus denselben umzusehen" [R, VI, 6n; see also: VIII, 399n]. This notion of our practical reason as guided by such a meta-interest in its own effectiveness offers a starting point for explaining the existence of a constraint, valid for all rational beings, to make use of the means that are appropriate to realize their chosen ends—i.e. a starting point for an explanation of the real possibility of hypothetical imperatives. For reason's interest in its own effectiveness could function as the ground for the rational constraint that we see ourselves under to act in a way that allows the intentions of our will, i.e. our practical reason, to become effective in the world[60].

Yet, even if this is accepted, the troubles arising for Kant's theory of the will from the notion of a hypothetical imperative do not end there. For once we rec-

---

[60] We will discuss the notion of an interest of reason in its own effectiveness in more detail in Chapter 9 below.

ognize that the hypothetical imperative is marked by the same characteristics of necessity and universality that characterize the categorical imperative, it becomes puzzling why Kant believes that his deduction of transcendental freedom requires our moral experience as its starting point. As we have seen above, the features of necessity and universality, which mark the moral experience according to Kant, function as a crucial premise in his fact-of-reason argument. Yet, if our experience of being subject to the demands of the hypothetical imperative is characterized by the same features, this opens the possibility of offering a parallel deduction of our transcendental freedom from purely non-moral premises. However, as we have argued above, in his later work Kant clearly dismisses this possibility. If he wishes to take that position, he has to explain what distinguishes the categorical imperative from the hypothetical imperative in a way that only our experience of being subject to the first, but not that of being subject to the second, can function as the premise in a fact-of-reason-style argument.

One reason why such an explanation is not forthcoming might be that Kant's discussion of the hypothetical imperative takes place in *Grundlegung*—that is, at a point in time in which he still believes in the possibility of a deduction of transcendental freedom from purely non-moral premises. Once he has rejected this possibility from *Kritik der Praktischen Vernunft* onwards, he never returns to discuss the hypothetical imperative in detail[61]—and never explains how we can make his claim that we are subject to hypothetical imperatives consistent with his new view that we can deduce the objective reality of our own transcendental freedom only on the basis of our moral experience[62]. Yet, a consistent defence of his fact-of-reason argument would require such an explanation.

– The second problem that marks Kant's theory of the will is that he is less than clear in his use of the notion of the determining ground of our maxims. There are, as we have seen above, two elements that determine the choice of

---

[61] Yet, there is a brief reference to the hypothetical imperative in [KpV, V, 20].
[62] However, note Kant's discussion of the difference between moral-practical rules (i.e. the categorical imperative) and technical-practical rules in *Kritik der Urteilskraft*, in which he argues that only the former belong to the discipline practical philosophy, while the latter, strictly speaking, are corollaries of theoretical philosophy, in that they inform us about which means are effective in promoting our ends in the world around us [KU, V, 172]. In the context of the present discussion, this could be read as Kant's attempt to eliminate the notion of a hypothetical imperative (i.e. the notion of a rational constraint that we are faced with in the technical-practical use of our reason)—and thus the problems that we have discussed in this section. Yet, the position he appears to be taking in *Kritik der Urteilskraft* fails to provide an explanation of how we can account for the common sense observation that, as rational agents, we see ourselves confronted with the rational demand to choose the appropriate means to our end (i.e. the phenomenon to which Kant had given the label of "hypothetical imperative" in his discussion in *Grundlegung*).

maxim: on the one hand, the feeling of pleasure (or displeasure) linked to a mental representation of a possible state of affairs or a rule of action (in the case of a moral action) that gives us an incentive to adopt a certain maxim; on the other hand, there is the underlying principle, our highest maxim, on the basis of which we decide which incentives to incorporate into our maxims (i.e. on which incentives to act).

Kant unhelpfully refers to both of these elements in the determination of action as the determining ground (*Bestimmungsgrund* or *Bewegungsgrund*), thus obfuscating the distinction between them[63]. That is, sometimes the term "determining ground" is used to refer to the feeling of pleasure that leads us to adopt a certain maxim[64], while in other passages, he uses it to refer to our highest maxim—i.e. the idealistic-fictitious principle of choice determining whether we give precedence to sensuous or moral incentives when deciding on how to act[65].

What adds to the confusion is that Kant also distinguishes between the subjective determining ground of the will (which he also calls *Triebfeder*, incentive) and the objective determining ground—but does not make consistent use of this distinction. Sometimes, he calls the subjective determining ground that which actually leads us to act and the objective determining ground the principles that objectively govern the use of our will (i.e. the moral law, that set of principles which would allow for the use of our will that is consistent with the interests of reason), as for instance in the following passage:

> Wenn nun unter Triebfeder (elater animi) der subjektive Bestimmungsgrund des Willens eines Wesens verstanden wird, dessen Vernunft nicht schon vermöge seiner Natur dem objektiven Gesetze notwendig gemäß ist, so wird erstlich daraus folgen: dass man dem göttlichen Willen gar keine Triebfedern beilegen könne, die Triebfeder des menschlichen Willens aber (und des von jedem erschaffenen vernünftigen Wesen) niemals etwas anderes

---

[63] Is the determining ground Kant refers to the determining ground of our will, that of our maxim or that of our action? In fact, Kant uses all three expressions synonymously, referring without any discernible distinction to the "determining ground of the will" [KpV, V, 21; R, VI, 21n], the "determining ground of the action" [KpV, V, 57; R, VI, 50] and the "determining ground of the maxim" [KpV, V, 34; KpV, V, 45].

[64] For example, in the following passage: "Denn der Bestimmungsgrund der Willkür ist alsdann die Vorstellung eines Objekts und dasjenige Verhältnis derselben zum Subjekt, wodurch das Begehrungsvermögen zur Wirklichmachung desselben bestimmt wird. Ein solches Verhältnis aber zum Subjekt heißt die Lust an der Wirklichkeit eines Gegenstandes" [KpV, V, 21; see also R, VI, 31].

[65] For example: "Ein unmittelbares Interesse nimmt die Vernunft nur alsdann an der Handlung, wenn die Allgemeingültigkeit der Maxime derselben ein genugsamer Bestimmungsgrund des Willens ist" [GMS, IV, 459].

> als das moralische Gesetz sein könne, mithin der objektive Bestimmungsgrund jederzeit und ganz allein zugleich der subjektiv hinreichende Bestimmungsgrund der Handlung sein müsse, wenn diese nicht bloß den Buchstaben des Gesetzes, ohne den Geist desselben zu enthalten, erfüllen soll. [KpV, V, 72]

On other occasions, however, Kant speaks of the objective determining ground of our will as that which actually leads us to act, while he uses the term "subjective determining ground" to denote motives for action based on our sensuous nature (i.e. desires). Under this reading, an action fails to have moral worth if the objective determining ground of our will is a subjective determining ground: "Man kann diesen Hang, sich selbst nach den subjektiven Bestimmungsgründen seiner Willkür zum objektiven Bestimmungsgrunde des Willens überhaupt zu machen, die Selbstliebe nennen" [KpV, V, 74].

In a third type of use of these terms, he treats the subjective determining ground as necessarily pathological (i.e. based on desires) and the objective determining ground as based on the interests of reason. Under this interpretation, a given action can either be triggered by a subjective or an objective determining ground—and is moral only in the latter case: "Der subjektive Grund des Begehrens ist die Triebfeder, der objektive des Wollens der Bewegungsgrund; daher der Unterschied zwischen subjektiven Zwecken, die auf Triebfedern beruhen, und objektiven, die auf Bewegungsgründe ankommen, welche für jedes vernünftige Wesen gelten. Praktische Prinzipien sind formal, wenn sie von allen subjektiven Zwecken abstrahieren; sie sind aber material, wenn sie diese, mithin gewisse Triebfedern zum Grunde legen" [GMS, IV, 427].

To dissolve this ambiguity in Kant's use of the term "determining ground", we should distinguish between three different elements in the determination of an action—the incentive, the subjective determining ground and the objective determining ground—in the following way:

a. The incentive is the emotional element in the determination of the action— that is, either the sensuous desire or the moral feeling[66];
b. The subjective determining ground is the highest maxim—i.e., the fundamental principle of choice determining whether we give precedence to moral or to sensuous incentives in the determination of our action;

---

[66] Beck claims that this is the use Kant makes of the term "incentive" in *Grundlegung:* in this work "Kant distinguished between 'incentive' and 'objective ground of volition' or motive, as between the desire for subjective ends and that for ends valid for every rational being" [Beck, 1960, 216]. However, in making this claim, Beck appears to be overlooking the following passage: "Wie nun aber reine Vernunft... für sich selbst eine Triebfeder abgeben... könne, das zu erklären, dazu ist alle menschliche Vernunft gänzlich unvermögend" [GMS, IV, 461].

c. The objective determining ground is the moral law—i.e. the set of principles that allows for the self-consistent use of our practical reason (that is, the use that is consistent with the interests of reasons).

These three aspects of the determination of our maxim have to be distinguished, in turn, from the material content—or object—of the maxim, namely the end that we are aiming to achieve with our action[67].

Using this terminology, we can state Kant's theory of the will in the following terms: the representation of an object or the awareness of a moral demand inspires in us a feeling—and whether or not we act on this feeling is determined by the subjective determining ground of our will, our highest maxim (though this is just a thought construct). A moral action is one in which the subjective determining ground of our will (our highest maxim) is in line with its objective determining ground (the moral law).

If this terminology is accepted, we would have to reject passages in which Kant equates incentives with the subjective determining ground of actions (as he does in [GMS, IV, 427] and [KpV, V, 72]) as well as those in which he speaks of duty as an incentive (as in [MS, VI, 218]). Furthermore, we should not say that there are actions that lack incentives (as Kant does in [GMS, IV, 462]), for given that the incentive is the feeling that leads us to adopt maxims to act and that Kant's theory is built on the notion that every action requires a feeling in this triggering role, there can be no action without an incentive. Lastly, we should distinguish between incentives—the feelings that lead us to adopt a certain maxim—and the material content of our maxim, that is, the end to be achieved through the action (something Kant fails to do in [R, VI, 36]).

---

[67] "Nun ist freilich unleugbar, dass alles Wollen auch einen Gegenstand, mithin eine Materie haben müsse; aber diese ist darum nicht eben der Bestimmungsgrund und Bedingung der Maxime" [KpV, V, 34; see also: Allison, 1990, 189]. Unfortunately, there are other passages in which Kant equates the end of an action with its determining ground ("[Man könnte] den Willen durch das Vermögen der Zwecke definieren... , indem sie jederzeit Bestimmungsgründe des Begehrungsvermögens nach Prinzipien sind" [KpV, V, 59; see also KpV, V, 27]). However, there are good reasons for him not to do so. In particular, as we will see below, his theory of moral value is best understood as centered on the notion that the moral value of an action is determined by the (subjective) determining ground of the will. However, if Kant equates the end of an action with its determining ground, it would follow that the moral value of an action depends on the end it is set to achieve, a conclusion that Kant explicitly rejects [GMS, IV, 399]. Wood overlooks the ambiguities involved in Kant's statements about the relation between the end of our action and the determining ground of our will when he writes of "Kant's insistence that the determining ground of a rational will must always be an end (Zweck)" [1999, 112].

– The third problem with Kant's theory of the will is the lack of clarity about the answer to the question of whether we can be aware of our own maxims. This doubt arises as an implication of the following two statements Kant makes in discussing his theory of moral value:

a) *The moral value of our action depends on the maxim on which it is based*
Kant repeatedly states that the moral value of an action depends not on the end for which it is committed, but on the maxim on the basis of which it is done: "Eine Handlung aus Pflicht hat ihren moralischen Wert nicht in der Absicht, welche dadurch erreicht werden soll, sondern in der Maxime, nach der sie beschlossen wird, hängt also nicht von der Wirklichkeit des Gegenstandes der Handlung ab, sondern bloß von dem Prinzip des Wollens, nach welchem die Handlung unangesehen aller Gegenstände des Begehrungsvermögens geschehen ist" [GMS, IV, 400; see also: R, VI, 31; MS, VI, 404].

b) *We can never be certain about the moral value of our actions*
Kant holds that it impossible for us to know with certainty whether our actions have moral value or not. The reason for this is not that we are in any doubt about the *standard* of moral value (the principle of adjudication—i.e. the moral law). In fact, Kant thinks that even the untrained mind is perfectly aware of these standards [KpV, V, 36]. Rather, the uncertainty about the moral value of our actions is due to the fact that we can never be certain about the subjective determining ground of our action.

> [Es ist] schlechterdings unmöglich, durch Erfahrung einen einzigen Fall mit völliger Gewissheit auszumachen, da die Maxime einer sonst pflichtmäßigen Handlung lediglich auf moralischen Gründen und auf der Vorstellung seiner Pflicht beruht habe. Denn es ist zwar bisweilen der Fall, dass wir bei der schärfsten Selbstprüfung gar nichts antreffen, was außer dem moralischen Grunde der Pflicht mächtig genug hätte sein können, uns zu dieser oder jener guten Handlung und so großer Aufopferung zu bewegen; es kann aber daraus gar nicht mit Sicherheit geschlossen werden, dass wirklich gar kein geheimer Antrieb der Selbstliebe unter der bloßen Vorspiegelung jener Idee die eigentliche bestimmende Ursache des Willens gewesen sei. [GMS, IV, 407; see also: R, VI, 21n; MS, VI, 447]

Given that Kant does not doubt that we are aware of the standard of moral value, it seems to follow from the claims that, first, the moral value of our actions depends on our maxims and, second, that we can never be certain of the moral value of our actions, that we can never be certain about the maxims we are acting on.

In fact, some commentators have accepted this conclusion. Wood, for instance, claims that "Kant denies that we can know even in our own case the principles on which we act" [1999, 200]. Similarly, O'Neill holds that "[l]ike other aspects of intelligible character, [our] maxims are not objects of knowledge" [1989, 71][68]. I will call this claim that Kant holds that we cannot know our own maxim *agnosticism about maxims*. This position is supported by the fact that there are indeed passages in which Kant explicitly says that we cannot be aware of our own maxims ("Aber die Maximen kann man nicht beobachten, sogar nicht allemal in sich selbst, mithin das Urteil, dass der Täter ein böser Mensch sei, nicht mit Sicherheit auf Erfahrung gründen" [R, VI, 20]). Furthermore, defenders of *agnosticism about maxims* can point to the common sense observation that in many of the actions we commit we are not aware of having formed any maxim before acting[69].

However, in spite of the textual evidence in favour of *agnosticism about maxims*, I believe that it makes it impossible to understand key aspects of Kant's moral philosophy and that, in our attempt to develop a well-grounded and self-consistent interpretation of Kant's theory of action, we should reject it. First, Kant holds that maxims are rules that we give to ourselves (*selbst auferlegte Regeln* [GMS, IV, 438]). This means that those subscribing to *agnosticism about maxims* have to explain how we can give rules to ourselves without being aware of them. This is not as hopeless a task as it might sound. The defenders of this position can point to the fact that Kant also calls the moral law self-imposed [GMS, IV, 434]—without us being aware of such an act of self-imposition. Thus, the notion of a subject imposing rules on itself without being aware of doing so does not seem to be foreign to the Kantian philosophical project. In fact, this parallel would support O'Neill's implicit suggestion that first-order maxims—just like the moral law and the highest maxim—are part of our intelligible character, i.e. mere ideas of reason that we can have no experience of[70].

---

[68] The reference to the intelligible character is interesting, given that it suggests that for O'Neill our first-order maxims are mere ideas, i.e. mere thought constructs used to make sense of our predicament as agents. I have argued above that we should regard our highest maxims as ideas in this sense. Yet, O'Neill seems to hold that not only our highest maxims, but also our first-order maxims are ideas. I will argue against this view below. Note that later in her text, O'Neill seems to endorse a different interpretation of Kant's view, namely one according to which "agents are not always aware of, nor ever infallible about, what their maxims are" [1989, 151]. Unlike the first view (i.e. the one that "maxims are not objects of knowledge"), this second interpretation seems to allow for the possibility that we are, at least sometimes, aware of our maxims.

[69] "Die Auffassung, dass wir immer nach Maximen handeln, die wir uns bewusst gemacht haben, ist empirisch falsch" [Köhl, 1990, 60].

[70] See note 68 above. However, we should note that while Kant employs language that suggests that the highest maxim is a mere idea of reason (as we have explored above), there is to my knowledge no part of his work that speaks about our first-order maxims in the same way.

Yet, there is a crucial difference between the imposition of the moral law and our highest maxim, on the one hand, and our first-order maxims, on the other. While the self-imposition of the moral law and the choice of the highest maxim have to be conceived of as choices by our timeless, noumenal self (a thought construct necessary to achieve a coherent view of ourselves as agents), Kant's language in discussing our choice of maxims suggests that this choice is one that the subject itself is aware of (and that, hence, happens in time, rather than being a mere idea of reason[71]). He writes, for instance, that "we become aware of the moral law (as soon as we compose our maxim of the will)" [KpV, V, 29] and that our choice of maxims "is in the moment of action in the power of the subject" [R, VI, 49]. This suggests that Kant regards the choice of our first-order maxim as something that happens in time, rather than it being a mere thought construct like the self-legislation of the moral law and our choice of the highest maxim. Thus, it seems that treating the choice of our first-order maxims as a mere idea—like the choice of our highest maxim—is not a promising interpretative strategy. This makes it difficult to see how we could account for them as rules we impose on ourselves without being aware of them.

Secondly, *agnosticism about maxims* turns the centrepiece of Kant's moral philosophy—the categorical imperative—into an incoherent demand. The imperative states that we should only adopt a maxim if we could also want it as a universal law—and reject it if we could not so want it: "Der kategorische Imperativ ist also nur ein einziger und zwar dieser: handle nur nach derjenigen Maxime, durch die du zugleich wollen kannst, dass sie ein allgemeines Gesetz werde" [GMS, IV, 421]. Yet, if we were not aware of what our maxims are, it would be impossible for us to comply with this demand. Similarly, passages in which Kant discusses the "universalizability test" [Allison, 1990, 205]—i.e. the test which determines whether a given maxim has lawlike form[72]—only make sense under the assumption that Kant takes us to be aware of our own maxims. The following passage is a good example:

> Welche Form in der Maxime sich zur allgemeinen Gesetzgebung schicke, welche nicht, das kann der gemeinste Verstand ohne Unterweisung unterscheiden. Ich habe z. B. es mir zur Maxime gemacht, mein Vermögen durch alle sichere Mittel zu vergrößern. Jetzt ist ein Depositum in meinen Händen, dessen Eigentümer verstorben ist und keine Handschrift darüber zurückgelassen hat. Natürlicherweise ist dies der Fall meiner Maxime. Jetzt will ich nur wissen, ob jene Maxime auch als allgemeines praktisches Gesetz gelten könne. Ich wende

---

[71] This point is highlighted by Guyer [2010, 138], but missed by Rosen [1993, 61]. See note 42 in Chapter 4 above.
[72] We will discuss the universalizability test in more detail below.

jene also auf gegenwärtigen Fall an und frage, ob sie wohl die Form eines Gesetzes annehmen. [KpV, V, 27]

Kant's demand that we test whether our maxim can function as a universal law is only intelligible if we assume that we are aware of our own maxims, while those subscribing to *agnosticism about maxims* must regard it as an absurd demand. Hence, to claim that we are unaware of our maxims is to assert that one of the hallmarks of Kant's philosophy (the categorical imperative) is condemned to uselessness by his own theory of action[73]—and makes the passages in which Kant discusses the related test of our maxims for universalizability unintelligible.

To understand the third reason for rejecting *agnosticism about maxims* we have to appreciate Kant's distinction between the legality and the morality of an action. We have just touched on the notion of legality: a maxim (and the action resulting from it) has legality (i.e. lawlike form) if it is consistent with the moral law (i.e. it is such that if all rational beings acted on it, the interests of reason in systematic unity would be satisfied[74]). In this sense, the universalizability test we have just encountered is a test for the legality of maxims. The morality of an action, on the other hand, depends on the agent's ground for adopting his maxim (i.e. the subjective determining ground of the agent's will; his highest maxim[75]): "Man nennt die bloße Übereinstimmung oder Nichtübereinstimmung

---

[73] I believe it is incoherent for O'Neill, who claims that we do not know our own maxims, to treat the categorical imperative as a still workable part of Kant's philosophy: "The Categorical Imperative can... most plausibly be construed as a test of moral worth rather than of outward rightness, and must always be applied with awareness that we lack certainty about what an agent's maxim is in a given case (and we have no guarantee against self-deception)" [1989, 98].
[74] There appears to be a consensus among commentators that an act that has legality (i.e. its maxim is consistent with the moral law) but not morality (i.e. it has not been adopted out of duty) is not evil. Allison, for instance, writes that "Moral evil itself... must consist for Kant in the adoption of maxims contrary to the law" [1990, 147]. Similarly, Korsgaard claims that "Kant's analysis identifies the rightness of the action essentially with the legal character of its maxim" [1996, 61]. While this interpretation might appeal to common sense, it is not Kant's position. As we will discuss in the text below, Kant holds that the moral value of an action depends only on its subjective determining ground—i.e. its highest maxim. Furthermore, he holds that an agent's highest maxim (his *Gesinnung*) is either good or evil: "[Z]wischen einer bösen und guten Gesinnung (innerem Prinzip der Maximen), nach welcher auch die Moralität der Handlung beurteilt werden muss, gibt es... nichts Mittleres" [R, VI, 22]. It follows from this—*pace* Allison and Korsgaard—that an action committed by an agent whose highest maxim is the principle of self-love is evil, regardless of whether it has legality or not.
[75] We will discuss this point about the morality of an action as determined by the subjective determining ground of the will in more detail in the text below.

einer Handlung mit dem Gesetze ohne Rücksicht auf die Triebfeder derselben die Legalität (Gesetzmäßigkeit), diejenige aber, in welcher die Idee der Pflicht aus dem Gesetze zugleich die Triebfeder der Handlung ist, die Moralität (Sittlichkeit) derselben" [MS, VI, 219].

This definition of legality as determined by the formal properties of our maxims in combination with *agnosticism about maxims*—i.e. the claim that we cannot know what these maxims are—should lead us to expect Kant to hold that we can never be certain about the legality of our actions. However, he embraces exactly the opposite position, namely that we have no doubt concerning the legality of our actions, even if we can never be certain of their morality: "[E]s ist dem Menschen nicht möglich so in die Tiefe seines eigenen Herzens einzuschauen, dass er jemals von der Reinigkeit seiner moralischen Absicht und der Lauterkeit seiner Gesinnung auch nur in einer Handlung völlig gewiss sein könnte; *wenn er gleich über die Legalität derselben gar nicht zweifelhaft ist*" [MS, VI, 292; my emphasis][76]. That is to say, Kant sees no reason for any doubt on our part about the formal properties of our maxims. This is difficult to square with the suggestion that we do not know what these maxims are.

A last reason for rejecting *agnosticism about maxims* is that we clearly are—at least sometimes—consciously choosing principles on which to act ("I will go to

---

[76] Kant highlights that given our apparently impeccable behavior might be due not to the moral quality of our character, but merely to moral luck (i.e. our not having been exposed to temptations that would have revealed our true character): "[W]elcher Mensch kennt sich selbst, wer kennt andre so durch und durch, um zu entscheiden: ob, wenn er von den Ursachen seines vermeintlich wohlgeführten Lebenswandels alles, was man Verdienst des Glücks nennt, als sein angebornes gutartiges Temperament, die natürliche größere Stärke seiner obern Kräfte (des Verstandes und der Vernunft, um seine Triebe zu zähmen), überdem auch noch die Gelegenheit, wo ihm der Zufall glücklicherweise viele Versuchungen ersparte, die einen andern trafen; wenn er dies alles von seinem wirklichen Charakter absonderte… ; wer will dann entscheiden, sage ich, [ob er] … seinem innern moralischen Werte nach… noch irgend einen Vorzug vor dem andern habe" [ED, VIII, 329–30]. In fact, he points out, uncertainty about the determining ground of our will opens up the possibility that there might never have been, in the history of mankind, a single fully moral action: "Vielleicht mag nie ein Mensch seine erkannte und von ihm auch verehrte Pflicht ganz uneigennützig (ohne Beimischung anderer Triebfedern) ausgeübt haben; vielleicht wird auch nie einer bei der größten Bestrebung so weit gelangen" [TP, VIII, 284–5].

Timmerman misunderstands Kant's concern about the uncertainty of the determining ground of our will by interpreting it as a concern about the uncertainty of our ends: "Kant sieht… prinzipielle Schwierigkeiten [im] Bereich der Selbsterkenntnis, denn es muss oft unklar bleiben, welche Zwecke man tatsächlich mit seinem Tun verfolgt" [2003, 154]. This points to a failure to heed the important distinction between the notion of an end, on the one hand, and that of the determining ground of the will, on the other, which we have discussed in note 67 above.

the bank to get some money"), in a way that the suggestion that these principles are by their very nature unknowable is simply implausible (which makes attributing such a view to Kant uncharitable, to say the least).

I take all of this to suggest strongly that we should reject interpretations of Kant's notion of maxims according to which it is impossible for us to know our own maxims[77]. While this conclusion sounds innocuous (which non-philosopher would think it is contentious to say that it is not impossible for us to know the principles on which we act?), it has important implications for Kant's conception of moral value. Most importantly, it forces us to reject Kant's suggestion that the moral value of our actions depends on our maxims, as we will discuss in the following point.

- The fourth problem with Kant's theory of action is his insistence that the moral value of our actions depends on the maxims on which they are based. As we have seen above, the suggestion that we cannot be aware of our own maxims flows directly from the two claims that, first, the moral value of our actions depends on our maxims and, second, that we can never be certain of the moral value of our actions. Hence, if we want to resist the conclusion that we cannot be aware of our own maxims, we have to reject one of the two premises that lead to it. I will argue that it is the claim that the moral value of our actions depends on our maxims that we can—and should—do without (*pace* Frierson[78]). To see why this is the case, we have to focus on two further claims that Kant makes in discussing his theory of moral value:

c) *The moral value of our actions depends on the determining ground of our will*
As we have seen, Kant holds that a given action has moral value if the determining ground of our will in committing the action has been duty, i. e. our commitment to following the moral law: "Das Wesentliche alles sittlichen Werts der Handlungen kommt darauf an, dass das moralische Gesetz unmittelbar den Willen bestimme" [KpV, V, 71; see also KpV, V, 151]. That is, in the terminology that we

---

[77] A possible escape route of those holding that, according to Kant, we cannot know our maxims is to claim that there is not one kind of maxim, but that Kant is operating with many kinds of maxims [Allison, 1990, 93]. I believe there is some truth to this claim, as my endorsement of the distinction between the notions of first-order maxims and the highest maxim shows. However, this simple distinction between first-order maxims and the highest maxim would not suffice to solve the problems here discussed. That is, those holding that we don't know (at least some kinds of) our maxims would have to offer further distinctions between different kinds of maxims—distinctions that are simply not made by Kant himself.
[78] "For Kant, the moral status of an action depends on the maxim that underlies that action" [Frierson, 2003, 72].

have settled on above, the moral value of our action depends on the subjective determining ground of our will (i.e., our highest maxim, the principle determining which kind of incentives we act on)[79].

d) *In deciding on how to act, we "incorporate" the determining ground of our will into our maxim*
Kant often speaks as if choosing a maxim on the basis of a certain determining ground involves "incorporating" that determining ground into the maxim. One example is the following passage in *Religion:* "[Je nachdem ob] er die Triebfedern, die diese Anlage enthält, in seine Maxime aufnimmt oder nicht (welches seiner freien Wahl gänzlich überlassen sein muss), macht er, dass er gut oder böse wird" [R, VI, 44; see also: R, VI, 29].

Claim c) is the central element of Kant's theory of moral value: what gives moral value to an action is not the end for which it is committed, but the subjective determining ground of our maxim—i.e. that which moves us to commit the action. An action only has moral value if it is motivated by duty, i.e. the thought that committing the action is demanded by the moral law. That is, what matters, morally speaking, is our ground for adopting our maxims (namely, our highest maxim).

If Kant also claims that the moral value of our action depends on the maxim on which it is committed, then it is because of claim d)—namely, the claim that the determining ground of our maxim is "incorporated" into, i.e. is part of, the maxim[80]. Thus, the moral value of our actions depends on the subjective deter-

---

[79] In the context of our discussion concerning the three types of determining ground of our will we can note that the moral value of our actions does not depend on the objective determining ground of our actions, for the objective determining ground would be the same for all wills and all actions (the set of principles allowing for the proper use of our practical reason, namely the moral law). Furthermore, the moral value of our action cannot be determined by our incentives, for in any situation, both incentives for selfish and for moral action are present, as Kant emphasizes in *Religion:* "Der Mensch (selbst der ärgste) tut, in welchen Maximen es auch sei, auf das moralische Gesetz nicht gleichsam rebellischerweise (mit Aufkündigung des Gehorsams) Verzicht. Dieses dringt sich ihm vielmehr Kraft seiner moralischen Anlage unwiderstehlich auf... Er hängt aber doch auch vermöge seiner gleichfalls schuldlosen Naturanlage an den Triebfedern der Sinnlichkeit und nimmt sie (nach dem subjektiven Prinzip der Selbstliebe) auch in seine Maxime auf... Da er nun natürlicherweise beide in dieselbe aufnimmt, da er auch jede für sich, wenn sie allein wäre, zur Willensbestimmung hinreichend finden würde... [muss] der Unterschied, ob der Mensch gut oder böse sei, nicht in dem Unterschiede der Triebfedern, die er in seine Maxime aufnimmt (nicht in dieser ihrer Materie), sondern in der Unterordnung (der Form derselben) liegen: welche von beiden er zur Bedingung der andern macht" [R, VI, 36].
[80] See, for instance, the following passage: "Nun ist zwar klar, dass diejenigen Bestimmungsgründe des Willens, *welche allein die Maximen eigentlich moralisch machen* und ihnen einen sit-

mining ground of our maxim; yet, it also depends on our maxim, given that the determining ground is part of the maxim. Thus, claim a)—i.e., the claim that the moral value of our action depends on the maxim on which it is based—follows from claims c) and d)—and leads when combined with claim b)—i.e., the claim that we can never be certain about the moral value of our actions—to the problematic conclusion that we cannot know our maxim, which we have rejected above.

However, there is good reason to hold that claim d) is suspicious: if we formulate a maxim of action, it is plausible to assume that it contains the specification of a means to achieve an end ("I will jump into the river to save the girl's life")—but the suggestion that such a rule of action also contains the reason for its own adoption (i.e. that the determining ground of our decision to adopt a certain maxim is "incorporated" into the maxim) is questionable, especially in light of the fact that Kant believes that we can never be certain what that reason is. It seems far more in the spirit of his approach to say that we choose a maxim that specifies a certain action in a given context to achieve a certain end without us being able to know with certainty what led us adopt this maxim (this was precisely the reason for which Kant introduced the notion of the highest maxim as the merely postulated determining ground of our choice of maxim in the first place)[81].

That is, there is a good reason to reject claim d)—i.e., the claim that choosing a maxim involves "incorporating" the determining ground of our will into our maxim. However, as we have just seen, claim d) is the basis for accepting claim a)—i.e. the notion that the moral value of our maxims depends on the maxim on which it is based. Thus, if we reject claim d), we have little reason to accept claim a). Hence, on reflection, in spite of Kant's assertions to the contrary, we should reject the notion that the moral value of our action depends on our maxims.

According to the resulting account of Kant's theory of action, our maxim would simply specify the action we intend to conduct and the end it is set to ach-

---

tlichen Wert geben, die unmittelbare Vorstellung des Gesetzes und die objektiv notwendige Befolgung desselben als Pflicht, als die eigentlichen Triebfedern der Handlungen vorgestellt werden müssen" [KpV, V, 151, my emphasis].

81 This is supported by Allison's observation that the agent's reason for adopting a given maxim does typically not feature in the examples Kant gives of maxims (yet, he cites [GMS, IV, 422] as an exception: "Seine Maxime aber ist: ich mache es mir *aus Selbstliebe* zum Princip, wenn das Leben bei seiner längern Frist mehr Übel droht, als es Annehmlichkeit verspricht, es mir abzukürzen" [my emphasis]). Allison's suggests we should understand the underlying determining ground as being only "implicit in the maxim" and as being "part of its 'deep structure'" [1990, 90]. However, there is nothing in Kant's texts to support this suggestion.

ieve—yet, it would not specify the underlying subjective determining ground that leads us to adopt the maxim. We would be aware of our maxim; however, we could not know with certainty what led us to adopt it (i.e., what our highest maxim is)[82]—and, hence, would be unable to be sure about the moral value of our action. Furthermore, it would be possible for two agents to act on the same maxim in two different cases—and yet for the resulting action to have moral value in one case but not in the other (depending on what led the agents to adopt their maxims in each case). An example could be two persons who save a third from drowning, acting on the maxim "I will jump into the water to save Peter"—either because they believe it is morally demanded of them or because they want to be admired as heroes. The maxims would be the same in both cases, yet the moral value of the action would not[83].

Under this interpretation of Kant's theory of action, it still makes sense to test our maxims for their universalizability. However, the moral value of the action does not depend on the maxim, but rather on why we have chosen it. That is, merely from the fact that a certain maxim passes the universalizability test, it does not follow that an action based on that maxim has moral value. Rather, an action has moral value only if we have chosen it *because* it has the form of a law (i.e. would not have chosen it had it not passed the universalizability test). In consequence, uncertainty about the moral value of our actions is due to uncer-

---

82 This crucial distinction between a maxim and the determining ground of a maxim is not respected by O'Neill when she writes: "It may not be easy to tell on which maxim a given act was performed. For example, a person who helps somebody else in a public place may have the underlying intention of being helpful—or alternatively the underlying intention of fostering a certain sort of good reputation" [1989, 85]. One explanation for her view, though, could be that she operates on the assumption—rejected above—that the determining ground of the maxim is part of the maxim.

83 This is consistent with Allison's emphasis on the "the intuition (central to Kant's moral theory) that we can adopt a given maxim for a number of distinct reasons, not all of which are of equal moral significance" [1990, 189]. Timmermann chooses a different solution. He holds that we should regard the underlying determining ground to be part of the maxim—in a way that actions of different moral quality have to be regarded as based on different maxims: "Es ist das entscheidende Merkmal von Maximen (im Gegensatz zu bloßen Regeln), dass sie nicht nur (a) die Absicht spezifizieren, dies oder das zu tun, wenn (b) eine bestimmte Situation gegeben ist, sondern auch (c) den zugrunde liegenden Zweck, den man mit der Absicht verfolgt... [So führen die] drei Arten der Motivation [im Krämer Beispiel] zu drei verschiedenen Maximen. Nur so ist erklärlich, dass Kant immer wieder die Maximen als den locus moralischer Bewertung anführt" [2003, 78n]. As I have pointed out above, this position in combination with Kant's claim that we cannot be certain about the moral value of our actions leads to the undesirable conclusion that we cannot know our own maxims. This, I have argued, is a good reason to reject Timmermann's suggestion.

tainty about the reason for which we choose our maxims—not uncertainty about which maxims we have chosen.
– Fifthly, there are at least three problems that arise from Kant's use of the notion of the highest maxim. The first is linked to the claims that: a) the moral value of our action is determined by the subjective determining ground of our will (i.e. our highest maxim), and b) that this highest maxim is a single principle of choice on the basis of which we select our first-order maxims[84].

The problem is that, taken together, these two specifications of the role played by the notion of the highest maxim imply that all actions of a given agent have the same moral value. For Kant suggests that we have to think of the highest maxim as a single principle governing our individual decisions to adopt or not to adopt a given maxim [R, VI, 25]. Yet, if there is, for a given agent, just one highest maxim and if, furthermore, the moral value of a given action depends on the subjective determining ground of the maxim (i.e., the highest maxim), then all actions of a given individual have the same moral value. This clearly is a counter-intuitive claim, for it implies that a single evil action by a given agent would make it impossible for him to commit any actions that have moral value. However, there is some evidence that Kant is willing to accept this implication of his theory, for instance when he writes that a single evil act of a given agent allows us to infer that his actions generally are guided by an evil highest maxim: "[Der böse Mensch kann] nicht in einigen Stücken sittlich gut, in andern zugleich böse sein. Denn ist er in einem gut, so hat er das moralische Gesetz in seine Maxime aufgenommen; sollte er also in einem andern Stücke zugleich böse sein, so würde, weil das moralische Gesetz der Befolgung der Pflicht überhaupt nur ein einziges und allgemein ist, die auf dasselbe bezogene Maxime allgemein, zugleich aber nur eine besondere Maxime sein: welches sich widerspricht" [R, VI, 24].

The second problem with the notion of the highest good is linked to Kant's claim, discussed above, that we have to conceive our highest maxim as the product of a noumenal choice—i.e. a choice that we do not actually make as empirical agents, but that is a mere projection, a mere idea of reason (i.e. to arrive at a coherent conception of ourselves as free agents we have to regard the choices of our first-order maxims *as if* they were made on the basis of a highest maxim).

---

[84] As we have highlighted above, the highest maxim is a mere postulate: while we are aware of ourselves as choosing our maxims, we can never be certain what moved us to choose a certain maxim—and the thought construct of the highest maxim is a way to conceive of this choice as free, as grounded in a free choice by our own noumenal self concerning our fundamental moral disposition.

However, allowing for the possibility of a noumenal choice of the principle of self-love as our highest maxim involves Kant in a *prima facie* contradiction. For, as we have seen above, he holds that we have to regard our noumenal self as pure practical reason, unaffected by the influence of our desires and, hence, necessarily guided in its activity by the interests of reason. This means that Kant's conception of our noumenal self has no resources to explain what could lead this necessarily-moral noumenal self to adopt the principle of self-love as its highest maxim, in a way that it would give priority to the interests of our sensuous nature over those of our reason.

We could try to argue that Kant should be understood here to be operating with two different thought constructs—on the one hand, the ideal vision of ourselves as free intelligences whose activities are necessarily governed by the moral law and, on the other, the notion of the non-empirical choice of our fundamental maxim as an idea of reason, a mere projection required for us to make sense of our predicament as agents. We could then claim that once these two thought constructs are carefully distinguished, the contradiction apparently involved in the notion of a noumenal choice in favour of the principle of self-love disappears. However, the problem with this solution is that it effectively denies that we can attribute the choice of our fundamental maxim to our noumenal self. This then raises the question of who exactly should be conceived as the author of this choice—and Kant's theory of the will has no resources to answer this question.

The third problem with the notion of the highest maxim is that conceiving it both as the determinant of the moral value of our actions and the product of a timeless choice makes it difficult to account for the possibility of moral progress. For the notion of moral progress involves that of improving the moral quality of our actions over time. Yet, it is difficult to see how this is possible if the moral quality of our actions is dependent on a timeless choice. Nonetheless, Kant explicitly allows for the possibility of moral progress (i.e., the transition of a state in which our highest maxim is the principle of self-love to one in which our highest maxim is the moral law[85]). He admits, though, that his theory cannot explain

---

[85] "Dass aber jemand nicht bloß ein gesetzlich, sondern ein moralisch guter (Gott wohlgefälliger) Mensch, d. i. tugendhaft nach dem intelligiblen Charakter (virtus Noumenon), werde, welcher, wenn er etwas als Pflicht erkennt, keiner andern Triebfeder weiter bedarf, als dieser Vorstellung der Pflicht selbst: das kann nicht durch allmähliche Reform, so lange die Grundlage der Maximen unlauter bleibt, sondern muss durch eine Revolution in der Gesinnung im Menschen (einen Übergang zur Maxime der Heiligkeit derselben) bewirkt werden; und er kann ein neuer Mensch nur durch eine Art von Wiedergeburt gleich als durch eine neue Schöpfung... und Änderung des Herzens werden" [R, VI, 47].

how such progress is possible. However, he holds that this difficulty should not be regarded as a shortcoming of his theory, but rather as due to the fact that the possibility of moral progress is simply not amenable to explanation:

> Wie es nun möglich sei, dass ein natürlicherweise böser Mensch sich selbst zum guten Menschen mache, das übersteigt alle unsere Begriffe; denn wie kann ein böser Baum gute Früchte bringen? Da aber doch nach dem vorher abgelegten Geständnisse ein ursprünglich (der Anlage nach) guter Baum arge Früchte hervorgebracht hat und der Verfall vom Guten ins Böse (wenn man wohl bedenkt, dass dieses aus der Freiheit entspringt) nicht begreiflicher ist, als das Wiederaufstehen aus dem Bösen zum Guten: so kann die Möglichkeit des letztern nicht bestritten werden. [R, VI, 45]

- A last problem with Kant's account of action on maxims is the important—yet, underdiscussed—question of whether it is a descriptive or a normative account. That is, it is not clear whether Kant's position is that acting on maxims is simply something that we do, or whether he thinks it is something that we have a talent for, that we can do and *should* do—and, hence, something that we can fail to do. That is, it is not clear whether our acting on maxims is a simple fact about us as agents (if one that only appears from the practical perspective) or whether our acting on maxims constitutes an achievement that we have to struggle to establish and maintain.

On the face of it, there is no problem here, given that Kant clearly states that a maxim is a principle on which the subject acts (for instance, "[Die Maxime ist] der Grundsatz, nach welchem das Subjekt handelt" [GMS, IV, 420n; see also: E, 1924, 52]). Yet, there are other passages in which the ability to act on maxims is portrayed not as a mere given, but as an achievement. In *Metaphysik der Sitten*, for instance, Kant writes: "Es ist [dem Menschen] Pflicht: sich aus der Rohheit seiner Natur, aus der Tierheit..., immer mehr zur Menschheit, durch die er allein fähig ist sich Zwecke zu setzen, empor zu arbeiten" [MS, VI, 387]. This suggests that our ability to set ends for ourselves (i.e. to act on maxims) is not simply a given, but something that we have to make an effort to achieve.

A similar point is made in Kant's lectures on pedagogy: "Die moralische Kultur muss sich gründen auf Maximen, nicht auf Disziplin... Man muss dahin sehen, dass das Kind sich gewöhne, nach Maximen und nicht nach gewissen Triebfedern zu handeln... Die erste Bemühung bei der moralischen Erziehung ist, einen Charakter zu gründen. Der Charakter besteht in der Fertigkeit, nach Maximen zu handeln" [IX, 480]. Here Kant not only describes the ability to act on maxims as a goal of education (i.e., something that can either be achieved or missed), but also defines "character" as the ability to act on maxims[86]. Given that for Kant our character is the result of a lifelong effort [A, VII, 321], this again suggests that our ability to act on maxims is not a mere fact about us, to be taken for granted, but rather a talent that we have to nurture and develop.

Both passages suggest that Kant considers acting on maxims as a skill that has to be developed—and that we can fail to develop. *Prima facie*, this suggestion seems to be inconsistent with the *Incorporation Thesis*, highlighted above, according to which we only act on the basis of maxims. However, if we read Kant's own statement of that *Thesis* carefully, we find that he does not actually say that all action is based on maxims, but rather that action on maxims is a mark of the *free* will: "Die Freiheit der Willkür ist von der ganz eigentümlichen Beschaffenheit, dass sie durch keine Triebfeder zu einer Handlung bestimmt werden kann, als nur sofern der Mensch sie in seine Maxime aufgenommen hat (es sich zur allgemeinen Regel gemacht hat, nach der er sich verhalten will)" [R, VI, 23].

Hence, the *Incorporation Thesis* is consistent with the normative reading of maxims: according to this reading we sometimes act on impulse or out of habit—and yet have the capacity to make rules that guide our action. However, this is a capacity we have to train and practice, not something we can count on as a given. This thought is in line with Kant's overall teaching, which highlights that our rational faculties are a recent development in human existence, that our rational control over our own lives is still shaky and that we are faced with the task of improving it[87].

Thus, although the textual evidence is far from clear, there appears to be some basis for understanding Kant's account of maxims as a normative account, according to which we have the talent for acting on maxims, but do not always realize this talent[88]. On this interpretation of Kant's position, the ability to act on

---

[86] This definition is partial. Other passages make it clear that Kant regards one's character as defined not only by the fact that we act on maxims, but also by the (moral) quality of the maxims we act on (see, for instance, [KpV, V, 152]). We will discuss the notion of a character in more detail in Chapter 8 below.

[87] We will discuss this topic in more detail in Chapter 8 below.

[88] This view is shared by Beck: "The Willkür, however, can fail to exercise its freedom or realize its potentiality of being free in a negative sense; then it gives way to the importunities of sense and is a will in name only, really being an aribitrium brutum" [1960, 203]). Wood's discussion of the topic is less clear, but he also seems to agree that we should not ascribe to Kant the position that all action is action on maxims: "The Incorporation Thesis ... does not say that volitional agency consists merely in the adoption of maxims... The most Kant needs (or wants) to claim... is that to be a volitional agent one must have the *capacity* to adopt maxims, and to respond to desires by incorporating (or refusing to incorporate) them into maxims" [1999, 52, my

rules chosen by reflective thought is an achievement—and a fragile one at that: we have managed to lift ourselves out of our animal condition of being guided in our actions by our sensuous desires, but nothing assures that we will not slip back into this condition ("Der Gang der Menschengattung zur Erreichung ihrer ganzen Bestimmung scheint daher unaufhörlich unterbrochen und in kontinuierlicher Gefahr zu sein, in die alte Rohheit zurückzufallen" [MAM, VIII, 116]).

If this is right, we should reject interpretations of the Kantian opus according to which "Kant holds that (mere reflex action apart) we always act on some maxim" [O'Neill, 1989, 151]. Rather, we should read Kant as demanding two things from us: first, that we act on maxims (i.e. that we make an effort to determine our actions on the basis of reflectively endorsed rules)—and that we act on *moral* maxims (i.e. that we make the moral law, rather than the principle of self-love, the subjective determining ground of our actions)[89].

Once we accept this normative reading of Kant's theory of acting on maxims, we are able to account the common sense observation, noted above, that we are often not aware of having formed any maxim before engaging in an action: we often act out of habit, perhaps by repeating acts for which at some point we reflected on an appropriate rule of action and which since then we have come to execute automatically. That is, we often fail to comply with Kant's first demand, i.e. to guide our action on the basis of rules chosen on the basis of reflection. For Kant, good action is action guided by self-reflective thought on the basis of the demands of our reason. By often failing consciously to reflect on the rules on which we act, we do not always meet the standard he sets for us.

---

emphasis; see also: Timmermann, 2003, 178]. Lastly, Köhl agrees that there is a question here that requires an answer: "Es ist nicht klar, ob Kant der Meinung war, dass jedes Handeln ein Handeln nach Maximen ist" [1990, 59].

89 O'Neill recognizes this double demand: "The test that Kant's Formula of Universal Law proposes for the moral acceptability of acts has two aspects. In the first place it enjoins us to act on a maxim; secondly, it restricts us to action on those maxims through which we can will at the same time that they should be universal laws" [1989, 83]. Yet, her recognition sits uncomfortably with her claim that "acting on a maxim does not require explicit or conscious or complete formulation of that maxim. Even routine or thoughtless or indecisive action is action on some maxim" [1989, 84]. For the latter position strongly suggests that O'Neill holds that any action for Kant counts as action on a maxim (i.e. that she subscribes to the descriptive reading of Kant's notion of acting on maxims, as is also suggested by the quote of hers we just encountered in the text above). However, if any action were by default an action on a maxim then it is difficult to understand why Kant would "enjoin us to act on a maxim".

Conclusion

The following account of Kant's theory of the will emerges from our discussion: according to Kant, we have the ability to guide our actions on the basis of maxims, i.e. rules chosen by self-reflective thought (yet, sometimes we fail fully to make use of this talent, by acting from habit or on impulse, rather than going through the trouble of consciously forming rules of action). Actions on maxims have two different determining grounds: one based in our sensuous nature, namely the incentive (either a desire—or the feeling of respect) that gives us an interest in the action in the first place and one based on self-reflective thought, namely the subjective determining ground of our maxims (i.e. the principle underlying the choice of our maxim). Kant calls the latter our highest maxim. The choice of this highest maxim is a mere idea of reason—a mere postulate required to explain the possibility of free action in a world of natural necessity. Consequently, we can have no experience of this choice—and can never be certain what actually leads us to choose one maxim rather than another. Thus, while we are aware of the maxims on which we act, we can never be sure about our reasons for adopting them. Given that, for Kant, the moral value of our actions depends on this reason for adopting our maxims (i.e. depends on the subjective determining ground of our maxims), this means that we can never be certain about the moral value of our actions. Hence, even where our actions and their underlying maxims are in line with the demands of the moral law (i.e. even if our maxim has legality) and even if we are confident that we have adopted the maxims *because* they were demanded by the moral law, we can never exclude the possibility that another motive—self-love—has played a part in the determination of our action.

6 Value

In Chapter 4, we traced the structure of Kant's argument establishing our consciousness of the moral law as a fact of pure reason. As a corollary, this argument grounds the objective reality of our transcendental freedom, if only from a practical point of view (in the sense explained above). Kant calls this status of ours as transcendentally free agents, certified by our moral consciousness, our personality. In the present chapter, we will explore Kant's claims that human beings, insofar as they are endowed with personality, have to be regarded as ends-in-themselves (i. e., as beings to which we have to attribute value, regardless of which idiosyncratic interests we happen to have)—and as the final end of creation (i.e. that for the purpose of which the whole of the natural world exists). In this process, I will try to show that these claims are not the extravagant dogmas they first appear to be, but are rather well grounded in Kant's theory of value.

The predispositions of human nature

Before we start our discussion of Kant's theory of value, we have to introduce some new terminology. As we have seen in Chapter 5 above, Kant distinguishes not only between our physical nature and reason, but also between a technical-practical use of reason (reason insofar as it is used as a tool for satisfying our interests as natural beings) and a moral-practical use of reason (reason insofar as it aims at satisfying its own essential interests). In *Religion*, he calls the resulting three aspects of our existence the three predispositions (Anlagen) of human nature, referring to them as animality (*Tierheit*), humanity (*Menschheit*) and personality (*Persönlichkeit* [R, VI, 26]). *Tierheit* is our physical nature, the entirety of our drives and desires [MS, VI, 420][1], while *Menschheit* "encompasses all our rational capacities having no specific reference to morality" [Wood, 1999, 118]. In particular, it involves our ability to set ends [MS, VI, 392] and, thus, to guide our actions on the basis of conscious thought. That is, *Menschheit* is our talent for the technical-practical use of reason (linked to the notions of reflective distance and negative freedom, discussed in Chapter 5 above). It is the ability to step back from, and reflect on, our desires and act only on those that we reflectively endorse. Lastly, *Persönlichkeit* is our status as transcendentally free agents,

---

[1] For a discussion in the secondary literature on Kant's notion of *Tierheit*, see [Allison, 1990, 148].

as certified by the fact of reason[2]. Insofar as we have *Persönlichkeit* we are capable of guiding our actions on the basis of our essential interests rather than being determined in our actions by natural necessity—and, hence, are accountable for these actions [MS, VI, 223].

As we have highlighted in our discussion of Kant's shift away from the *Grundlegung* account of the foundations of morality to the fact-of-reason argument offered in *Kritik der Praktischen Vernunft*, Kant in his mature work is adamant on the distinction between the technical-practical and the moral-practical use of reason—or, in our new terminology, between *Menschheit* and *Persönlichkeit*[3]:

> Daraus, dass ein Wesen Vernunft hat, [folgt] gar nicht, dass diese ein Vermögen enthalte, die Willkür unbedingt durch die bloße Vorstellung der Qualifikation ihrer Maximen zur allgemeinen Gesetzgebung zu bestimmen und also für sich selbst praktisch zu sein: wenigstens so

---

[2] "Wenn wir die genannten drei Anlagen [Tierheit, Menschheit, Persönlichkeit] nach den Bedingungen ihrer Möglichkeit betrachten, so finden wir, dass die erste keine Vernunft, die zweite zwar praktische, aber nur andern Triebfedern dienstbare, die dritte aber allein für sich selbst praktische, d. i. unbedingt gesetzgebende, Vernunft zur Wurzel habe" [R, VI, 28]. On the notion of personality, see also [KpV, V, 87] and [MS, VI, 239].

[3] Given the hybrid structure of Kant's anthropology, we should expect him to offer us a picture of human nature built around two elements: our physical nature and reason. In fact, this is still the case in his essay on the conjectural history of mankind, published in 1786 [MAM, VIII, 116n]. However, once Kant takes the position that the validity of the moral law and our status as transcendentally free cannot be directly inferred from our status as rational beings (as explored in Chapter 4 above), he sees himself forced to distinguish between our capacity for rational agency, on the one hand, and our status as transcendentally free agents, on the other—i.e. to adopt the distinction between humanity and personality he offers in *Religion*. However, there are at least two problems with seeing humanity and personality as distinct predispositions of human nature. First, it is difficult to make sense of the notion of humanity as a self-standing predisposition, given that it would, by itself, be a defective form of reason, one not guided by its own interests, in spite of the fact that Kant holds, as we have seen in Chapter 1, that reason is essentially an interested faculty. Secondly, some of the uses Kant makes of the term 'humanity' are inconsistent with the distinction between personality and humanity, for instance when he writes that "Mit dem Zwecke der Menschheit in unserer eigenen Person ist also auch der Vernunftwille, mithin die Pflicht verbunden, sich um die Menschheit durch Kultur überhaupt verdient zu machen" [MS, VI, 392]. This last issue can be addressed by assuming that Kant is operating with a narrow and a wide conception of humanity, where the former is distinct from personality, while the latter includes the notion of personality, in the same way in which he is best understood as operating with a narrow and a wide conception of reason (see Chapter 1). Such an interpretation seems to be supported by passages like the following in *Metaphysik der Sitten:* "Die Menschheit selbst ist eine Würde; denn der Mensch kann von keinem Menschen... bloß als Mittel... gebraucht werden, und darin besteht eben seine Würde (die Persönlichkeit), dadurch er sich über alle andere Weltwesen... erhebt" [MS, VI, 462; see also: MS, VI, 239]).

viel wir einsehen können. Das allervernünftigste Weltwesen könnte doch immer gewisser Triebfedern, die ihm von Objekten der Neigung herkommen, bedürfen, um seine Willkür zu bestimmen; hiezu aber die vernünftigste Überlegung, sowohl was die größte Summe der Triebfedern, als auch die Mittel, den dadurch bestimmten Zweck zu erreichen, betrifft, anwenden: ohne auch nur die Möglichkeit von so etwas, als das moralische, schlechthin gebietende Gesetz ist, welches sich als selbst und zwar höchste Triebfeder ankündigt, zu ahnen. Wäre dieses Gesetz nicht in uns gegeben, wir würden es als ein solches durch keine Vernunft herausklügeln [R, VI, 26n].

As a consequence, Kant insists that our mere status as rational beings is not sufficient to ascribe transcendental freedom to ourselves (in a way that our being endowed with humanity would be a sufficient ground for ascribing personality to ourselves); rather, a further element is required to secure the objective reality of the latter (this further element being, as we have seen above, our awareness of being subject to the demands of morality)[4].

It is personality alone that allows us to breach the immanence of the empirical world: if we were endowed with only *Tierheit* and *Menschheit*, this would be consistent with us being fully and only part of the empirical world. The assumption of a noumenal character would be neither necessary nor warranted. Without personality, that is, our existence could be explained as a purely physical-mechanical phenomenon (for even our negative freedom, without the guarantee of the objective reality given to our transcendental freedom by the fact of reason argument, could, for all we know, just be "nature again" [KrV, III, 521][5]). Thus, it

---

4 This crucial point is not always respected in the secondary literature. An example is Guyer, who writes that: "[I]t is precisely the capacity to set and consent to ends and the capacities necessary for us to pursue those ends in which humanity as Kant conceives it consists; the idea of humanity as an end in itself, in other words, is identical to the idea of the incomparable dignity of human autonomy or freedom governed by the law that we give to ourselves" [2000, 10]. This sentence, apart from containing a *non sequitur* (why should it follow from the fact that humanity consists in our ability to set ends that the idea of humanity is identical to the idea of dignity?), rides roughshod over Kant's distinction between humanity and personality: the sentence starts by focusing on humanity (our ability to set ends) and finishes by speaking about personality (our transcendentally freedom, which, as we will see below, is the ground for our status as ends in ourselves), without acknowledging any transition. Rosen [1993, 65], Wood [1999, 120] and Rawls [2004, 30 – 31] provide further illustrations of the dangers of not respecting the distinction between humanity and personality. We will discuss these passages in some more detail in the text below. Allison, on the other hand, is clear in highlighting the importance of the distinction: "Kant regards [personality] as a separate predisposition, distinct from the predisposition to humanity. In so doing, he affirms that our status as persons in the full sense, that is as moral agents, cannot be derived from our status as rational animals" [1990, 149].

5 In this case, our negative freedom would collapse into merely psychological freedom, in the sense discussed in note 52 in Chapter 5 above.

is only the attribution of personality that elevates us above the status of mere things of nature[6].

Kant's theory of value

With our account of the human predispositions in place, we can start exploring Kant's theory of value, in which—as we will see—the notion of personality plays a central role. In fact, only a good grasp of that notion will allow us to make sense of Kant's assertions that human beings are ends in themselves, have absolute value and have to regard themselves as the final end of creation.

The first important point to establish in discussing Kant's theory of value is that value, for Kant, is not a natural property (i.e., a property of the world as it is independent of us), but something that we project onto the world. Consequently, nature by itself is without value [KrV, III, 371; see also: MAM, VIII, 115]. There is only value because we project it into the world[7]. That is to say, the only kind of value there is in the world is value *for us*[8]. We project value, Kant holds, by willing—that is, by choosing something as our end. To choose something as our end is to attribute value to it, to regard it as good [KU, V, 207][9]. In this sense, the good is the object of the will ("Denn das Gute ist das Objekt des Willens" [KU, V, 209]).

Crucially, there are for Kant two types of the good[10], related to the two aspects of our will that we have discussed in Chapter 5:

---

6 Kant holds that our moral experience is both elevating and humbling. It elevates us in that it justifies us in attributing to ourselves noumenal existence—and, hence, transcendental freedom: "[Die]echte Triebfeder der reinen praktischen Vernunft beschaffen... ist keine andere als das reine moralische Gesetz selber, so fern es uns die Erhabenheit unserer eigenen übersinnlichen Existenz spüren lässt" [KpV, V, 88]. Yet, our moral experience is also humbling in that it involves the demand that we give up our self-love (i.e. our tendency to make the pursuit of happiness the highest principle of our will) [KpV, V, 74].
7 "Denn (so urteilt ein jeder): Bestände die Welt aus lauter leblosen, oder zwar zum Teil aus lebenden, aber vernunftlosen Wesen, so würde das Dasein einer solchen Welt gar keinen Wert haben, weil in ihr kein Wesen existierte, das von einem Werte den mindesten Begriff hat" [KU, V, 449]. Rawls comments: "[F]or Kant,... practical reason constructs for the will its own object out of itself and does not rely on a prior and antecedent order of values" [2000, 230].
8 Just as there is space and time only from the perspective of human beings [KrV, III, 55], so there is value only from the perspective of rational beings.
9 Hence, the good, for Kant, is a practical notion: not something to be contemplated, but something to be created [KU, V, 443; see also: Beck, 1960, 134; Korsgaard, 1996, 246].
10 In fact, Kant distinguishes between three types of good: the unconditional-objective (moral) good, the subjective good (our material ends, i.e. those ends that are chosen because they satisfy our sensuous desires) and that which functions as a means to achieve one of the other goods

- The empirical will that we have experience of and that is focused on obtaining that which allows us to satisfy our sensuous desires;
- The noumenal will of which we have no experience and which is a mere idea —yet, an idea whose objective reality we have to accept to make sense of the moral demands we find ourselves confronted with.

Corresponding to the two types of the will, we have two types of interests: our sensuous interests, on the one hand, and the interests of our reason, on the other [KU, V, 209][11]. With each of these types of interests is associated a type of object of the will:
- The object of the empirical will is material: the material object or state of affairs we want to achieve by means of our actions in order to satisfy our sensuous interests [GMS, IV, 427];

(the useful, [KU, V, 207]). The moral good and the subjective good are intrinsically good, i.e. we choose them for the satisfaction (either moral or sensuous) they afford us and not as a means for any further ends, while the useful is an extrinsic good (for it is chosen as a means for a further end). Consequently, Wood is mistaken when he denies that happiness—the ideal conception of the complete achievement of all of our material ends—is an intrinsic good [1999, 312]. Allison, on the other hand, recognizes that Kant considers happiness an intrinsic good [1990, 107n]. We will discuss Kant's notion of happiness in more detail in Chapter 7 below. Of the three types of good —the moral good, the subjective good and the useful –, only the former two are relevant for our present discussion. Hence, in the text we will only be dealing with these.

11 Kant holds that each of these interests is linked to a specific kind of pleasure (*Wohlgefallen*) which we experience when these interests are satisfied: "Das Angenehme und Gute haben beide eine Beziehung auf das Begehrungsvermögen und führen sofern, jenes ein pathologisch-bedingtes (durch Anreize, stimulos), dieses ein reines praktisches Wohlgefallen bei sich, welches nicht bloß durch die Vorstellung des Gegenstandes, sondern zugleich durch die vorgestellte Verknüpfung des Subjekts mit der Existenz desselben bestimmt wird. Nicht bloß der Gegenstand, sondern auch die Existenz desselben gefällt" [KU, V, 209]. That is, as we have seen in our discussion of the notion of the moral feeling in Chapter 5 above, Kant recognizes a pleasure *sui generis* that we experience when satisfying the interests of our rational faculties: "Das Wohlgefallen an einer Handlung um ihrer moralischen Beschaffenheit willen ist dagegen keine Lust des Genusses, sondern der Selbsttätigkeit und deren Gemäßheit mit der Idee seiner Bestimmung. Dieses Gefühl, welches das sittliche heißt, erfordert aber Begriffe und stellt keine freie, sondern gesetzliche Zweckmäßigkeit dar, lässt sich also auch nicht anders als vermittelst der Vernunft und, soll die Lust bei jedermann gleichartig sein, durch sehr bestimmte praktische Vernunftbegriffe allgemein mitteilen" [KU, V, 292]. This is linked to the notion of *Selbstzufriedenheit*, the state of contentment afforded to an agent who has managed to establish rational control over his own actions [KpV, V, 118]. We will discuss the notion of *Selbstzufriedenheit* in more detail in Chapter 8 below.

- The object of the noumenal will is formal: those conditions that allow for a use of our rational faculties in line with the interests of reason [R, VI, 5; see also: GMS, IV, 428].

Lastly, corresponding to these two types of object of the will there are two types of good:
- The subjective good that is the object of our empirical will—i.e. the material end that we choose in order to satisfy our sensuous desires [KU, V, 208][12];
- The objective good that is the satisfaction of the interests of reason, as codified in the moral law [KpV, V, 62–3].

The crucial difference here is between that which is only subjectively valuable (i.e. only from the viewpoint of the subject and linked to his idiosyncratic desires) and that which is objectively valuable (i.e. from the viewpoint of every rational being, by virtue of the fact that the principles determining its value are

---

[12] Kant sometimes speaks as if only the objective good were to count as the good ("Was wir gut nennen sollen, muss in jedes vernünftigen Menschen Urteil ein Gegenstand des Begehrungsvermögens sein" [KpV, V, 60]). Furthermore, he spends a considerable amount of time distinguishing between the good and the pleasant (for instance [GMS, IV, 413] and [KU, V, 210]). One could take this as evidence for the claim that he has no intention to recognize such a thing as a subjective good. However, he also wants to distinguish between relative ends, which only have value because of the specific desires of an individual agent, and objective ends that are valuable for all rational agents [GMS, IV, 427]. For this purpose, he requires a distinction between the ends that only have subjective value (i.e. those that give us pleasure because they satisfy a sensuous desire) and those that have objectively value (i.e. those that satisfy an interest of reason) of the kind he hints at in [KU, V, 209]. To the extent to which this essay is right to use the expressions "to have value" and "to be good" synonymously, this would require him to drop his suggestion that only the objectively good deserves to be called "good" and rather to adopt the distinction between the subjective good and the objective good. Kant frequently—and correctly—insists that the pleasant should not be considered good, because the good is a notion of reason and thus pleases indirectly (or, as Kant puts, it by means of a concept: "Gut ist das, was vermittelst der Vernunft durch den bloßen Begriff gefällt" [KU, V, 214]), while the pleasant is an object of our senses and thus pleases directly: "Der Zweck selbst, das Vergnügen, das wir suchen, ist im letzteren Falle nicht ein Gutes, sondern ein Wohl, nicht ein Begriff der Vernunft, sondern ein empirischer Begriff von einem Gegenstande der Empfindung" [KpV, V, 62]. However, this only means that we should not call the pleasant as such the subjectively good, but rather only consider it as the subjective good insofar as it has been adopted by the will as its end (i.e. insofar as it has become an object of the will). There is at least one passage in *Kritik der Urteilskraft* in which Kant appears to be accepting this position: "Das Angenehme, das... den Gegenstand lediglich in Beziehung auf den Sinn vorstellt, muss allererst durch den Begriff eines Zwecks unter Prinzipien der Vernunft gebracht werden, um es als Gegenstand des Willens gut zu nennen" [KU, V, 208].

valid for all rational beings[13]): "Praktisch gut ist aber, was vermittelst der Vorstellungen der Vernunft, mithin nicht aus subjektiven Ursachen, sondern objektiv, d. i. aus Gründen, die für jedes vernünftige Wesen als ein solches gültig sind, den Willen bestimmt" [GMS, IV, 413].

The objectively valuable is thus not a feature of the things in the world, but determined by the interests of our reason—and, hence, by the moral law (which codifies the conditions under which the interests of reason can be satisfied): "Hier ist nun der Ort, das Paradoxon der Methode in einer Kritik der praktischen Vernunft zu erklären: dass nämlich der Begriff des Guten und Bösen nicht vor dem moralischen Gesetze (dem er dem Anschein nach sogar zum Grunde gelegt werden müsste), sondern nur (wie hier auch geschieht) nach demselben und durch dasselbe bestimmt werden müsse" [KpV, V, 63; see also: GMS, IV, 436].

More specifically, the good in the objective sense, according to Kant, is the full satisfaction of the interests of reason. It is that which we would will—i.e. that which would be the object of our will—if we had a holy will, i.e. a will not distorted by the influence of our sensuous nature[14]. Yet, as finite rational beings whose wills are affected by desires we do not necessarily act in accordance with the good. Rather, it confronts us as an obligation—a demand which takes the form of an unconditional imperative [GMS, IV, 413-4]: "Duty is only the form in which the good appears to beings like man who do not necessarily desire the good and must be constrained to seek it" [Beck, 1960, 128][15]. In this sense, the objectively good is the practically necessary [GMS, IV, 412], that which we are obliged to do, even though we might fail to do it.

From what we have said so far, it follows that there is only such a thing as objective value in the world because of our being endowed with personality. If there were nothing to our existence but our *Tierheit* without our humanity and our personality there would be no freedom and hence no value at all in the world. In this sense, Kant says that while for animals there is such a thing as pleasure, only for rational beings there is such a thing as the good: "Annehmlichkeit gilt auch für vernunftlose Tiere... das Gute aber für jedes vernünftige

---

13 Wood overlooks this crucial distinction when he claims that for Kant any adoption of an end involves the attribution of *objective* goodness: "Kant's argument... requires us to concede that setting an end for ourselves involve ascribing objective goodness to it" [1999, 126]. This mistake is linked—and might even have led to—Wood's misunderstanding of Kant's argument establishing human beings as ends in themselves (see note 38 below).
14 We discuss the notion of a holy will in more detail in Chapter 8 below.
15 "Kants Platz in der Geschichte der Ethik wird mit der Weigerung identifiziert anzuerkennen, dass die Begriffe der Verpflichtung und des Werts voneinander getrennt werden können" [Herman, 2004, 154].

Wesen überhaupt" [KU, V, 210][16]. If, on the other hand, we had *Tierheit* and humanity but no personality—i.e. if we lacked that aspect of our existence that breaks the immanence of the empirical world and opens the space for a non-empirical aspect of our existence –, there would only be subjective ends and relative values[17]. We would see our ends as valuable, but the value of these ends would be contingent on us having certain desires—and would expire as soon as these desires did. Hence, without personality, there would be no objective values in the world[18].

To say that something has objective value is to say that, as rational beings, we have to regard it as valuable, independently of whatever other idiosyncratic interests we happen to have. Yet, to regard something as valuable is to accept it as an end. Thus, to say that there is something that has objective value is to say that there are objective ends—i.e. ends that we have to adopt, regardless of which other subjective ends we are pursuing. Thus, the first result of our survey of Kant's theory of value is that thanks to our personality there is such a thing as objective value in the world—and, hence, that there are objective ends.

This raises the question: what, according to Kant, are these objective ends that have objective value? Before we can answer this question, we have to introduce a crucial distinction—that between the unconditional-objective good and the merely conditional-objective good. As we have seen, an objective good is something to which each rational being has to attribute value—i.e. something which each rational being has to adopt as an end. However, there are some things that have the status of objective good only conditionally. The most important example of such conditionally-objective goods are the subjective ends of

---

16 This is linked to Kant's claim that only rational beings have interests, while animals merely have physical drives: "Interesse ist das, wodurch Vernunft praktisch, d. i. eine den Willen bestimmende Ursache, wird. Daher sagt man nur von einem vernünftigen Wesen, dass es woran ein Interesse nehme, vernunftlose Geschöpfe fühlen nur sinnliche Antriebe" [GMS, IV, 459n]. This highlights the link—discussed in the text above—between the notions of interest and value.
17 Given that our negative freedom is for its possibility dependent on our positive freedom (in the absence of which it is mere comparative freedom, in the sense explained in note 52 in Chapter 5 above), the notion of a subjective end would be a peculiar one under the scenario discussed in the text (i.e. one in which we had humanity without personality): it would be an end in the sense that we chose it on the basis of our conscious thought; however, in the absence of transcendental freedom (personality), this choice would itself have to be conceived as determined by natural necessity.
18 Given that our personality is revealed to us by our awareness of the demands of morality, it is this awareness—the fact of reason—that ultimately underpins Kant's theory of value. In this sense, Kemp Smith is right when he asserts that for Kant "the moral consciousness is the key to the meaning of the entire universe as well as of human life. Its values are the sole ultimate values" [2003, 571].

other rational beings. Kant holds that we have a duty to help other rational beings to achieve their ends [MS, VI, 388], as long as they have developed a good will (i.e. have adopted the moral law as their highest maxim). As he puts it, we are to adopt their subjective ends as our own [GMS, IV, 430] (i.e. attribute value to them). Given that this duty is valid for all rational beings, this is equivalent to saying that the subjective ends of rational beings with a good will have objective value (for all rational beings, regardless of their idiosyncratic interests, have to attribute value to them)[19]. Yet, these ends of other rational beings (and, hence, the realization of their ends, i.e. their happiness[20]) have objective value only conditionally, because their status as objectively valuable is dependent on the moral quality of their wills[21]: "Glückseligkeit [ist] immer etwas, was dem, der sie besitzt, zwar angenehm, aber nicht für sich allein schlechterdings und in aller Rücksicht gut ist, sondern jederzeit das moralische gesetzmäßige Verhalten als Bedingung voraussetzt" [KpV, V, 111; see also KU, V, 208–9]. However, in addition to these merely conditionally objective goods, Kant holds that there are some things that have objective value unconditionally, i.e. they have objective value without that value being dependent on any additional conditions. Thus, within the class of things that have objective value, we have to distinguish between those that have unconditional-objective value and those that have conditional-objective value[22].

---

19 However, Kant is adamant that the happiness of an evil person—i.e. one who has chosen the principle of self-love as his highest maxim—does not have objective value. See our discussion of this point in note 13 in Chapter 7 below.
20 For the link between the notion of subjective ends and that of happiness, see our discussion in Chapter 7.
21 Consequently, Herman is doubly mistaken when she claims that ends that are willed in accordance with the categorical imperative are unconditionally good: "Handlungen und Zwecke, die in Übereinstimmung mit den Prinzipien des [Kategorischen Imperativs] gewollt werden, sind unbedingt gut" [2004, 125]. First, for these ends to be willed in accordance with the categorical imperative only ensures the legality, not the morality of the associated action (with morality requiring in addition that the ends be chosen by a will that has adopted the moral law as its highest maxim, as discussed in Chapter 5 above)—and it is morality that matters for the moral worth of an action. Secondly, even if the action had moral (and, hence, objective) value, it would —contrary to Herman's assertion—not be unconditional-objective value, for the reasons discussed in the text.
22 This important distinction is overlooked by many commentators, but noted by Formosa: "Although Kant is not particularly clear on this point he must be committed to the existence of two classes of objective ends: those with unconditional and absolute worth and those with conditional and non-absolute worth. The objective ends which Kant thinks have conditional and non-absolute worth are our own self-perfection, the happiness of others and the self-given permissible ends of rational agents. These are objective ends because they are valuable for all ra-

We have to be careful in the use of our terminology at this point in order to avoid confusion. For Kant wants to distinguish between that which has subjective value (i.e., is linked to our interests as sensuous beings) and that which has objective value (i.e. is linked to the interests of our reason). However, he also wants to allow for the possibility that some of the things that have subjective value also have conditional-objective value (namely, the happiness of rational beings if these have developed a good will). In this sense, the happiness of rational beings with a good will is an objective good. This statement undercuts the neat distinction between the objective and the subjective good that we started out with. For happiness is now considered both a subjective—and an objective good (at least in so far as the agent in question has a good will). Consequently, we have to be careful to refer to the rational good as the unconditional-objective good and to happiness as the subjective good, which, under certain circumstances (namely, if the individual in question has developed a good will) is also a conditional-objective good.

We can now return to our question of what are objective ends, i.e. the things that we have to regard as objectively good. As we will discuss below, Kant holds that the conditional-objective goods are dependent for their value on the unconditional-objective goods[23]. Consequently, we have to start by focusing on the unconditional-objective goods—and have to ask: what, according to Kant, are the ends that have unconditional-objective value? Kant gives two seemingly contradictory answers to this question. On the one hand, he holds that: "Es ist überall nichts in der Welt... was ohne Einschränkung für gut könnte gehalten werden, als allein ein guter Wille" [GMS, IV, 393]. This answer seems to leave little space for misunderstanding: the only thing that can be said to be an unqualified (i.e. unconditional) objective good is the good will, i.e. our will insofar as it has adopted the moral law as its main determining ground [KU, V, 443]. Yet, in other passages Kant asserts that our personality—i.e. our status as transcendentally free agents—has absolute (i.e. unconditional) value[24]:

[D]er Mensch, als Person betrachtet, d. i. als Subjekt einer moralisch-praktischen Vernunft, ist über allen Preis erhaben; denn als ein solcher (homo noumenon) ist er nicht bloß als Mittel zu anderer ihren, ja selbst seinen eigenen Zwecken, sondern als Zweck an sich selbst zu schätzen, d. i. er besitzt eine Würde (einen absoluten innern Wert), wodurch er allen andern

---

tional agents independently of their inclinations. These are not, however, unconditionally or absolutely valuable ends because we may sometimes act against or be indifferent to these ends" [2013, 178].

23 See note 27 below.
24 For evidence that Kant uses the terms "absolute value" and "unconditional-objective value" synonymously, see [KU, V, 209].

vernünftigen Weltwesen Achtung für ihn abnötigt, sich mit jedem Anderen dieser Art messen und auf den Fuß der Gleichheit schätzen kann. [MS, VI, 435]

Thus, there is, in Kant's works, a tension between the claims, first, that only the good will (i.e. our will insofar as it has adopted the moral law as its highest maxim) has unconditional-objective value and that, second, every human being as a bearer of personality (i.e., transcendental freedom) has unconditional-objective value. However, once we look into the arguments underlying these claims, this tension largely disappears.

The argument for the claim that the good will is an unconditional-objective good is relatively straightforward. We have seen above that, for Kant, only when our will is guided by the moral law is it certain to will in a self-consistent manner, i.e. not to fall into self-contradiction—and, hence, to will in a way that is consistent with the interests of reason. That is, having a good will is to be in a condition in which the interests of reason are satisfied[25]. Yet, given that for Kant the objective good is precisely that which satisfies the interests of reason, a good will is objectively good[26]. Furthermore, there is no circumstance in which a good will can fail to be an objective good. Hence, it is an unconditional-objective good.

Kant's argument for the claim that human beings have absolute value simply by virtue of being endowed with personality is more involved than—but also presupposes—the previous one. The first premise of his argument is that there only is such a thing as objective value in the world because of our noumenal freedom. For without this freedom—i.e. without our personality—there could be no such thing as a good will (i.e. a will guided by the interests of reason)[27]. In this

---

[25] To be precise, to have a good will is a necessary—but not sufficient—condition for the complete satisfaction of the interests of our reason. We will discuss the conditions for such a complete satisfaction of the interests of our reason at the end of this chapter—and in Chapter 7 below.

[26] My interpretation of Kant here disagrees with that offered by Schönecker & Wood, who hold that Kant never offered a reason for his regarding our personality as unconditionally valuable: "Kant hat nie eine echte Werttheorie entwickelt. Er sagt weder, was genau überhaupt Werte im ethischen Kontext sind, noch, wie wir solche Werte erkennen. Er begründet daher auch überhaupt nicht, warum es autonome Vernunftwesen sind, die absoluten Wert (Würde) besitzen" [2002, 145].

[27] A different way of putting the same point is to highlight that it is only by virtue of having personality, i.e. autonomy, that there is such a thing as the moral law in the first place. Given that the moral law determines what has objective value (in that it codifies the conditions required for the satisfaction of the interests of reason), that which allows us to give the moral law to ourselves is the condition of all (objective) value: "Denn es hat nichts einen Wert als

sense, noumenal freedom—our personality—is the condition of the possibility of objective value[28].

The second premise is the claim that that which is the condition of the possibility of objective value has itself objective value [GMS, IV, 435]. The validity of this premise follows directly from the fact that it is impossible to ascribe value to the good will without ascribing value to our personality (i.e. treating it as an end), given that the good will *is* the realization (of the interests) of our personality. In committing to realize our own good will (i.e. to treat our good will as an end), we commit to realizing the interests of our own personality (i.e. the ideal vision of ourselves as transcendentally free) in the empirical world, i.e. to treat the realization of the interests of our noumenal will as an end. Given that treating something as an end and ascribing value to it is the same thing, it follows that in necessarily ascribing value to the good will, we are necessarily ascribing value to our own personality (i.e. adopt the realization of its interests as our end). In this sense, we have to treat that which is the condition of the possibility of objective value (i.e. our personality) as itself having objective value.

We should note that the arguments establishing the unconditional-objective value of the good will and our personality do not only apply to our personal case, i.e. do not only establish the unconditional-objective value of our own good will and our own personality, but that of the good will and the personality of every rational being. This follows from Kant's doctrine of the *underlying identity of all rational beings*, according to which all rational beings are the same in their status as bearers of pure practical reason, i.e. their transcendentally free will. While we as finite rational beings differ in our empirical features and desires [KpV, V, 21], the moral personality that is our "proper self" is the same for all rational beings. Thus, Kant's account of rational nature implies what Brandt calls the underlying "identity of [all] rational beings" ("Identität der Ver-

---

den, welchen ihm das Gesetz bestimmt. Die Gesetzgebung selbst aber, die allen Wert bestimmt, muss eben darum eine Würde, d. i. unbedingten, unvergleichbaren Wert, haben, für welchen das Wort Achtung allein den geziemenden Ausdruck der Schätzung abgibt, die ein vernünftiges Wesen über sie anzustellen hat. Autonomie ist also der Grund der Würde der menschlichen und jeder vernünftigen Natur" [GMS, IV, 436].

28 This focus on the conditions of the possibility of necessary features of our experience makes Kant's argument establishing personality as an absolute value similar in structure to the transcendental deduction of the categories in *Kritik der Reinen Vernunft:* "Die transzendentale Deduktion aller Begriffe a priori hat also ein Prinzip, worauf die ganze Nachforschung gerichtet werden muss, nämlich dieses: dass sie als Bedingungen a priori der Möglichkeit der Erfahrung erkannt werden müssen (es sei der Anschauung, die in ihr angetroffen wird, oder des Denkens). Begriffe, die den objektiven Grund der Möglichkeit der Erfahrung abgeben, sind eben darum notwendig" [KrV, III, 105].

nunftwesen" [2007, 356]). Given that we thus all share in the same reason, a case in which different individual wills enter into conflict as a consequence of at least one of them failing to attribute value to the personality of the other (i.e. by treating him as a mere object, rather than as a self-guided agent) involves a contradiction of reason—and, hence, a frustration of reason's interest in systematic unity[29]. The only reliable way to avoid such conflict—and, hence, to satisfy of our reason's interest in systematic unity (which, as we have seen, is the objective good)—is to attribute value to the personality of all rational beings. In this sense, the personality of all rational beings has unconditional-objective value[30].

Thus, we achieve the unconditional-objective good for ourselves by establishing ourselves as a fully free agents, i.e. agents whose wills are guided by the moral law as their main determinant (given that the moral law codifies the conditions that allow for the satisfaction of the interests of our practical reason). Yet, given the underlying identity of all rational beings, we would impede the complete satisfaction of the interests of reason if we acted in ways that made it impossible for other rational beings to establish themselves as fully free agents as well. Hence, realizing the objective good for a given individual involves not only taking an interest in maintaining and enhancing his own status as a free agent, able to choose and pursue his own ends—but also taking an interest in maintaining and enhancing the status of all other rational beings as free agents. Yet, as we have seen above, to take an interest in the realization of an object, for Kant, is to treat this object as valuable—i.e. to treat it as an end. Hence, realizing the objective good involves attributing value to the status of all other rational beings as free agents (i.e. their personality)—that is, to regard their personality as an end[31].

---

[29] See our discussion of this point in Chapter 3 above.

[30] This argument helps clarify Kant's contention that immorality involves self-contradiction: for to commit an immoral act is to sacrifice something that has absolute value for something that is a mere contingent end and of qualified value. It is to sacrifice that which is the condition of all value to that which is thus conditioned. This is noted by Korsgaard [1996, 123], although as I note below Korsgaard is mistaken in assuming that humanity, not personality, is the basis of Kant's ascription of the status of ends in themselves to rational beings.

[31] In this sense, freedom—as the condition for the possibility of value—is itself the most fundamental value in the Kantian system. This is recognized by Guyer, who emphasizes "Kant's commitment to the normative thesis that freedom is our fundamental value" [2000, 7]. Yet, Guyer fails to explain how this position of Kant's is based in his theory of value. Wood comments: "Perhaps the most fundamental proposition in Kant's entire ethical theory is that rational nature is the supreme value and the ground of whatever value anything else might possess" [1999, 121]. Note, though, that I am taking issue with Wood's reading of what grounds this position of Kant's in the text below.

Hence, Kant holds, human beings insofar as they are endowed with personality have unconditional-objective value. Kant calls this specific type of unconditional-objective end—that which is the condition of the possibility of all objective ends—an end in itself. Kant specifies three conditions that have to be met for something to be an end in itself: 1) it has to have objective value [GMS, IV, 431]; 2) it can never be treated merely as a means, but always has to be treated also as an end [GMS, IV, 428]; 3) it is the only kind of thing that can itself have ends—and, hence, is the condition for the possibility of all objective ends [GMS, IV, 437]. The first condition is met (tautologically) by all things that have objective value, the second by those which have unconditional-objective value (which, under no circumstances, can legitimately be treated as not having intrinsic value)—and the third only by those which are the source of all objective value. Hence, the set of the ends in themselves is a perfect subset of the unconditional-objective ends, which in turn is a subset of the objective ends.

Our discussion so far suggests that there is no contradiction between Kant's claims that our good will has unconditional-objective value and that our personality has unconditional-objective value. Yet, it is important to note these they are different claims. The good will is an objective end in the sense that it is something that we have a duty to achieve. The value attaching to our personality, on the other hands, is a value that we are endowed with regardless of any effort on our part[32]. This difference matters—but is easily misunderstood. This happens to Prauss, for instance, who writes: "Was sollte es wohl heißen, sich Selbstzweck könne der Mensch nur unter der Bedingung sei, dass er zunächst einmal die anderen Menschen als Selbstzwecke sich selber zum Zwecke macht" [1982, 139]. To think that we are ends in ourselves only insofar as we respect the status of others as ends in themselves is precisely to overlook that the ground for regarding human beings as ends in themselves is that they have personality (i.e., a status that does not require any effort on their part), not that they have a good will.

Unfortunately, Kant himself is confused on this point when he claims that the only thing of objective value is a good will. For if that were true, we would only be required to respect moral individuals (given that respect is the attitude required when faced with objective value, in the sense discussed below). Furthermore, given that nothing can be an end in itself without it having objective

---

[32] This suggests that Beck is mistaken when he suggests our personality could be "rendered ineffective" ("Even in an evil man, one who voluntarily embraces other maxims than those conforming to the moral law, the predisposition to personality is not lost; it has only been rendered ineffective by a free choice against the demands of the moral law" [1960, 227]). On our interpretation of the Kantian notion of personality, this would mean that we could somehow temporarily lose our transcendental freedom, which is not an option that Kant contemplates.

value, we would at most be required to treat those individuals with a good will as ends in themselves, while not being required to treat those with moral shortcomings in this way. To the degree to which these conclusions are fundamentally at odds with the spirit of Kant's moral philosophy, we should reject the assertion that the good will is the only thing that has objective value[33]. Rather, we should say that while a good will—as the condition in which our will operates in a way that is consistent with the interests of our practical reason—has objective value (and, in fact, is the "supreme good"[34] [KpV, V, 110]), the condition for the possibility of achieving this good will (namely, our personality) has to be considered as having objective value as well (and, in fact, as being an end in itself), for the reasons highlighted above[35].

The argument we have just explored is sometimes misstated in the secondary literature as seeking to establish the claim that human beings are ends in themselves merely because of their ability freely to choose their ends. This seems to be the position attributed to Kant by Wood who, summarizing an argument by Korsgaard, writes that: "Kant's reasoning here takes the form of a 'regress on conditions'. It begins from the value we place on the ends we set, and infers that this value is grounded in the rational nature of the being who

---

[33] Another problematic passage by Kant in this context is the following from *Kritik der Urteilskraft*: "Also ist es nur das Begehrungsvermögen: aber nicht dasjenige, was ihn von der Natur (durch sinnliche Antriebe) abhängig macht, nicht das, in Ansehung dessen der Wert seines Daseins auf dem, was er empfängt und genießt, beruht: sondern der Wert, welchen er allein sich selbst geben kann, und welcher in dem besteht, was er tut, wie und nach welchen Prinzipien er nicht als Naturglied, sondern in der Freiheit seines Begehrungsvermögens handelt; d. h. ein guter Wille ist dasjenige, wodurch sein Dasein allein einen absoluten Wert und in Beziehung auf welches das Dasein der Welt einen Endzweck haben kann" [KU, V, 443]. This passage can be rendered acceptable if we understand Kant as saying that only our ability to have a good will (i.e. our personality) is what gives us absolute value, rather than the more natural interpretation of his words, namely that we only have objective value insofar as we have achieved a good will.

[34] While the good will for Kant is the *supreme* good, it is not the *highest* good. That label is preserved for the ideal vision of the empirical world in which a complete rational order has been established: i.e. it is a vision of the world as populated by rational beings with good wills, coordinated by shared laws, and in which, consequently, all interests of reason in systematic unity and completeness are fully satisfied. That is, once a good will has been achieved and the interests of reason with respect to that will have been satisfied, it is still possible that much else about the world at large remains at odds with the interests of reason. The highest good is the ideal state of affairs in which these interests are completely satisfied. We will discuss Kant's notion of the highest good in Chapter 7.

[35] There is a third thing that, from the point of view of Kant's theory of value, we should regard as having unconditional-objective value, namely the highest good. We will discuss this notion—and the grounds for attributing unconditional-objective value to it—in Chapter 7 below.

sets the end, which... possesses a 'value-conferring status' in relation to the end. Because humanity or rational nature is the source of all such value, it is regarded as absolutely and unconditionally valuable, and an end in itself [Wood, 1999, 127][36]. Similarly, Rosen renders Kant's argument in the following manner: "All objects in the world possess whatever value they have solely because they are 'means' to the attainment of some human goal... Human choices are 'value conferring'. Suppressing human choices therefore means suppressing not only the creation of specific instrumental goods but also the source of all value in the world" [1993, 65]. Lastly, Guyer claims that, according to Kant, "a systematic realization of happiness [is] the ultimate object of morality, because freedom is, essentially, the capacity to set our own ends, and happiness is, essentially, the realization of our freely set ends" [2000, 13][37].

The problem with these interpretations of Kant's argument is that they fail to take serious the distinction, explored earlier in this chapter, between humanity and personality. If Kant's argument for human beings' status as ends in themselves were based on the claim that our choice confers value, as suggested by Wood and Rosen, and that, hence, a disruption of our ability to choose would undermine that which is the source of all value in the world, then it should be our faculty of choice, i.e. humanity, which Kant regards as the basis for

---

36 The argument by Korsgaard that Wood is summarizing here seems to endorse the same position, though it is not presented with the same conciseness: "Kant's answer, as I understand him, is that what makes the object of your rational choice good is that it is the object of a rational choice... [W]e are supposing that rational choice itself *makes* its object good. His idea is that rational choice has what I will call value-conferring status... If you view yourself as having a value-conferring status in virtue of your power of rational choice, you must view anyone who has the power of rational choice as having, in virtue of that power, a value-conferring status. This will mean that what you make good by means of your rational choice must be harmonious with what another can make good by means of her rational choice—for the good is a consistent, harmonious object shared by all rational beings. Thus, regressing upon the conditions, we find that the unconditioned condition of the goodness of anything is rational nature, or the power of rational choice. To play this role, however, rational nature must itself be something of unconditional value—an end in itself" [1996, 122–23]. In fairness, Korsgaard is here merely concerned with Kant's position in *Grundlegung*, that is, a text that was published before he endorsed the distinction between humanity and personality, which, as I will argue, is inconsistent with this interpretation of his position. However, nowhere does Korsgaard indicate that she is aware of Kant's position in his mature work on the question of what grounds our status as ends in ourselves.

37 As we will discuss in Chapter 7, Guyer is right that, for Kant, "happiness is, essentially, the realization of our freely set ends", a point that is not always appreciated by commentators. However, Guyer is mistaken in his suggestion that, for Kant, "a systematic realization of happiness [is] the ultimate object of morality", for Kant does not hold that "freedom is, essentially, the capacity to set our own ends", as we will discuss in the text below.

our status as ends in ourselves. For humanity is our faculty of choice, i.e. our ability to set ends for ourselves rather than being determined in our action by our sensuous desires.

Yet, Kant makes it very clear that if we were only endowed with humanity, there would be no objective value in the world: "Wären dagegen auch vernünftige Wesen, deren Vernunft aber den Wert des Daseins der Dinge nur im Verhältnisse der Natur zu ihnen (ihrem Wohlbefinden) zu setzen, nicht aber sich einen solchen ursprünglich (in der Freiheit) selbst zu verschaffen im Stande wäre: so wären zwar (relative) Zwecke in der Welt, aber kein (absoluter) Endzweck, weil das Dasein solcher vernünftigen Wesen doch immer zwecklos sein würde" [KU, V, 449][38]. Consequently, the mere ability to attribute subjective value—i.e. to choose between different objects suggested to us by our desires by adopting them as ends—does not ground our status as ends in ourselves, as would be the case if Kant's argument were built on the premise that "value confers choice". Rather, as we have explored above, it is our personality (i.e. our ability

---

38 See also [KpV, V, 61]: "Denn im Werte über die bloße Tierheit erhebt ihn das gar nicht, dass er Vernunft hat, wenn sie ihm nur zum Behuf desjenigen dienen soll, was bei Tieren der Instinkt verrichtet; sie wäre alsdann nur eine besondere Manier, deren sich die Natur bedient hätte, um den Menschen zu demselben Zwecke, dazu sie Tiere bestimmt hat, auszurüsten, ohne ihn zu einem höheren Zwecke zu bestimmen". The same conclusion is reached in [MS, VI, 435]. Schönecker & Wood are careful to emphasize this point: "[D]er Status des Menschen, Zweck an sich selbst zu sein, [wird] nicht mit der Fähigkeit begründet, rational Zwecke setzen zu können, sondern mit der Autonomie" [2002, 103]. Amazingly, Wood directly contradicts this insight in his own monograph on Kant's moral theory, writing that "Kant has at least two reasons for choosing humanity rather than personality as the end in itself" [1999, 120], in spite of the overwhelming textual evidence to the contrary. The two reasons he states are that "first, preserving and respecting rational nature means preserving and respecting it in all its functions, not merely in its moral function of giving and obeying moral laws; furthering rational nature requires furthering all the (morally permissible) ends it sets, not merely the ends it sets in response to duty. Second, it follows necessarily from the role played by the concept of an end in itself in grounding the categorical imperative that rational beings cannot be ends in themselves only insofar as they are virtuous or obedient to moral laws". The first of these reasons is directly contradicted by Kant's own assertion that rational choice where it only serves to satisfy sensuous desires has no objective value. The second is based on a conflation of Kant's notion of personality and the good will, for Wood argues against the claim that human beings are ends in themselves "only insofar as they are ... obedient to the moral law" (i.e. have a good will), while Kant's actual position is, as highlighted in the text, that they are ends in themselves insofar as they regard themselves as transcendentally free (i.e. have personality). This highlights neatly the danger of not distinguishing carefully between Kant's notions of personality, on the one hand, and the good will, on the other, that we discussed above (see note 13 above).

to guide ourselves on the basis of the interests of reason and, hence, our ability to develop a good will) that grounds this status[39].

Kant calls the unconditional-objective value that we have because of our personality our dignity (*Würde*, [MS, VI, 436; see also: GMS, IV, 436]). In line with the observation that this is a value that we have regardless of any moral achievement, Kant holds that we cannot lose or forfeit our dignity [MS, VI, 436][40].

---

[39] This is not to deny that there is a sense in which rational choice confers objective value: those ends that are chosen by a good will thereby become objectively good (albeit in a conditional manner, as highlighted in our discussion in the text above). In the extreme case, the entire empirical world would, when organized by an ethical community of rational beings mutually sharing and supporting one another's ends, become objectively good (this is Kant's notion of the highest good, which we will discuss in Chapter 7). Yet, it is to deny that rational choice (in the sense of consciously choosing an end) is a sufficient condition for the resulting end to be regarded as objectively good.

[40] However, there are some passages in which Kant asserts that certain immoral forms of behavior are inconsistent with our dignity, in a way that committing them equates to "throwing away" our dignity [MS, VI, 429] and turning us into "Nichtswürdige" (literally, "those that do not have dignity", [R, VI, 4]). In other passages, Kant—unfortunately from the viewpoint of consistency—suggests that our dignity is determined by the moral quality of our actions: "Wahrhaftigkeit im Inneren des Geständnisses vor sich selbst und zugleich im Betragen gegen jeden Anderen, sich zur obersten Maxime gemacht, ist der einzige Beweis des Bewusstseins eines Menschen, dass er einen Charakter hat; und da diesen zu haben das Minimum ist, was man von einem vernünftigen Menschen fordern kann, zugleich aber auch das Maximum des inneren Werts (der Menschenwürde)" [A, VII, 295]. This ambiguity concerning the notion of dignity—i.e. whether our dignity is given to us merely by virtue of our status as transcendentally free or whether it is something that we have to earn through moral behaviour—reflects the tension underlying his theory of objective value more generally, which we have encountered above in our survey of his assertions about the value of the good will and personality. This tension is due to the fact that he uses the term "dignity" in his attempt to communicate each of the following two central tenets of his moral philosophy: first, that we have to treat human beings as ends in themselves, regardless of how they behave, and, second, that it is important for us to achieve moral worth by virtue of making the moral law the highest determining ground of our actions. Different commentators have, in their attempts to distil the essence of Kantian moral theory, tended to highlight one or the other of these two positions, with Wood, for instance, emphasizing the first ("Kant's conception of human dignity: the absolute, hence equal, worth of all rational beings", [1999, xiv]) and Guyer the second ("Kantian morality is based on nothing less than the supposition that we can respect ourselves only by attempting to live up to the ideal of free rationality, the guidelines for the realization of which are expressed by the moral law", [2000, 275]). Yet, while both positions are rooted in the logic of his overall project, it is unfortunate that Kant is using the term "dignity" to express both these notions. Given the term's central role in marking our status as ends that impose constraints on all other rational beings, it would be preferable to speak of dignity as the objective value rational beings have merely by virtue of their personality and use the term "moral worth" to express the notion of a value that we have to earn through the moral quality of our will.

Thus, while from the perspective of a rational being only endowed with humanity in the narrow sense, other human beings appear either as instruments or obstacles in the pursuit of his personal interests[41], from the perspective of the rational being endowed with personality they appear as invested with dignity, that particular type of unconditional-objective value[42] which imposes limiting conditions on the actions of all other rational beings[43].

Kant calls the attitude with which we respond to this experience of absolute value respect (Achtung)[44]. The problem with this term is that Kant uses it in two different ways. As we have discussed in Chapter 5 above, he uses Achtung to denote the moral feeling that provides the emotional basis for a moral action. As such, Achtung is a feeling, something that is linked to our sensuous nature. In the present context, however, Achtung has a different meaning without Kant highlighting (or perhaps even noting) the difference: it is an intellectual attitude, namely the recognition—independently of whether we have a corresponding feeling or not—that the dignity of human beings as bearers of personality (i.e. bearers of a transcendentally free will) imposes duties on us regarding the ways in which we can and cannot treat them[45]. In this sense, respect is "eine

---

41 From the perspective of humanity, "I perceive the other as a subject, not as a mere object in the world; and it is precisely because he is subject and as a subject that I want to subdue him to my will, treating him as a mere instrument for the accomplishment of my aspiration" [Yovel, 1989, 150].

42 The logic of Kant's argument commits him to the position that if we somehow knew that these other rational beings were only invested with humanity, but not personality, they would not have this value for us. In fact, as we will see in Chapter 9, it is only because other rational beings are endowed with personality that we have to regard them as having rights, i.e. a claim on us to refrain from certain actions where these affect their external freedom.

43 "Dieses Prinzip der Menschheit und jeder vernünftigen Natur überhaupt, als Zwecks an sich selbst, (welche *die oberste einschränkende Bedingung der Freiheit der Handlungen eines jeden Menschen* ist) ist nicht aus der Erfahrung entlehnt" [GMS, IV, 430; my emphasis]. Kant is using ‚humanity' here in the wide sense of the term, as discussed in note 3 above.

44 Kant himself notes that the respect we feel for the dignity of others is respect for a mere idea. For the object of respect is the personality of rational beings—and this personality is a mere idea (i.e. a concept of whose object we can have no experience): "[H]ierin liegt eben das Paradoxon: dass bloß die Würde der Menschheit als vernünftiger Natur ohne irgend einen andern dadurch zu erreichenden Zweck oder Vorteil, mithin die Achtung für eine bloße Idee dennoch zur unnachlaßlichen Vorschrift des Willens dienen sollte" [GMS, IV, 439].

45 This ambiguity does not appear to have been noted in the secondary literature. However, the rendition some writers give of the Kantian notion of respect clearly brings out this second, purely conceptual (i.e. non-emotional) aspect of respect. Examples include Wood ("Respect is directed at something whose worth we recognize by reason from within ourselves, and we recognize that worth as essentially greater than the worth of any object of inclination" [1999, 46]) and Schönecker & Wood ("Achtung reflektiert einen objektiven Wert:... Achtung kann man nur für

Maxime der Einschränkung unserer Selbstschätzung durch die Würde der Menschheit in eines anderen Person" [MS, VI, 449] and "die Anerkennung einer Würde... an anderen Menschen, d. i. eines Werts, der keinen Preis hat, kein Äquivalent, wogegen das Objekt der Wertschätzung... ausgetauscht werden könnte" [MS, VI, 462]. That is, rather than denoting an emotion, it refers to the way we form our maxims to ensure they are consistent with the status of other rational beings as ends in themselves.

The fact that Kant is in fact operating with two different conceptions of the notion of respect becomes most obvious when he writes in *Kritik der Praktischen Vernunft* that a divine being, as a non-sensuous rational being, would not have any emotions and, hence, would not be capable of respect [KpV, V, 76][46], while stating some pages later in the same work that even a divine being would have to regard us as ends-in-ourselves [KpV, V 87]. Yet, accepting our status as ends-in-ourselves, and hence recognizing our dignity, is precisely what it is to have respect for our personality ("[Der Mensch] ist verbunden, die Würde der Menschheit an jedem anderen Menschen praktisch anzuerkennen, mithin ruht auf ihm eine Pflicht, die sich auf die jedem anderen Menschen notwendig zu erzeigende Achtung bezieht" [MS, VI, 462]). That is, this second passage (i.e. the one in [KpV, V, 87]) implies that we should conceive of a divine being as having respect for our personality. The fact that Kant in *Kritik der Praktischen Vernunft* effectively both denies and affirms that a divine being would have respect for our personality suggests strongly that he is operating with two different conceptions of the notion of respect—and that he would have done better to use two different terms in order to distinguish more clearly between them[47].

---

das haben, was ‚Grund' und ‚Tätigkeit eines Willens' ist, also für das ‚bloße Gesetz in sich'" [2002, 82].

46 "Hierbei ist nun zu bemerken: dass, so wie die Achtung eine Wirkung aufs Gefühl, mithin auf die Sinnlichkeit eines vernünftigen Wesens ist, es diese Sinnlichkeit, mithin auch die Endlichkeit solcher Wesen, denen das moralische Gesetz Achtung auferlegt, voraussetze, und dass einem höchsten, oder auch einem von aller Sinnlichkeit freien Wesen, welchem diese also auch kein Hindernis der praktischen Vernunft sein kann, Achtung fürs Gesetz nicht beigelegt werden könne" [KpV, V, 76].

47 A further passage that suggests that Kant is operating with two conceptions of the notion of respect is the following: "Ein jeder Mensch hat rechtmäßigen Anspruch auf Achtung von seinen Nebenmenschen" [MS, VI, 462]. Given, first, that for Kant rights are the flipside of duties (see Chapter 9 below) and, second, that he holds that we cannot have the duty to have certain feelings [MS, VI, 399], we should not understand him to be speaking here about a right that we have concerning the emotional state of others, but rather about the attitude they take towards us (i.e. the way they form their maxims to ensure that they are consistent with our dignity as transcendentally free rational beings). Given the passages discussed in Chapter 5, according to which we

Value and teleology

We have now explored the meaning of—and justification for—Kant's assertions that human beings have objective value and are ends in themselves. This leaves us with the task of explaining his claim that we also have to regard human beings as "the final end (*Endzweck*) of creation" [KU, V, 443]. However, to understand the notion of a final end of creation, we first have to spend a moment to explore Kant's account of teleology.

While Kant's metaphysics commits him to regarding the world as the product of the blind processes of Newtonian physics, he was struck from early on by the fact that it is difficult to conceive of many natural objects—in particular, living organisms—as the product of such mechanical processes [Yovel, 1989, 128]. These organisms seem, rather, to be products of a teleological cause, i.e. a cause that creates with an end result in mind. The second half of *Kritik der Urteilskraft* aims at integrating such a teleological view of the world with the mechanistic picture of the world developed in *Kritik der Reinen Vernunft*. To understand this enterprise, we have to appreciate the fundamental difference between the two forms of causality:
- Mechanical causality involves the blind playing-out of the laws of nature, in a process that is indifferent to the resulting states of affairs;
- Teleological causality, on the other hand, is a type of causality in which the idea of the end result precedes and determines the action in question. Teleological causality, unlike the mechanical variety, involves the notion of mental mediation: the process in question begins with a mental representation of the end result, which then leads to the realization of that result [KU, V, 220].

As just highlighted, the guiding thought in Kant's reflections on teleology is that there are certain objects—namely, living organisms—whose possibility we can only explain if we conceive of them as the products of teleological causality. Kant holds, for instance, that it is impossible for us to explain how the human body can be the product of merely mechanical forces [KU, V, 389]. Such an organism and its part must, Kant holds, appear to us as natural ends (*Naturzwecke*), the products of purposeful activity [KU, V, 405]. In regarding an eye, for instance, we conceive of it as having been made for the purpose of seeing [KU, XX, 240]. It

---

should conceive of "respect" as a kind of feeling, this offers independent evidence for the claim that Kant is operating with two different conceptions of the notion of respect.

is impossible for us to think about an eye as merely the accidental product of blind mechanical processes[48], while ignoring the purposes it serves[49].

We conceive of a teleological cause in analogy with the causality of our own will—that is, as involving an intelligent mind acting on the basis of a preconception of the result to be realized [KU, V, 360]. Hence, in regarding some parts of the natural world as the products of teleological causality, we have to see them as the products of an intelligent designer, i.e. God [KU, V, 400]. What is more, in order to be able to regard some parts of the natural world as products of a teleological causality, Kant maintains, we have to apply this maxim consistently, i.e. we have to regard the entirety of nature as the product of such causality [KU, V, 376]. Consequently, once we posit an intelligent author as the creator of some parts of nature, we have to ascribe the creation of all of nature to him (unless, of course, we wanted to come up with a story of different types of causality bringing about different parts of empirical reality).

To see the natural world as the product of teleological causality, Kant holds, is to regard it as a *system of ends* [KU, V, 378–9]: in positing a rational author of nature, we envisage a world structured according to means-ends relation. The reason for this is that we think of such a rational creator of the world as a being with a fully rational will, i.e. a kind of causality exclusively guided by reason's interest in systematic unity. Given that reason is a teleological, i.e. end-directed, faculty (see Chapter 1), the highest systematic unity—that is, the order most pleasing to a rational mind—is one in which the particulars are ordered teleologically: "Die höchste formale Einheit, welche allein auf Vernunftbegriffen beruht, ist die zweckmäßige Einheit der Dinge" [KrV, III, 452][50]. Hence, we conceive of the work of the author of nature not as a patchwork of unconnected ends, but rather as a harmonious whole of means-end relations, in which nothing is in vain and all ends are coordinated according to one common plan[51].

---

48 As Wood point out, this is exactly where Kant's thought is vulnerable to the onslaught of the theory of evolution [1999, 23].

49 This inability to understand natural ends as the products of purely mechanistic processes, Kant claims, is due to the limitations of our own epistemic abilities, in a way that epistemically more powerful beings might, for all we know, be able to comprehend how living organisms can be the product of merely mechanical processes [KU, V, 405–6].

50 Kant defines a "system" as a "purposeful" (i.e. end-directed) order [KrV, III, 456]. That is, the notion of a teleological order is already part of the notion of systematic unity. Consequently, it should not be surprising that only a teleological interpretation of the world is found, in our discussion below, fully to satisfy the interest of reason in organizing our knowledge in a systematic fashion.

51 In this sense, mechanical causality is associated with a *bottom-up* view of the world (a given whole is conceived of as a mere aggregate of its individual constituent items; so, what is given

This raises the question: how is such a teleological view of the world as a system of ends consistent with the Newtonian physics that Kant's epistemology is based on? Kant's answer is that the teleological viewpoint is a merely regulative one [KU, V, 379]. The mechanical laws of nature describe the way in which the world of our experience is constituted, while the teleological viewpoint is one that we adopt in response to subjective needs of ours, namely that of giving a satisfactory account of the possibility of natural ends[52]. Properly understood, the resulting judgments do not tell us anything about how the empirical world is constituted, but merely about how we have to structure our knowledge of it[53]: "Wir haben… unentbehrlich nötig, der Natur den Begriff einer Absicht unterzulegen, wenn wir ihr auch nur in ihren organisierten Produkten durch fortgesetzte Beobachtung nachforschen wollen; und dieser Begriff ist also schon für den Erfahrungsgebrauch unserer Vernunft eine schlechterdings notwendige Maxime" [KU, V, 398].

The faculty allowing us to adopt this teleological viewpoint, Kant holds, is the faculty of judgment. To judge is to think particular items as subsumed under general categories [KU, V, 179]. In this sense, it is the ability to apply rules (and, hence, to use concepts): for concepts, as rules, are by their nature general, i.e. apply to many similar cases, independently of their specific differ-

---

first are the individual items—and the whole is just what we get when these individual items are brought together). Teleological causality, on the other hand, is associated with a *top-down* view of the world (what is given first is the idea of the whole—and everything that is individual merely appears a function of that whole): "Wenn wir nun ein Ganzes der Materie seiner Form nach als ein Produkt der Teile und ihrer Kräfte und Vermögen sich von selbst zu verbinden (andere Materien, die diese einander zuführen, hinzugedacht) betrachten: so stellen wir uns eine mechanische Erzeugungsart desselben vor. Aber es kommt auf solche Art kein Begriff von einem Ganzen als Zweck heraus, dessen innere Möglichkeit durchaus die Idee von einem Ganzen voraussetzt, von der selbst die Beschaffenheit und Wirkungsart der Teile abhängt, wie wir uns doch einen organisierten Körper vorstellen müssen" [KU, V, 408].

52 Kant argues that the tension between these two ways of interpreting reality—the mechanical and the teleological—could be seen to give rise to what he calls the "antinomy of the faculty of judgment". The thesis in this antinomy would be the position that the creation of all material things is possible according to mechanical laws, while the antithesis would be that the creation of some material things is impossible according to mechanical laws [KU, V, 387]. This antinomy is resolved, however, once we note that the use of the teleological principle guiding our scientific inquiries is merely regulative, not constitutive—i.e., such that they do not make a statement about the world, but about our requirements for structuring our knowledge of the world.

53 "The natural, cosmological world follows pure mechanistic laws and has, as such, no teleological significance. Only human reason and praxis endow it with ends" [Yovel, 1989, 135]. What makes this distinction less neat than it at first appears is that the order in the natural world is itself the product of reason, as we have discussed in Chapter 1.

ences—and to make a judgment is precisely to apply a general rule to a given particular[54]. In *Kritik der Urteilskraft*, Kant distinguishes between two functions of the faculty of judgment: the *determining* faculty of judgment (*bestimmende Urteilskraft*) operates when a rule is given independently—and individual items of experience have to be subsumed under this rule (for instance, when I recognize a certain movement of physical objects as governed by the law of gravity). Yet, Kant holds there is also a second, merely *reflective* use of our faculty of judgment (*reflektierende Urteilskraft*), in which the faculty of judgment itself furnishes the general rule to fit the individual observations it is provided with [KU, V, 179].

The postulation of a teleological order governing the world results from this reflective use of the faculty of judgment. The teleological principle is a general rule that is not grounded in how the empirical world itself is constituted, but is a mere ordering principle, based on our own epistemic requirements:

> Es versteht sich, dass [die Idee der gesamten Natur als eines Systems nach der Regel der Zwecke] nicht ein Prinzip für die bestimmende, sondern nur für die reflektierende Urteilskraft sei, dass es regulativ und nicht konstitutiv sei, und wir dadurch nur einen Leitfaden bekommen, die Naturdinge in Beziehung auf einen Bestimmungsgrund, der schon gegeben ist, nach einer neuen gesetzlichen Ordnung zu betrachten und die Naturkunde nach einem andern Prinzip, nämlich dem der Endursachen, doch unbeschadet dem des Mechanismus ihrer Kausalität zu erweitern. [KU, V, 379]

The teleological order is one that we project onto the world in order to make it fit with our cognitive needs[55]. In fact, Kant holds, only by regarding the world as

---

[54] The introduction of this new cognitive faculty in the late *Kritik der Urteilskraft* comes as a surprise. In the earlier *Kritik der Reinen Vernunft*, Kant had told us that judging is a function of the understanding (and had, in fact, equated judging with thinking [KrV, III, 86]). Now, however, he claims that it is thanks to a specialized faculty of judgment that we are able to judge. This is noted by Schopenhauer: "Man könnte auch einen Vorwurf großer Inkonsequenz daraus nehmen, dass, nachdem in der Kritik der reinen Vernunft unablässig wiederholt ist, der Verstand sei das Vermögen zu urteilen, und nachdem die Formen seiner Urteile zum Grundstein aller Philosophie gemacht sind, nun noch eine ganz eigentümliche Urteilskraft auftritt, die von jenem völlig verschieden ist" [*Die Welt als Wille und Vorstellung*, Erster Band, Anhang].

[55] Thus, the problematic notion of a teleological order in the world receives a re-interpretation that makes it acceptable from a critical point of view, namely one that sees it concerned with the requirements of our own epistemic apparatus rather than with the features of the world outside us: "Wir verfahren aber mit [einem Begriffe] bloß kritisch, wenn wir ihn nur in Beziehung auf unser Erkenntnisvermögen, mithin auf die subjektiven Bedingungen ihn zu denken betrachten, ohne es zu unternehmen über sein Objekt etwas zu entscheiden" [KU, V, 395]. As Yovel notes, this integration of problematic metaphysical notions—critically re-interpreted—into our worldview is a standard Kantian move: "[I]t is typical of the critical mode of thinking to change

teleologically ordered can we conceive of it as a systematic whole—and thus structure our knowledge of the world in a way that satisfies the interests of our reason [KU, V, 398]. As we have seen above, empirical nature is a coherent whole, a system, structured by the laws of nature. Yet, although it is our own intellect that gives these laws, Kant holds, it does not follow that we can easily grasp its systematic structure. On the contrary, in regarding nature we are confronted with a bewildering multiplicity of different laws, without fully understanding how they fit into a coherent structure [KU, V, 185][56]. This must leave frustrated our reason's demand to structure its knowledge into a systematic whole. As we have seen above, reason, for Kant, is essentially a teleological, end-directed faculty (see Chapter 1). Consequently, Kant holds that the only order that fully satisfies its needs is a teleological order. Thus, only by regarding the world as structured according to means-end relations can our reason's need for systematic unity of its knowledge fully be satisfied[57]. In this sense, the notion of the teleological order of reality is a mere idea—a tool that we use to satisfy the demands of reason and whose validity is based not on any correspondence to an objective reality, but rather on our own subjective needs to regard the world as a unified system [KU, V, 404].

---

the function of many dogmatic concepts, transferring them from a context in which they have no validity to a context in which they gain a legitimate if limited use... [T]he claims of transcendent metaphysics (totality, God, supersensible matters) are translated from their spurious cognitive expression into genuine expressions in the spheres of morality, aesthetics, and history" [1989, 158–9].

56 See also: "[D]ie Erfahrung [muss], nach allgemeinen so wohl als besonderen Gesetzen, so wie sie überhaupt, objektiv betrachtet, möglich ist, (in der Idee) ein System möglicher empirischer Erkenntnisse ausmachen... Daraus folgt aber nicht, dass die Natur, auch nach empirischen Gesetzen, ein für das menschliche Erkenntnisvermögen fassliches System sei, und der durchgängige systematische Zusammenhang ihrer Erscheinungen in einer Erfahrung, mithin diese selber als System, den Menschen möglich sei. Denn es könnte die Mannigfaltigkeit und Ungleichartigkeit der empirischen Gesetze so groß sein, [dass es uns unmöglich wäre], diese empirischen Gesetze selbst zur Einheit der Verwandtschaft unter einem gemeinschaftlichen Prinzip zu bringen, wenn nämlich... uns an diesen ein rohes chaotisches Aggregat und nicht die mindeste Spur eines Systems darlegte, ob wir gleich ein solches nach transzendentalen Gesetzen voraussetzten müssen" [KU, XX, 209]. The same thought is elaborated in [KU, V, 386].
57 The suggestion that only a teleological reading of reality fully satisfies the interests of our reason already appears in Kritik der Reinen Vernunft: "Die höchste formale Einheit, welche allein auf Vernunftbegriffen beruht, ist die zweckmäßige Einheit der Dinge, und das spekulative Interesse der Vernunft macht es notwendig, alle Anordnung in der Welt so anzusehen, als ob sie aus der Absicht einer allerhöchsten Vernunft entsprossen wäre. Ein solches Prinzip eröffnet nämlich unserer auf das Feld der Erfahrungen angewandten Vernunft ganz neue Aussichten, nach teleologischen Gesetzen die Dinge der Welt zu verknüpfen, und dadurch zu der größten systematischen Einheit derselben zu gelangen" [KrV, III, 452].

Once we regard the world as teleologically ordered—i.e. as a system in which every item is a means to an end and every end itself the means to a higher end—we are confronted with the question: what is the final end for which all the other ends are means? When regarded from a mechanical point of view, the world presents itself as a blind flow of causes and effects, in which any question about the purpose of the whole is meaningless [KU, V, 434]. When we regard the world from a teleological viewpoint, however, the question about the ultimate purpose of the whole of creation not only becomes possible, but even necessary: if we have to regard the whole world as a purposeful system, in which everything is a means to an end, we are immediately confronted with the question: what is the world as a whole there for? Or, in Kant's terminology, what is the final end (*Endzweck*) of creation [KU, V, 443–4]? If we have to regard the world as a system of means and ends, then such a system would be incomplete, Kant holds, if there were no *Endzweck* for the sake of which the whole system of means and ends existed. Without an *Endzweck* grounding all other ends [R, VI, 6], the entire compound of means and ends would itself not be properly grounded [KU, V, 435].

In addressing the question concerning the *Endzweck* of creation, Kant lays out three criteria an *Endzweck* must fulfil. First, it must be an end that requires, for its justification, no reference to another, higher end (for otherwise we would not have reached the last element in the chain of means-end relations, [KU, V, 434]). Secondly, it must be the end for which all other ends are, in turn, means—that is, the end that justifies the existence of the entire complex of means and ends that is the empirical world when viewed from a teleological perspective [KU, V, 443]. Lastly, it cannot be an item in the empirical world, for everything that is empirical is necessarily of conditional value [KU, V, 378]. Hence, the *Endzweck* must be an idea of reason (i.e. something of which we cannot have any experience in the empirical world [KU, V, 435]).

In our discussion at the beginning of this chapter, we have noted an ambiguity in Kant's account of the ground for the ascription of objective value to human beings, with Kant declaring both that we have objective value because of our personality (i.e., our ability to guide ourselves on the basis of the interests of reason) and that we have objective value insofar as we have developed a good will (i.e., have made the moral law the highest determining ground of our maxims). A similar ambiguity affects his discussion of the *Endzweck* of creation. The difference is that this time there are three different candidates that Kant declares, at different points, to be the *Endzweck* of creation. The first of these is humans beings insofar as they are endowed with personality: "Die moralischen Gesetze aber sind von der eigentümlichen Beschaffenheit, dass sie etwas als Zweck ohne Bedingung, mithin gerade so, wie der Begriff eines Endzwecks es bedarf, für die

Vernunft vorschreiben: und die Existenz einer solchen Vernunft, die in der Zweckbeziehung ihr selbst das oberste Gesetz sein kann, mit andern Worten die Existenz vernünftiger Wesen unter moralischen Gesetzen, kann also allein als Endzweck vom Dasein einer Welt gedacht werden" [KU, V, 449–50][58].

Yet, Kant also claims that a good will, rather than our personality, is the *Endzweck* of creation: "[E]in guter Wille ist dasjenige, wodurch sein Dasein allein einen absoluten Wert und in Beziehung auf welches das Dasein der Welt einen Endzweck haben kann" [KU, V, 443][59]. Lastly, there are passages in which Kant declares that the final end (*Endzweck*) of creation is the same as the final end of our practical reason ("[D]er Endzweck der Schöpfung ist diejenige Beschaffenheit der Welt, die zu dem, was wir allein nach Gesetzen bestimmt angeben können, nämlich dem Endzwecke unserer reinen praktischen Vernunft, und zwar so fern sie praktisch sein soll, übereinstimmt" [KU, V, 445; see also: KU, V, 453–4; R, VI, 6])—and, as we will discuss in Chapter 7, the final end of our practical reason is the condition of the empirical world in which the interests of our practical reason are fully satisfied. Kant calls this condition the highest good ("das höchste Gut" [KpV, V, 125]). This suggests that the highest good is to be regarded as the *Endzweck* of creation[60].

Our discussions of the notion of the interests of reason and of Kant's theory of value provide us with a good basis from which to resolve the tension between these different claims. As we have seen, the notion of an *Endzweck* of creation is first introduced when we regard the world as created by an intelligent author, i.e. a pure rational will guided in its efforts by the interests of reason. Given the structure of rational thought, we have to conceive of such an author as acting

---

58 See also: [KU, V, 435–6] and [KU, V, 442].
59 However, assertions like this one are directly contradicted by at least one passage in *Kritik der Urteilskraft*, in which Kant explicitly states that a good will cannot be the ground for our status as *Endzweck*: "Nicht der Mensch nach moralischen Gesetzen, d. i. ein solcher, der sich ihnen gemäß verhält, ist der Endzweck der Schöpfung. Denn mit dem letztern Ausdrucke würden wir mehr sagen, als wir wissen: nämlich dass es in der Gewalt eines Welturhebers stehe, zu machen, dass der Mensch den moralischen Gesetzen jederzeit sich angemessen verhalte… [N]ur vom Menschen unter moralischen Gesetzen [i.e. one who has personality] können wir, ohne die Schranken unserer Einsicht zu überschreiten, sagen: sein Dasein mache der Welt Endzweck aus" [KU, V, 448n]. We will clarify the meaning of the quote in the text in our discussion below.
60 The identification of the highest good as the final end of creation is also made in [R, VI, 6] ("Moral also führt unumgänglich zur Religion, wodurch sie sich zur Idee eines machthabenden moralischen Gesetzgebers außer dem Menschen erweitert, in dessen Willen dasjenige Endzweck (der Weltschöpfung) ist, was zugleich der Endzweck des Menschen sein kann und soll") and [TP, VIII, 279n] ("[Wir haben das] Bedürfnis, ein höchstes auch durch unsere Mitwirkung mögliches Gut in der Welt als den Endzweck aller Dinge anzunehmen").

with a final end in mind. Given that the good (and, hence, the end) for a fully rational mind is the satisfaction of the interests of reason, we have to conceive such an author as aiming at satisfying the interests of reason. The *final* end of such a being would be a condition in which all his ends are realized, i.e. a condition in which the interests of reason are *completely* satisfied. This suggests that the *Endzweck* of creation, in its strictest sense, is the realization of the highest good—i.e. the state of affairs in the world in which the interests of reason are completely satisfied[61].

In fact, this notion of the full satisfaction of the interests of reason meets all criteria for being an *Endzweck* outlined above. First, it has unconditional-objective value (for, as we have seen above, the satisfaction of the interests of our reason, for Kant, is objectively good—and does not depend for its goodness on any further conditions). Secondly, it is the ground for the possibility of objective value (for the interests of reason ground the possibility of objective value)—and, hence, the ground for the value of all other ends. Lastly, as we will see in our discussion in Chapter 7, the notion of the full satisfaction of the interests of reason is a mere idea of reason (i.e. not an object of possible experience).

However, our argument establishing the highest good as the *Endzweck* of creation does not imply that we have to reject his suggestions that the good will and of our personality are to be regarded as the *Endzweck* of creation. Rather, once we understand the logic underlying Kant's argument, we find that—in spite of the apparent contradiction—these claims are in fact mutually consistent. As we will see in Chapter 7, the achievement of a good will is a necessary condition for the realization of the highest good. In fact, in Kant's view the highest good can only be realized if all rational beings have achieved a good will. In this sense, it is correct that "ein guter Wille ist dasjenige, wodurch... das Dasein der Welt einen Endzweck haben kann", as the quote above puts it.

Furthermore, as we will discuss in Chapter 7 Kant holds that the realization of the *Endzweck* of creation (i.e. the creation of a fully rational order in which the interests of our reason are completely satisfied) is only possible as the product of human action guided by the moral law. In this sense, the existence of human beings endowed with personality is the condition of the possibility of realizing the *Endzweck* of creation. Furthermore, as we will discuss in Chapter 8, bringing about the *Endzweck* of creation involves fully realizing our own rational nature. Thus, human beings are *Endzweck* of creation in the broad sense that their full

---

61 The same conclusion is reached by Yovel [1989, 176], who is among the few commentators to note the ambiguities in Kant's identification of the final end of creation, as well as Wood [1999, 311].

self-realization is the purpose for which the world as a whole exists[62]: "[D]er von uns zu bewirkende höchste Endzweck [ist] das, wodurch wir allein würdig werden können selbst Endzweck einer Schöpfung zu sein" [KU, V, 469][63].

In order for this not to appear mystifying, we have to remember the starting point of our discussion: values and ends only exist from the perspective of reason. There is no such thing as an end—and, hence, no such thing as a final end (*Endzweck*) of creation—in the world as it is independent of our conscious thought[64]. In identifying that which has value, we are not making factual statements about the natural world, but are describing a structure our practical reason projects onto the world. Similarly, in discussing the purpose for which the world exists, we are not making statements of fact about the intentions of an actual creator, but are describing a framework, projected by our conscious thought, in which we can coherently think about our experience of the world—and our

---

[62] This is recognized by Yovel: "Man enjoys a central position not by virtue of what he is, but by virtue of what he ought to do and to become. He must make himself the center of creation by using his practical reason to determine its end and by consciously acting to realize it" [1989, 180].

[63] In identifying the final end of creation with the final end of our own moral mission, Kant's account of teleology connects the two realms of nature and freedom: our epistemic needs bring us to regard the world as a teleological structure—and in thinking through the logic of this structure, we discover man in so far as he is subject to the moral law as the final justification for the existence of this world [KU, V, 453]. This highlights the practical orientation of Kant's philosophical project: it is because of our will—our free will as a noumenal existence—that we are *Endzweck* of creation, not because of our theoretical faculties: "Ohne den Menschen [würde] die ganze Schöpfung eine bloße Wüste, umsonst und ohne Endzweck sein [...]. Es ist aber... nicht das Erkenntnisvermögen... (theoretische Vernunft), in Beziehung auf welches das Dasein alles Übrigen in der Welt allererst seinen Wert bekommt, etwa damit irgend Jemand da sei, welcher die Welt betrachten könne... Also ist es nur das Begehrungsvermögen... dasjenige, wodurch sein Dasein allein einen absoluten Wert und in Beziehung auf welches das Dasein der Welt einen Endzweck haben kann" [KU, V, 442–3]. Yovel comments: "[T]he metaphysical question of what the universe at large exists for... Although this question is legitimate and even necessary for critical reason, the answer is to be sought on the level not of existence, but of moral ought. For questions about the world as a whole have no critical answers in cognitive terms, only in terms of the metaphysics of praxis... [W]hen speaking of the moral idea, we are not dealing with a Platonic idea in itself, but with an end projected by man's rational will... Here we have an excellent example of the dynamics of the critical system, translating the ultimate metaphysical questions from their delusory, cognitive form into their proper expression in the field of praxis" [1989, 178–9; see also: Korsgaard, 1996, 246].

[64] "Endzweck ist bloß ein Begriff unserer praktischen Vernunft und kann aus keinen Datis der Erfahrung zu theoretischer Beurteilung der Natur gefolgert, noch auf Erkenntnis derselben bezogen werden. Es ist kein Gebrauch von diesem Begriffe möglich, als lediglich für die praktische Vernunft nach moralischen Gesetzen" [KU, V, 454–5].

place within this world. It is not surprising that within this framework, created around the interests of reason, the complete satisfaction of the interests of reason appears as the final end for which all other things exist. In Kant's theory of value, as in his theory of cognition, "pure reason is ultimately concerned only with itself" [KrV, III, 448][65]—or, more precisely, with the satisfaction of its own essential interests[66].

We have reached the highest expression of the hybrid notion of the world and of human nature that Kant's philosophy is built around: based on the idea of ourselves as transcendentally free wills, we regard ourselves as endowed with a dignity, as ends in ourselves and, consequently,—in the context of a teleological interpretation of the world—as the final end of creation[67]. This interpretation elevates man from the indifferent position he occupied in a purely mechanical interpretation of the world [Wicks, 2007, 239] and places him at the center of the world, as that which justifies the existence of the world as a whole[68]. Conversely, it reduces the rest of nature to the status of a mere means to be used by man to achieve the ends he sets for himself: "Von dem Menschen

---

[65] "Dass eben dadurch aber der Mensch einen 'Wert', ja sogar einen 'inneren' und 'absoluten' Wert darstellt, bedeutet somit lediglich, dass er als theoretisches und praktisches Selbstverhältnis jeweils immer wieder zunächst einmal allein 'sich selber wert ist'" [Prauss, 1982, 137].

[66] In the light of our results, Kant's claim that the rational has a higher value than the merely physical does not look like an *ad hoc* assertion, but rather appears solidly grounded in his theory of values: for values, like ends, only appear in the world from the perspective of reason.

[67] The fact that we have this status as the final end of creation only insofar as we are endowed with personality—a condition disclosed to us by means of the fact-of-reason argument, based on our awareness of the moral demands we are facing—makes our moral consciousness the starting point for answering the question about the meaning of existence: "The moral consciousness, like sense-experience, discloses upon examination a systematic unity of presupposed conditions... The underlying conditions... of practical experience have from the start a purely noumenal reference. They have no other function than to define, in terms of the moral consciousness, the ultimate meaning of reality as a whole. They postulate a universe in which the values of spiritual experience are supported and conserved" [Kemp Smith, 2003, 571].

[68] However, to attribute objective reality to our status as *Endzweck* of creation we need one further step in our argument. As we have highlighted in the text above, regarding the world as teleologically ordered is so far merely a regulative viewpoint we have adopted for the purpose of ordering our knowledge of the world. That is, we need some independent grounds for regarding this notion as constitutive (in a way that we can attribute objective reality to it). This is the role played by Kant's moral proof of God, which we will discuss in Chapter 7. The aim of this proof is to establish the objective reality of God on practical grounds. If the proof succeeds, allowing us to attribute objective reality to the notion of an intelligent author of the world, this would ground the objective reality of notion of the world as teleologically ordered—and, hence, our status as the *Endzweck* of creation. However, as we will see, Kant's proof fails. We will discuss the implications of this failure in Chapter 7 below.

nun... als einem moralischen Wesen, kann nicht weiter gefragt werden: wozu... er existiere. Sein Dasein hat den höchsten Zweck selbst in sich, dem, so viel er vermag, er die ganze Natur unterwerfen kann" [KU, V, 435][69].

Conclusion

In order to understand Kant's assertions that human beings have objective value, are ends in themselves and are the final end of creation, we require a good grasp of the central Kantian notion of personality (i.e. our status as transcendentally free agents)—and the ways in which it is distinguished from the notion of humanity (i.e., our ability to guide our actions by conscious thought), on the one hand, and that of a good will (i.e., a will that has adopted the moral law as its highest maxim), on the other. Furthermore, we have to appreciate the way in which the good (i.e. value) for Kant is not a natural property, but something that appears only from the perspective of reason, as something that is projected onto the world by our practical reason (i.e. our will). More specifically, the good, for Kant, is the object of our will—i.e. that which we choose as our end to satisfy our interests. Corresponding to the two types of interest that we have as finite rational beings, Kant distinguishes two types of goods: the subjective good (i.e., the object of our empirical will, i.e. that which we want in order to satisfy a sensuous desire) and the objective good (i.e. the object of pure practical reason, i.e. that which we want in order to satisfy an essential interest of reason).

To say that human beings insofar as they are endowed with personality are ends in themselves is to say that we have to attribute unconditional-objective value to them—that is, have to treat them as ends, regardless of which idiosyn-

---

[69] Brandt appears to overlook this passage when he writes: "Nie ist [bei Kant] davon die Rede, der Mensch sei zur Herrschaft über die Natur bestimmt" [2007, 168]. Shell, on the other hand, correctly notes that "Kant's philosophic development, and his critical thought in particular, can be understood as an explanation and defense of man's appropriation of the world" [1980, 185]. In thus asserting its control over the world around it, the human will turns the tables on its other—physical nature—from whose control it struggled to liberate itself: "Der Unterschied [ist] zwischen den Gesetzen einer Natur, welcher der Wille unterworfen ist, und einer Natur, die einem Willen (in Ansehung dessen, was Beziehung desselben auf seine freie Handlungen hat) unterworfen ist" [KpV, V, 44]. Kant's assertion of the right of rational beings to subject nature to their will highlights how his advocacy of equality among rational beings is coupled with a radical inequality between the rational and the non-rational: any thing and animal, for Kant, exists only for the purposes of satisfying the desires of the rational beings. Non-rational things only have one purpose—that given to them by rational beings. Their legitimate fate, Kant holds, is to be exploited as rational beings see fit.

cratic empirical interests we happen to have. The reason for awarding them this status is that personality itself is the condition for the possibility of all objective value—and, as we have seen above, only by treating the condition of objective value as itself being objectively valuable can we avoid a self-contradiction of the will.

Kant also holds that we have to regard human beings (insofar as they have personality) as the final end (*Endzweck*) of creation. Only by regarding the natural world as the product of teleological causality—i.e. as designed by an intelligent author –, Kant believes, can we account for the possibility of living organisms. Yet, he emphasizes that in assuming this teleological viewpoint, we are not making judgments about the way in which the natural world is actually constituted, but rather structure our experience of this world in a way that corresponds to our own subjective cognitive requirements. Once we regard the world in this way as a purposeful system, created by an intelligent author, we are faced with the question of what this system itself is there for—i.e. the question regarding the final end (*Endzweck*) of creation. Given that we have to conceive of such an intelligent author as guided in his efforts by the interests of reason, the logic of Kant's theory of value suggests that the final purpose of his creation must be the state of affairs in the world in which the interests of reason are completely satisfied. Kant calls this state of affairs the "highest good". Thus, the highest good is the *Endzweck* of creation in its strict sense. However, given that—as we will discuss below—the realization of the highest good is the highest level of human self-realization (i.e. the realization of our personality, our proper self, in the empirical world) we can conceive of human beings insofar as they are endowed with personality as the *Endzweck* of creation in the broad sense.

7 The highest good

In the previous chapter, we have explored how the notion of the objective good is linked to that of the satisfaction of the interests of reason. In the context of that discussion, we have already hinted at the distinction between a narrow and a wide sense in which the interests of reason can be satisfied. The good will is the notion of the narrow satisfaction of the interests of reason. It is the notion of a will which has made the moral law the highest determining ground of its maxims—and which, hence, acts in a way that satisfies the interests of reason. Yet, having developed a good will is consistent with the interests of our rational faculties being frustrated in other ways—through a conflict with other, non-moral wills, for instance, or because of other obstacles in our attempts to realize our ends in the world around us. This opens the door to a wider notion of the satisfaction of the interests of reason: namely, the ideal conception of a state of the world in which all interests of reason are completely satisfied. This ideal vision of the world is what Kant calls the "highest good" (*das höchste Gut*).

This chapter explores Kant's notion of the highest good. In particular, it argues, following Beck, that Kant inadvertently operates with two different conceptions of that notion—the juridical conception (according to which the highest good is happiness distributed according to virtue) and the maximal conception (according to which the highest good consists in the combination of the highest degree of happiness with the highest degree of virtue). I will argue that only the maximal conception constitutes a defensible conception of the highest good. This has important implications for Kant's overall philosophical project, for only the juridical conception would allow him to complete his moral proof of the existence of God. To the degree to which the juridical conception of the highest good is rejected, the proof must seen to be unsuccessful.

The ambiguity in Kant's conception of the highest good

As we have discussed in the last chapter, Kant distinguishes between two types of interests that we have as finite rational beings: material interests linked to our sensuous nature and those linked to our rational nature. Related to these two sets of interests, there are two kinds of good, namely the subjective good (happiness, the satisfaction of our material interests) and the objective good (virtue, the satisfaction of our rational interests). The best possible state of the world, which Kant calls the highest good, is the one in which we enjoy both the objective and the subjective good: "Nach meiner Theorie ist weder die Moralität des Menschen für sich, noch die Glückseligkeit für sich allein, sondern das höchste in der Welt mögliche Gut, welches in der Vereinigung und Zusammenstimmung beider besteht, der einzige Zweck des Schöpfers" [TP, VIII, 279][1].

This, however, leaves open the question: what is the proper relation between these two kinds of good in the ideal state of affairs[2]? As Beck notes, Kant offers two different replies to this question, without clearly distinguishing between these (in fact, nothing in the texts suggests he is aware of the difference himself)[3]. Beck calls these the juridical and the maximal conception of the highest good [1960, 268]. According to the juridical conception, the proper relation of virtue and happiness consists in happiness being distributed among rational beings according to their moral merit ("Glückseligkeit, ganz genau in Proportion der Sittlichkeit... ausgeteilt", [KpV, V, 110][4]), while the maximal conception is the notion of all rational beings having achieved a good will and enjoying the

---

1 While Kant rejects the notion that happiness is the all-encompassing human good, he does not deny that it is an important ingredient in the highest good (and thus in the fulfilled human life). That said, he is careful to emphasize two different ways in which we can attribute undue importance to our happiness: the first involves choosing the principle of self-love (i.e. that of promoting our own happiness) as our highest maxim, something which—as we have seen in Chapter 5—is inconsistent with the demands of morality. Secondly, Kant insists that an existence of effortless happiness (the life of the happy savage), far from being an enviable condition, is one in which we fail to realize the ideal conception of ourselves as fully rational beings—and, hence, one in which we fail to satisfy the demands of our reason. We will discuss this point in more detail in note 33 in Chapter 8 below.

2 Kant faults the ancients for not seeing the importance of this question, but rather assuming an analytical relation between the notions of virtue and happiness, with the Stoics holding that virtue *just is* happiness and the Epicureans claiming that happiness *just is* virtue [KpV, V, 111–3]. However, within the framework of Kantian philosophy this must appear as a gross mistake, for virtue and happiness are linked to two fundamentally different aspects of our existence—reason and our sensuous nature, respectively—in a way that precludes the possibility of an analytical relation of this kind [KpV, V, 112]. By mistakenly assuming such an analytical relation, Kant holds, the ancients lost sight of the important question of what precisely the relation is of the rational good and the sensuous good in the best possible human life.

3 Yovel also complains about "[t]he ambiguous character of Kant's discussion of the highest good... No single text is an adequate summary, and some texts provide varying definitions of the concept or reduce it to a single aspect" [1989, 48; see also: Reath, 1988, 594].

4 Further passages in which Kant is operating with the juridical conception of the highest good include: [KrV, III, 528; KpV, V, 119; KU, V, 471n; R, V, 5]. The juridical conception of the highest good is defended by O'Connell [2012].

highest possible degree of happiness ("die größte Glückseligkeit mit dem größten Maße sittlicher (in Geschöpfen möglicher) Vollkommenheit", [KpV, 129][5]).

Before exploring the difference between the two conceptions of the highest good Kant is operating with—and, hence, the appropriate relation between happiness and virtue in the best possible state of affairs in the world—we have to take a step back and ask what exactly Kant means when he speaks about "happiness". As with other key concepts in Kant's works, there is an important, yet hidden ambiguity in his use of this notion. Kant sometimes speaks of happiness as the *complete satisfaction of our desires and inclinations*, as for instance, when he says "Glückseligkeit ist die Befriedigung aller unserer Neigungen" [KrV, III, 523] or that "in dieser Idee [der Glückseligkeit vereinigen sich] alle Neigungen zu einer Summe" [GMS, IV, 399][6]. In other passages, however, he speaks of happiness as consisting in the *realization of our ends*, as when he refers to "[die]

---

5 Admittedly, in this passage Kant also makes reference to a key characteristic of the juridical conception, namely the notion of the exact proportion between virtue and happiness: "[I]n dem Begriffe des höchsten Guts als dem eines Ganzen [wird] die größte Glückseligkeit mit dem größten Maße sittlicher (in Geschöpfen möglicher) Vollkommenheit als in der genausten Proportion verbunden vorgestellt". However, the fact that Kant here understands the notion of the highest good to involve the "highest" happiness in combination with "highest" moral perfection suggests that this conception of the highest good is meaningfully different from the juridical conception, which does not involve any such maximizing aspects. Furthermore, other passages in which Kant is operating with the maximal conception do not make reference to the notion of the "exact proportion", which, in any case, in a scenario of both maximal happiness and maximal virtue is a redundant condition, as will be discussed below. These passages include: [KU, V, 453] and [TP, VIII, 279]. Among commentators, Guyer ("Kant ... describes [the highest good] as the conjoint maximization of virtue and happiness", [2000, 334]) characterizes the notion of the highest good in terms that suggest he subscribes to the maximal conception. However, he does not appear to note the distinction between the juridical and maximal conception. Rawls also offers at least one account of the notion of the highest good that suggests the maximal conception ("The highest good is... that world in which each person both has a completely good will and is fully happy", [2000, 313]). However, many other of his comments suggest he is in fact operating with the juridical conception (see notes 16 and 21 as well as note 59 in Chapter 9 below). Reath [1988] also defends the maximal interpretation of the highest good. Unlike Guyer and Rawls, he is aware of the ambiguity in Kant's conception of the highest good.
6 Other passages in which Kant uses the term "happiness" as denoting the most complete satisfaction of our desires and inclinations are to be found in *Kritik der Praktischen Vernunft* ("Alle Neigungen zusammen (die auch wohl in ein erträgliches System gebracht werden können, und deren Befriedigung alsdann eigene Glückseligkeit heißt) machen die Selbstsucht... aus" [KpV, V, 73]) and *Kritik der Urteilskraft* (where Kant refers to happiness as "[die] Summe aller Neigungen", [KU, V, 434n]). See also [R, VI, 58]. Among commentators, Prauss [1982, 29], Yovel, [1989, 51], Allison [1990, 123], Rosen [1993, 190] and Reath [2010, 36] interpret Kant as subscribing to the conception of happiness as the complete satisfaction of our inclinations and desires, without highlighting (or, indeed, showing awareness of) the ambiguity in Kant's use of the term.

Summe aller Zwecke, deren Erreichung Glückseligkeit genannt wird" [TP, VIII, 282][7].

This difference might seem innocuous—but it is, in fact, crucial. For it determines, whether we think of happiness as being principally linked to our *Tierheit* or our humanity[8]. For inclinations and desires are, for Kant, part of our sensuous nature (i.e. our *Tierheit*), while an end is something we choose for ourselves, with the help of our reason in its technical-practical use (i.e. our humanity). Consequently, if happiness were understood to consist in the satisfaction of our desires and inclinations, it would be linked only to our physical existence—and, hence, would be something we enjoy merely by virtue of being endowed with a physical body. However, in this case it would be impossible to explain why it should be regarded as a good (given that Kant operates with a very technical notion of the good as that which satisfies the interests of reason), rather than as merely something pleasant (with pleasure defined as the emotional response to the satisfaction of a desire [KpV, V, 21]). Hence, if we accept the conception of happiness as the satisfaction of our desires, the notion that happiness should form part of a completely good state of affairs might appear straightforward on an intuitive level, but would be hard to explain on a technical level.

If we regard happiness as consisting in the realization of our ends, on the other hand,—and, hence, as being linked to the activity of our practical reason—establishing the status of happiness as a (subjective) good becomes unproblematic, given that, for Kant, choosing an object as our end and attributing subjective value to it is the same thing[9]. Thus, only by linking happiness to reason (as happens under the conception of happiness as the realization of our ends,

---

[7] Others passage in which Kant speaks of happiness as linked to the realization of our ends can be found in *Kritik der Urteilskraft* ("die Glückseligkeit auf Erden [ist] der Inbegriff aller durch die Natur außer und in dem Menschen möglichen Zwecke desselben... das ist die Materie aller seiner Zwecke auf Erden", [KU, V, 431]) and *Religion* [R, VI, 5]—as well as [TP, VIII, 282]. This conception of happiness, which will be endorsed in the text, is ascribed to Kant by Beck ("Happiness, unlike pleasure, is a concept belonging to understanding, not to feeling", [1960, 97]), Guyer ("[H]appiness just consists in the fulfillment of ends", [2000, 386]), Wood [1999, 326], Rawls [2000, 225] and Formosa [2013, 186]. As before, however, none of these writers identifies the ambiguity in Kant's use of the term "happiness". Surprisingly, Rosen also attributes to Kant the conception of happiness as the realization of our ends [1993, 69], in spite of the fact that later in the same work he claims that for Kant happiness involves the satisfaction of our desires (see previous note).

[8] For a discussion of the difference between *Tierheit* and humanity, see Chapter 6 above.

[9] Establishing happiness as our subjective good in this way opens the way for regarding it as having conditional-objective value in the case of individuals that have developed a good will, in the sense explained in Chapter 6—and, hence, for grounding our duty to promote the happiness of others.

but not under the conception of happiness as the satisfaction of our desires) can we explain why happiness should be considered as a good from the viewpoint of Kant's theory of value. This strongly suggests that we should adopt the conception of happiness as the realization of our ends (and avoid language that suggests a direct link between our inclinations and desires, on the one hand, and happiness, on the other, without the mediation of practical reason)[10]. We would then regard the unconditional-objective good as linked to our moral-practical reason, concerned with the formal quality of our will (i.e. its highest maxim), while the subjective good would be linked to our technical-practical reason, concerned with the material content of our will (i.e. the realization of our ends)[11].

---

10 There are further reasons for assuming that Kant's notion of happiness should be conceived of as linked to the realization of our ends, rather than the satisfaction of our desires. Firstly, in at least one passage, Kant explicitly says that the notion of happiness is not directly based in our Tierheit ("Der Begriff der Glückseligkeit ist nicht ein solcher, den der Mensch etwa von seinen Instinkten abstrahiert und so aus der Tierheit in ihm selbst hernimmt", [KU, V, 430]). Secondly, as Yovel notes, both morality and happiness "have a unifying function in their respective domains" [1989, 51; see for instance: KrV, III, 520; see also: Guyer, 2000, 100]. For Kant, reason is the faculty that generates order and unity among naturally uncoordinated elements. This suggests that the ordering function involved in the notion of happiness is linked to reason (as it would be under the conception of happiness as linked to the realization of our ends), rather than directly to our sensuous nature (as it would be under the conception of happiness as the satisfaction of our desires). Lastly, in defining the notion of justice in *Metaphysik der Sitten* Kant writes that "an action is just if... its maxim is such that our freedom of will is consistent with everybody else's freedom according to a universal law" [MS, VI, 230]. In an earlier essay, he had expressed the same idea by saying that "everybody is entitled to seek his happiness in the way he sees fit, provided he does not interfere with the freedom of others to pursue a similar end, as long as it [this latter freedom] is consistent with the freedom of everybody else according to a possible universal law" [TP, VIII, 290]. This implies that justice, for Kant, concerns the protection of each rational being's freedom to pursue his own happiness. However, given the prominent role Kant thus implicitly assigns to the pursuit of happiness (by making it central to his conception of justice), it would be odd if that happiness turned out to consist in the satisfaction of whatever desire happened to grip us in the moment. In fact, nothing in Kant's writings would justify assigning a special protection to our self-gratification. If the pursuit of happiness is understood as consisting in our realizing our freely chosen ends, on the other hand, such a right —and the importance attached to it—flow naturally from Kant's philosophical framework. One implication of choosing this conception of happiness as linked to our humanity, i.e. our ability to choose ends, rather than our physical nature (our ability to fulfill our desires), would be that non-rational beings (i.e. animals) would not be seen to be capable of happiness.

11 This is obviously not to claim that happiness is not linked to our sensuous nature at all. Under the conception of happiness argued for in the text, happiness concerns the realization of our subjective ends, i.e. those ends we adopt on the basis of sensuous incentives [KpV, V, 25]. However, what this interpretation does deny is that happiness is linked *directly* to our sen-

The juridical conception of the highest good

We are now in a position to explore the respective merits of Kant's different conceptions of the highest good. Kant's argument aimed at establishing the plausibility of the juridical conception is built on the premise, explored in the last chapter, that happiness, our subjective good, is also a conditional-objective good. More precisely, its value is conditional on the moral quality of the will of the person experiencing it[12]. While happiness is always valuable for the person enjoying it (i.e. is always a subjective good), from an objective point of view it only has value (is only a good) to the degree to which the will of the person experiencing has a good will [KpV, V, 111]. If that were not the case—i.e. if the objective value of my happiness were unconditional and, in particular, were not

---

suous nature, without mediation by our technical-practical reason. The resulting conception of happiness is both subjective and empirical. It is subjective in the sense that what the happiness of each individual consists in depends on his idiosyncratic desires ("Worin nämlich jeder seine Glückseligkeit zu setzen habe, kommt auf jedes sein besonderes Gefühl der Lust und Unlust an" [KpV, V, 25]). It is empirical in the sense that we need experience to find our what the desires are whose satisfaction we are to adopt into our maxims as our ends ("Nur die Erfahrung kann lehren, was uns Freude bringe" [MS, VI, 215; see also KrV, III, 523–4; GMS, VI, 418]).

We should note that the conception of happiness as linked to the realization of our ends is not without problems. It leaves no conceptual space, for instance, for the possibility that we get what we want (i.e. realize our subjective ends)—and are still unhappy. Conversely, it cannot account for the common experience of being happy for no particular reason (i.e. without having realized any particular end). The common ground for these two problems is the fact that when we speak about happiness we typically refer to a particular emotional state. Yet, the conception of happiness as the realization of our ends defines happiness without reference to emotions, thus allowing for the divergence between the common use of the term and the use suggested by our technical definition. The most plausible solution to this problem is to admit that we are actually speaking about two different concepts here: one that it relevant from an ethical and political perspective (namely, happiness as the success in the exercise of our free will in its technical-practical application) and one that involves a particularly holistic experience of pleasure. Given that, from a Kantian perspective, these two concepts are linked to two different aspects of our existence—reason and our sensuous nature, respectively—it is not surprising that they are not necessarily realized in the same instances.

12 In this sense, there is a clear hierarchy among the two elements of the highest good. The formal component of the highest good (virtue) is its "first condition" [KpV, V, 109]: "[Sittlichkeit ist] das oberste Gut (als die erste Bedingung des höchsten Guts)... , Glückseligkeit [macht] dagegen zwar das zweite Element desselben [aus], doch so, dass diese nur die moralisch bedingte, aber doch notwendige Folge der ersteren sei. In dieser Unterordnung allein ist das höchste Gut das ganze Objekt der reinen praktischen Vernunft, die es sich notwendig als möglich vorstellen muss, weil es ein Gebot derselben ist, zu dessen Hervorbringung alles Mögliche beizutragen" [KpV, V, 119]. Yovel notes that "here, as elsewhere, the right order is the priority of the formal principle over any content" [1989, 33].

conditional on the moral quality of my will –, then by obtaining happiness through an immoral act, I would do something that has objective value. Yet, for Kant something has objective value only to the degree to which it is consistent with the satisfaction of the interests of reason, in a way that an act violating the moral law cannot have objective value (or bring about something of objective value). Hence, happiness cannot be of unconditional-objective value. Rather, it only has objective value when it is enjoyed by a person with a good will[13].

In the second step of the argument, Kant holds that we have to conceive of an ideal state of the world (i.e. the highest good) as the state of affairs that would be created by a fully rational being (i.e. a being guided only by the interests of reason) [KpV, V, 110][14]—for in such a world everything would be ordered in a way that would satisfy the interests of reason, and, hence, this world would be fully good. Given that happiness only has objective value when it is enjoyed by individuals with a good will, such a world-creating rational being would only grant happiness to the virtuous. Hence, in the ideal state of the world, happiness would be distributed according to virtue. In this sense, we can think of being virtuous as deserving to be happy [KpV, V, 130], which is just to say that to be vir-

---

13 Consequently, the happiness of the evil person (i.e., one who has chosen the principle of self-love as his highest maxim) is objectively undesirable: "Ein vernünftiger unparteiischer Zuschauer [kann] am Anblicke eines ununterbrochenen Wohlergehens eines Wesens, das kein Zug eines reinen und guten Willens ziert, nimmermehr ein Wohlgefallen haben kann" [GMS, V, 393; see also: KU, V, 443]. This is overlooked by Reath, who writes: "The value of an individual's ends is not determined by that individual's degree of virtue, but by the good of the ends themselves" [1988, 605]. Conversely, the pain of the evil person is considered objectively good: "Wenn... jemand, der friedliebende Leute gerne neckt und beunruhigt, endlich einmal anläuft und mit einer tüchtigen Tracht Schläge abgefertigt wird: so ist dieses allerdings ein Übel, aber jedermann gibt dazu seinen Beifall und hält es an sich für gut" [KpV, V, 61].
There is at least one passage in which Kant writes that we should promote the "permitted" ends of others: "Wenn es also auf Glückseligkeit ankommt, worauf als meinen Zweck hinzuwirken es Pflicht sein soll, so muss es die Glückseligkeit anderer Menschen sein, deren (erlaubten) Zweck ich hiermit auch zu dem meinigen mache" [MS, VI, 388]. This suggests that what determines whether we have a duty to promote a given end of another rational being (and, hence, whether this end has conditional-objective value in the sense discussed in Chapter 6) is whether it is "permitted", i.e. whether it is chosen by means of a legal maxim (i.e., a maxim that is consistent with the moral law). However, as we have discussed in Chapter 5, what determines the moral (i.e. objective) value of a given end is not the legality of the maxim on the basis of which it has been chosen, but the moral quality of the agent in question (i.e., the subjective determining ground on which it was chosen). Given that we only have a duty to promote the ends of others if these have objective value, this means if an evil person pursues a "permitted" end, we have no duty to promote that end—contrary to Kant's assertion in [MS, VI, 388].
14 This notion of an all-powerful, rational being distributing happiness in proportion with virtue is anticipated in *Kritik der Reinen Vernunft* [KrV, III, 528]. It also recurs in *Religion* [R, VI, 5].

tuous is to be entitled to happiness from the viewpoint of a fully rational being. Thus, according to the juridical conception, the highest good is a world in which there is a necessary link between a person's virtue and his happiness, in that each person's happiness is proportionate to his virtue[15].

The second conception of the highest good is the maximal conception. According to this conception, the highest good—i.e. the ideal state of the world—is a condition in which all rational beings enjoy both the unconditional-objective good (i.e. a good will) and the conditional-objective, or subjective, good (i.e. happiness) to the highest degree possible. To see why this is the best possible state of affairs, we have to note that in a world in which at least some rational beings have not developed a good will, the unconditional-objective good would not be fully realized. Hence, it would be a condition that, from the perspective of Kant's theory of value, could be improved upon. Similarly, in a world in which all rational beings have developed a good will, but at least some of them have not achieved happiness (i.e. fail in their efforts to realize their subjective ends), the conditional-objective good would not be fully realized. Again, it would be a condition that could be improved upon. Only a world in which both the unconditional-objective good (i.e. a good will) and the conditional-objective good (i.e. happiness) of all rational beings have been fully realized is in a condition that could not be improved upon, for it is a world in which the interests of our reason would be completely satisfied. Hence, this would be the best possible world[16].

---

[15] This claim that we have to conceive of the best possible state of affairs in the world as marked by a necessary link between virtue and happiness leads Kant to speak about an "antinomy of practical reason", which he describes in the following manner: "Es muss also entweder die Begierde nach Glückseligkeit die Bewegursache zu Maximen der Tugend, oder die Maxime der Tugend muss die wirkende Ursache der Glückseligkeit sein; das erste ist schlechterdings unmöglich; das zweite ist aber auch unmöglich" [KpV, V, 113]. In our discussion in the text below, we will reject the claim that the best possible state of affairs in the world involves that of a necessary link between virtue and happiness, in a way that undermines the very premise that leads Kant to assert the existence of the antinomy of practical reason. However, even Beck, who accepts the juridical conception of the highest good—and, hence, the notion that we have to accept the postulation of such a link—has little time for Kant's alleged antinomy: "[W]e can hardly attach to an antinomy in the concept of the highest good the importance which Kant professes to find in it... [T]he antinomy... is really quite a poor thing, wholly unable to carry this great historical and systematic burden... Kant's usual high-quality workmanship is not much in evidence in the discussion of the antinomy" [1960, 245–6].

[16] The term of the "best possible world" is reminiscent of Leibniz. In fact, Leibniz is Kant's inspiration for his notion of the highest good, as Kant himself acknowledges [KrV, III, 527]. The relation between Leibniz' and Kant's conception of the best possible world is explored by Yovel, who highlights that "the theory of the highest good is Kant's version of the Leibnizian har-

So far, we have explored the content of the two conceptions of the highest good Kant is operating with—the juridical and the maximal conception. We are now faced with the question: which of these should we regard as most consistent with Kant's overall project? In his writings, Kant himself gives more prominence to the juridical conception. Beck—who is among the few commentators surveyed for this work to note that Kant is operating with two different conceptions of the highest good—also declares a preference for the juridical conception, complaining that "neither the Kantian text nor the Christian doctrine, which Kant is here rationalizing, nor the voice of duty itself requires the maximal conception" [1960, 270]. However, in the following I will try to show that, on the basis of Kant's conception of the good that we have discussed in Chapter 6, only the maximal conception is a plausible candidate for being considered the highest good, while the juridical conception should be rejected as a flawed conception of the best possible state of the world.

To understand the problems surrounding the juridical conception of the highest good, it helps to trace its origins. The notion of the highest good is first mentioned in *Kritik der Reinen Vernunft* (1781), which was written before Kant's breakthrough conception of morality as autonomy[17]. According to the account of morality proposed in the *Kritik der Reinen Vernunft*, the moral imperative must be backed by a threat or a promise in order to motivate us to action: "[Die moralischen Gesetze könnten nicht als Gebote angesehen werden], wenn sie nicht a priori angemessene Folgen mit ihrer Regel verknüpften und also Verheißungen und Drohungen bei sich führten" [KrV, III, 527]. Consequently, there is only hope that rational beings will behave morally if there can be shown to be a necessary link between virtue and an emotional reward (happiness)—and, more specifically, if it could be shown that happiness (as a reward) is necessarily distributed in accordance with virtue. However, if we conceive of the world as gov-

---

mony between the realms of nature and grace" [1989, 77]. The important difference between Leibniz' and Kant's use of the notion of the best possible world lies in the fact that "in Leibniz this harmony exists actually" [1989, 77], while "in Kant, Leibniz's idea is historicized: the harmonious, best world does not actually exist as the product of divine goodness, but should be realized progressively by human praxis" [1989, 91n]. Rawls also notes the debt Kant's notion of the highest good owes to Leibniz' work, but regards this link as problematic: "I view the idea of the highest good as a Leibnizian element in Kant's philosophical theology... which he never reworked so as to make it consistent with his moral philosophy" [2000, 317]. However, Rawls' complaints about inconsistencies are based on his acceptance of the juridical conception of the highest good, as discussed in note 21 below.

17 It is notable, however, that Kant continues to operate with the old ethical framework in the second edition of *Kritik der Reinen Vernunft*, published in 1787, i.e. after he has introduced his conception of morality as autonomy in *Grundlegung* (1785).

erned by the laws of nature, i.e. if we look at the world as it appears from the viewpoint of theoretical reason, no such link between virtue and happiness can be established [KrV, III, 526]. We can only hope for the appropriate distribution of happiness if we assume, first, the existence of a just ruler of the world, God, who has the benevolence and the power to distribute happiness according to virtue and, second, the reality of a next life in which this just distribution of happiness is to take place. The resulting ideal of happiness distributed in proportion to virtue in an assumed next life is, Kant holds, the highest good [KrV, III, 528][18].

Hence, in order for morality to be possible within the moral framework of *Kritik der Reinen Vernunft*, we have to assume the existence of God and the immortality of the soul (the condition for the possibility of a next life) as practical ideas of reason, i.e. as beliefs not backed by empirical fact, but adopted because they are necessary for the possibility of morality. Thus, according to the ethical theory of *Kritik der Reinen Vernunft*, the ideas of God and immortality are necessary conditions for the possibility of morality. Without these, Kant holds, the demands of morality would be mere illusions ("leere Hirngespinste", [KrV, III, 526]).

However, the move to the conception of morality as autonomy in *Grundlegung* undermines the usefulness of the juridical conception of the highest good, in a way that Kant might have failed to appreciate. According to his new conception of morality, the moral law motivates us simply because we recognize it as an expression of the interests of our own reason. The threats and promises that appeared as necessary conditions for the possibility of morality in *Kritik der Reinen Vernunft*, are now seen not only as unnecessary—but even as undermining an action's moral quality (for if a threat or a promise constitute the determining ground of an action, the action thereby becomes a heteronomous one, i.e. one motivated by material, rather than moral concerns [GMS, IV, 444]]). Consequently, the notion that God, the benevolent power dispensing happiness in proportion with moral value, is the ground of the validity of the moral law is now rejected ("Die Ideen von Gott und Unsterblichkeit sind... nicht Bedingungen des moralischen Gesetzes" [KpV, V, 4])[19].

---

[18] The origin of the juridical conception of the highest good within the ethical framework of *Kritik der Reinen Vernunft* is not generally appreciated in the secondary literature, with Rawls [2000, 314–5] and Guyer [2000, 119], for instance, struggling to make sense of the demand that happiness be distributed in accordance to virtue.

[19] See also [KpV, V, 129]. However, Kant's position on this point is not entirely consistent. For in *Kritik der Praktischen Vernunft* he also holds that if it were impossible to realize the highest good in the empirical realm, this would imply the invalidity of the moral law: "Ist also das höchste

However, in spite of the change in his ethical theory, Kant continues to operate with the juridical conception of the highest good. Yet, in the context of his new ethical framework the highest good is no longer considered as a reward waiting for us in a next world (as was the case in *Kritik der Reinen Vernunft*), but rather as the best possible state of affairs in the this world, which we are to realize with our own powers[20]. Kant now describes the highest good as our

---

Gut nach praktischen Regeln unmöglich, so muss auch das moralische Gesetz, welches gebietet dasselbe zu befördern, phantastisch und auf leere eingebildete Zwecke gestellt, mithin an sich falsch sein" [KpV, V, 114]. The reasoning underlying this claim is that by demanding of us something that is impossible to realize, the moral law generates a contradiction of reason. Yet, the very ground for the validity of the moral law is that it codifies the conditions under which the interests of reason—and, in particular, the interest of reason in systematic unity—can be satisfied. Thus, by generating a contradiction of reason the moral law would undermine the very justification for its validity. However, as we will see below, Kant also wants to hold that a necessary condition for being able to conceive of the possibility of our realizing the highest good in the empirical world is a belief in God [KpV, V, 126]. Hence, we can only consider the moral law as valid if we believe that it is possible to realize the highest good—and we can only believe that it is possible to realize the highest good if we believe in God. Consequently—and contrary to his claim in [KpV, V, 4], cited in the text above –, acceptance of the objective reality of the idea of God seems to be a necessary condition for the acceptance of the validity of the moral law. The same problem recurs in *Kritik der Urteilskraft*, where Kant holds that a disbelief in the existence of God should not affect our acceptance of the validity of the moral law [KU, V, 451], while also claiming that without a belief in God the highest good would appear unattainable and that the impossibility of the realization of the highest good would imply that we would have to regard the moral law as a mere "illusion of our reason": "die spekulative Vernunft... muss [die Möglichkeit des höchsten Gutes] ... ohne Gott und Unsterblichkeit anzunehmen, für eine ungegründete und nichtige, wenn gleich wohlgemeinte Erwartung halten und, wenn sie von diesem Urteile völlige Gewissheit haben könnte, das moralische Gesetz selbst als bloße Täuschung unserer Vernunft in praktischer Rücksicht ansehen" [KU, 471n]. Among commentators, Yovel [1989, 35] focuses on the first element in this pair of contradictory claims (i.e. Kant's claim that the validity of the moral law is not influenced by whether or not it is possible to realize the highest good), while Beck [1960, 245] and Korsgaard [1996, 169] focus on the second (i.e. the claim that the possibility of the realization of the highest good is a necessary condition for the validity of the moral law). Beck is the only one to note that Kant's position on this topic is internally inconsistent.

20 This change is noted by Yovel, who, however, mistakenly claims that it takes place between *Kritik der Praktischen Vernunft* and *Kritik der Urteilskraft*: "In the first two Critiques, Kant tends to think of the highest good as a separate world, transcendent to our world and, in fact, a sort of critical and rational version of the next world... However, from the third Critique on, Kant's conception changes. The highest good becomes the 'final end of creation' itself, i.e. the consummate state of *this* world" [1989, 72]. In fact, this new conception of the highest good as a state of affairs we are to bring about in the empirical world is already present in *Kritik der Praktischen Vernunft*. In that work, Kant speaks of "actions that aim at realizing the highest good" ("Handlungen, die darauf abzielen, das höchste Gut wirklich zu machen" [KpV, V, 119]) and "realization of the high-

"final end" in this world, the goal towards which all our efforts should be directed [KU, V, 450]. Instead of holding that we have to earn the happiness we are to receive in the next life by being moral in this one, as he did in *Kritik der Reinen Vernunft*, he now states that we have the duty to work towards the realization of the highest good as the best possible state of affairs in the empirical world [KpV, V, 129; see also: KU, V, 450].

Yet, this attempt to integrate the juridical conception of the highest good, a remnant of Kant's pre-*Grundlegung* ethics, into the new framework leads to a series of problems. The first problem is that the juridical conception is simply an implausible candidate for the best possible state of affairs in empirical world. According to the juridical conception, any state in which there is a necessary link between happiness and virtue (with happiness being distributed according to virtue) counts as the highest good. That is, the juridical conception involves the claim that such a link is a sufficient condition for a given state of affairs to count as the highest good (given that, under this conception of the highest good, the latter is defined as a condition in which "happiness is distributed in exact proportion to virtue" [KpV, V, 110]). Yet, this claim is implausible. For a world in which all rational beings are evil and (as a consequence) unhappy would meet this condition, in spite of the fact that it is clearly not an ideal state of affairs in any meaningful sense. Thus, the suggestion that the juridical conception of the highest good offers a vision of the best possible state of affairs is not convincing.

The second problem is that Kant is eager to show that we have a duty to promote the highest good. However, assuming the juridical conception, such a duty is unintelligible. For the duty to promote the highest good under the juridical conception would be a duty to work towards a state of affairs in which happiness is necessarily distributed according to virtue. Yet, what could we possibly do to comply with this duty[21]? One option would be to support the virtuous in realizing

---

est good in the world" ("Bewirkung des höchsten Guts in der Welt" [KpV, V, 122]), phrases that indicate that he already understands the highest good as a state of affairs to be realized in the empirical realm, rather than one postulated to exist in a transcendent world.

21 Beck agrees that, once one accepts the juridical conception, it is hard to make sense of the duty to promote the highest good: "Suppose I do all in my power—which is all any moral decree can demand of me—to promote the highest good, what am I to do? Simply act out of respect for the law, which I already knew. I can do absolutely nothing else toward apportioning happiness in according with desert—this is the task of the moral governor of the universe… It is not *my* task; my task is to realize the one condition of the *summum bonum* which is within my power [i.e. virtue]" [1960, 244–5]. Consequently, Beck regards Kant's attempt to establish the existence of a duty to promote the highest good as unsuccessful. Yet, as I will try to show below, once we adopt the maximal conception of the highest good, the notion of a distinct duty to promote

their ends (and thus in achieving happiness). However, as we have seen in our discussion of the Kant's notion of human beings as ends in themselves, such a duty to support others in the pursuit of their (moral) ends has already been independently established (see Chapter 6 above). Another option would be for us to inflict pain and frustration on the wicked, actively sabotaging their projects to ensure that their lack of virtue is compensated with the appropriate amount of unhappiness. However, apart from the fact that such a duty to disrupt the lives of the wicked would be a distinctly odd one, there is no trace in Kant's writings of any willingness to endorse this apparent implication of taking seriously the juridical conception of the highest good. Overall, we can conclude that under the juridical conception Kant's claim that we have a duty to promote the highest good appears to be highly problematic[22].

The third problem for the juridical conception of the highest good is that it is not clear how the necessary link between happiness and virtue could be made consistent with a scientific picture of reality. While in the account offered in *Kritik der Reinen Vernunft* the highest good was to be realized in the next life (a claim whose truth-value cannot be decided scientifically), Kant's new account

---

it becomes not only intelligible, but also flows quite naturally from Kant's previously established positions. Thus, Beck fails to appreciate that the problem of establishing such a duty is specifically linked to the juridical conception of the highest good, which he endorses, rather than being due to a general problem with the notion of a duty to realize the highest good.

Yovel also states that the postulation of such a duty is not properly grounded in Kant's ethical framework, and, hence, arbitrary: "The inevitable conclusion is that on this crucial issue extraneous moralistic considerations are brought in, deriving probably from a vague feeling of justice, but not rooted in Kant's basic ethics" [1989, 63]. Like Beck, Yovel is operating with the juridical conception of that notion ("The three critiques only reassert in different ways that reward [i.e. happiness as a reward for virtue] is a moral claim, without supplying a reason why" [1989, 62])—though unlike Beck, he does not note that there is an alternative conception of the highest good to be found in Kant's writings. Rawls, who subscribes to the juridical conception of the highest good as well, also finds the claim that we have a duty to promote the highest good puzzling: "I do not believe... that the content of the moral law... enjoins that in a realm of ends people are to act so as to make happiness strictly proportionate to virtue. It is striking that Kant never tries to show this; in the Dialectic of the second Critique, he simply takes it for granted" [2000, 313]. As I will try to show the claim that we have a duty to promote the highest good only appears puzzling if we accept the juridical conception of the highest good—but is unproblematic if we assume the maximal conception.

22 Furthermore, as Rawls points out, the difficulty of judging the moral quality of anybody's will (including our own), which Kant himself emphasizes, makes it difficult to decide how much happiness any particular individual deserves in the first place: "the generalized precept to match happiness with virtue... requires more knowledge than we could ever expect to have" [2000, 316]. Admittedly, though, the same problem afflicts our duty to promote the happiness of others insofar as they have developed a good will.

involves the notion that a necessary link between happiness and virtue is to be established in the empirical world. Yet, as Kant himself admits, in a world governed by the laws of nature such a necessary link between happiness and virtue would be impossible [KpV, V, 119][23]. Hence, Kant holds we have to accept the belief in the possibility of the highest good as a practical truth. That is, we have to accept that it is possible to realize the highest good in the empirical world not because we have any empirical evidence that it can in fact be realized (on the contrary, as we have just seen, according to a scientific account of reality a necessary link between happiness and virtue is impossible), but rather because doing so is required by a necessary practical interest of ours (namely, the moral demand to realize the highest good in the empirical world).

Kant's argument for this claim involves the notion that we have a duty to promote the highest good. I have just argued that such a duty is unintelligible under the juridical conception. However, to gain clarity about a further problem with this conception—namely, its inconsistency with a scientific view of reality –, let us assume for a moment that this premise can be made sense of. Here, then, is Kant's argument:

1. We have a necessary practical interest in the possibility of the highest good (understood as a state of affairs in which there is a necessary link between happiness and a good will)—and, hence, a moral duty to work towards its realization (by assumption);
2. If we have a moral duty to realize the highest good, then it must be possible to realize the highest good [KpV, V, 125] (Kant's doctrine that "can follows from ought", as discussed in Chapter 4 above);
3. Hence, it must be possible to realize the highest good (from 1 and 2);
4. However, according to our theoretical understanding of empirical reality, such a necessary link between happiness and a good will is impossible;
5. If the truth of a proposition a) cannot not be determined by theoretical means, b) does not lead to logical contradiction and c) is linked to a necessary practical interest, then we are warranted to accept the truth of this proposition, if only as a practical truth (Kant's doctrine of practical knowledge, as discussed in Chapter 2);
6. Hence, we are warranted to accept the truth of the proposition that the realization of the highest good in the empirical realm is possible (from 3, 4 and 5).

---

[23] As highlighted above, the notion that a necessary link between virtue and happiness is impossible in a world governed by the laws of nature is first introduced in *Kritik der Reinen Vernunft* [KrV, III, 526]. It also recurs in *Kritik der Praktischen Vernunft* [KpV, V, 128] and *Kritik der Urteilskraft* [KU, V, 450].

The problem with this argument is that it contains a fallacy. For Kant's theory of practical knowledge (i.e. premise 5) clearly specifies that the attribution of truth-values to judgments on the basis of necessary practical interests is only possible where these truth-values cannot be decided by theoretical means (see Chapter 2 for more details)[24]. However, in the present context, the truth-value of the proposition in question (namely, the proposition "The establishment of a necessary link between a good will and happiness is possible in the empirical realm") is not indeterminate at all. Our best scientific account of reality falsifies the proposition, as Kant himself readily admits. Hence, the argument to establish the possibility of realizing the highest good under its juridical conception in the empirical world does not, as intended by the logic of practical knowledge, involve assuming the truth of a proposition whose truth-value is indeterminate from a theoretical perspective. Rather, it simply overrides available theoretical knowledge. This is a misapplication of the doctrine of practical knowledge.

Consequently, instead of allowing us to develop a self-consistent view of the world in which all our experience—theoretical and practical—is incorporated in a consistent manner (with the gaps left by theoretical knowledge filled by practical knowledge), the adoption of the notion of the highest good in the juridical conception would lead to a contradiction in our worldview. For now it would be both possible and impossible to realize the highest good in the empirical world[25].

---

[24] Thus, for instance, insofar as we regard ourselves as physical beings, our actions are determined by natural necessity. Yet, this leaves open the possibility that we are transcendentally free insofar as we have noumenal existence. No scientific evidence can show this to be impossible—and given that we have a necessary practical interest in assuming our own transcendental freedom, we are, by Kant's logic of practical knowledge, entitled to assume the objective reality of our freedom. Kant is adamant, however, in holding that if transcendental freedom could be shown to be impossible from a theoretical perspective, then we would have to give up our attempts to ascribe such freedom to us on the strength of the doctrine of practical knowledge: "Gesetzt nun, die Moral setze notwendig Freiheit (im strengsten Sinne) als Eigenschaft unseres Willens voraus, indem sie praktische in unserer Vernunft liegende, ursprüngliche Grundsätze als Data derselben a priori anführt, die ohne Voraussetzung der Freiheit schlechterdings unmöglich wären, die spekulative Vernunft aber hätte bewiesen, dass diese sich gar nicht denken lasse: so muss notwendig jene Voraussetzung, nämlich die moralische, derjenigen weichen, deren Gegenteil einen offenbaren Widerspruch enthält, folglich Freiheit und mit ihr Sittlichkeit (denn deren Gegenteil enthält keinen Widerspruch, wenn nicht schon Freiheit vorausgesetzt wird) dem Naturmechanismus den Platz einräumen" [KrV, III, 18].

[25] Consequently, the acceptance of the juridical conception would lead precisely to the kind of paradoxical metaphysical questions that Kant set out to eliminate in *Kritik der Reinen Vernunft*: how would the ideal state of affairs that is the highest good be realized if it is, by Kant's own confession, impossible according to the laws of nature? Would the laws of nature have to be sus-

Thus, far from helping to satisfy the interests of reason in systematic unity and completeness (which is the proper purpose of the use for the ideas of reason), the idea of the highest good under its juridical conception would lead to a frustration of these interests.

The fourth problem linked to the juridical conception is that postulating a necessary link between happiness and virtue is simply unnecessary in Kant's mature ethical framework[26]. At the beginning of this chapter, we have seen that the juridical conception draws some plausibility from the correct observation that a state of affairs in which the virtuous are unhappy or the wicked enjoy happiness cannot count as an objectively good one from the viewpoint of Kant's theory of value. However, it simply does not follow from this that in a good state of affairs happiness must be distributed *according to* virtue (let alone "*necessarily*"). In the highest good under the maximal condition, for instance—in which all rational beings have achieved a good will and enjoy the greatest possible happiness—the virtuous would not be unhappy nor would the wicked be happy (for in this ideal scenario, all rational beings have developed a good will—and there simply would be no wicked people)[27]. Yet, the maximal conception does not involve the postulation of a necessary link between happiness and virtue. Thus, while the necessary link between happiness and virtue that marks the juridical conception of the highest good was necessary for the account of morality proposed in *Kritik der Reinen Vernunft* (in which our virtue in this world was the cause of our happiness in the next world), such a strong causal relationship—and, hence, the juridical conception of the highest good—is simply not necessary in his mature ethical framework[28].

---

pended or modified? Would there be a Christian Judgment Day at the end of time (i.e. when natural laws no longer apply) in which happiness would finally be distributed according to merit?

26 This is noted by Reath: "The description of [the content of the notion of the highest good] in terms of a proportionality of happiness and virtue has no apparent basis in Kant's moral view" [1988, 613].

27 This is noted by Rawls [2000, 313].

28 In fact, Kant's position involves a confusion between the claim, which is valid in the context of Kant's theory of value, that having a good will is the ground for the objective value of our happiness and the problematic claim that our having a good will must be the cause of our happiness. Thus, a debunking of the juridical conception of the highest good involves the insight that a good will can be the condition for the objective value of one's happiness without being the cause of that happiness.

The maximal conception of the highest good

All these considerations should lead us to regard the juridical conception of the highest good as an unfortunate anachronism in Kant's late ethical writings. The maximal conception of the highest good, on the other hand—according to which the best possible state of affairs in this world is one in which all rational beings have developed a good will and enjoy happiness (i.e. the realization of their ends)—is not only consistent with Kant's mature ethical theory, but is also consistent with many (though not all) of the uses to which Kant intends to put the notion of the highest good. This becomes clear if we subject the maximal conception of the highest good to the same tests that led us to reject the juridical conception.

Firstly, unlike the juridical conception, the maximal conception of the highest good is a recognizable vision of the best possible state of the world: given that, as we have discussed above, the happiness of a person who has developed a good will (as is, by definition, the case under the highest good) is not only a subjective good, but also a conditional-objective good, the highest good is the condition in which both the unconditional-objective good (i.e. the good will) and the conditional-objective good (i.e. the happiness) of each rational being has been realized. This complete realization of the good both in its unconditional-objective and its conditional-objective form is not only a completely good state of affair—but, crucially, also one that could not possibly be improved upon, given Kant's conception of the good. In this sense, from the perspective of Kant's theory of value it is quite recognizably the best possible state of affairs in the world.

Secondly, given the maximal conception of the highest good, establishing the duty to promote the highest good is straightforward. According to the Grounding Thesis, discussed in Chapter 3, duties are based on the interests of pure reason. Furthermore, as we have seen in Chapter 6, if something is identified as an interest of pure reason, its realization is an objective good. Yet, to say that something is an objective good is to say that it is something a fully rational being would want—and a duty is simply the will of a fully rational being, presenting itself to us finite rational beings in the form of obligation [GMS, IV, 413–4]. From this it follows that we have a duty to realize the objective good. Yet, if we are under an obligation to pursue the objective good in every particular instance, then we have an obligation to bring about the state of affairs in which the complete objective good is realized. This state of affairs is the highest good— that is, the state of affairs in which all interests of reason are fully satisfied. Hence, we have a duty to work towards a state of affairs in which all rational beings have achieved a good will (the satisfaction of the interests of our moral-practical reason) as well as enjoying the highest possible degree of happiness (the realization of the ends of our technical-practical reason)[29]. Consequently, if we adopt the maximal conception of the highest good, it is easy to make sense of the claim that we have a duty to promote the highest good[30].

While the demands made on us by the categorical imperative regard the formal quality of our individual maxims, the duty to promote the highest good is concerned with the impact that all our actions taken together have on the world: "The duty to promote the highest good no longer means that a person should make himself good, but that he should also make the *world* good. He ought to transcend the limits of his private morality and posit to himself, as the subject of moral progress, not only his own personality, but also the entire world" [Yovel, 1989, 74]. In this sense, the duty to promote the highest good should be regarded, in Yovel's words, as the "second stage" of Kant's moral theory [1989, 32][31]: while the first stage is concerned with the moral quality of our character, the second maps out an *Endzweck*, a final end that our actions in their entirety are set to realize in the world: "Das Bedürfnis eines durch reine Vernunft aufgegebenen, das Ganze aller Zwecke unter einem Prinzip befassenden Endzwecks (eine Welt als das höchste auch durch unsere Mitwirkung mögliche Gut) ist ein Bedürfnis des sich noch über die Beobachtung der formalen Gesetze zu Hervorbringung eines Objekts (das höchste Gut) erweiternden

---

29 The argument in this form is not to be found in Kant's texts—but it does, I believe, flow naturally from his overall position once we accept the maximal conception of the highest good. The closest Kant comes to making the case for a duty of promoting the highest good under the maximal conception is at the beginning of *Religion*. His argument starts by noting that all willing involves the willing of an end, i.e. a desired state of affairs that our willing is aimed at bringing about [R, V, 4]. Consequently, even moral willing—i.e. the application of our will to satisfy a rational, not a material interest—involves the willing of an end, "for our reason can certainly not be indifferent towards the question: what will be the result of our acting morally" [R, V, 5]. The answer to that question is: the end of moral willing is the state of affairs in which all the interests of our reason—i.e. both in its technical-practical application and its moral-practical application—are satisfied. That is, the end of moral willing is the highest good. Hence, the highest good is the state of affairs that would be willed by a perfectly rational, all-powerful being. At this point, the last step we need to establish the duty to promote the highest good is the observation that duty simply is the willing of a perfectly rational being which presents itself in the form of an imperative to finite rational beings [GMS, IV, 414], i.e. beings whose will does not necessarily do that which is objectively good. Surprisingly, though, Kant does not take this step—but rather branches out into a long, rather cryptical footnote, at the end of which he claims to have established the duty to promote the highest good [R, VI, 6n].
30 We will discuss the duty to promote the highest good in more detail in Chapter 9 below.
31 See also: [Rawls, 2000, 146] and [Guyer, 2000, 78] We will explore Yovel's notion of the two stages of Kant's ethical system more closely in Chapter 9 below.

uneigennützigen Willens. Dieses ist eine Willensbestimmung von besonderer Art, nämlich durch die Idee des Ganzen aller Zwecke" [TP, VIII, 279n; see also: KU, V, 453].

Thirdly, there is no problem in making the ambition to realize the highest good under the maximal conception consistent with our scientific view of the world. For neither developing a good will, nor achieving happiness, nor doing both at the same time is impossible in the world of our experience. In *Kritik der Urteilskraft*, Kant seems to be suggesting the opposite in his tale of the virtuous man who struggles to be moral but finds himself confronted with evil and treachery, sees other virtuous men perish—and finally concludes that only faith in the existence of God and in divine justice can allow him to regard the joint achievement of virtue and happiness as possible [KU, V, 452]. Yet, Kant surely overstates his case here: while it is true that without divine intervention it is difficult to see how virtue could be the *cause* of happiness (as it would be required under the juridical conception of the highest good), it is by no means impossible to conceive of virtuous men being happy even in a world governed by the laws of nature[32].

However, our conclusion about the possibility of realizing virtue and happiness in the empirical world comes with two important caveats. First, Kant holds that, as we have seen, that we can never be sure about the true moral quality of our will (i.e. we can never be sure whether we have achieved a good will, for the reasons highlighted in Chapter 5). The highest moral achievement that is possible for finite rational beings is *virtue*—i.e. embattled morality, a condition in which we have to guard the uncertain moral quality of our will against the continuous onslaughts and attempts at seduction from our inclinations (we will discuss this notion in more detail in Chapter 8 below). Second, Kant holds that happiness is an ideal condition of complete realization of all our ends that will never be fully realized [KU, V, 430], given the ever-changing nature of our inclinations and desires (which are the incentives on the basis of which we adopt these ends, as discussed in Chapter 5).

Thus, the ideal conception of the world embedded in the maximal conception of the highest good should not be understood as a state of affairs that will be achieved at some point, but rather as an ideal towards which we are striving (and have the duty to strive) constantly—without ever reaching it. Consistent

---

32 Kant himself admits that achieving virtue and happiness together is not impossible in *Kritik der Praktischen Vernunft*: "Denn dass eine dem moralischen Gesetze angemessene Würdigkeit der vernünftigen Wesen in der Welt, glücklich zu sein, mit einem dieser proportionierten Besitze dieser Glückseligkeit in Verbindung an sich unmöglich sei, kann doch niemand behaupten wollen" [KpV, V, 144].

with Kant's insistence on the importance of constant activity (discussed in Chapter 8 below), it is a goal towards which we are travelling, rather than a blissful state that we reach once and for all[33]. However, what matters for our purposes here is that there is no reason to think that coming infinitely close to realizing this goal in the world of our experience is inconsistent with a scientific conception of reality[34].

Overall, the maximal conception—unlike the juridical conception—offers a coherent vision of the completely good state of affairs in the empirical world, which flows naturally from Kant's theory of value and makes it easy to explain why we have a duty to work towards its realization. This should lead us to discount Kant's use of the juridical conception in his mature ethical works as the unfortunate preservation of a notion rooted in a superseded ethical framework —and to attempt to build our understanding of his mature ethical theory around the maximal conception of the highest good.

However, precisely because of the third point discussed above—the obvious ease with which the highest good in its maximal conception fits into our scientific view of reality—the attempt fully to integrate it into Kant's system creates significant havoc. For Kant intends to use the duty to realize the highest good as the foundation for his "moral proof" of the objective reality of the notion of God [KU, V, 458] (as he did in *Kritik der Reinen Vernunft*[35]). However, once we accept the maximal conception of the highest good, the argument aiming to establish the objective reality of the notion of God breaks down.

To understand why this is so, we have to remember that the idea of God— which plays a central role both in the mechanical worldview, discussed in Chap-

---

[33] Readers should not be disturbed if, on the one hand, we speak about our duty of realizing the highest good in the empirical world, while claiming, on the other, that the highest good is an idea that can never be fully realized. What is meant by the former is that we have the duty to bring about a state of affairs that resembles as closely as possible the vision of an ideal rational order in which both the unconditional-objective good (virtue) and the subjective good (happiness) are fully realized, even though the complete realization of the highest good in the empirical world is a limit condition we are never to reach (or can never know to have reached, given the epistemic uncertainty regarding the moral quality of our will).

[34] The fourth argument against the juridical conception—that the necessary link it postulates between happiness and virtue is simply unnecessary and implausible—also does not apply to the maximal conception.

[35] This is slightly imprecise. More correctly, we should say that in *Kritik der Reinen Vernunft*, Kant argues that we need the assume the objective reality of the notion of God to establish the real possibility of the highest good (as a good to be achieved in the next life) and, hence, the validity of the moral law, while in *Kritik der Urteilskraft* he holds that we need it to establish the objective reality of the notion of God to show that it is possible to comply with our duty to realize the highest good in the empirical world.

ter 1, and the teleological worldview, discussed in Chapter 6—has a merely regulative status in these theoretical contexts. As Kant establishes in his epistemological studies, which we have discussed in Chapter 2 above, we cannot have theoretical knowledge of the objects of concepts if there are no intuitions from our senses corresponding to these concepts (i.e. we cannot ascribe real possibility to these concepts from a theoretical perspective [KpV, V, 139]). Concepts we use for regulative purposes (i.e. to structure our knowledge of the world) in spite of the fact that they cannot be given real possibility are mere ideas of reason. However, we have seen as well that Kant allows for the ascription of objective reality to these ideas on the basis of the doctrine of practical knowledge. According to that doctrine, we can regard a given concept as having real possibility if it can be shown that doing so is required to make sense of our predicament as agents in the world. Kant hopes that this allows him to establish the articles of traditional metaphysics, which he had removed from the sphere of possible theoretical knowledge, as objects of practical knowledge[36].

In this sense, the moral proof of the objective reality of the notion of God aims at grounding the objective reality of the idea of God from a practical point of view[37]. It is, in fact, an extension of the argument for the possibility

---

36 "Der Akt der negativen Aufhebung war die Aufgabe der KrV, die positive Kehrseite der resurrectio Gottes und der Unsterblichkeit aus moralischer Notwendigkeit ist Sache der Gegenkritik, der KpV" [Brandt, 2007, 378].
37 In addition, it aims at securing the full content of that notion (i.e., benevolence, omnipotence and omniscience). Kant holds that the notion of God as an idea of theoretical reason is a meager one that lacks many of the features that we associate with divinity: "Der Begriff von Gott bleibt also auf dem empirischen Wege (der Physik) immer ein nicht genau bestimmter Begriff von der Vollkommenheit des ersten Wesens, um ihn dem Begriffe einer Gottheit für angemessen zu halten (mit der Metaphysik aber in ihrem transzendentalen Teile ist gar nichts auszurichten)" [KpV, V, 139]. Thus, any theoretical argument merely establishes, as a regulative assumption, the existence of a "non-sensuous something" that functions as the ground of the empirical world ("[D]er Begriff von einem nichtsinnlichen Etwas..., welches den letzten Grund der Sinnenwelt enthalte, der noch kein Erkenntnis (als Erweiterung des Begriffs) von seiner inneren Beschaffenheit ausmacht" [KU, V, 466]). Only the moral proof of the existence of God allows us to establish the complete notion of God: "Ich versuche nun diesen Begriff an das Objekt der praktischen Vernunft zu halten, und da finde ich, dass der moralische Grundsatz ihn nur als möglich unter Voraussetzung eines Welturhebers von höchster Vollkommenheit zulasse. Er muss allwissend sein, um mein Verhalten bis zum Innersten meiner Gesinnung in allen möglichen Fällen und in alle Zukunft zu erkennen; allmächtig, um ihm die angemessenen Folgen zu erteilen; eben so allgegenwärtig, ewig u. s. w.. Mithin bestimmt das moralische Gesetz durch den Begriff des höchsten Guts, als Gegenstandes einer reinen praktischen Vernunft, den Begriff des Urwesens als höchsten Wesens, welches der physische (und höher fortgesetzt der metaphysische), mithin der ganze spekulative Gang der Vernunft nicht bewirken konnte. Also ist der Begriff von Gott ein ursprünglich nicht zur Physik, d. i. für die spekulative Vernunft, sondern zur Moral

of the highest good, which we have examined in the context of our discussion of the juridical conception of the highest good above. As we have seen, the argument takes the following form:

1. We have a necessary practical interest in establishing the possibility of the highest good—and, hence, a moral duty to work towards its realization in the empirical world (as we have just argued);
2. If we have a moral duty to realize the highest good, then it must be possible to realize the highest good (Kant's doctrine that "can follows from ought");
3. Hence, it must be possible to realize the highest good (from 1 and 2);
4. However, according to our theoretical understanding of empirical reality, it is impossible to realize the highest good;
5. If the truth of a proposition a) cannot not be determined by theoretical means, b) does not lead to logical contradiction and c) is linked to a necessary practical interest, then we are warranted to accept the truth of this proposition, if only as a practical truth (Kant's doctrine of practical knowledge);
6. Hence, we are warranted to accept the truth of the proposition that the realization of the highest good in the empirical realm is possible (from 3, 4 and 5).

To establish the objective reality of the idea of God, three further steps are required:

7. If we are warranted to assume the objective reality of a given idea of reason, then we are also warranted to assume the objective reality of the conditions of its possibility [KU, V, 471n];
8. We can only conceive of the possibility of the highest good if we assume the existence of God, that is, an omnipotent, omniscient and benevolent power that underwrites the proper distribution of happiness according to virtue [KU, V, 450][38];
9. Hence, we are warranted in accepting the objective reality of the notion of God, if only as a practical truth (from 6, 7 and 8)[39].

---

gehöriger Begriff, und eben das kann man auch von den übrigen Vernunftbegriffen sagen, von denen wir als Postulaten derselben in ihrem praktischen Gebrauche oben gehandelt haben" [KpV, V, 140; see also: KU, V, 444; R, VI, 139].

38 See also: [KpV, V, 124] and [R, VI, 6n].

39 Kant offers this argument in [KpV, V, 124–25], [KU, V, 450] and [R, VI, 139]. The presentation of his argument is shortened to fit our purposes here. For a more detailed statement of the argument, see Beck [1960, 274].

I have argued above that Kant's attempt to run the first part of this argument with the juridical conception of the highest good breaks down once the doctrine of practical knowledge comes into the picture, given that a necessary condition for the application of that doctrine—namely, that the truth-value of the proposition in question not be settled from a theoretical perspective—is not met in this case (for we can already decide the truth-value of the proposition "The establishment of a necessary link between a good will and happiness is possible in the empirical realm" from a theoretical perspective).

However, if we replace the juridical conception with the maximal conception, the argument also fails. This time, it breaks down at step 4, for with the maximal conception in place the realization of the highest good is no longer inconsistent with the laws of nature, as discussed above[40]. That is, the argument aims to show that we need to believe in the existence of God to convince ourselves that it is possible to realize the highest good in the empirical realm. Yet, once we adopt the maximal conception of the highest good, there is no reason to doubt that proposition in the first place—and, hence, no need to introduce the notion of God to assuage the doubt. God, who was supposed to appear on the scene as the guarantor of the logical possibility of the highest good [Yovel, 1989, 95], is no longer needed once we operate with the maximal conception of the highest good.

If this is correct, it is a severe blow for Kant's overall project for two reasons. First, as we have just highlighted, Kant aims to integrate the articles of traditional metaphysics (such as the notions of freedom and God), critically re-interpreted as ideas of practical reason, into his philosophical system [KU, V, 473 – 4][41]. While his case for the objective reality of freedom has been endorsed in Chapter 4, his attempt to give a coherent account of the objective reality of the notion of God must be seen to be failure[42]. Secondly, and more importantly, Kant's wider proj-

---

40 In this context, Kant's rather awkward attempt to convince his readers of the impossibility of being both virtuous and happy in [KU, V, 452], discussed in the text above, could be read as an attempt to reconstruct the moral proof of the existence of God on the basis of the notion of the highest good under the maximal conception—an attempt, one must conclude, that is more courageous than convincing.
41 See our discussion in note 55 in Chapter 6 above.
42 The third article of traditional metaphysics Kant is seeking to integrate into his system is the notion of the immortality of the soul. As with the idea of God, the idea of the immortality of the soul is treated as a postulate: that is, a proposition that is incapable of theoretical proof (or disproof), but whose objective reality we are required to assume for practical reasons. As in the case of the idea of God, assuming the objective reality of the notion of the immortality of the soul is held to be a necessary condition for the possibility of realizing the highest good. Kant states the argument for this claim in *Kritik der Praktischen Vernunft*: the notion of the highest

good involves that of a will that has achieved moral perfection ("die völlige Angemessenheit der Gesinnungen zum moralischen Gesetze" [KpV, V, 122]). This moral perfection is the holiness of the will, i.e. a condition in which the will is no longer affected by sensuous desires (we will discuss the notion of a holy will in more detail in Chapter 8 below). Thus, our duty to bring about the highest good involves a duty to attain a holy will. However, as Kant himself points us, no finite (and, hence, embodied) rational being can ever attain a holy will, i.e. completely free his will from the influence of his sensuous desires. The best we can hope for is a constant and infinite approximation towards the ideal of a holy will. Given that this is the only way in which we can comply with our duty to develop a holy will, we have to assume the possibility of such a constant and infinite approximation to the ideal condition of holiness: "[Die Heiligkeit des Willens kann] nur in einem ins Unendliche gehenden Progress zu jener völligen Angemessenheit angetroffen werden, und es ist nach Prinzipien der reinen praktischen Vernunft notwendig, eine solche praktische Fortschreitung als das reale Objekt unseres Willens anzunehmen" [KpV, V, 122]. Yet, such an infinite progress is only possible under the assumption of an infinite life span, i.e. if we assume the immortality of the soul. Given the doctrine of practical knowledge, this warrants us to postulate the immortality of the soul—not as the object of theoretical cognition, but of practical faith (i.e. as an objectively valid assumption made on necessary practical grounds).

There is much that is problematic about this argument—and it has come in for general criticism from commentators ("The postulate of immortality of the soul is the most problematic in Kant's own terms and the least adequate to its intended purpose" [Yovel, 1989, 295n; see also: Beck, 1960, 270–1; Allison, 1990, 171–73]. We will only focus on two flaws here. First, the argument is built on the postulation of a duty to attain holiness. But there is no good reason to assume that we have such a duty. As we will discuss in the text below, the best finite rational beings can aim for is virtue, i.e. a sensuously affected will that makes the moral law its highest determining ground in spite of being subject to temptation. A holy will, on the other hand, is a will that is not subject to any sensuous desires. Hence, to achieve a holy will we would somehow have to get rid of our sensuous nature (this is reminiscent of Kant's occasional throw-away remarks in *Grundlegung* [GMS, IV, 428] and *Kritik der Praktischen Vernunft* [KpV, V, 118] that finite rational beings should be happy if they could get rid of their desires). Yet, to ask finite rational beings to rid themselves of their sensuous nature is a meaningless demand (what could we possibly do to comply with it?). It is notable that there is no other context in which Kant speaks about a duty to achieve holiness. On the contrary, in *Metaphysik der Sitten,* he writes that "[d]ie größte moralische Vollkommenheit des Menschen ist: seine Pflicht zu tun und zwar aus Pflicht"[MS, VI, 392; see also TP, VIII, 285]. That is, for us to reach moral perfection it is sufficient that we do our duty out of duty (i.e. have a good will). The implication is that moral perfection for finite rational beings does not require holiness (i.e. the additional condition that our will be free from any kind of sensuous temptation). The only reason for assuming a duty to develop a holy will is the need to get the argument for the immorality of the soul off the ground. Without the assumption of such a duty, it collapses at the first step [Guyer, 2000. 352]. Given that this not a strong reason for accepting the postulation of such a duty, the claim that we have a duty to develop a holy will should be rejected.

The second problem with the argument for the immortality of the soul is that the notion of constant and infinite progress towards a holy will that continues after our physical death is inect is to unify our theoretical worldview with our practical experience of the world (see Chapter 2 above). His final move in that project is to identify the intelligent mind that we have to assume as the cause of the teleological order in the world (see Chapter 6 above) with the moral God whose existence we have to assume to be able to account for the possibility of realizing the highest good [KU, V, 454–5]. This would entitle us to ascribe moral intentions to the creator of the teleological order in the world—and, hence, to regard the world as created for a moral purpose [KU, V, 458; see also: KpV, V, 145]. This, in turn, grounds the identification of the highest good (and, hence, of ourselves as those whose self-realization the highest good consists in) as the final end of creation (for only if we assume that the world has been created by a moral intelligence do we have grounds to ascribe to the world a moral-teleological structure) [KU, V, 453–4]. Unfortunately, this happy ending for Kantian philosophy remains unrealized as long as the moral proof for the existence of God remains unsuccessful, as our analysis above suggests it is.

---

coherent, given that what prevents us from attaining a holy will in the empirical world is the influence of our sensuous nature on our will. Once our body dies, this obstacle is removed immediately—and no further progress of any kind is required [Yovel, 1989, 113]. This is another way of saying that our noumenal will is always already a holy will (i.e. not subject to sensuous influences). Hence, the notion of a constant progress by our noumenal will after our death towards the ideal condition of holiness is inconsistent with Kant's own conception of our noumenal will.

There are two more points that we should be aware of in this context: First, the notion of the immortality of the soul was in fact a crucial feature of the account of the highest good Kant operated with in *Kritik der Reinen Vernunft*, where, as discussed in the text above, the highest good was conceived not as a state of affairs to be attained in the empirical world, but rather as a reward waiting for us in a next life. The role played by this notion of the next life in fact made the assumption of our continued existence after our death (and, hence, the immortality of the soul) necessary. However, with Kant's switch to his new conception of the highest good as the ideal state of affairs in this world, the notion of the immortality of the soul loses both its usefulness and its legitimacy. Secondly, Beck correctly points out that Kant's argument for the immortality of the soul implicitly operates with the maximal conception of the highest good [1960, 268]: for the notion of the highest good Kant uses in the first premise of the argument is one involving not merely the distribution of happiness according to virtue (as would be the case under the juridical conception), but rather moral perfection. That is, it contains the element of maximization that distinguishes the maximal conception from the juridical conception (which is marked by the notion of proportionate distribution). Thus, the fragile state of Kant's arguments for the postulates—the idea of God and the immortality of the soul—can be gauged from the fact that he is forced to operate with the juridical conception of the highest good to build his argument for the objective reality of the idea of God, only then to switch to the maximal conception to make the case for the objective reality of the idea of the immortality of the soul.

For the purposes of our discussion, the failure to establish the objective reality of the notion of God has two implications:
- First, we have no grounds for holding that the world is designed for the purpose of aiding us in our moral mission to realize the highest good. This is less problematic than it might sound. To see why this is so, we should note that Kant mentions two different purposes the notion of God serves in our project of pursuing the highest good. On the one hand, it is to ensure the logical possibility of the realization of the highest good. As we have seen above, Kant (with the juridical conception of the highest good in mind) holds that from our theoretical understanding of the world, it would appear impossible to realize the highest good. Hence, to avoid a contradiction of reason with itself (as would happen if we were subject to a moral demand to do something that is impossible), we need to assume the objective reality of God to ensure that that which we are morally required to do (i.e., realize of the highest good) can in fact be done: "[Die Vernunft] wird ... für ihr eigenes praktisches Gesetz und die dadurch auferlegte Aufgabe, also in moralischer Rücksicht, [die Idee von Gott] als real anerkennen müssen, um nicht mit sich selbst in Widerspruch zu kommen" [KU, V, 471n].

On the other hand, the notion of God serves to *sustain our hope that we will be rewarded* appropriately for our moral efforts. This is highlighted by the following dialogue from the moral catechism in *Metaphysik der Sitten*:

> [Lehrer:] Wenn wir uns aber auch eines solchen guten und tätigen Willens, durch den wir uns würdig (wenigstens nicht unwürdig) halten glücklich zu sein, auch bewusst sind, können wir darauf auch *die sichere Hoffnung* gründen, dieser Glückseligkeit teilhaftig zu werden?
> [Schüler:] Nein!...
> [Lehrer:] Hat die Vernunft wohl Gründe für sich, eine solche die Glückseligkeit nach Verdienst und Schuld der Menschen austeilende, über die ganze Natur gebietende und die Welt mit höchster Weisheit regierende Macht als wirklich anzunehmen, d. i. an Gott zu glauben?
> [Schüler:] Ja. [MS, VI, 482; my emphasis][43]

On this second interpretation of the role played by the notion God, it serves to entitle us to the "certain hope" that we will be rewarded with happiness for our efforts to develop a good will.

---

43 See also: „Die Gottseligkeitslehre kann also nicht für sich den Endzweck der sittlichen Bestrebung ausmachen, sondern nur zum Mittel dienen, das, was an sich einen besseren Menschen ausmacht, die Tugendgesinnung, zu stärken, dadurch dass sie ihr (als einer Bestrebung zum Guten, selbst zur Heiligkeit) *die Erwartung des Endzwecks*, dazu jene unvermögend ist, *verheißt und sichert*" [R, VI, 183; my emphasis].

Thus, God can either be seen to ensure that realizing the highest good is logically possible—or to guarantee that our moral efforts will be met with the appropriate reward. Under the juridical conception of the highest good, these two roles played by the notion of God coincide. For under that conception, the highest good consists precisely in a moral distribution of happiness, which, in the absence of God, could not be seen to be possible. Thus, God, by functioning as the guarantor of the dispensation of happiness according to moral effort, ensures the logical possibility of the highest good.

However, from the viewpoint of the maximal conception of the highest good —which has been endorsed in this essay and according to which the best possible state of affairs is one in which all rational beings have developed a good will and enjoy the greatest possible happiness—neither of these two functions played by the notion of God is required. The notion that we should expect to be rewarded with happiness for our moral efforts—which, in any case, appears to be profoundly at odds with the spirit of Kant's ethical project—plays no role under this conception of the highest good. Given that all that is required for the highest good to be logically possible under the maximal conception is that neither the pursuit of a good will nor the pursuit of our happiness (nor the joint pursuit of both) is impossible, there is no reason to believe that we need the notion of God in order to be able to secure the logical possibility of the highest good. Furthermore, with the maximal conception in place, we require no guarantees of any kind: no guarantee that we will succeed in developing a good will, no guarantee that our efforts will be rewarded with happiness. This is the irony of Kant's failed attempt to make the moral proof of God work: the reason the proof fails is that, under the maximal conception, God simply is not needed.

- The second implication of the failure of Kant's moral proof of God is more problematic. It is the fact that the objective reality of the notion of God, which we were aiming to establish, is the ultimate ground for regarding ourselves as the final end of creation, in the sense discussed in Chapter 6. For the objective reality of the notion of God allows us to accept the notion of the empirical world as teleologically ordered not merely as a regulative idea (as is the case if we accept it on purely theoretical grounds), but as objectively real (if only as a practical truth). That is, once we have reason to attribute objective reality to the notion of God as the intelligent author of creation, the idea of a teleologically structured world turns from a merely regulative idea into a constitutive one, i.e. one that also has objective reality for us. This notion of the objective reality of a teleologically ordered world, in turn, grounds the objective reality of our status of *Endzweck* of creation. If the notion of God does not have objective reality, then neither does that of the teleological order of reality nor our status as *Endzweck* of creation[44]. Put differently, if we have no grounds for believing that there is an intelligent creator of the world (even if only as an item of practical knowledge), then we have no grounds for holding that the world has been created for a purpose—and, thus, that we are the purpose it has been created for.

What remains is the regulative use of the idea of God in its theoretical application (both in the context of regarding the world as governed by mechanical laws of nature, as discussed in Chapter 1, and in that of regarding it as teleologically structured, as discussed in Chapter 6). However, the attribution of objective reality to the idea of God and the unification of practical and theoretical philosophy has to wait until the moral proof for the existence of God can be made to work. As long as this proof is not forthcoming, we find ourselves faced with the moral demand to create the best possible state of affairs—in which all rational beings have achieved both virtue and happiness—in a world in which such a project is possible (i.e. not inconsistent with the governing laws of nature), but which, for all we know, is utterly indifferent to this plan of ours (rather than being the creation of a morally inspired God).

Conclusion

Kant calls the best possible state of affairs in the world the "highest good". The notion of the highest good combines the unconditional-objective good (virtue) with the subjective good (happiness). However, Kant is unclear about how we are to conceive of the relation of virtue and happiness in the highest good. In fact, he appears to be operating with two different conceptions of that notion: according to the juridical conception, the highest good is the state of affairs in which happiness is distributed in exact proportion to virtue, while according to the maximal conception, it is the condition in which all rational beings have developed a good will and enjoy the highest possible degree of happiness.

I have argued that we should reject the juridical conception of the highest good, given that: a) the necessary link between happiness and virtue it postulates is neither a necessary nor a sufficient condition for a given state of affairs to count as the best possible state of affairs; b) the juridical conception makes it

---

[44] "Wohl…können wir sagen: dass nach der Beschaffenheit unseres Vernunftvermögens wir uns die Möglichkeit einer solchen auf das moralische Gesetz und dessen Objekt bezogenen Zweckmäßigkeit, als in diesem Endzwecke ist, ohne einen Welturheber und Regierer, der zugleich moralischer Gesetzgeber ist, gar nicht begreiflich machen können" [KU, V, 455].

difficult to account for the claim that we have a duty to promote the highest good; and c) it seems impossible to make the juridical conception of the highest good consistent with a scientific account of reality. The maximal conception of the highest good, on the other hand, does not suffer from similar defects, as: a) it is built around the notion of the complete satisfaction of the interests of reason—and, hence, from the perspective of Kant's theory of value, quite recognizably the best possible state of affairs in the world; b) it allows us to explain why we have a duty to promote the highest good; and c) it is consistent with a scientific account of reality.

Consequently, we should accept the maximal conception of the highest good. However, once we do so, Kant's moral proof of the objective reality of the notion of God is doomed to failure. This makes it impossible to complete the last step in Kant's philosophical enterprise—namely, to establish the objective reality of the notion of God as the benevolent, omnipotent and omniscient author of nature, entitling us to regard the world as created for a moral purpose.

8 *Aufklärung*

Kant conceives of enlightenment (*Aufklärung*) as the process by which we become increasingly aware of, and capable of acting in line with, the requirements for the proper use of both our technical-practical reason (i.e. our ability to realize our ends) and our moral-practical reason (i.e. our ability to choose good ends), thus coming closer to realizing the highest good in the empirical world. Introducing the notion of *Aufklärung* allows us to make the important distinction between the two conceptions of the good human life Kant is operating with: on the one hand, the highest good as the ideal condition of the complete satisfaction of all the interests of reason—and, on the other, our actual existence spent in the attempt to realize this ideal condition, overcoming the weakness of our imperfect wills and the temptation posed by our sensuous nature. The latter form of existence—the struggle to come increasingly close to an ideal condition that we can never fully achieve—is, Kant holds, the best possible life that we can hope to be leading as finite (and, hence, flawed) rational beings in the empirical world.

The history of reason

Aufklärung, for Kant, is the process in which we come to understand the proper requirements for the use of our rational faculties—and learn to employ our rational faculties in accordance with these requirements [SDO, VIII, 146n]. This conception of *Aufklärung* is linked to Kant's account of our rational faculties as not fully emancipated from the influence of our physical nature—nor entirely aware of the proper conditions for their use. To appreciate Kant's conception of *Aufklärung*, we will explore his speculative account of the development of our rational faculties, as presented in his 1786 essay "Mutmaßlicher Anfang der Menschengeschichte". We will paraphrase this account in terms of the three predispositions of human nature (*Tierheit*, humanity and personality) introduced in Chapter 6. In doing so, we will re-visit some of the themes we have encountered in previous chapters. This should help us to connect the different strands of our discussion so far.

At the first stage of our development—that of *Tierheit* –, reason plays no role and our actions are guided by instinct. Human beings are simply animals, passive, determined directly by their physical desires[1]—and without any reflective distance. At the same time, though, they live in harmony, both in the sense

---

[1] "Die Kausalität der Vernunft ist Freiheit. Die bestimmende Kausalität der Sinnlichkeit: Tierheit" [R 5619, XVIII, 258].

that their desires are well-coordinated by their instinct and in that this instinct guides them safely through the world. This instinct, Kant holds, is not a magic faculty that we lose at later stages of development, but rather our sensual nature before the advent of our reason [MAM, VIII, 111]. This is one of the ironies of Kant's anthropology: the same desires which in combination with our not yet fully developed rational powers are a constant source of conflict and strife, are identified as that which allows for peaceful coordination in our pre-rational existence on the stage of *Tierheit*.

At the second stage of development, our rational faculties awaken [MAM, VIII, 111]. This is the stage at which we achieve *Menschheit*. We gain not only self-awareness—but also the talent for reflective distance from our desires, i.e. the ability to set ends for ourselves [MS, VI, 392]. Yet, which ends we set is still determined by our desires. That is, we have reason, but we use it as a mere tool for the satisfaction of our physical desires [R, VI, 45], without challenging their authority to determine which objects are valuable and are hence to be pursued by means of our actions. At this stage, Kant thinks, our reason is still too weak, too entangled with our physical nature [KU, V, 430] and too little aware of its own essential interests to guide itself on the basis of these[2]. Consequently, the use of reason at the stage of mere *Menschheit* is "lawless" ("gesetzloser Gebrauch der Vernunft" [SDO, VIII, 145]). It is not guided by reason's essential interests; rather, our desires function as the main determining factor of our will. Kant calls this a condition of heteronomy [KpV, V, 33]—which, properly speaking, is a misnomer, given that this other ("hetero") of reason (the desires) does, according to Kant, not provide any rules or laws ("nomoi"), but merely prevents reason from guiding itself by its own laws.

Given that our reason is still "shaky" ("wankend" [R 1466, XV, 645]) at this stage, our new freedom comes with dangers and frustrations. Among these, Kant suggests, is that, first, our newly developed rational faculties are initially less than well suited for the task of managing our lives [MAM, VIII, 114], in a way that the emergence of reason positively endangers our existence. Where our instincts reliably provided for our needs, our actions, guided by our still

---

[2] This feature of Kant's conjectural account of the development of reason is important, given that it motivates his insistence on the need for reason to become increasingly aware of its own interests, limitations and modes of functioning. "Reason does not immediately possess the full, though limited scope that it can attain in principle, but must be actualized in a progressive move of self-explication" [Yovel, 1989, 14]. Kant emphasizes how slowly and tentatively the development of reason proceeds: "[Die Vernunft] wirkt aber selbst nicht instinktmäßig, sondern bedarf Versuche, Übung und Unterricht, um von einer Stufe der Einsicht zur andern allmählich fortzuschreiten" [IAG, VIII, 19].

weak rational faculties, often go awry. In particular, Kant highlights, reason's lust for experimentation not only functions as an engine of progress, but is also a source of perils for the early humans [MAM, VIII. 111][3].

Second, Kant emphasizes the sense of terror that comes with the first experience of freedom. In the instincts, under whose tutelage he had hitherto lived, man had a clear guide on which steps to take in the world (which foods and mates to choose etc.). Through reason, man acquires the responsibility of choice. He loses the certainty of instinct and stares into the existential abyss of having to choose among a myriad of options [MAM, VIII, 112][4]. Through reason, he also acquires awareness of himself as a fragile creature in a violent world: while animals blissfully graze in the narrow horizon of the present moment, man—now endowed with self-awareness—sees himself as confronted with an uncertain future filled with dangers, suffering and death [MAM, VIII, 113].

Lastly, Kant highlights the contribution reason makes to the corruption of man. As we have seen, reason spurns man to try and invent new pleasures—and urges him not to accept the prohibitions given to him from the outside. In consequence, he commits barbarities, which at an earlier stage his instincts would have prevented and which at a later stage a fully developed reason will shield him against [MAM, VIII, 115]. It is thus that Kant, the ardent advocate of human freedom, blames freedom, where it is "lawless", not constrained by the requirements of its proper use, as the main source of evil in the world: "Alle Übel in der Welt kommen aus der Freiheit" [E, 1924, 153].

In sum, the step from *Tierheit* to *Menschheit* is marked by the emergence of reason (even though, at this stage, we still lack the ability to use reason according to its own requirements) and a weak form of freedom (negative freedom, in the form of self-reflective distance). Yet, it is also marked by a loss of the harmony that characterized our earlier animal condition: our existence becomes conflict-ridden and our actions incoherent and volatile[5].

The next step in the development of reason Kant highlights is that of human beings seeing themselves as confronted with moral demands [MAM, VIII, 113], as

---

3 However, this is not to say that Kant disapproves of this process of experimentation, as Yovel points out: "[Reason] gives rise to 'artificial desires' (luxuries), which Kant considers as genuine humanizing factors...[c]ontrary to Rousseau (and partly also to Marx), who sees such artificial needs as signs of derangement or alienation" [1989, 191].

4 "Reason, regarded as an empirical sign of our freedom, is precisely our capacity for an indeterminate mode of life, one that is open-ended and self-devised, in contrast with the life of other animals, which is fixed for them by instinct" [Wood, 2003, 17].

5 "Das erste, was der Mensch tun muss, ist, dass er die Freiheit unter Gesetze der Einheit bringt; denn ohne dieses ist sein Tun und Lassen lauter Verwirrung" [R 7202, XIX, 280].

well as their becoming aware of their ability to guide themselves on the basis of these demands. This discloses to them their status not only as physical beings, but also as transcendentally free[6]. Like the first transition—the one from *Tierheit to Menschheit*—this step introduces something radically new into the world. In the first transition, the new element was the emergence of reason, of self-aware agents, who see themselves as capable of choosing for themselves the ways in which they satisfy their natural desires. In the second transition, the new element is the notion of an end that we give to ourselves—i.e., an end of an action that is not suggested to us by something external to our reason (such as our desires), but one that reason generates for itself. Humans are the only beings that can give ends to themselves in this sense—and this only thanks to their personality, i.e. their ability to guide their will on the basis of the interests of reason [KU, V, 431]. Yet, our having personality—and, hence, being aware of the demands of the moral law on us—is still consistent with our not acting on these demands. It is only at the last stage of human development—namely, that at which we develop a good will—that we make the moral law the highest determining ground of our will.

In addition to making the distinction between personality and the good will, discussed in Chapter 5 above, Kant also distinguishes between a good will and a holy will. To have a holy will is to have a good will that is constitutionally incapable of adopting a maxim that is contrary to the moral law [KpV, V, 32]. Only disembodied rational beings would be capable of a holy will, for only they would not be subject to the distorting influence of sensuous desires. Hence, such beings would necessarily follow the moral law (i.e. necessarily have a holy will). Consequently, for them the moral law would not present itself in the form of an imperative [GMS, IV, 414]. Finite rational beings—whose will is "affected" (though not determined) by their desires—are incapable of reaching the state of holiness. No amount of good intentions can change the fact that we feel the temptation of our desires to make exceptions for ourselves from the demands of the moral law. Thus, while we feel that it is within our powers to act according to these demands [R, VI, 49], we can never guarantee that, at any given moment, we will not be knocked off course by the surreptitious influence of our desires. In this sense, our propensity to evil in our will is "radical" [R, VI, 37]: the tendency of giving influence to our desires is not an accidental feature, but lies in our will's very nature [R, VI, 32]. Consequently, the moral law presents itself to finite (i.e. physically embodied) rational beings such as ourselves in the form of an im-

---

[6] For the link between moral consciousness and awareness of our transcendental freedom, see our discussion in Chapter 4 above.

perative: i.e. a demand that we will follow not by necessity, but following which requires effort and struggle.

Thus, while we can achieve a good will—i.e. reach a condition in which the moral law determines our will –, a holy will is unachievable for us [KpV, V, 122]. The idea of a holy will is the projection of an ideal condition we are never to reach—and which we nonetheless require as a reference point to orient ourselves in our efforts and which, by fighting the influence of our desires on our will, we can come increasingly close to: "Diese Heiligkeit des Willens ist gleichwohl eine praktische Idee, welche notwendig zum Urbilde dienen muss, welchem sich ins Unendliche zu nähern das einzige ist, was allen endlichen vernünftigen Wesen zusteht" [KpV, V, 32][7].

This, thus, is the basic dialectic of Kant's practical philosophy: we have to win peace and harmony (in the form of full rational control over our lives) by means of a prolonged struggle (against the temptations of our desires)—with the special twist that we are never to reach the state of peaceful bliss. The latter is a mere bait, the grail that we continue to travel towards, without us ever being able to reach it. Thus, the desired state of activity, marked by full rational control (in the sense explained below), is never realized—yet, our life is nonetheless marked by activity, namely the constant effort of self-discipline, of battling against the temptations of our physical nature to come closer to this desired state.

Kant sees us as expulsed from the certainties of a life guided by our natural instincts and not yet arrived at the certainty of a life guided by fully competent rational powers. In this sense, we find ourselves in a *Zwischenraum* [MAM, VIII, 116], a conflict-ridden transitional stage between two forms of existence in which we are at peace with ourselves and the world around us, the passive-harmonious condition of our animal condition and the active-harmonious condition of an ideal rational order[8]. We are left to our still fledgling, erring rational abilities, bound to plunge into sin and degeneration[9]. Just like the early humans, we easily come to see reason as a burden. We are constantly lured into trying to escape

---

[7] For the role played by Kant's notion of a holy will in his unsuccessful attempt to establish the objective reality of the immortality of the soul, see note 42 in Chapter 7 above.

[8] As Kant puts it in R 1501: "Tierheit und Instinkt ist gut. Tierheit und Freiheit (mit Vernunft) ist böse, bringt aber vermittelst der Vernunft das Gute" [XV, 790].

[9] In describing the fragile condition of our rational faculties, Kant writes that "[D]ie Vernunft [ist noch nicht] zu der gehörigen Stärke gelangt... , den Zügel zu führen" [A, VII, 253]. He also speaks about "[den] mit der Einbildungskraft und den Sinnen verwickelten Verstand... " [KU, V, 430], "[den] angebornen Hange zur Verkehrung der Triebfedern in den Maximen unserer Willkür" [R, VI, 60] and "[die] Macht der die Vernunft schwächenden Neigungen" [MS, VI, 384].

from the responsibility of using our own reason to guide our lives [WA, VIII, 35]. We are, furthermore, tempted into misology, the hatred of reason [GMS, IV, 395]—and embrace prejudices and superstitions where these promise less demanding routes in life than the hard school of self-discipline afforded by reason.

Aufklärung

As we have seen, Kant conceives of reason as the new element that breaks into the harmony of our animal existence[10]. He emphasizes how little prepared we are to use it and how easy it is for us to slip into the misuse of reason (or to despair of the task of using it responsibly). The only chance he sees for us to move on from our current troubled condition, the *Zwischenraum*, is for us to learn how to use this new instrument responsibly and according to its own requirements. Yet, we are not given any manual from which we could glean what these requirements are. Rather, we have to find out for ourselves how to use our rational faculties, through inquiry and reflection. This is the process of *Aufklärung* (enlightenment): the increasing understanding of how to make proper use of our reason—and the reform of our lives that results from applying this understanding in practice[11].

In its practical dimension, this process of *Aufklärung* involves three elements, which Kant highlights in the following passage from his lectures on anthropology:

> Der Mensch ist durch seine Vernunft bestimmt, in einer Gesellschaft mit Menschen zu sein und in ihr sich durch Kunst und Wissenschaften zu kultivieren, zu zivilisieren und zu moralisieren, wie groß auch sein tierischer Hang sein mag, sich den Anreizen der Gemächlichkeit und des Wohllebens, die er Glückseligkeit nennt, passiv zu überlassen, sondern vielmehr tätig, im Kampf mit den Hindernissen, die ihm von der Rohheit seiner Natur anhängen, sich der Menschheit würdig zu machen. [A, VII, 325]

---

10 O'Neill notes correctly that "Kant's developmental account of reason fits well with an evolutionary view of cognition" [1989, 43].
11 Enlightenment understood in this way is not so much the apotheosis of reason, as rather the process whereby reason discovers itself as a problem, realizes that it is not fully aware of its own requirements and limits. Yovel comments: "[T]he emergence of Enlightenment as a vehicle of progress represents a true revolution in itself. It is a conversion... of the mode of consciousness, whereby reason frees itself from dependence on the blind natural dialectic and, becoming aware of its own structure and precepts, it projects them as a conscious historical plan and makes this awareness an actual agent of change" [1989, 153]. The important social dimension of this process of *Aufklärung* will be discussed in Chapter 9 below.

The key elements in this passage are the three verbs at the beginning—to cultivate, to civilize and to moralize –, which Kant understands in the following way[12]:
- Cultivation is the perfection in the use of our technical-practical reason, i.e. the ability to realize the ends we have set for ourselves;
- Moralization is the perfection in the use of our moral-practical reason, i.e. the ability to set our ends properly (that is, in line with the requirements of our pure practical reason);
- Civilization is the process of entering into political and ethical community with other human beings.

We will have achieved the highest good in the sense discussed in Chapter 7—and thus will have fully completed the task of *Aufklärung*—if we have fully cultivated, civilized and moralized ourselves. For the highest good would be realized if we achieved perfection in both the moral-practical use of our reason (i.e. developed a good will) and the technical-practical use of reason (which allows us to secure our happiness), with civilization being necessary to achieve either[13]. In the following, we will look at the different elements of *Aufklärung* in more detail. We will discuss culture and morality in this chapter, while leaving civilization for the next chapter on Kant's conception of social life.

Culture, for Kant, is the perfection in the use of our technical-practical reason, i.e. perfection in our ability to achieve the ends that we have set for ourselves: "Die Hervorbringung der Tauglichkeit eines vernünftigen Wesens zu beliebigen Zwecken überhaupt (folglich in seiner Freiheit) ist die Kultur" [KU, V, 449]. That is, in urging us to cultivate ourselves, Kant is demanding that, in addition to perfecting our ability to choose good ends, we ensure that our will is effective, i.e. capable of bringing about the ends we have chosen. Given the definition of happiness as the realization of our ends that we have arrived at in Chapter 7, culture in this sense is the ability to bring about our own happiness.

Kant identifies two elements to culture: self-discipline and skill (*Geschicklichkeit*) [KU, V, 431–2]. *Skill* is the ability to choose and conduct our actions in a way that they are effective in bringing about the desired end. This involves both the knowledge of the appropriate means for realizing a given end—and the powers and talents required to apply that knowledge. In order to realize a

---
12 Kant's use of these three terms is discussed by Wood [2003, 20].
13 Yet, as we have seen, the highest good is an ideal condition that it is impossible for us ever to reach fully. The good life that we are actually capable of is not one of realized perfection, but rather one of constant struggle to come increasingly close to the ideal condition of the highest good, against the obstacles of temptation, laziness and error.

given end, we need to be aware of the causal structure of reality to choose the means that are appropriate for bringing about the end[14]. Yet, this knowledge of the relevant causal relations by itself would help us little if we did not also have the talents and powers to apply this knowledge in practice[15]. Given that, in contrast to animals, man is marked by the indeterminacy of his ends (as choosing our ends is an act of freedom), he needs to develop his talents broadly to ensure that whichever of these he requires for the realization of his ends will be available [GMS, IV, 415][16].

The second element of culture is self-discipline. In the context of culture (i.e. the use of our technical-practical reason), self-discipline refers to the ability to work towards the realization of our ends without being distracted and disrupted

---

14 In this sense, Kant says, the rules of our technical-practical reason should be understood to be part of theoretical, not practical philosophy—i.e. as concerned with the causal relations that govern the world we want to manipulate, rather than our ability to be guided by the ideas of reason [KU, V, 172].

15 Kant counts among these talents the ability "to have influence on other men and their wills" [KU, V, 172]. Wood, in particular, highlights how Kant shows himself aware of the important social dimension in our ability to realize our ends—i.e. of the fact that in the context of many of our projects, other people will be essential instruments in our ventures: "We are social beings whose chief means to happiness lies in controlling and manipulating other people" [1999, 260; see also: Brandt, 2007, 198]. Moralization for Kant crucially involves not just regarding the others as tools. Yet, this should not be confused with the claim that we are not to regard them as tools at all. In fact, it is legitimate to regard others as instruments for the realization of our ends (i.e. make use of them as taxi drivers, tennis partners and tax lawyers)—as long as we also regard them as ends in themselves, in the sense discussed in Chapter 6 above.

16 Kant even postulates a duty to develop our talents on this basis: "Mit dem Zwecke der Menschheit in unserer eigenen Person ist also auch der Vernunftwille, mithin die Pflicht verbunden, sich um die Menschheit durch Kultur überhaupt verdient zu machen, sich das Vermögen zu Ausführung allerlei möglichen Zwecke, so fern dieses in dem Menschen selbst anzutreffen ist, zu verschaffen oder es zu fördern" [MS, VI, 392]. What is surprising about this is that Kant often denies that we have a duty to work towards our own happiness: "Ein Gebot, dass jedermann sich glücklich zu machen suchen sollte, wäre töricht; denn man gebietet niemals jemanden das, was er schon unausbleiblich von selbst will" [KpV, V, 37; see also: MS, VI, 386]. Yet, as happiness for Kant consists in the realization of our ends, this commits him to the rather odd position of claiming that we have a duty to develop our talents to be able to realize our happiness, in spite of the fact that we do not have a duty to pursue our happiness. However, there are some passages in which he asserts that we do have a duty to promote our own happiness—either indirectly, to avoid that our own misery diminishes our ability to act morally [KpV, V, 93; see also: Allison, 1996, 123], or directly, given that the duty to promote the happiness of all as part of our effort to realize the highest good involves the promotion of our own happiness [MS, VI, 451; see also: Guyer, 2000, 341]. We will discuss the justification for the claim that we have a duty to develop our talents in Chapter 9 below.

in our efforts by the influence of our desires[17]. Adopting an end and pursuing it often involves working towards a desired state of affairs over a prolonged period of time. All the while, our will is subject to the influence of our ever-changing desires, luring and tempting it with new objects of interest. Without self-discipline in the use of our technical-practical reason, the pursuit of our ends, whatever these might be, would constantly be at risk of being aborted due to the emergence of new desires pulling us into new directions[18].

While culture concerns the ability to realize the ends we have chosen, morality concerns the ability to choose good ends (i.e. those that are consistent with the interests of reason)[19]. Given the central role played by morality in Kant's overall philosophical project, it is not surprising that his discussion of this notion is more sprawling and less easy to summarize than that of the notion of culture. However, the following four points are central to Kant's notion of moralization:

– First, moralization involves the development of self-discipline, which we have already encountered in the context of our discussion of culture above. In the context of morality (i.e. the use of our moral-practical reason), self-discipline is our will's ability to ensure that the process of choosing our ends is not compromised or hijacked by the influence of our inclinations and desires. Crucially, this does not mean that we are not to pursue our own subjective ends (and,

---

17 While Kant asserts that self-discipline is part of culture [KU, V, 432], many of his descriptions of self-discipline involve our ability to free ourselves from the influence of our desires thanks to the influence of the moral law. These passages would suggest that self-discipline would be an aspect of morality (i.e. our moral-practical reason) rather than culture (i.e. our technical-practical reason). As I try to show in the text, the logic of Kant's position implies that we should be operating with two different notions of self-discipline, one related to the use of our technical-practical reason, one related to the use of our moral-practical reason.

18 This is the problem of the weakness of the will that Kant discusses in *Religion:* "Die Gebrechlichkeit (fragilitas) der menschlichen Natur ist selbst in der Klage eines Apostels ausgedrückt: Wollen habe ich wohl, aber das Vollbringen fehlt, d. i. ich nehme das Gute (das Gesetz) in die Maxime meiner Willkür auf; aber dieses, welches objektiv in der Idee (in thesi) eine unüberwindliche Triebfeder ist, ist subjektiv (in hypothesi), wenn die Maxime befolgt werden soll, die schwächere (in Vergleichung mit der Neigung)" [R, VI, 29].

19 Note that the claim that morality is concerned with our ability to choose good ends is not inconsistent with our assertion in Chapter 5 that the moral worth of an action, for Kant, is not concerned with ends, but with the subjective determining ground of our will. For if we act on the basis of the demands of the moral law (i.e. choose the moral law as our highest maxim), this will lead us to pursue certain ends (such as the highest good) because we recognize them to be objectively good. So, what matters for the moral quality of our will is which highest maxim we adopt—but the consequence of our adopting the moral law as our highest maxim will be that we pursue ends that we recognize to be objectively good (and pursue them *because* they are objectively good).

hence, our own happiness). Rather, it means that we only pursue our subjective ends if doing so is consistent with the demands of the moral law: "[Z]uerst muss ich sicher sein, dass ich meiner Pflicht nicht zuwider handle; nachher allererst ist es mir erlaubt, mich nach Glückseligkeit umzusehen, wie viel ich deren mit jenem meinem moralisch- (nicht physisch-) guten Zustande vereinigen kann" [TP, VIII, 283; see also: KpV, V, 93].

To understand the importance of the notion of self-discipline for Kant's account of moralization, we have to spend a moment highlighting its links to the notions of our rational thought as an autonomous activity, on the one hand, and of the flawed condition of our rational faculties, on the other. Conscious thinking, for Kant, is a rule-governed activity. We only use our conscious thought correctly, whether in its theoretical or its practical application, if we follow the appropriate rules of thought—that is, the rules that allow for a non-contradictory and complete use of our rational faculties. However, nothing guarantees that we identify these rules correctly or, even if we have identified them, apply them in a proper and consistent manner. That is, we do not benefit from any form of guidance or oversight from a higher authority in the use of our reason[20]. This is what Kant means when he says that reason has to oversee the use of all our faculties (i.e. we have to reflect consciously on how to make use of our various faculties), without there being, in turn, another faculty overseeing it [KpV, V, 120]. The only guide reason has in its application is reason itself.

This motivates the focus on the notion of a critique of reason [KrV, III, 484]: in the absence of any guidance in the use of our conscious thought, our thinking has to provide its own guidance, reflecting on itself, identifying the rules for its

---

20 Kant argues that the absence of such oversight is what makes the free use of reason possible in the first place: "[W]ürden Gott und Ewigkeit mit ihrer furchtbaren Majestät uns unablässig vor Augen liegen [dann würde die] Übertretung des Gesetzes... freilich vermieden, das Gebotene getan werden; weil aber die Gesinnung, aus welcher Handlungen geschehen sollen, durch kein Gebot mit eingeflößt werden kann... so würden die mehrsten gesetzmäßigen Handlungen aus Furcht, nur wenige aus Hoffnung und gar keine aus Pflicht geschehen, ein moralischer Wert der Handlungen aber, worauf doch allein der Wert der Person und selbst der der Welt in den Augen der höchsten Weisheit ankommt, würde gar nicht existieren. Das Verhalten der Menschen, so lange ihre Natur, wie sie jetzt ist, bliebe, würde also in einen bloßen Mechanismus verwandelt werden, wo wie im Marionettenspiel alles gut gestikulieren, aber in den Figuren doch kein Leben anzutreffen sein würde" [KpV, V, 147]. Thus, as Yovel puts it, the negative result of Kant's transcendental metaphysics (the existence of God is not subject of a possible theoretical proof) has an important positive practical corollary: "Although the supreme objects of traditional metaphysics (God, the soul, the cosmos as a whole) must be declared cognitively problematic, this negative result does a positive service to the practical interest of reason by barring the possibility of heteronomous morality based upon the will of a transcendent God, and thus by clearing the way for a moral law that man legislates himself" [1989, 259].

own proper use and putting these into practice[21]. What makes this process extraordinary is that not even the standards which determine what counts as success in the use of our conscious thought are given to us from the outside. Rather, the only standards by which we can guide our efforts are the interests of our reason [SDO, VIII, 146]. Yet, even once we have identified the proper rules for the use of our conscious thought, based on the interests of reason, we constantly run the risk of misapplying these, especially in the realm of practice, due to the temptations we are subject to from our sensuous nature. As we have seen above, evil for Kant is precisely the inability to follow the correct rules of willing, the propensity to fall into a lawless use of our practical reason [R, VI, 57n].

This leads us to the importance of self-discipline. Self-discipline in the use of our practical reason is the ability not to be distracted or corrupted in the application of the proper rules of willing by any temptations or desires ("Man nennt den Zwang, wodurch der beständige Hang von gewissen Regeln abzuweichen eingeschränkt und endlich vertilgt wird, die Disziplin" [KrV, III, 466–7]). It involves the ability of our will to give precedence to the lawful principles of proper (self-consistent) willing and resist the influence of our desires and inclinations, which by their nature are disorderly and lawless [R, VI, 57n]. Thus, the problem of self-discipline flows directly from Kant's hybrid anthropology—i.e. his conception of man as endowed with both a physical body and reason, without the interests of these two elements of human nature being naturally coordinated[22].

However, we have to be careful not to misunderstand the nature of the conflict between these two elements of human nature. Kant sometimes speaks as if the development of self-discipline involved taming—and establishing order among—our inclinations ("Die ethische Gymnastik besteht... in der Bekämpfung der Naturtriebe" [MS, VI, 485; see also: KpV, V, 73; TP, VIII, 312]). This is linked to his tendency to conceive of the inclinations and desires as the source of evil [A, VII, 144]. Both these positions suggest a battle-of-the-forces model, according to

---

[21] The antinomies are useful precisely because, as contradictions of reason, they indicate that we are making some mistake in the use of our reason, thus forcing us to inquire into the rules we follow in applying our reason, allowing us to discover our mistakes and leading us to gain a better understanding of the proper rules for the use of our reason: "[Di]e Vernunft [wird] genötigt, diesem Scheine nachzuspüren, woraus er entspringe, und wie er gehoben werden könne, welches nicht anders als durch eine vollständige Kritik des ganzen reinen Vernunftvermögens geschehen kann; so dass die Antinomie der reinen Vernunft, die in ihrer Dialektik offenbar wird, in der Tat die wohltätigste Verirrung ist, in die die menschliche Vernunft je hat geraten können, indem sie uns zuletzt antreibt, den Schlüssel zu suchen, aus diesem Labyrinth herauszukommen" [KpV, V, 107].

[22] It is also linked to Kant's effort, discussed in Chapter 1, to distinguish carefully between the empirical and the rational element in both cognition and practice.

which the problem of morality somehow involves a struggle between the forces of good (our reason) and evil (our sensuous nature) for control over our will. As Allison puts it: "[M]uch of Kant's language... reinforces the view that he conceives of the moral life as essentially one of conflict between the psychic forces in which the human will is playing field and prize rather than autonomous arbitrator" [1990, 126][23].

Luckily, this extravagant picture of the struggle between reason and inclination fighting for control over our will is not Kant's settled view. Rather, as we have seen above, he holds that the problem of evil (and, hence, of self-discipline) is entirely internal to the will (i.e. practical reason itself): the will, still shaky in the use of its own freedom [A, VII, 229] and hazy about the proper rules for its application, finds itself subject to the lure of our inclinations [KpV, V, 74]. Not yet fully isolated from the influence of sensuous desire, it is suffering from a "continuous inclination to violate the law" ("einen kontinuierlichen Hang zur Übertretung... des Gesetzes" [KpV, V, 128]). The solution to this problem is self-discipline, i.e. the will's ability to isolate itself from this temptation [MS, VI, 408]. Discipline is, thus, the will's self-liberation from the tyranny of foreign interests [KU, V, 432]. Hence, on Kant's considered view, the will is not the battleground on which a conflict of forces takes place, but rather the active protagonist in the fight for its own reformation.

Kant is careful to emphasize the element of struggle in this process. It is, he holds, "not enough to let the seeds of goodness develop in an unimpeded manner", but rather it is required for us to "fight against the cause of evil, which lies within us" [R, VI, 57]. The will of finite rational beings such as ourselves is necessarily "affected" ("affiziert" [MS, VI, 213]) by the influence of our desires—and, hence, subject to temptation. We require "sacrifice" ("Aufopferung") and "inner coercion" ("innere Nötigung", [KpV, V, 83]) to resist that temptation. Kant calls this *Selbstzwang:* the ability to force ourselves to do that which does come neither naturally, easily nor with pleasure—but which we nonetheless recognize as the right thing [KpV, V, 83–4].

To the degree to which we are able to discipline ourselves in this way, we achieve *virtue (Tugend)*: not the peaceful, temptation-free holiness of the will enjoyed by a noumenal will, but "moral disposition in conflict" ("moralische Gesinnung im Kampfe" [KpV, V, 84; see also R, VI, 93; MS, VI, 383]), a ceaseless struggle to make the moral law the highest determining ground of our will

---

[23] Similarly, Ameriks notes "the unfortunate picture, which Kant himself sometimes encourages, of noumenal dutifulness and phenomenal inclination in its entirety pushing against each other in an absurd quasi-physical battle in a veritable no-man's-land" [2000, 320].

and to resist the siren calls of our desires. This is the best, the most moral condition that we as sensuously affected—and, hence, continuously tempted—beings can aspire to: to come as close as possible to the ideal of a holy will, without ever being able to reach it [MS, VI, 446]:

> [A]lle moralische Vollkommenheit, zu welcher der Mensch gelangen kann, [ist] immer nur Tugend..., d. i. gesetzmäßige Gesinnung aus Achtung fürs Gesetz, folglich Bewusstsein eines kontinuierlichen Hanges zur Übertretung, wenigstens Unlauterkeit, d. i. Beimischung vieler unechter (nicht moralischer) Bewegungsgründe zur Befolgung des Gesetzes, folglich eine mit Demut verbundene Selbstschätzung und also in Ansehung der Heiligkeit, welche das christliche Gesetz fordert, nichts als Fortschritt ins Unendliche dem Geschöpfe übrig [lassend]. [KpV, V, 128][24]

In this sense, the holy will is our "unachievable destiny" ("unerreichbare Bestimmung" [KpV, V, 112]), while virtue (*Tugend*) is precisely the never-ending struggle to come closer to a moral perfection that will be forever denied us [KpV, V, 84].

Developing moral self-discipline, Kant holds, results in a purification of the will. By reducing the influence of sensuous impulses on the will, we increasingly replace the confusion of motivating factors with a tidy hierarchy, in which rational determining grounds of our will dominate the sensuous ones [KpV, V, 93]. In thus struggling to impose the "purity of the moral principle" [KpV, V, 156] on our actions we set out on the path to good will, which is also a "pure will", i.e. one whose supreme determining ground is the moral law [KpV, V, 109][25]: "In dieser Reinigkeit [ist] der wahre Wert der Moralität anzutreffen" [TP, VIII, 284][26].

---

24 I have argued that the notion of a duty to attain a holy will („Heiligkeit, welche das christliche Gesetz fordert") is incoherent—and should be rejected (see note 42 in Chapter 7 above).
25 In the picture Kant is operating with here the influence of physical nature is that which "contaminates and weakens" [VT, VIII, 395n] our moral disposition, while the moral law is marked by "purity" [GMS, IV, 390]. This is another variation on Kant's hybrid anthropology, this time cloaked in the terminology of hygiene.
26 In *Religion*, Kant suggests that the process of moralization involves "the restoration, in its entire purity, of the predisposition to the good in the human heart" ("Die Anlage zum Guten im menschlichen Herzen in ihrer Reinigkeit wieder herzustellen", [R, VI, 50]). This is misleading, for it suggests that this purity is a condition that we enjoy in some initial state of moral bliss, only to lose it later on. However, a key element of Kant's account of the development of reason, which we have discussed in the text above, is that morality (just as rational order) is something artificial, something that presents itself as an ideal and which we have to impose as a foreign element onto our animal existence. Thus, the achievement of moral purity is not a "restoration" of a purity we have lost, but the establishment of something radically new. Kant himself recognizes this in the same work, when he writes that the moment we become conscious of ourselves as beings who can determine their own actions, our will is already corrupted (due to its tendency

Furthermore, given that for Kant the empirical-physical element is that which is subjective and idiosyncratic, while the rational element is that which is objective and shared, this process of purifying our will also involves an *objectification of the will*—i.e. is a process in which we reduce the influence on our willing of that which is subjective and idiosyncratic, while increasing the influence of that which is objective and shared[27]. In acting morally, we subject our maxims to the "principle of universality" ("Prinzip der Allgemeingültigkeit" [KU, V, 471]) and prioritise our shared rational interests over our "private goals" ("Privatabsicht" [GMS, IV, 396; see also A, VII, 329]), by learning to consider the latter not from our own biased viewpoint, but rather "impartially, as if from the perspective of a stranger" [R, VI, 6][28].

- Secondly, moralization is a process in which we establish ourselves as *fully unified* agents. While a will that is only guided by technical-practical reason, without any influence of moral-practical reason (as in Kant's thought-experiment of humanity without personality, discussed in Chapter 6), can achieve some measure of harmony among our different projects, it is nonetheless potentially self-contradictory, as nothing prevents it from acting against the essential interests of reason, leading to the forms of self-contradictions discussed in Chapter 3. Only as moral agents, guided by the moral law (and, thus, the interests of reason) and pursuing the realization of the highest good can we ensure that our will becomes fully self-consistent, with all our ends integrated into a systematic unified whole [GMS, IV, 437]. In fact, in following the moral law, our reason aims to achieve the same systematically unified order in the field of practice that it strives for in its theoretical

---

to be guided by sensuous desires). The best thing we can do is start from this condition of original evil (not one of initial purity) and attempt to purify our will: "[S]o früh wir auch auf unsern sittlichen Zustand unsere Aufmerksamkeit richten mögen, so finden wir: dass mit ihm es nicht mehr res integra ist, sondern wir davon anfangen müssen, das Böse, was schon Platz genommen hat (es aber, ohne dass wir es in unsere Maxime aufgenommen hätten, nicht würde haben tun können), aus seinem Besitz zu vertreiben: d. i. das erste wahre Gute, was der Mensch tun kann, sei, vom Bösen auszugehen, welches nicht in den Neigungen, sondern in der verkehrten Maxime und also in der Freiheit selbst zu suchen ist" [R, VI, 57n].

27 An ethical mindset, for Kant, is one in which subjective (i.e. idiosyncratic) ends are subordinated to objective (i.e. shared) ends: "Der Begriff eines Zwecks, der zugleich Pflicht ist, welcher der Ethik eigentümlich zugehört, ist es allein, der ein Gesetz für die Maximen der Handlungen begründet, indem der subjektive Zweck (den jedermann hat) dem objektiven (den sich jedermann dazu machen soll) untergeordnet wird" [MS, VI, 389].

28 This is linked to Kant's more general theme that correct thought is thought which takes into account the viewpoint of all other rational beings, a topic we will discuss in more detail in Chapter 9 below.

employment: "So werden die Bestimmungen einer praktischen Vernunft... den Kategorien des Verstandes gemäß, aber nicht in der Absicht eines theoretischen Gebrauchs desselben, um das Mannigfaltige der (sinnlichen) Anschauung unter ein Bewusstsein *a priori* zu bringen, sondern nur um das Mannigfaltige der Begehrungen der Einheit des Bewusstseins einer im moralischen Gesetze gebietenden praktischen Vernunft oder eines reinen Willens *a priori* zu unterwerfen, Statt haben können". [KpV, V, 65][29]

Kant calls this process of establishing ourselves as unified agents under the guidance of the moral law the formation of a character ("[D]ie Gründung eines Charakters... ist absolute Einheit des inneren Prinzips des Lebenswandels überhaupt" [A, VII, 295]). To develop a character, for Kant, involves not only achieving harmony among the different aspects of our existence (our reason and our desires) at any given point in time, but also consistency in our actions across time, due to our acting on firm, unchangeable principles. In this sense, he defines a character as "praktische konsequente Denkungsart *nach unveränderlichen Maximen*" [V, 152; my emphasis][30].

- Thirdly, in the process of moralization we establish ourselves as *fully active* agents. Kant's characterizes our pre-moral condition as one of passivity, in that our will is under the dominion of our sensuous desires [A, VII, 267]. In moralizing ourselves, we free ourselves from this condition of passivity. We bring our lives under rational control—and thus for the first time gain full dominion over ourselves: "Die Tugend also, so fern sie auf innerer Freiheit gegründet ist, enthält für die Menschen... ein bejahendes Gebot, näm-

---

29 This analogy is noted by Allison: "Just as in the theoretical realm the proper, regulative function of reason is to guide enquiry by framing an ideal order involving the systematic connection of phenomena under laws, so too, in the practical realm, its proper function is to guide conduct by framing an order of ends or ought-to-bes. Like its theoretical analogue, this activity is an expression of the spontaneity of reason because it goes beyond what is dictated by the sensible data, which in this case are the desires and inclinations of the agent" [1990, 40; see also: Beck, 1960, 143].

30 Kant considers the stability and regularity that comes with acting on firm principles to be so valuable that he sometimes suggests that doing so is commendable even if the principles we act on are of questionable moral quality: "Einen Charakter aber schlechthin zu haben, bedeutet diejenige Eigenschaft des Willens, nach welcher das Subjekt sich selbst an bestimmte praktische Prinzipien bindet, die er sich durch seine eigene Vernunft unabänderlich vorgeschrieben hat. Ob nun zwar diese Grundsätze auch bisweilen falsch und fehlerhaft sein dürften, so hat doch das Formelle des Wollens überhaupt, nach festen Grundsätzen zu handeln (nicht wie in einem Mückenschwarm bald hierhin bald dahin abzuspringen), etwas Schätzbares und Bewundernswürdiges in sich; wie es denn auch etwas Seltenes ist" [A, VII, 292].

lich alle seine Vermögen und Neigungen unter seine (der Vernunft) Gewalt zu bringen, mithin... Herrschaft über sich selbst [zu erreichen]" [MS, VI, 408; see also A, VII, 144]. In this sense, success in the process of moralization allows us to achieve a condition in which "reason alone is in power" [KU, V, 433], guiding itself purely on the basis of its own interests [KpV, V, 118]. Given Kant's conception of reason as spontaneity (see Chapter 1 above), moralizing ourselves involves establishing the control over our lives by that which is active within us, while reducing the influence of that which is passive.

By thus learning to guide ourselves by means of our own reason, determining our ends on the basis of our own rational interests, we take responsibility for our own lives [MS, VI, 237]. Yet, for this purpose we have to overcome our natural laziness and our fear of the uncertainty that comes with making unguided use of our rational faculties [WA, VIII, 35][31]. It is tempting and comfortable to avoid taking responsibility and rather let others think and decide for us [A, VII, 229][32], thus making what Kant calls a merely "passive use of our reason" [L, IX, 76]. However, remaining in the resulting condition of "self-inflicted immaturity" [WA, III, 35]— due to a lack of self-discipline and courage, not a lack of ability—is to frustrate reason's need to guide itself on the basis of its own interests[33].

---

31 "The Enlightenment spirit... courageously accepts the anxiety, instability, discontent, and self-alienation that rational thinking inevitably brings with it" [Wood, 1999. 319].

32 "[D]ie Trägheit sehr vieler Menschen macht, dass sie lieber in Anderer Fußtapfen treten als ihre eigenen Verstandeskräfte anstrengen. Dergleichen Menschen können immer nur Kopien von Andern werden, und wären alle von der Art, so würde die Welt ewig auf einer und derselben Stelle bleiben" [L, IX, 46].

33 Consistent with his insistence on the importance of active self-determination, Kant rejects conceptions of the good human life centered on the notion of effortless happiness. Where life provides for our needs easily—as Kant believed was the case on the island of Tahiti, which was newly discovered in his days—our motivation further to develop our talents is blunted. Indulging in such easy happiness, Kant writes in his review of Herder's *Ideen zur Philosophie der Geschichte der Menschheit*, would lower us to the level of cattle: "Meint der Herr Verfasser wohl: dass, wenn die glücklichen Einwohner von Otaheite [Tahiti], niemals von gesittetern Nationen besucht, in ihrer ruhigen Indolenz auch tausende von Jahrhunderten durch zu leben bestimmt wären, man eine befriedigende Antwort auf die Frage geben könnte, warum sie denn gar existieren und ob es nicht eben so gut gewesen wäre, dass diese Insel mit glücklichen Schafen und Rindern, als mit im bloßen Genusse glücklichen Menschen besetzt gewesen wäre?" [VIII, 65]. A life lived in indulgence is, for Kant, one in which we fail to realize the ideal conception of ourselves as fully rational beings—and, hence, one that is devoid of value ("warum sie denn gar existieren"). We have seen how, for Kant, the good life is essentially one in which we constantly strive to impose rational order on our existences. The example of Tahiti serves, for Kant, to show

- Lastly, moralization, for Kant, is a form of self-realization. It is a process by which our empirical person is reformed to resemble as closely as possible our proper self, i.e. the ideal conception of ourselves as noumenal will [KpV, V, 43]. As we have seen in Chapter 3, the notion of a noumenal will is that of a will that necessarily makes the moral law (and, thus, the interests of reason) the highest determining ground of its action. In this sense, a noumenal will is a holy will. Given that our own sensuously affected will, unlike the idealized noumenal will, is subject to the temptations posed by our desires, we can never reach this ideal condition of holiness. However, in striving to make the moral law the highest determining ground of our will, we can come increasingly close to realizing the ideal condition of transcendentally free agency—i.e. our proper self—in the empirical realm [KpV, V, 32][34]. In this sense, by moralizing ourselves, we become what we most properly are (to borrow Nietzsche's phrase)[35].

Thus, we can summarize Kant's notion of moralization by saying that it involves achieving the self-discipline required to guide ourselves on the basis of the inter-

---

the danger of a condition in which this projecting power is absent: it is a state of stagnation—a fall back into the passive existence enjoyed by the grazing animal that fully lives in the present: "Im Leben (absolut) zufrieden zu sein, wäre tatlose Ruhe und Stillstand der Triebfedern, oder Abstumpfung der Empfindungen und der damit verknüpften Tätigkeit. Eine solche aber kann eben so wenig mit dem intellektuellen Leben des Menschen zusammen bestehen, als der Stillstand des Herzens in einem tierischen Körper, auf den, wenn nicht (durch den Schmerz) ein neuer Anreiz ergeht, unvermeidlich der Tod folgt" [A, VII, 235]. A corollary of this position is that paradise, as it is traditionally conceived of (a place of minimum required effort and maximum pleasure), is, for Kant, an unappealing place: any dream of easy happiness, as encapsulated in this notion of paradise, Kant suspects, reveals an underlying frustration with the burdens and responsibilities that come with the struggle of developing our rationality [MAM, VIII, 122; see also: ED, VIII, 335].

34 Allison [1996, 118] rejects the suggestion that the Kantian project is ultimately one of self-realization, in the sense proposed here. He acknowledges that this strand is present in Kant's works, but writes that: "I also believe that there is a somewhat different strand, yielding what might be termed an ethic of self-justification. According to this strand, on which my own interpretation is largely based, the ultimate question is always how a maxim is to be justified rationally. Once again, justification matters because as long as we take ourselves as rational agents, we cannot abandon it as a requirement." He does not, though, go on to provide any reasons for his preference for one of the strands he identifies in Kant's works over the other—or even to show why we should see these two aspects of Kant's work as standing in any meaningful conflict with one another.

35 Conversely, to reject the path of *Aufklärung* is to refuse to realize our proper self in the empirical realm. Doing so, Kant holds, would be a crime against "the holy rights of humanity" ("die heiligen Rechte der Menschheit verletzen und mit Füßen treten" [WA, VIII, 39]).

ests of our reason, which allows us to establish ourselves as fully unified and active agents, thus coming as close as possible to realizing the ideal conception of ourselves as noumenal agents in the empirical realm.

We have seen above how the process of moralization, for Kant, is linked to the ability to reject the demands for immediate gratification of our desires—and thus involves sacrifice and inner coercion. However, Kant is careful to emphasize that doing our duty is not altogether the austere misery it might at first appear to be. To start with, he insists that once we have developed a moral disposition, recognizing the moral demands as an expression of our essential interests rather than something forced onto us from the outside, we will do our duty with a "happy heart" [R, VI, 23n] and even with love [MS, VI, 484][36]. What is more, Kant holds that just as the successful employment of our practical-technical reason brings us happiness, there is a peculiar type of pleasure we experience as a consequence of the proper use of our moral-practical reason. He calls this *Selbstzufriedenheit*. It is a contentment we take in freeing our will from the tyranny of our sensuous desires [KpV, V, 118] and in the resulting "complete self-consistency" of our will [R 7202, XIX, 278]. Unlike happiness, our conception of which is constantly changing [KU, V, 430], *Selbstzufriedenheit*, which itself is not dependent on any sensuous input, affords us "invariable" contentment: "Freiheit und das Bewusstsein derselben als eines Vermögens, mit überwiegender Gesinnung das moralische Gesetz zu befolgen, ist Unabhängigkeit von Neigungen... und, so fern als ich mir derselben in der Befolgung meiner moralischen Maximen bewusst bin, der einzige Quell einer notwendig damit verbundenen, auf keinem besonderen Gefühle beruhenden, unveränderlichen Zufriedenheit" [KpV, V, 117]. Part of the contentment we derive from developing a good will is the pride we feel when discovering, through our awareness of the moral demands on us and our ability to act on these, the "sublimity of our own super-sensuous existence" [KpV, V, 88; see also: R, VI, 50; MS, VI, 435], which—in spite of being a mere idea of practical reason—inspires in us "veneration" for our higher self [KpV, V, 87] and, consequently, the "highest self-regard" [MS, VI, 436].

---

36 As Allison highlights, these late assurances about the graceful aspects of following the moral law are a response to Schiller's critique of the cheerless character Kant gives to morality in his early writings on the topic. However, as Allison notes, since Kant "fails to indicate his reason for holding [the view that genuine virtue consists in doing one's duty with a happy heart], he creates the impression that there is more agreement than is in fact the case" [1990, 182].

The possibility of progress

Looking back over the history of mankind, the development of our rational faculties appears as the surprising result of an unconscious historical process, almost as if by a "concealed plan" executed by the benevolent agency of "nature" [IAG, VIII, 27; see also KU, V, 433]. While the postulation of such an agency would be fallacious from a mechanical-scientific viewpoint, it is, Kant holds, permissible as an assumption by our reflective faculty of judgment in the context of developing a teleological reading of reality[37], that is, insofar as we regard the world as a system of means-ends relations directed at the realization of the highest good[38] (not claiming to describe an independent reality, but rather organizing our experience of that reality in a way most consistent with the requirements of our thought, in the sense explained in Chapter 6).

Once we regard nature from this perspective, as aiming at the development of our rational faculties (and our talents, more generally), Kant claims, many of the elements of our lives that we consider nuisances or outright evils turn out to be blessings [A, VII, 328]. The perennial absence of foodstuffs in the state of nature and the constant threat to our survival in an uncertain world, for instance, force us to be active and train our powers to ensure our survival. Furthermore,

---

[37] "Um sich also auch nicht der mindesten Anmaßung, als wollte man etwas, was gar nicht in die Physik gehört, nämlich eine übernatürliche Ursache, unter unsere Erkenntnisgründe mischen, verdächtig zu machen: spricht man in der Teleologie zwar von der Natur, als ob die Zweckmäßigkeit in ihr absichtlich sei, aber doch zugleich so, dass man der Natur, d. i. der Materie, diese Absicht beilegt; wodurch man...anzeigen will, dass dieses Wort hier nur ein Prinzip der reflektierenden, nicht der bestimmenden Urteilskraft bedeute und also keinen besondern Grund der Kausalität einführen solle, sondern auch nur zum Gebrauche der Vernunft eine andere Art der Nachforschung, als die nach mechanischen Gesetzen ist, hinzufüge, um die Unzulänglichkeit der letzteren selbst zur empirischen Aufsuchung aller besondern Gesetze der Natur zu ergänzen. Daher spricht man in der Teleologie, so fern sie zur Physik gezogen wird, ganz recht von der Weisheit, der Sparsamkeit, der Vorsorge, der Wohltätigkeit der Natur, ohne dadurch aus ihr ein verständiges Wesen zu machen (weil das ungereimt wäre); aber auch ohne sich zu erkühnen, ein anderes, verständiges Wesen über sie als Werkmeister setzen zu wollen, weil dieses vermessen sein würde" [KU, V, 383]. Yovel points out that it is only in *Kritik der Urteilskraft* that Kant advances this interpretation of the cunning of nature as a regulative assumption by our reflective faculty of judgment (rather than a dogmatic, constitutive claim), which allows him to integrate this notion into his critical system [1989, 8]. This is overlooked by Hill when he writes that the notion of nature's intentions "really has no place in a Kantian ethic given Kant's deepest assumptions and commitments about nature, agency and value" [2003, 198n].

[38] Yet, as we have seen in Chapter 7, to the degree to which Kant's moral proof for the existence of God is unsuccessful, we lose the right to assert the objective reality of a moral intelligence that has created the world for this purpose.

the constant conflict among individuals [A, VII, 322] and the wars among states force us to reflect on the rules and restraints that make social interaction possible, in the process leading us to discover the moral law as the expression of our rational interests [KU, V, 433–4]. In a condition of perfect bliss in which our desires are immediately satisfied by a generous environment, these powers would remain dormant—and we would lead the lives of contended animals, satisfied but passive [A, VII, 235]. While such a peaceful existence would allow us to take care of the needs of our physical nature without problems, the demands of our reason for self-development and self-realization as active and unified agents would go unheeded [MAM, VIII, 122; see also: VIII, 65], in a way that we would be likely to slip into an existence of passivity: "[I]m Leben (absolut) zufrieden zu sein, wäre tatlose Ruhe und Stillstand der Triebfedern, oder Abstumpfung der Empfindungen und der damit verknüpften Tätigkeit" [A, VII, 235]. Hence, in the early stages of our development, it is only because of the "cunning of nature" (in Yovel's phrase [1989, 8]), which exposes us to dangers and conflict, that we are forced down the road of development[39].

However, Kant holds that it is an important aspect of *Aufklärung*—i.e. the process by which we become conscious of, and start living in accordance with, the requirements for the proper use of our rational faculties—that we ourselves take charge of this process of development which so far has been driven by external forces. That is, once we reach the level at which we come to understand our historic mission of cultivation, civilization and moralization on the path towards realizing the highest good in the empirical world, we ourselves have to take responsibility for a process which up to now has been the product of the "cunning of nature": "Die Natur hat gewollt: dass der Mensch alles, was über die mechanische Anordnung seines tierischen Daseins geht, gänzlich aus sich selbst herausbringe und keiner anderen Glückseligkeit oder Vollkommenheit teilhaftig werde, als die er sich selbst frei von Instinkt, durch eigene Vernunft, verschafft hat" [IAG, VIII, 19; see also: R, VI, 100–1][40].

---

39 Kant holds that the aim of the "cunning of nature" is the development of our talent to be active agents (i.e. to be able set ends for ourselves and pursue them successfully [KU, V, 431]). He makes the same point by asserting that culture (i.e., the perfection of our technical-practical reason) is the ultimate end of nature ("der letzte Zweck der Natur" [KU, V, 431.]). Thus, Kant distinguishes between the ultimate end of nature and the final end (Endzweck) of creation, which we have discussed in Chapter 6 above. The former is an end within the natural world for which all others ends in nature in turn are means, while the latter is the end for which creation as a whole exists [KU, V, 426]. For a further discussion of the distinction between the final end of creation and the ultimate end of nature, see [Yovel, 1989, 175–7].
40 "The true ends of human life… are not posited for us by nature or providence, but by human reason once nature has brought it to historical maturity" [Wood, 1999, 230–1]. Brandt aptly calls

Will man prove capable of fulfilling his task of imposing a rational order on the world around him, on his own actions and on the interactions with his fellow human beings so as to create the best possible world in which all rational beings achieve virtue and happiness? We have seen above that doing so is possible according to the laws of nature—but this still leaves open the question of whether our limited powers and our fragile wills will allow us actually to bring it about. Kant admits that on purely theoretical grounds we cannot exclude the possibility that we fail at this task [A, VII, 328–9][41]. In fact, in his more pessimistic moments, he himself sounds far from assured that we will be successful ("Wie kann man aber erwarten, dass aus so krummem Holze etwas völlig Gerades gezimmert werde?" [R, VI, 100][42]).

However, given that we have a duty to promote the highest good, we are entitled to believe that we will be able to realize it [TP, VIII, 309], for otherwise our pursuit of the highest good would be irrational and the moral demand to work towards its realization would contain a contradiction of reason [KU, V, 471n][43].

---

this transition the "Übergang aus der Naturgeschichte in die Freiheitsgeschichte der Menschheit" [2007, 198; see also Yovel, 1989, 196].

41 See also: [ED, VIII, 336–7]. We should note that Kant does not doubt that there has been moral progress in the past: "[Es] lassen sich manche Beweise geben, dass das menschliche Geschlecht im Ganzen wirklich in unserm Zeitalter in Vergleichung mit allen vorigen ansehnlich moralisch zum selbst Besseren fortgerückt sei (kurz dauernde Hemmungen können nichts dagegen beweisen)" [TP, VIII, 310]. Thus, Brandt is mistaken when he asserts that "die unmittelbare Erfahrung lehrt, so die Meinung Kants, nur ein Hin und Her von Fortschritt und Rückschritt" [2007, 191]. (In fact, this is precisely the position, held by Moses Mendelssohn, which Kant argues *against* in his 1793 essay "Über den Gemeinspruch: Das mag in der Theorie richtig sein, taugt aber nicht für die Praxis" [TP, VIII, 307–9]). Thus, what is at stake in Kant's argument is not whether there has been progress in the past, but whether that progress will continue. Kant is careful to emphasize that having an answer to the former question helps us little in our attempt to deal with the latter: "Wenn das menschliche Geschlecht, im Ganzen betrachtet, eine noch so lange Zeit vorwärts gehend und im Fortschreiten begriffen gewesen zu sein befunden würde, so kann doch niemand dafür stehen, dass nun nicht gerade jetzt vermöge der physischen Anlage unserer Gattung die Epoche seines Rückganges eintrete" [SF, VII, 83]. This is recognized by Yovel: "The cunning of nature... is discovered *ex post facto*, and applies only to the past; with regard to the future, its a priori probability remains very slim... and so we have no valid ground for historical prediction, much less for a solid guarantee of political progress in the future" [1989, 277–8]. However, Kant also insists that there can be no proof that such progress is impossible [TP, VIII, 309].

42 See also: "Ich verdenke es Keinem, wenn er in Ansehung der Staatsübel an dem Heil des Menschengeschlechts und dem Fortschreiten desselben zum Besseren zu verzagen anhebt" [SF, VII, 93].

43 See also: "[M]an mag so schwergläubig sein, wie man will, so muss man doch, wo es schlechterdings unmöglich ist, den Erfolg aus gewissen nach aller menschlichen Weisheit

Thus, instead of empirical evidence for the possibility of moral progress, we only have "moral certainty" [A, VII, 329]—i.e. the acceptance of a notion as objectively real (namely, that of the possibility of ongoing moral progress) on merely practical grounds. This is, again, an application of Kant's doctrine of practical knowledge: the proposition that we can achieve our historic mission to impose rational order on the world is one we accept as true, on the basis that its truth-value cannot be determined by means of data available from a theoretical perspective and that we take a necessary practical interest in it.

Yet, while we are thus entitled, on practical grounds, to believe that we can be successful in our mission of self-guided moral progress, this by no means assures us that it will happen [EF, VIII, 336–7]. The handover from the cunning of nature to human rational self-control means that the further progress in our development is no longer mapped out for us, but depends on our own efforts. The best thing we can do is continue down the laborious and never-ending path of cultivation, civilization and moralization, struggling to reform human nature with the help of our growing rational powers and guided by the idealized vision of ourselves as fully rational beings[44]. Yet, whether we take this path or slip back into a lower, baser form of existence depends entirely on us[45].

(die, wenn sie ihren Namen verdienen soll, lediglich auf das moralische gehen muss) genommenen Mitteln mit Gewissheit voraus zu sehn, eine Konkurrenz göttlicher Weisheit zum Laufe der Natur auf praktische Art glauben, wenn man seinen Endzweck nicht lieber gar aufgeben will" [ED, VIII, 337].

44 Kant expresses this thought of the infinite progress towards a never-achievable goal by saying that while no human individual will ever reach mankind's destiny, mankind as a species can (in fact, he asserts that this is a distinguishing feature of man relative to animals—with each individual reaching the species' destiny, i.e. its highest possible development, while the same is not true for humans [A, VII, 329]). The reason for this is that the human species, unlike the individual human being, has a potentially unlimited life span [IAG, VIII, 20]. Thus, the notion of the species' achievement of the mankind's rational goal plays a role similar to that of the immortality of the soul (see note 42 in Chapter 7 above), in that in both cases an entity with an infinite life span is identified as a possible candidate for completing the infinite path of progress lying ahead of us.

45 "Kant's philosophy of history is... as Goldmann has rightly observed, totally future-oriented; it seeks the remedy and even the justification of the ills of the present in the historical world to come, not in a romantic and impossible return to a 'golden' past; it has no sentiment to spare in the longing (with some readers of Rousseau) for a lost paradise, the ideal state of nature that to Kant is the state of sheer animality" [Yovel, 1989, 193].

Conclusion

Kant understands *Aufklärung* as the process by which we gain an understanding of the appropriate rules for the use of our rational faculties, as well as the ability to guide our rational faculties on the basis of these rules. This notion of *Aufklärung* is built on his conception of our rational faculties as not yet fully developed, as still unduly entangled with our sensuous nature and unclear about the requirements for their own proper use.

Aufklärung, for Kant, involves civilization (the formation of a political and ethical community among rational beings), cultivation (the perfection in the use of our technical-practical reason) and moralization (the perfection in the use of our moral-practical reason). The notion of moralization is a particular focus of attention in Kant's writings: he understands it as involving the development of the self-discipline required to guide ourselves on the basis of the interests of our reason, which allows us to establish ourselves as fully unified and active agents, thus coming as close as possible to realizing the ideal conception of ourselves as noumenal agents in the empirical realm.

The notion of *Aufklärung* allows us to distinguish two different conceptions Kant offers of the good human life: on the one hand, there is the highest good, the perfect state of affairs in which all rational beings have developed a good will and have achieved the greatest possible degree of happiness; on the other, there is the best existence that we as finite (and, hence, flawed) rational beings are capable of—namely, that of striving to realize the ideal condition in the empirical world. While the best conceivable state is one of harmony and peace, the best life we can actually aspire to live is one of constant struggle in our effort to overcome the flaws inherent in our imperfect wills, thereby coming increasingly close to realizing the ideal vision of ourselves as perfectly rational agents.

9 Social life

Kant's focus on the notion of autonomy has led some commentators to regard his philosophical project as individualistic[1], as concerned narrowly with the individual's mission of achieving personal moral perfection, without social interaction being of particular importance. The task of this chapter will be to show that such an individualistic reading of Kant's philosophy is misguided. More specifically, it aims to establish the following three points:

1. Kant emphasizes the many ways in which we rely for our wellbeing and the development of our faculties on the interaction with our fellow human beings. In particular, he holds that we can only learn to make proper use of our rational faculties if we use them in concert with others;
2. Kant thinks we can only make effective use of our technical-practical reason (i.e. our ability to pursue our own happiness) in the context of a law-governed society that secures the external freedom of all individuals by setting and enforcing limits on the freedom of each;
3. Kant holds that the highest moral achievement consists in the foundation of an ethical community spanning all rational beings, in which each member is committed to respecting and promoting the status of all others as free choosers and pursuers of their own ends.

Our discussion of these three points will enable us to appreciate the important social dimension of Kant's notion of the highest good, which we have discussed in the previous two chapters: the realization of the highest good—i.e. the best possible state of the world in which the greatest happiness is combined with the greatest moral perfection—is possible only as the result of a collective effort. This makes the highest good an essentially social conception of the good human life.

Human beings are destined for society

Kant offers three distinct arguments for the claim that "human beings are destined for society" [MS, VI, 471; see also A, VII, 330]—i.e. that in order to make full use of their faculties human beings require social interaction. His first argument to establish this claim is based on man's inherent neediness. As beings

---

[1] For further discussions of the case against the clam that Kant's moral philosophy is individualistic, see Wood [1999, 281] and Wood [2003, 23].

with fragile physical bodies and limited powers, we are reliant on the help of others to achieve our projects or even assure our personal safety. We are, in Kant's words, "Bedürftige, auf einem Wohnplatz durch die Natur zur wechselseitigen Beihilfe vereinigte vernünftige Wesen" [MS, VI, 453][2].

The second argument is based on Kant's view that human beings are naturally lazy. If not forced to compete against others, we have little inclination to be active—and would rather spend our time indulging our desires, thus violating our duty to develop our talents. At our current stage of development, at which the notion of duty does not necessarily move us to act, it is our desire to compare favorably to others that pushes us to be active in order to compete against them successfully:

> Dieser Widerstand ist es nun, welcher alle Kräfte des Menschen erweckt, ihn dahin bringt seinen Hang zur Faulheit zu überwinden und, getrieben durch Ehrsucht, Herrschsucht oder Habsucht, sich einen Rang unter seinen Mitgenossen zu verschaffen... Ohne jene an sich zwar eben nicht liebenswürdige Eigenschaften der Ungeselligkeit, woraus der Widerstand entspringt, den jeder bei seinen selbstsüchtigen Anmaßungen notwendig antreffen muss, würden in einem arkadischen Schäferleben bei vollkommener Eintracht, Genügsamkeit und Wechselliebe alle Talente auf ewig in ihren Keimen verborgen bleiben. [IAG, VIII, 21]

That is, social interaction—and, more precisely, the competition among individuals in society—is an important motor of the development of our talents [IAG, VIII, 22][3].

Kant's third—and most important—argument for the claim that we need social interaction for our wellbeing and the development of our faculties is based on the notion that we can only make proper use of our rational faculties if we use them in concert with others. As we have seen in Chapter 1, reason is objective in that the rules for its correct use are the same for all agents. This is true both for the theoretical and the practical use of reason: if a given set of premises leads, by means of the correct application of the rules of reason, to a certain conclusion, this conclusion is valid, regardless of whether I run through the argument or you do[4]. Similarly, in the practical application of reason, a given act is objectively

---

[2] On Kant's conception of human beings as needy and non self-sufficient, see O'Neill [1989, 101], Rosen [1993, 199] and Wood [1999, 195].
[3] See also: Rosen [1993, 75], Williams [2003, 122] and Brandt [2007, 477].
[4] If the premises of this argument are true, the judgment reached by means of objectively valid inferences is also true. That is, truth is the property of judgments on which different reasoners must converge if only they make proper use of their rational faculties: "Wahrheit aber beruht auf der Übereinstimmung mit dem Objekt, in Ansehung dessen folglich die Urteile eines jeden Verstandes einstimmig sein müssen" [KrV, III, 532].

good if its maxim has been chosen because it has the form of a universal law, i.e. because it satisfies reason's essential interest in systematic unity, an interest shared by all rational beings. Hence, the practical laws governing the proper use of our practical reason are the same for every rational being.

As a consequence of the objective nature of the rules of reason, to reason properly is to abstract from our own subjective interests—and to look, as Kant puts it, at our own case "from the perspective of a stranger" [KU, V, 295][5] to ensure that we base the use of our rational faculties only on considerations and interests which are objectively valid[6]. However, given the way in which our rea-

---

[5] This ability to regard our actions from the perspective of a stranger, Kant holds, is our conscience (*Gewissen*): "Diese ursprüngliche intellektuelle und... moralische Anlage, Gewissen genannt, hat nun das Besondere in sich, dass, obzwar dieses sein Geschäfte ein Geschäfte des Menschen mit sich selbst ist, dieser sich doch durch seine Vernunft genötigt sieht, es als auf den Geheiß einer anderen Person zu treiben" [MS, VI, 438]. More specifically, Kant ascribes two functions to our conscience: First, to have a conscience is to be aware of the moral demands on us ("Gewissen ist die dem Menschen in jedem Fall eines Gesetzes seine Pflicht zum Lossprechen oder Verurteilen vorhaltende praktische Vernunft" [MS, VI, 400]). This links the notion of conscience to the fact-of-reason argument—i.e., the argument establishing the objective validity of the moral law on the basis of our awareness of being confronted with moral demands. In fact, we could rephrase the starting point of our argument in Chapter 4 by saying that it is an *a priori* fact of reason that we have a moral conscience. In the same way in which Kant holds that we cannot forfeit our moral personality, he asserts that while we can act against our conscience, it is impossible for us ever to lose it: "[Ein Mensch] kann es in seiner äußersten Verworfenheit allenfalls dahin bringen, sich [um die Stimme des Gewissens] gar nicht mehr zu kehren, aber sie zu hören, kann er doch nicht vermeiden" [MS, VI, 438]. Secondly, to have a conscience is to regard oneself as morally accountable for one's actions. In this sense, Kant likens our conscience to a tribunal in front of which we have to answer for the moral quality of our actions: "Das Bewusstsein eines inneren Gerichtshofes im Menschen...ist das Gewissen" [MS, VI, 438]. Consequently, morality involves, in a figurative sense, a splitting of our person into two—on the one hand, the agent, and, on the other, the moral judge, watching over the agent's deeds: "Die zwiefache Persönlichkeit, in welcher der Mensch, der sich im Gewissen anklagt und richtet, sich selbst denken muss: dieses doppelte Selbst, einerseits vor den Schranken eines Gerichtshofes, der doch ihm selbst anvertraut ist, zitternd stehen zu müssen, andererseits aber das Richteramt aus angeborener Autorität selbst in Händen zu haben" [MS, VI, 439n]. Like Kant's description of the critique of reason as a tribunal which adjudicates the self-contradictions of reason [KrV, III, 491], the discussion of conscience highlights Kant's tendency—noted by O'Neil [1989, 18]—of building his philosophy around juridical metaphors.

[6] Thus, to reason properly involves the process of objectification that we have explored in the previous chapter. Yovel points out that Kant's conception of proper reasoning combines individual spontaneity and objectivity: "To be rational, an attitude must fulfill both conditions: it must derive from a spontaneous act of the individual, and it must conform to a form shared by all" [Yovel, 1989, 246]. The reason why there is no tension between these two elements of proper reasoning is the one highlighted in the text above—namely that, in Kant's conception, the individ-

son is entangled with our sensuous nature, this ideal case of proper reasoning is rarely—if ever—realized in the actual world: more frequently, our sensuous nature impinges on our use of reason[7]. As discussed in Chapter 5, this impingement is often so subtle that we ourselves are not aware of the ways in which subjective factors distort the use of our reason. We engage in what Kant calls "vernünfteln": we convince ourselves that we are reasoning from an objective standpoint, while in fact serving our very subjective interests [A, VII, 265].

The combination of Kant's notion of reason as objective with the notion of the corruption of our actual use of reason by our sensuous nature leads to the important Kantian position that we can only make proper use of our reason when using our rational faculties in concert with others ("[W]ie viel und mit welcher Richtigkeit würden wir wohl denken, wenn wir nicht gleichsam in Gemeinschaft mit andern, denen wir unsere und die uns ihre Gedanken mitteilen, dächten" [SDO, VIII, 144]). For only if we compare our judgments with those of others, Kant claims, can we recognize and eliminate the impure, the subjective elements in our thought[8], thus managing to arrive at judgments that are objectively valid [L, IX, 57; see also: KrV, III, 532].

This makes the possibility of public debate—the "public use of reason"—crucial [WA, VIII, 37]. For only where it is possible to present our arguments publicly and to expose them to the critique of others, do we have a chance to purge them of their distorting subjective elements: "[M]an nimmt uns [durch das Verbot der Bücher], wo nicht das einzige, doch das größte und brauchbarste Mittel unsere eigene Gedanken zu berichtigen, welches dadurch geschieht, dass wir sie öffentlich aufstellen, um zu sehen, ob sie auch mit Anderer ihrem Verstande zusammenpassen; weil sonst etwas bloß Subjektives (z. B. Gewohnheit oder Neigung)

---

ual's spontaneous self (which, as we have seen in Chapter 1, is a mere idea of reason, a mere ideal conception of ourselves) guides itself on the basis of principles that are shared by all rational beings, and, hence, are objectively valid. That is, there is no tension between the two elements in Kant's account of proper reasoning because of the objective nature of the rules of reason.

[7] This is true of both the theoretical and the practical use of our reason. Discussing the transcendental illusion in *Kritik der Reinen Vernunft*, Kant writes: "Irrtum [wird] nur durch den unbemerkten Einfluss der Sinnlichkeit auf den Verstand bewirkt..., wodurch es geschieht, dass die subjektiven Gründe des Urteils mit den objektiven zusammenfließen und diese von ihrer Bestimmung abweichend machen" [KrV, IV, 235; see also: MS, VI, 463; A, VII, 146].

[8] Kant holds that when we are prevented from communicating with others, we are thereby deprived of "the only, the greatest and the most useful means of correcting our own thoughts" [A, VII, 219]. In this case, "something subjective (a habit or an inclination) can easily be regarded as objectively valid, which is precisely what constitutes the illusion of which it is said that… it leads us to deceive ourselves in the process of applying a rule" [A, VII, 219].

leicht für objektiv würde gehalten werden" [A, VII, 219]. Consequently, Kant regards reason as an essentially social faculty ("Der Verstand ist an sich schon gemeinschaftlich" [R 1871, XVI, 144]), depending for its very existence on the possibility of correcting criticism by others [KrV, III, 484][9].

A corollary of this position is that thought only counts as proper thought when it is communicable—or, in Kant's preferred phrase, when it is consistent with the conditions of publicity (*Publizität*, [EF, VIII, 386])[10]. If a maxim or judgment cannot be made public, the author thereby implicitly confesses that his thought has violated the character of universality that marks the correct use of our rational faculties. This might come about either because sharing the thought or the maxim in question is simply impossible (i.e. it is not a communicable thought or maxim)—or because sharing it would undermine its efficacy. In the first case, Kant holds the author of the maxim or thought in question shows signs of mental derangement—i.e. his thought lacks the mark of the healthy mind, namely that it is conducted according to the universal laws of reason: "Das einzige allgemeine Merkmal der Verrücktheit ist der Verlust des Gemeinsinnes (sensus communis) und der dagegen eintretende logische Eigensinn (sensus privatus)... [E]s ist ein subjektiv-notwendiger Probierstein der Richtigkeit unserer Urteile überhaupt und also auch der Gesundheit unseres Verstandes: dass wir diesen auch an den Verstand Anderer halten, nicht aber uns mit dem unsrigen isolieren und mit unserer Privatvorstellung doch gleichsam öffentlich urteilen" [A, VII, 219]. If, on the other hand, a maxim cannot be made public because doing so would undermine its efficacy, it is, in Kant's view, a sign of injustice:

---

9 "Kant... considers [the idea of publicity] to be intimately connected with the idea of rationality... the voice of reason is ultimately the voice of public opinion when it crystallizes into unanimous agreement as result of open and informed debate" [Rosen, 1993, 182n; see also: Arendt, 1992, 10; Wood, 1999, 302]. A similar idea is expressed by the economist John Maynard Keynes in the preface to his *General Theory:* "It is astonishing what foolish things one can temporarily believe if one thinks too long alone" [2008, 8].

10 Kant holds that it is our "natural vocation" to communicate our thoughts to others ("[E]s ist ein Naturberuf der Menschheit, sich vornehmlich in dem, was den Menschen überhaupt angeht, einander mitzuteilen" [TP, VIII, 305])—and that we "expect and demand" that others communicate their thoughts to us [KU, V, 297]. However, this need and demand for communication is partly counteracted by our awareness that we make ourselves vulnerable by communicating our thoughts too freely: "[Der Mensch] fühlt... mächtig das Bedürfnis sich Anderen zu eröffnen (selbst ohne etwas dabei zu beabsichtigen); andererseits aber auch durch die Furcht vor dem Missbrauch, den Andere von dieser Aufdeckung seiner Gedanken machen dürften, beengt und gewarnt, sieht er sich genötigt, einen guten Teil seiner Urteile (vornehmlich über andere Menschen) in sich selbst zu verschließen" [MS, VI, 471–2; see also: A, VII, 332]. On this tendency to disguise our thoughts, see Wood [2003, 14].

> [E]ine Maxime, die ich nicht darf laut werden lassen, ohne dadurch meine eigene Absicht zugleich zu vereiteln, die durchaus verheimlicht werden muss, wenn sie gelingen soll, und zu der ich mich nicht öffentlich bekennen kann, ohne dass dadurch unausbleiblich der Widerstand Aller gegen meinen Vorsatz gereizt werde, kann diese notwendige und allgemeine, mithin a priori einzusehende Gegenbearbeitung Aller gegen mich nirgend wovon anders, als von der Ungerechtigkeit her haben, womit sie jedermann bedroht [EF, VIII, 381][11].

Kant insists that the correct use of our rational faculties does not come natural to us: man—as a flawed, corruptible being, unaccustomed to the art of making self-guided use of his rational faculties—needs guidance and education. However, there is no external authority to provide such guidance. All we have are other flawed and corruptible beings with the same needs and shortcomings. Hence, Kant concludes, the best we can do is to guide one another in spite of the fragility from which we all suffer: "Der Mensch muss... zum Guten erzogen werden; der aber, welcher ihn erziehen soll, ist wieder ein Mensch, der noch in der Rohheit der Natur liegt und nun doch dasjenige bewirken soll, was er selbst bedarf". [A, VII, 325][12]

Thus, the very notion of *Aufklärung*, which we have encountered in the preceding chapter, is profoundly social. We have no other way, Kant insists, to identify the correct rules for the use of our reason but the achievement of consent among a multiplicity of finite rational beings whose thinking is impaired by their subjective interests and their personal shortcomings—yet who nonetheless have a talent for operating their rational faculties according to objectively valid rules [KrV, III, 492][13]. In this sense, social interaction is necessary for the full development of our rational faculties.

---

11 See also R 7818 („Handlungen, deren Maxime notwendig dissimuliert werden muss, sind unrecht. Die Maxime aller rechtmäßigen Handlungen muss öffentlich sein und von der Art, dass sie von jedem wenigstens angenommen werden kann" [XIX, 526]) and R 7822 („Das Prinzip der rechtlichen Pflicht ist: ich muss so handeln, als wenn meine Maximen eben so von jedermann wie von Gott gesehen würden... Würde einem jeden ins Herz gesehen werden können, so müsste er gute Maximen annehmen" [XIX, 526–7]).
12 Kant's faith in—and his belief in the importance of—education also transpires in his lectures on logic, where he asserts that "Der Mensch kann nur Mensch werden durch Erziehung. Er ist nichts, als was die Erziehung aus ihm macht" [L, IX, 443] and "[H]inter der Education steckt das große Geheimnis der Vollkommenheit der menschlichen Natur" [L, IX, 444]. This emphasis on the role of education for the development of man's faculties again hints at the centrality of social interaction in Kant's anthropology. On this point, see [Wood, 1999, 203].
13 The notion that social interaction is necessary for identifying the correct rules for the use of our rational faculties appears to be at odds with Kant's insistence that we always already know what our duties are (and, hence, what the principles of morality demand of us): "Was nach dem Prinzip der Autonomie der Willkür zu tun sei, ist für den gemeinsten Verstand ganz leicht und ohne Bedenken einzusehen" [KpV, V, 36; see also: GMS, IV, 403]. However, these latter assertions

The Kantian idea of the social aspect of reason comes with a strong, built-in notion of equality. For the process of communication that Kant has in mind is not restricted to a few learned men. Kant holds that everyone shares in the same reason—regardless of education or subtlety of mind. More important than erudition is the ability to think straight (to have *gesunde Vernunft* [SDO, VII, 142])—an ability that can easily be clouded by excessive sophistry and learning [II, 65]. When it comes to deciding between right and wrong, the simple man has no disadvantages vis-à-vis the learned one [KpV, V, 27]. In this sense, for Kant every rational being—regardless of his level of education—is a "colleague in the great counsel of human reason": "Die mitteilende Neigung der Vernunft ist nur unter der Kondition billig, dass sie zugleich mit der teilnehmenden verbunden sei. Andere sind nicht Lehrlinge, auch nicht Richter, sondern Kollegen im großen Rat der menschlichen Vernunft" [R 2566, XVI, 419–20][14].

---

are contradicted by others in which Kant explicitly allows for the possibility of us erring on the question of what is morally demanded of us: "[I]n dem objektiven Urteile, ob etwas Pflicht sei oder nicht, kann man wohl bisweilen irren; aber im subjektiven, ob ich es mit meiner praktischen (hier richtenden) Vernunft zum Behuf jenes Urteils verglichen habe, kann ich nicht irren" [MS, VI, 401]. According to this position, all that is morally required is for us to act according to our moral conscience: "Wenn aber jemand sich bewusst ist nach Gewissen gehandelt zu haben, so kann von ihm, was Schuld oder Unschuld betrifft, nichts mehr verlangt werden" [MS, VI, 401]. (For a discussion of the notion of conscience, see note 5 in Chapter 9). The latter position is more in keeping with the Kantian notion that the proper use of our rational faculties does not come natural to us, but requires effort and self-discipline. It is, consequently, more germane to his overall philosophical project.

14 The Kantian assumption that all human beings enjoy the same endowment of common rational ability is highlighted by Yovel ("[B]y virtue of sharing the same rationality, man enters a relation of equality with all other rational beings" [1989, 192]) and Kemp Smith ("Kant propounds one of his abiding convictions, namely, that in matters which concern all men without distinction nature is not guilty of any partial distribution of her gifts, and that in regard to the essential ends of human nature the highest philosophy cannot advance beyond what is revealed to the common understanding" [2003, 577; see also Williams, 2003, 82]. Brandt claims that "[Kant] ist wie Rousseau lebenslang der Auffassung, dass Frauen von Natur nicht dazu in der Lage sind, nach Grundsätzen zu handeln, sondern nach dem Gefühl oder dem männlichen Vorbild" [2007, 386]. Yet, the passage Brandt references in his context [A, VII, 306] contains no statement to this effect. Brandt makes reference to two further passages in an accompanying footnote. However, the first of these [XV, 936] does not exist (at least not according to the online version of the *Akademieausgabe*, used for research on this work), while the second [MS, VI, 314] refers not to women's ability to act on principles, but their status as passive citizens (as discussed in note 37 below).

The highest achievement in the use of our rational faculties, Kant holds, is to develop common sense (or *sensus communis*)[15], the ability to internalize the purifying process that allows us to use our rational faculties correctly by freeing ourselves from the distorting subjective elements in our thought processes:

> Unter dem sensus communis... muss man die Idee eines gemeinschaftlichen Sinnes, d. i. eines Beurteilungsvermögens verstehen, welches in seiner Reflexion auf die Vorstellungsart jedes andern in Gedanken (a priori) Rücksicht nimmt, um gleichsam an die gesamte Menschenvernunft sein Urteil zu halten und dadurch der Illusion zu entgehen, die aus subjektiven Privatbedingungen, welche leicht für objektiv gehalten werden könnten, auf das Urteil nachteiligen Einfluss haben würde. Dieses geschieht nun dadurch, dass man sein Urteil an anderer nicht sowohl wirkliche als vielmehr bloß mögliche Urteile hält und sich in die Stelle jedes andern versetzt, indem man bloß von den Beschränkungen, die unserer eigenen Beurteilung zufälliger Weise anhängen, abstrahiert: welches wiederum dadurch bewirkt wird, dass man das, was in dem Vorstellungszustande Materie, d. i. Empfindung ist, so viel möglich weglässt und lediglich auf die formalen Eigentümlichkeiten seiner Vorstellung oder seines Vorstellungszustandes Acht hat. [KU, V, 293–4][16]

In summary, Kant emphasizes the centrality of social interaction for human wellbeing and the development of our faculties, based on the three arguments from neediness, laziness and the essentially social constitution of our rational faculties. However, Kant also shows an awareness of the downsides of sharing our lives with others. He notes that the restrictions on our freedom that come with social life induce in us an impulse to flee the society of others. This is what Kant calls our "unsocial sociability" (*ungesellige Geselligkeit*[17]): while we cherish

---

15 O'Neill points to a subtle difference between Kant's notion of the 'sensus communis' and our modern notion of 'common sense': "[W]hereas 'common sense' is used to refer to understandings that are actually shared, in an *actual* community or more widely, the sensus communis consists of three principles or maxims that constrain understandings, indeed practices of communication, that can be shared in any *possible* community" [1989, 25]. The three maxims O'Neill mentions are Kant's "three maxims of thought", which we briefly discuss in note 16 below.
16 The notion of the 'sensus communis' is linked to the second of Kant's three maxims of correct thought: always to „think from the perspective of all other rational beings" („An der Stelle jedes andern denken" [KU, V, 294]—the other two maxims are to think for oneself and to think consistently)—and thus to the notion of the objectification of the self, discussed in the previous chapter. O'Neill correctly links the notion of sensus communis to that of self-discipline, describing it as „the self-discipline of thinking that will be required if there is to be communication among a plurality whose members are not antecedently coordinated, who form a merely possible community" [1989, 25]. Kant defines madness as a loss of common sense, marked by „an inability to judge one's own thoughts from the standpoint of another" [R 1506, XV, 813–4].
17 "Ich verstehe hier unter dem Antagonismus die ungesellige Geselligkeit der Menschen, d. i. den Hang derselben in Gesellschaft zu treten, der doch mit einem durchgängigen Widerstande, welcher diese Gesellschaft beständig zu trennen droht, verbunden ist. Hiezu liegt die Anlage

and need interaction with others to develop our talents, our impulse to be in charge of our environment and our unwillingness to be subject to the constraints that come with being part of a social group drive us into solitude. Eager to enjoy our freedom, we want everything in the world around us to be ordered according to our own will—and resent the limits to our will arising from the presence of others [A, VII, 327; see also IAG, VIII, 21].

In the most extreme case, in interacting with others we run the risk of being dominated by their wills—and of being used as mere tools for their purposes. Following Rousseau, Kant emphasizes the distress that results for an individual from coming under the control of others [A, VII, 268; see also: TP, VIII, 293–4][18]. The attempt to protect ourselves against the domination by the will of other human beings leads us preemptively to seek power over them [A, VII, 273]. The resulting struggle for domination is intensified by the fact that in society other individuals are often the best tools available for satisfying our desires [R 1500, XV, 788; see also: Wood, 1999, 260]. In consequence, we easily develop a fixation with achieving control over those around us[19]. In fact, Kant holds, some of the most powerful vices arise in the context of our interaction with others [A, VII, 270]—and, in particular, from the fact that man's self-reflexivity leads him to compare himself to others and to derive his feeling of self-worth not from what is shared, but from that which is different from, and superior to, others[20].

---

offenbar in der menschlichen Natur. Der Mensch hat eine Neigung sich zu vergesellschaften: weil er in einem solchen Zustande sich mehr als Mensch, d. i. die Entwickelung seiner Naturanlagen, fühlt. Er hat aber auch einen großen Hang sich zu vereinzeln (isolieren): weil er in sich zugleich die ungesellige Eigenschaft antrifft, alles bloß nach seinem Sinne richten zu wollen, und daher allerwärts Widerstand erwartet, so wie er von sich selbst weiß, dass er seinerseits zum Widerstande gegen andere geneigt ist" [IAG, VIII, 20].

18 Yovel: "[T]he hostility [a human being] feels initially to his fellow men and his inability to 'tolerate' them arise not from any threat to his life but from the danger they pose to his will. As an ego-centered principle of will, I, like every other man, want everything to be run according to my subjective wishes... [W]e have... the inclination to power and to impose one's personal will and consciousness upon the social system" [1989, 148–9].

19 "Denn anderer Menschen Neigungen in seine Gewalt zu bekommen, um sie nach seinen Absichten lenken und bestimmen zu können, ist beinahe eben so viel als im Besitz anderer, als bloßer Werkzeuge seines Willens, zu sein. Kein Wunder, dass das Streben nach einem solchen Vermögen, auf Andere Einfluss zu haben, Leidenschaft wird" [A, VII, 271]. Similarly, in R 1522 Kant writes: "Davon dass alle Menschen Überlegenheit über einander suchen, kommt alles Böse, aber auch alles Gute der Kultur her" [XV, 894; see also: R, VI, 93].

20 "Die Anlagen für die Menschheit können auf den allgemeinen Titel der zwar physischen, aber doch vergleichenden Selbstliebe (wozu Vernunft erfordert wird) gebracht werden: sich nämlich nur in Vergleichung mit andern als glücklich oder unglücklich zu beurteilen. Von ihr rührt die Neigung her, sich in der Meinung anderer einen Wert zu verschaffen; und zwar ur-

Thus, Kant emphasizes that interaction with others leads to a desire to flee their company and has the potential to corrupt our character by leading us to base our sense of self-worth on subjective-comparative, rather than objective-moral, considerations. Yet, in spite of recognizing this dialectic of social life, he insists that only through social interaction—and by exposing ourselves to, and overcoming, the risks it brings—can we can hope to develop our rational faculties and advance on the path of *Aufklärung*.

Entering civil society

The second essentially social aspect of Kant's conception of human existence is his claim that we can only achieve perfection in the use of our technical-practical reason in the context of a civil society (*bürgerliche Gesellschaft*). He defines a civil society as a social group in which the equal external freedom of each is secured by laws agreed on by all and backed by coercive state power [R, VI, 98; see also: MS, VI, 305–6; TP, VIII, 292]. External freedom is defined as an individual's "independence from the coercive influence of another person's will" ("Unabhängigkeit von eines Anderen nötigender Willkür" [MS, VI, 237])[21]. To see why a civil society should be required in order for us to be able to make full use of our technical-practical reason—i.e. to pursue our personal projects successfully–, we have to spend a moment to prepare the ground for Kant's argument. This discussion will be somewhat technical, but it will be important for our subsequent argument to develop a good grasp of Kant's position here.

The starting point for this argument is Kant's claim that we, as beings endowed with moral personality, have an "innate right" ("angebornes Recht"

---

sprünglich bloß den der Gleichheit: keinem über sich Überlegenheit zu verstatten, mit einer beständigen Besorgnis verbunden, dass andere darnach streben möchten; woraus nachgerade eine ungerechte Begierde entspringt, sie sich über Andere zu erwerben" [R, VI, 27; see also: Wood, 1999, 135].

[21] This is the fourth important conception of freedom we encounter in Kant's works—in addition to the notions of transcendental freedom, negative freedom and moral freedom, as discussed in Chapter 5 above. As happens frequently in his works, Kant here simply uses the term "freedom", in a way that makes it difficult for his readers to distinguish his different conceptions of that term. In this text, we will use the term "external freedom" to make the distinction clear. Kant explicitly uses the term "external freedom" in [MS, VI, 316], [MS, VI, 406] and [TP, VIII, 289] (in the latter case, he refers to it as "Freiheit im äußeren Verhältnisse der Menschen zu einander").

[MS, VI, 238][22]) to external freedom. What does it mean to say that we have innate rights[23]? In *Metaphysik der Sitten,* Kant distinguishes between "natural" and "positive" external laws [MS, VI, 224] (where external, or juridical, laws concern the regulation of actions, while inner, or ethical, laws concern the maxims and the ends on the basis, and for the purpose, of which these actions are conducted [MS, VI, 214]). Positive external laws are legislated by human authority to regulate social interactions. Natural external laws, on the other hand, are valid "a priori and without any explicit legislation" ("[Gesetze], zu denen die Verbindlichkeit auch ohne äußere Gesetzgebung a priori durch die Vernunft erkannt werden kann" [MS, VI, 224]). That is, natural external laws are laws which are concerned with regulating actions and whose validity is not grounded on human authority, but which are instead valid *a priori*. We have already learnt that *a priori* laws, for Kant, are based on the interests of reason. Consequently, if Kant is right in claiming that there are natural external laws, then these are laws that are valid for us because we require them for the proper use of our rational faculties.

Before proceeding, we have to note that rights, for Kant, are the flipside of obligations. To say that I have a right to go about my projects without being coerced by others into serving as a tool for theirs is to say that all other rational beings have an obligation not to coerce me in this way [MS, VI, 237]. Yet, we already know that obligations are grounded in laws[24]. This implies that rights are grounded in law. Thus, if there are innate rights (i.e. rights we have before the

---

22 Kant also refers to this right as our "innate equality" [MS, VI, 237], the "only original right which every person has by virtue of their humanity" ("dieses einzige, ursprüngliche, jedem Menschen kraft seiner Menschheit zustehende Recht" [MS, VI, 238]), the "principle of innate freedom" [MS, VI, 238] and "these innate, irrevocable rights, which necessarily belong to humanity" ("diese angebornen, zur Menschheit notwendig gehörenden und unveräußerlichen Rechte" [EF, VIII, 350]). In spite of Kant's claim that the right to external freedom is the only innate right we have ("Das angeborne Recht ist nur ein einziges" [MS, VI, 237]), earlier in the same work he also states that children have an "innate right" to be looked after by their parents: "Kinder als Personen haben... ein ursprünglich-angeborenes (nicht angeerbtes) Recht auf ihre Versorgung durch die Eltern, bis sie vermögend sind, sich selbst zu erhalten" [MS, VI, 280].
23 Guyer justly criticizes Kant for not explaining of how exactly we are to conceive of innate rights: "Kant spells out several consequences of this innate right, but does not explain why or in what sense it is innate or original" [2000, 278]. In the text above we will reconstruct answers from Kant's writings to both the question of what is meant by an "innate right"—and what the justification is for claiming that we are bearers of innate rights.
24 More precisely, all obligation is based on self-imposed laws—and, hence, all obligation, for Kant is self-imposed obligation: "Denn was meine Freiheit betrifft, so habe ich selbst in Ansehung der göttlichen, von mir durch bloße Vernunft erkennbaren Gesetze keine Verbindlichkeit, als nur so fern ich dazu selber habe meine Beistimmung geben können" [EF, VIII, 350n].

advent of any positive legislation), these must be established by natural external law.

Thus, we can state Kant's position in the following terms: we have a right to act without being subjected to the coercive influence of the will of others—and this right is established by a natural external law, based on the interests of reason. Our right to external freedom is "innate" in the sense that no positive legislation is required to establish it, but that we enjoy it merely by virtue of our rational nature and the *a priori* laws governing the use of our rational faculties.

This raises the question: in which sense do the interests of reason ground our right to external freedom? In Chapter 5 above, we have argued that we should ascribe to Kant the position that reason has an essential interest in its own effectiveness. For, in his view, reason demands that we fully realize the ideal conception of ourselves as noumenally free wills in the empirical world [R, VI, 61]. Doing so requires that we establish ourselves as agents capable of using their rational faculties to achieve the ends they set for themselves. An existence in which we were incapable—either because of a lack of skill or because of external constraints—of achieving the ends we choose for ourselves would be one in which we would have failed to realize the ideal conception of ourselves as noumenally free agents. Hence, only where we are in a position to act successfully on the projects we have chosen for ourselves—i.e. where reason is effective in choosing and realizing our ends—can we be said to satisfy reason's demand to actualize our essential nature as free rational beings in the empirical world. That is, Kant's conception of the demands of reason gives us ground for ascribing to reason an essential interest in its own effectiveness.

As we have highlighted in Chapter 3, the interests of reason generate duties. In this sense, we should understand our duty to develop our talents and skills, discussed in Chapter 8 above, as based on reason's interest in its own effectiveness[25]. For given the indeterminacy of our ends as rational beings, it is only by developing a broad range of skills that we can ensure that we will be able to pursue and realize whatever end we happen to choose (that is, only in this way can we ensure reason's effectiveness in choosing and realizing ends).

Yet, on the same grounds reason's interest in its own effectiveness also imposes a duty on all other rational beings not to interfere with my reason's role as the active chooser and pursuer of my own projects. That is, it generates a duty for others not to impose their will on mine and to coerce me to function as a tool for their projects. For were they to impose their will in this manner, (their) reason

---

[25] See note 16 in Chapter 8 above. Note that Kant himself does not offer any justification for his claim that we have such a duty.

would frustrate (my) reason's essential interest in its own effectiveness—in a way that would lead to a self-contradiction of reason (in the sense discussed in Chapter 3 and Chapter 7 above). To make proper use of their own rational faculties—and, hence, to avoid such contradictions—all rational beings have to respect the right of others to choose and pursue their own ends. That is, rational beings have an obligation to respect the external freedom of others. My innate right to external freedom is just the flipside of this obligation. For to say that others have a moral obligation not to impose their will on my life is to say I have a natural right to act in a way that is unencumbered by the coercive influence of the wills of others. Thus, Kant holds that each of us—before the advent of any positive legislation—has an innate right, by virtue of his moral personality, to pursue his own projects without suffering the coercive interference by the will of others.

The reference to moral personality—and, hence, to our noumenal freedom—is crucial in this context. For Kant holds that it is only because of our moral personality that we have any rights at all: "Wir kennen unsere eigene Freiheit (von der alle moralische Gesetze, mithin auch alle Rechte sowohl als Pflichten ausgehen) nur durch den moralischen Imperativ, welcher ein pflichtgebietender Satz ist, aus welchem nachher das Vermögen, andere zu verpflichten, d. i. der Begriff des Rechts, entwickelt werden kann" [MS, VI, 239]. That is, it is just because we ourselves, as bearers of moral personality, can be subject to obligations that we can, in turn, impose obligations on others (i.e. enjoy rights). Given that the fact of reason is the basis for our self-ascription of moral personality (see Chapter 4 above), our innate right to external freedom is thus ultimately grounded in the fact of reason[26]. Kant holds, furthermore, that the validity of positive external laws is based on the validity of natural external law: "[Die natürliche Rechtslehre muss] zu aller positiven Gesetzgebung die unwandelbaren Prinzipien hergeben" [MS, VI, 229]. Hence, the fact of reason and the moral law are the basis for the validity of natural external laws, which, in turn, ground the validity of positive external laws.

We are now in a position to discuss Kant's claim that we can only make full use of our technical-practical reason in the context of a civil society. The problem with our innate right to external freedom is that in the absence of positive legislation and state authority it is not secured against infringement. For the fact that others have a moral obligation to respect my right to external freedom does not mean they will necessarily act accordingly. To illustrate this point, Kant, follow-

---

26 This is noted by Rosen [1993, 46].

ing Hobbes, uses the thought construct of a state of nature[27], i.e. a condition in which the lack of natural coordination among the actions of different human beings is not made up for by any shared laws or authorities[28]. In the state of nature, each individual enjoys what Kant calls "wild freedom" [IAG, VIII, 22]: given the absence of any coercive authority, the individual is free to engage in any act he pleases, provided he has the requisite powers (i.e. provided he is not blocked in his efforts by other, stronger individuals): "[Im Naturzustand gibt] jeder sich selbst das Gesetz, und es ist kein äußeres, dem er sich samt allen andern unterworfen erkennte… [Jeder ist] sein eigner Richter, und es ist keine öffentliche machthabende Autorität da, die nach Gesetzen, was in vorkommenden Fällen eines jeden Pflicht sei, rechtskräftig bestimme und jene in allgemeine Ausübung bringe" [R, VI, 95; see also MS, VI, 346][29].

The problem with the state of nature is that it is a condition of permanent latent conflict: in the absence of any rules coordinating the actions of the different individuals, the external freedom of each is permanently at risk of being undermined by the act of another [R, VI, 97n][30]. Each individual, in the attempt to promote and protect his own interests, becomes a threat for the plans of others. Even where this does not result in direct clashes among individuals, any peace

---

27 The state of nature is an idea of reason ("die Vernunftidee eines solchen nicht-rechtlichen Zustandes" [MS, VI, 312]), in the sense discussed in Chapter 1 above.

28 Compare this to the state of nature reason is said to find itself in before being subjected to the critique of reason in *Kritik der Reinen Vernunft*: "Man kann die Kritik der reinen Vernunft als den wahren Gerichtshof für alle Streitigkeiten derselben ansehen… Ohne dieselbe ist die Vernunft gleichsam im Stande der Natur und kann ihre Behauptungen und Ansprüche nicht anders geltend machen oder sichern, als durch Krieg. Die Kritik dagegen, welche alle Entscheidungen aus den Grundregeln ihrer eigenen Einsetzung hernimmt, deren Ansehen keiner bezweifeln kann, verschafft uns die Ruhe eines gesetzlichen Zustandes, in welchem wir unsere Streitigkeit nicht anders führen sollen, als durch Prozess" [KrV, III, 491]. On the many variations of the theme of the state of nature as a field of lawless struggle in Kant's work, see Saner [1973, 272 and 308].

29 Kant also refers to the notion of wild freedom as "lawless freedom" [MS, VI, 316; see also: IAG, VIII, 25], "brutal freedom" [R, VI, 97; see also: IAG, VIII, 24], "crazy freedom" ("tolle Freiheit" [EF, VIII, 354]), "natural freedom" ("natürliche Freiheit" [MS, VI, 343]), "unbound freedom" ("ungebundene Freiheit" [IAG, VIII, 22]), "unconditional freedom" ("unbedingte Freiheit" [A, VII, 327]) and "mutually conflicting freedom" ("einander wechselseitig widerstreitende Freiheit" [KU, V, 432]).

30 Kant reflects on our status as naturally uncoordinated agents in R 1500: "Die Ursache liegt in seiner Freiheit, da er nicht durch den Instinkt der Natur, alle Glieder einer Gattung einstimmig macht, sondern durch Launen und Einfälle (oder durch Grundsätze) getrieben wird, die keine Einheit verstatten. Aber diese Freiheit ist es nicht allein, sondern ein gewisser Hang, sich der Richtschnur der Ordnung zu entziehen, die die Vernunft vorschreibt, und sich seinen Einfällen und Neigungen zu gefallen davon auszunehmen" [XV, 785].

under these circumstances must be regarded as fragile and temporary, given that the interaction of many uncoordinated agents can lead to the outbreak of conflict at any moment [EF, VIII, 349]. That is, in the state of nature our innate right to external freedom is constantly at risk of being infringed [R, VI, 97n][31]. This is what we might call the *paradox of freedom:* in a condition of perfect freedom, in which each individual is free to do as he pleases, freedom undermines itself, as no individual can make a secure and effective use of his freedom. Because each individual enjoys unrestricted freedom, the freedom of each is constantly at risk[32].

Note that nothing in this situation hinges on the evil intentions of the individuals involved (in a way that it could be solved if these intentions were sufficiently benign). Rather, uncertainty is a structural property of the state of nature: there are no generally recognized rules of interactions and no means to resolve conflict, in a way that even with the best of intentions naturally uncoordinated individuals are bound to clash in the pursuit of their individual projects [MS, VI, 312]. What is more, because each individual is aware of the fragility of his own external freedom, each has an incentive to undermine the freedom of others to ensure that they do not use it to undermine his own[33].

Civil society is Kant's solution to the problem of uncoordinated freedom. It involves establishing a state authority that restricts the external freedom of each individual in a way that it is consistent with the greatest equal freedom of all other individuals. This leads to a "harmonization" ("durchgängige Zusammenstimmung", [TP, VIII, 290]) of the previously fragmented freedom of the different individuals: "[D]ie Gesetze sind hier auch nur Einschränkungen unsrer

---

[31] As a consequence, the state of nature is, from a Kantian perspective, necessarily unjust [KrV, III, 492]. "According to Kant, justice requires a guarantee that personal rights and liberties will be protected, and because there is no impartial method of settling quarrels in the state of nature, such an assurance is impossible there. The state of nature is consequently unjust in the sense that it is always devoid of justice, even if it is not always a condition of active injustice. It is worth stressing that the state of nature is not unjust as a result of any evil in human nature... It is unjust for the more basic, more structural reason that justice can exist only when there is some systematic means of protecting individual rights" [Rosen, 1993, 10].

[32] This paradox motivates Kant's statement that "Freiheit ist das größte Gut und das größte Übel" [R 7217, XIX, 288]. Rosen comments: "In connection with external freedom Kant's attitude is decidedly mixed as is shown by his repeated claim that the unbridled freedom of the state of nature is destructive and must be replaced by the controlled freedom of civil society... As much as any other political philosopher, Kant recognizes the dangers of unrestricted freedom and the harm it may produce" [1993, 41].

[33] "Die Menschen haben eine Fähigkeit und Trieb, in Gesellschaft zu treten; aber sie misstrauen einander wegen der Gewalttätigkeit. Daher sucht einer dem anderen aus Furcht zuvor zu kommen" [R, 1501, XV, 790].

Freiheit auf Bedingungen, unter denen sie durchgängig mit sich selbst zusammenstimmt" [KrV, III, 239]. Each individual loses his wild, insecure freedom and instead comes to enjoy a more restricted, but secure freedom. This is what we might call the corollary of the *paradox of freedom:* for a group of finite rational beings, the freedom of each can only be secured by restricting the freedom of all [TP, VIII, 290; see also Williams, 2003, 81]. Only restricted external freedom can be secure—and, hence, effective—external freedom (i.e. freedom that does not risk being disrupted at any given moment). The best possible state for us as finite rational beings, insofar as our external freedom is concerned, is not one of a complete absence of restraints on our freedom, but one in which the freedom of all is maximized by restricting the freedom of each ("die größte Freiheit... und doch die genauste Bestimmung und Sicherung der Grenzen dieser Freiheit" [IAG, VIII, 22][34].

To achieve this determining and securing of the greatest possible equal freedom of each, Kant argues a political society has to have the following characteristics. First, the interaction between the different individuals in the society—the citizens—has to be regulated by public (positive external) laws that apply to each citizen in the same way. That is, the citizens enjoy what Kant calls "civil equality" ("bürgerliche Gleichheit" [MS, VI, 314][35]). Each surrenders his wild freedom and gains an equal degree of secure freedom under shared laws. The legal relation between the citizens under a civil constitution is thus one of reciprocity: by entering into a condition in which we can legally oblige others, we accept that we

---

34 "Independence comes only within a framework of rules that we accept as our own. It is not itself a complete absence of restraint, but rather an acceptance of certain obligations which allows us to act without restraint in certain specified directions" [Williams, 2003, 140].
35 Kant emphasizes that this equality before the law is consistent with considerable material inequality [TP, VIII, 291–2; see also: Saner, 1973, 31; Rosen, 1993, 29; Wood, 1999, 154]. In his *Mutmaßlicher Anfang der Menschengeschichte*, he even dates the rise of material inequality among human beings with the foundation of civil society: "Von dieser ersten und rohen Anlage konnte sich nun nach und nach alle menschliche Kunst, unter welcher die der Geselligkeit und bürgerlichen Sicherheit die ersprießlichste ist, allmählich entwickeln... Mit dieser Epoche fing auch die Ungleichheit unter Menschen, diese reiche Quelle so vieles Bösen, aber auch alles Guten, an und nahm fernerhin zu" [MAM, VIII, 119]. Furthermore, in *Kritik der Urteilskraft*, Kant argues that material inequality is necessary for the advancement of culture: "Die Geschicklichkeit kann in der Menschengattung nicht wohl entwickelt werden, als vermittelst der Ungleichheit unter Menschen: da die größte Zahl die Notwendigkeit des Lebens gleichsam mechanisch, ohne dazu besonders Kunst zu bedürfen, zur Gemächlichkeit und Muse anderer besorgt, welche die minder notwendigen Stücke der Kultur, Wissenschaft und Kunst, bearbeiten" [KU, V, 432]. However, as in his discussion of passive citizenship (see note 37 below), Kant insists that those at the losing end of the material distribution range must have the chance to improve their lot through "talent, hard work and luck" [TP, VIII, 292].

can equally be legally obliged by them: "Keiner [kann] den andern wozu rechtlich verbinden..., ohne dass er sich zugleich dem Gesetz unterwirft, von diesem wechselseitig auf dieselbe Art auch verbunden werden zu können" [EF, VIII, 350n; see also: MS, VI, 237; Shell, 1980, 117][36].

Secondly, the citizens have to be authors of the laws to which they are subject [MS, VI, 314; see also: SF, VII, 86n][37]. Only under this condition are they not subject to the will of another (i.e. suffer no infringement of their innate right to external freedom). Kant holds that laws decided on by all ensure that each citizen will be treated with justice, for he will be subject only to rules which he has co-legislated (and, Kant holds, no one can do injustice to himself [MS, VI, 313]). Only a set of laws in which those who have to obey them are also the legislators, Kant insists, is consistent with our natural right to external freedom (i.e. the right to be free from coercive influence of the will of others): "Die Idee einer mit dem natürlichen Rechte der Menschen zusammenstimmenden Constitution: dass nämlich die dem Gesetz Gehorchenden auch zugleich, vereinigt, gesetzgebend sein sollen" [SF, VII, 90].

---

36 The notion of legal equality is inspired by Newtonian physics. In civil society, as in the physical realm, there is a perfect coincidence of cause and effect ("[die] Gleichheit der Wirkung und Gegenwirkung einer dem allgemeinen Freiheitsgesetze gemäß einander einschränkenden Willkür, (welches der bürgerliche Zustand heißt)" [TP, VIII, 292]. In this sense, Kant also refers to the "mechanical uniformity" of life under a civil constitution [SF, VII, 80]. Shell notes that "[t]he impersonality of mechanics, as (an external) system of body, is paralleled by the impartiality of right, as an external system of wills" [1980, 125n]. We have discussed the manner in which Kant's ethical thought is inspired by Newton in note 17 in Chapter 3 above.

37 In practice, however, Kant thinks the legislation should be conducted not by the citizens themselves, but by their delegates [MS, VI, 341] (see note 41 below). Furthermore, Kant qualifies his statement about the right to participate in legislation by distinguishing between active and passive citizens, apportioning the right to participate in the legislative process only to the latter. To be an active citizen, one has to be an adult male and enjoy "civil personality" [MS, VI, 314; see also: Saner, 1973, 35]. By this latter terms Kant means that an individual has to be economically independent and not have been convicted of certain criminal offences [MS, VI, 331]. The former of these conditions is meant to exclude apprentices and servants from active citizenship, though Kant admits that in practice "it is a bit difficult" to determine which professions exactly should be seen to confer the right to active citizenship [TP, VIII, 295n]. Passive citizens continue to enjoy the equal protection of their right to external freedom, but do not have the right to participate in legislation. Yet, Kant insists that it must be possible for them to work their way up to achieve the status of active citizen [MS, VI, 315; see also: Brandt, 2007, 159]. That said, it is rather unclear how this demand could be satisfied in the case of women, whom Kant excludes from active citizenship merely by virtue of their sex. The distinction between active and passive citizenship seems to have been overlooked by Rosen, who writes that Kant regards "political freedom as an a priori right belonging to each person in virtue of her humanity" [1993, 212]. The use of the female possessive pronoun is particularly ironic here, given the point just discussed.

Thirdly, the positive external laws in the civil society are backed up by coercive powers. To ensure that each individual follows the laws that secure the freedom of all, the state has to be able to avail itself of "irresistible force", to be applied against those who violate these laws: "[Eine vollkommen gerechte bürgerliche Gesellschaft ist] eine Gesellschaft, in welcher Freiheit unter äußeren Gesetzen im größtmöglichen Grade mit unwiderstehlicher Gewalt verbunden angetroffen wird" [IAG, VIII, 22][38]. In this sense—and rather paradoxically—state coercion is the necessary condition for the possibility of effective external freedom[39]. Given that the citizens are themselves the authors of the laws to which they are subject, these laws—and the coercion used to enforce them—do not confront the citizens as a foreign imposition, but are the expression of their own rational will (namely, the expression of their own rational interest in creat-

---

38 The notion of irresistible state power, for Kant, implies an absolute prohibition of any attempt to overthrow the sovereign. His argument for this claim is rooted in his understanding of the logic of the law under civil society. For us to escape from the state of nature, we have to create a common authority that can adjudicate all conflicts—and that is equipped with irresistible power to enforce its decisions [EF, VIII, 382]. Thus, the existence of irresistible state force is, Kant holds, a necessary condition for the possibility of a civil society: "[E]s existiert kein rechtlich bestehendes gemeines Wesen ohne eine solche Gewalt" [TP, VIII, 299]. Yet, the logic of this construct implies that that there can be no right within the legal code to overthrow the adjudicating authority, for if there were, the society in question would lack the hallmark of a civil society, namely a sovereign authority equipped with irresistible force [MS, VI, 372]. Kant holds that resistance against sovereign power is a severe crime ("das höchste und strafbarste Verbrechen im gemeinen Wesen" [TP, VIII, 299]), given that it undermines the condition of the possibility for the protection of everyone's external freedom. Rosen [1993, 144] argues that Kant's argument defending absolute sovereign powers is inconsistent with his own republicanism, i.e. his conception of the state powers as split into its executive, legislative and judicative functions (on Kant's republicanism, see note 41 below). Rosen also points out [1993, 150] that in several passages, Kant seems to be endorsing resistance to state authority, for instance, when in *Metaphysik der Sitten* he writes that we are to obey the sovereign in everything *as long as doing so it is not inconsistent with our inner morality* ("Gehorchet der Obrigkeit (in allem, was nicht dem inneren Moralischen widerstreitet)" [MS, VI, 371]) or when he suggests in *Kritik der Praktischen Vernunft* that the honest man who is ordered by his sovereign to slander an innocent man should resist that demand [KpV, V, 155–6].

39 Kant argues that the right to coercion follows analytically from the right to external freedom: "[W]enn ein gewisser Gebrauch der Freiheit selbst ein Hindernis der Freiheit nach allgemeinen Gesetzen (d. i. unrecht) ist, so ist der Zwang, der diesem entgegengesetzt wird, als Verhinderung eines Hindernisses der Freiheit mit der Freiheit nach allgemeinen Gesetzen zusammen stimmend, d. i. recht: mithin ist mit dem Rechte zugleich eine Befugnis, den, der ihm Abbruch tut, zu zwingen, nach dem Satze des Widerspruchs verknüpft" [MS, VI, 231; see also: MS, VI, 396; TP, VIII, 299; Wood, 1999, 322n; Guyer, 2000; 412n].

ing the conditions of secure external freedom)[40]. State coercion enforces our own laws against ourselves—or, to put it differently, it enforces the laws of our higher, noumenal self against our erring, empirical self. A coercive state, for Kant, is not one that violates our autonomy, but is rather a necessary condition for the realization of our freedom. This is why, Kant claims, the use of state violence is not only compatible with, but required for the maintenance of, our ability to lead self-guided lives: "[D]ie bürgerliche Verfassung [ist] ein Verhältnis freier Menschen... , die (unbeschadet ihrer Freiheit im Ganzen ihrer Verbindung mit anderen) doch unter Zwangsgesetzen stehen" [TP, VIII, 290].

Fourthly, the only legitimate purpose for which the freedom of each can be restricted is the securing of freedom itself. The state, Kant holds, is not concerned with promoting any particular conception of happiness, but merely to generate the formal condition under which we can successfully pursue our own projects [TP, VIII, 290; see also: TP, VIII, 302][41].

The resulting civil condition is one of right or justice (*Recht*)[42]: "Recht ist die Einschränkung der Freiheit eines jeden auf die Bedingung ihrer Zusammenstim-

---

[40] "Kant ... thinks there is liberty only within the civil condition. The restraints that the civil condition imposes upon us... have to be seen as constraints we put on ourselves, and so as internal to our political freedom" [Williams, 2003, 82; see also: Shell, 1980, 126].

[41] In addition to the four characteristics of the civil society mentioned in the text, Kant also emphasizes the importance of a republican constitution, by which he understands a representative system of government [MS, VI, 341] that separates the executive functions of the state from the legislative and judicative ones [EF, VIII, 352], thus reducing the scope for a despotic use of state power: "Die bürgerliche Verfassung in jedem Staate soll republikanisch sein" [EF, VIII, 349]. A republican constitution, Kant holds, reduces the likelihood that the state will start wars [SF, VII, 85; see also: EF, VIII, 351] and is "the only one fully consistent with upholding the rights of men" ("[D]ie republikanische Verfassung [ist] die einzige, welche dem Recht der Menschen vollkommen angemessen... ist" [EF, VIII, 366). In many passages, Kant appears to use the terms "civil constitution" and "republican constitution" as synonymous, for instance when he writes, in a discussion of the notion of a republican constitution, that only it truly deserves to be called a "civil constitution" [A, VII, 331] or when he says that the kind of constitution resulting from the idea of the original contract is a republican one [EF, VIII, 350]. Kant is explicit that he does not equate republicanism with democracy, which he regards as a form of despotism [EF, VIII, 352; see also: Rosen, 1993, 34].

[42] O'Neill highlights how the Kantian notion of justice is connected to his wider theme of achieving unity among a multiplicity of agents who are not naturally coordinated: "The reason why Kant is drawn to explicate the authority of reason in political metaphors is surely that he sees the problems of cognitive and political order as arising in one and the same context. In either case we have a plurality of agents or voices and no transcendent or pre-established authority. Authority has in either case to be constructed. The problem is to discover whether there are any constraints on the mode of order (cognitive or political) that can be constituted. Such constraints (if they can be discovered) constitute respectively the principles of reason and of justice.

mung mit der Freiheit von jedermann, in so fern diese nach einem allgemeinen Gesetze möglich ist" [TP, VIII, 289–90]. That is, a just state is one in which the freedom of each is curtailed by laws that apply to each individual in the same way to ensure the greatest possible secure freedom for all[43]. Under the resulting laws, each individual loses his wild, unconstrained freedom in return for a more restricted, yet secure and protected freedom. While he is now subject to state coercion, he can nonetheless consider himself free, given that, first, he himself is a co-legislator of the laws that are being enforced against him, and, second, this coercion is a necessary condition for giving his freedom practical reality (for otherwise he would live with the constant threat of his actions being disrupted by the interference of others)[44].

Borrowing a term from Rousseau, Kant conceives the foundation of a civil society as the unification of the individuals' particular wills into a common

---

Reason and justice are two aspects to the solution of the problems that arise when an uncoordinated plurality of agents is to share a possible world" [1989, 16].

43 As Kant puts it, this condition combines freedom, law and coercion [A, VII, 330–1]. He distinguishes it from anarchy (freedom, law, no coercion), despotism (law, coercion, no freedom) and barbarism (coercion, no freedom, no law).

44 However, Kant argues that the task of setting up a "perfect civil constitution" is only completed once the problem of lawless freedom has been solved not only in the relations among the citizens within the state, but also in those among the different states: "Das Problem der Errichtung einer vollkommnen bürgerlichen Verfassung ist von dem Problem eines gesetzmäßigen äußeren Staatenverhältnisses abhängig und kann ohne das letztere nicht aufgelöst werden" [IAG, VIII, 24; see also: KU, V, 432; Guyer, 2000, 411]. Kant argues that the different sovereign states, just like the individuals in their pre-civil condition, live a state of nature, which is marked by the absence of an authority to adjudicate conflicts, leading to a constant latent threat of clashes among the states [MS, VI, 344; EF, VIII, 354]. The solution to this problem, Kant holds, is not the merging of all peoples into one super-state (for it would be impossible to enforce common laws in such a vast state—and the reduced opportunities for participation would risk making the state despotic [EF, VIII, 367]) or establishing a state of states, in which the individual states are subjects (for this would be incompatible with the monopoly of power held by the sovereigns of the individual states [EF, VIII, 355–6]). Rather, the individual states, Kant suggests, are to come together in a voluntary federation of states, in which they agree to preserve peace [EF, VIII, 356], not to interfere with their respective internal affairs and to help protect one another against possible external attacks [MS, VI, 344]. However, this solution is vulnerable to his own insight that the central problem in the state of nature is the absence of an adjudicating authority with the power to enforce its decisions. The establishment of such an authority, Kant argues when discussing the state of nature among individuals, is central to solving the paradox of freedom. However, in discussing the same paradox on the inter-state level, his solution notably fails to establish an authority of this kind, a problem that Kant himself seems to acknowledge in [EF, VIII, 357].

will ("allgemeiner Wille" [R, VI, 98; see also: MS, VI, 269])⁴⁵. The individual wills, which are in conflict in the state of nature, are now integrated into a condition of systematic unity. The positive laws of the state are understood as the maxims of this common will, which allow for the coordination of the individual wills. Kant calls the initial act, in which the individual wills generate a common reference point by which to adjudicate their conflicts, the writing of an original contract [TP, VIII, 297]. He does not, however, conceive of this as an actual historical event. Rather, the original contract is a mere idea of reason—and, like most ideas of reason, must appear abstruse if we take it too literally. The notion of the original contract suggests that we have to regard the positive laws of the civil society *as if* they were the expression of a common will, of our need for a common framework of rules that allow us to escape our wild freedom and enable us to live together and interact without the permanent latent threat of conflict⁴⁶.

We are now in a position to understand Kant's claim that we can only achieve perfection in the use of our technical-practical reason in the context of a civil society. We have found that Kant regards civil society as the only manner of organizing our social interactions in that allows us to enjoy secure external

---

45 When referring to the notion of the common will, Kant also uses the terms "gemeinschaftlicher Wille" [EF, VIII, 371], "allgemeingültiger Wille" [IAG, VIII, 23], "vereinigter Wille" [TP, VIII, 297; see also: MS, VI, 302] and "allgemein wirklich vereinigter Wille" [MS, VI, 264]. Kant is explicit that the notion of the common will is a mere idea of reason: "[E]s ist eine bloße Idee der Vernunft, die aber ihre unbezweifelte (praktische) Realität hat: nämlich jeden Gesetzgeber zu verbinden, dass er seine Gesetze so gebe, als sie aus dem vereinigten Willen eines ganzen Volks haben entspringen können" [TP, VIII, 297].

46 Kant concedes that the most likely empirical origin of state authority is violence and oppression: "[I]n der Ausführung jener Idee (in der Praxis) [ist] auf keinen andern Anfang des rechtlichen Zustandes zu rechnen, als den durch Gewalt" [EF, VIII, 371]. In order for this insight not to undermine the power of the sovereign, citizens should refrain from investigating into the historical origins of state power [MS, VI, 318]. Kant admits, furthermore, that in practice there will often be a significant gap between the ideal civil constitution and the actual political set-up in historically embodied states [EF, VIII, 371]. Yet, to be able to live together at all and to be able to make use of our freedom in a secure and effective manner, we need state authority to solve the paradox of freedom. The best course of action is to push—by means of a public discussion about the shortcomings of the actually existing political set-up [TP, VIII, 304]—for a constant approximation of the flawed political reality to the standards of the ideal civil constitution [MS, VI, 340; see also: MS, VI, 372], even if this approximation takes a long time [R, VI, 188n]. In this process we are to use the idea of the original contract as a touchstone ("Probierstein" [TP, VIII, 297]) to assess the quality of the laws legislated in the current political system. Rosen points out that Kant's position amounts to a qualified defense of the unjust state as historically necessary: "[Kant believes that] a just state can develop only after a prolonged period of political injustice, and that since unjust states are therefore historically necessary precursors of just states, they be accorded a degree of legitimacy" [1993, 4; see also: Shell, 1980, 172–3].

freedom. Given that the technical-practical use of our rational faculties is concerned with choosing and realizing our personal projects (i.e. working towards our happiness), external freedom—the ability to pursue our projects without the interference by others—is precisely the freedom to make unimpeded use of our reason in this sense.

As needy and vulnerable creatures, we require a stable social background, ordered by shared laws, to develop and exercise our rational powers. We cannot thrive in the chaotic state of nature [IAG, VIII, 25], in which each individual follows his own standards of right and wrong, making it impossible for all ever to be safe from threats of conflicts and attacks [IAG, VIII, 22; see also A, VII, 329]. In this sense, existence in a civil society is the necessary formal condition for us to be able to make proper use of our rational faculties to pursue the ends we have chosen for ourselves: "Die formale Bedingung, unter welcher die Natur... ihre Endabsicht allein erreichen kann, ist diejenige Verfassung im Verhältnisse der Menschen untereinander, wo dem Abbruche der einander wechselseitig widerstreitenden Freiheit gesetzmäßige Gewalt in einem Ganzen, welches bürgerliche Gesellschaft heißt, entgegengesetzt wird; denn nur in ihr kann die größte Entwickelung der Naturanlagen geschehen" [KU, V, 432].

Given reason's interest in its own effectiveness and given, furthermore, the way in which this effectiveness is structurally threatened in the state of nature, Kant argues that we have a duty to leave the state of nature—and enter the civil condition, in which the external freedom of each is secured[47]: "Aus dem Privatrecht im natürlichen Zustande geht nun das Postulat des öffentlichen Rechts hervor: du sollst im Verhältnisse eines unvermeidlichen Nebeneinanderseins mit allen anderen aus jenem heraus in einen rechtlichen Zustand, d. i. den einer austeilenden Gerechtigkeit übergehen" [MS, VI, 307; SF, VII, 91][48].

---

[47] "What was for Hobbes and Locke primarily a selfish impulsion to quit the state of nature becomes for Kant a non-selfish imperative of duty as well. We have a duty to protect ourselves from wrongful injury and to refrain from injuring others" [Shell, 1980, 153].

[48] Kant offers a more complex argument for the duty to enter into civil society based on the notion of property: we can only make effective use of our will if we can employ the things we find in the world around us as tools [MS, VI, 246]. That is, property—the ability to own and thus reliably make use of things—is a necessary condition for the effective use of our external freedom. However, in the state of nature the only form of possession that is possible is empirical or provisional possession [MS, VI, 256]. That is, I only own a thing as long as it is physically under my control. Yet, nothing ensures that it will not be snatched from me by a stronger individual. Consequently, my claim on any possession—and, by extension, my ability to make effective use of my will—in the state of nature is always fragile and only provisional. Kant contrasts merely provisional possession with the notion of intelligible property, i.e. the property claim in which a given thing is mine regardless of whether it is in my hands or miles away from me [MS,

Ethical community

The third important social aspect of Kant's moral philosophy is the notion that accomplishing moral perfection requires the founding of an ethical community. For Kant, entering a civil society is only one part of the solution to the problem of achieving coordination among the naturally uncoordinated wills of finite rational beings[49]. For submitting to shared external laws (i.e., laws governing our actions, rather than being concerned with our intentions) as the best policy to secure one's own external freedom is consistent with us remaining indifferent about, or even hostile to, the interests of others[50]. That is, it is consistent with us continuing to consider others from the perspective of our technical-practical reason, from which they appear merely as obstacles in, or tools for, our pursuit of

---

VI, 254]. The claim I have on a given thing is independent of empirical possession—but rather consists of a relation between my will and that of all other wills, committing the latter to respect my claim on the object in question [MS ,VI, 261; Guyer, 2000, 236]. Only in such a condition, in which all others are committed to respect my property right, are peremptory, intelligible property claims possible and I can reliably make use of the objects around me—and, by extension, can make effective use of my will. Yet, such agreements for the mutual recognition of property claims are only possible in a state of law (i.e. a state in which individuals have come together to follow shared rules of interaction—and in which there is an authority to enforce these rules [MS, VI, 312]). That is, they are possible only in a civil condition: "[D]enn bürgerliche Verfassung ist allein der rechtliche Zustand, durch welchen jedem das Seine... gesichert wird" [MS, VI, 256; see also: MS, VI, 264]. Hence, given that a) the interests of reason ground duties; b) our reason has an essential interest in ensuring its own effectiveness; c) our reason can only be effective if it is possible for us to make reliable use of the things around us; d) we can only make such reliable use of the things around us in a civil condition, it follows that we have a duty to enter into a civil condition. On this point, see [Dodson, 1997, 102]. In addition to postulating a duty to enter into the civil society, Kant also holds that we have the right to force others to enter into a civil condition with us [MS, VI, 312; see also: Rosen, 120, 1993; Guyer, 2000, 283].

49 Kant insists that entering into a civil society is a *necessary* condition for achieving moral unity among the naturally uncoordinated wills of finite rational beings: "Wenn ein ethisches gemeines Wesen zu Stande kommen soll, so müssen alle Einzelne einer öffentlichen Gesetzgebung unterworfen werden" [R, VI, 98; see also: EF, VIII, 366; Yovel, 1989, 111]. However, he also holds that it is not a *sufficient* condition [R, VI, 97]. "[C]ivil society... is only an external copy... of morality. It secures external freedom but does not abolish the subjective antagonism of wills. Even within the perfect constitution men may remain in the ethical state of conflict, using their political freedom immorally, conflicting within the law while each is trying to use the other only as a means, with no regard to his inherent worth as end in himself" [Yovel, 1989, 151; see also: Wood, 1999, 309n].

50 "A civil society based on right does require no moral commitment on the part of its members to respect one another's rightful freedom. It requires only a system of external legislation, backed by coercive sanctions sufficient to guarantee that rights will not be infringed" [Wood, 2000, 10].

our subjective projects[51]. Kant puts this point by saying that the problem of setting up a civil political system could be solved even by devils (that is, by beings lacking all interest in the well-being of others [EF, VIII, 366])[52], because such a system, operating through coercion, gives incentives to act in accordance with the laws even to those who are focused only on their narrow self-interest. That is, individuals' living in a civil society—i.e. having left the *juridical* state of nature—is consistent with them remaining in an *ethical* state of nature[53]:

> [S]o ist auch der ethische Naturzustand ein Zustand der unaufhörlichen Befehdung des guten Prinzips, das in jedem Menschen liegt, durch das Böse, welches in ihm und zugleich in jedem andern angetroffen wird, die sich... einander wechselseitig ihre moralische Anlage verderben, und selbst bei dem guten Willen jenes einzelnen, durch den Mangel eines sie vereini-

---

[51] Yovel points out that an important aspect of this ethical state of nature is the "conflict between pure subjective consciousness, each of which refuses to recognize the other and seeks to subordinate it and eliminate its status" [1989, 110], while Kant's solution involves "the foundation of an ethical community whose founding principle is the mutual recognition of all consciousness and the constant decision of each to regard all the others as equal in status and as ends in themselves" [1989, 111].

[52] Whether the assertion that the problem of setting up a civil political system could be solved by devils is consistent with Kant's theory of rights depends on how one conceives of devils. If devils are understood to be beings that are only endowed with technical-practical reason, but not with moral-practical reason—that is, if they are conceived as beings endowed with the instrumental reason, but do not see themselves confronted with any moral demands (making them the kind of beings Kant discusses in [R, VI, 26n], a passages we have discussed in Chapter 4 above)—then the assertion is not consistent with his theory of rights. For as we have discussed in the text above, Kant holds that we only have rights by virtue of our moral personality—that is, as beings endowed with moral-practical reasons. Devils conceived of as lacking moral-practical reasons would not be bearers of rights (either based on natural or positive law). Hence, they would lack a necessary condition for the possibility of entering a civil society (that is, a society built for the purpose of the protection of rights). Brandt interprets the notion of a "devil" in this way—but does not note the resulting inconsistency [2007, 384–5]. If, on the other hand, devils are conceived of as beings which are endowed with moral-practical reason, but which simply decide to ignore the moral demands they see themselves confronted with, Kant's suggestion is unproblematic.

[53] The distinction between justice and ethics, which underlies that between the juridical and the ethical state of nature, is parallel to that between legality and morality, discussed in Chapter 5 above: the former member in each pair is only concerned with the regulation and the evaluation of that which is external (i.e. actions), while the latter member in each pair is concerned with that which is internal (i.e. the determining grounds of actions). "Diese Gesetze der Freiheit heißen zum Unterschiede von Naturgesetzen moralisch. So fern sie nur auf bloße äußere Handlungen und deren Gesetzmäßigkeit gehen, heißen sie juridisch; fordern sie aber auch, dass sie (die Gesetze) selbst die Bestimmungsgründe der Handlungen sein sollen, so sind sie ethisch, und alsdann sagt man: die Übereinstimmung mit den ersteren ist die Legalität, die mit den zweiten die Moralität der Handlung" [MS, VI, 214].

genden Prinzips sie, gleich als ob sie Werkzeuge des Bösen wären, durch ihre Misshelligkeiten von dem gemeinschaftlichen Zweck des Guten entfernen. [R, VI, 96]

In the ethical state of nature, we continue to frustrate our reason's interest in the systematic unity with other wills [KrV, III, 525]. This unity is only achieved if our willing is based on shared universal (*allgemeingültig*) principles [KU, V, 471]. Kant calls the ideal state of moral unity in which all individuals determine their wills on the basis of shared moral principles a realm of ends (*Reich der Zwecke*):

> Ich verstehe aber unter einem Reiche die systematische Verbindung verschiedener vernünftiger Wesen durch gemeinschaftliche Gesetze. Weil nun Gesetze die Zwecke ihrer allgemeinen Gültigkeit nach bestimmen, so wird, wenn man von dem persönlichen Unterschiede vernünftiger Wesen, imgleichen allem Inhalte ihrer Privatzwecke abstrahiert, ein Ganzes aller Zwecke (sowohl der vernünftigen Wesen als Zwecke an sich, als auch der eigenen Zwecke, die ein jedes sich selbst setzen mag) in systematischer Verknüpfung d. i. ein Reich der Zwecke, gedacht werden können. [GMS, IV, 433]

The members of this realm of ends recognize one another as ends in themselves and adopt the (morally permitted) ends of others as their own [MS, VI, 450], committing themselves to supporting their fellow human beings in their realization of their projects[54]. Just as in the civil society the external freedom of each individual is restricted in a way so as to be consistent with the equal external freedom of all others, in the realm of ends each will restricts itself "to the conditions under which it is consistent with the autonomy of all other rational beings" [KpV, V, 87; see also: MS, VI, 449][55].

---

[54] Wood points out that Kant's conception of friendship is the model for his notion of the realm of ends [1999, 279]. Kant defines friendship as "Vereinigung zweier Personen durch gleiche wechselseitige Liebe und Achtung. Man sieht leicht, dass sie ein Ideal der Teilnehmung und Mitteilung an dem Wohl eines jeden dieser durch den moralisch guten Willen Vereinigten sei" [MS, VI, 469]. This "sharing in the well-being of the other" is similar to the sympathy ("Wohlwollen") that Kant identifies as the emotional aspect of a truly moral attitude towards others: "Wohlwollen ist das Vergnügen an der Glückseligkeit (dem Wohlsein) Anderer" [MS, VI, 452]. He calls the practical attitude linked to this moral sympathy "practical love": "Die Liebe wird aber hier nicht als Gefühl (ästhetisch)... verstanden (denn Gefühle zu haben, dazu kann es keine Verpflichtung durch Andere geben), sondern muss als Maxime des Wohlwollens (als praktisch) gedacht werden, welche das Wohltun zur Folge hat" [MS, VI, 449; see also: EF, VIII, 338]. On the importance of the notions of sympathy and practical love for Kant's late moral philosophy, see Allison [1990, 167] and Guyer [2000, 299].
[55] It should be noted that the notion of a realm of ends already appears in *Grundlegung*. Here, however, it is not presented as an end to be realized in the empirical world. Rather, we are told that in determining our actions we are to act *as if* we were members in the realm of ends: "[E]in jedes vernünftige Wesen [muss] so handeln, *als ob* es durch seine Maximen jederzeit ein gesetz-

In the ideal condition of the realm of ends, the self-contradiction of practical reason that results from the conflict among individual wills is fully resolved and the ends of all are integrated into one systematic whole. In Kant's words, "die freie Willkür [der vernünftigen Wesen] unter moralischen Gesetzen [hat] sowohl mit sich selbst, als mit jedes anderen Freiheit durchgängige systematische Einheit" [KrV, III, 515]. Hence, the realm of ends is the condition in which reason's interest in systematic unity is fully satisfied. It is the closest finite rational beings can come to realizing the ideal conception of themselves as perfectly rational noumenal wills in the empirical world [KpV, V, 43]. Given the underlying identity of the reason of all rational beings (discussed in Chapter 6 above), the founding of the realm of ends constitutes a re-unification of reason with itself[56].

The focus on the notion of the realm of ends as the pinnacle of moral perfection highlights that the unilateral adoption of moral principles is not sufficient for the successful realization of our moral end. For where each individual commits to his personal moral code, there will be no coordination among the principles they are acting on [R, VI, 97]. Only if the principles by which we determine our actions are shared, can we hope to achieve our moral mission: "[D]as höchste sittliche Gut [wird nicht allein] durch die Bestrebung der einzelnen Person zu ihrer eigenen moralischen Vollkommenheit... bewirkt..., sondern [erfordert] eine Vereinigung derselben in ein Ganzes zu eben demselben Zwecke zu

---

gebendes Glied im allgemeinen Reiche der Zwecke wäre" [GMS, IV, 438; my emphasis]. In fact, Kant explicitly warns us that our making this commitment should not lead us to expect others to make the same effort [GMS, IV, 438.]. That is, while the notion of the realm of ends is already present in *Grundlegung*, it is used here as a guide for attaining the correct moral attitude, not a task to be accomplished in the empirical world. Thus, Yovel is right in observing that while the notion of the realm of ends is presented in *Grundlegung* as a mere thought construct helping us to orient ourselves in our attempt to achieve a good will, in Kant's latter work it is meant to be realized in the empirical world through the application of our powers [1989, 110].

56 The motive of achieving unity from a fragmented starting point is an important theme in the Kantian opus: "Das Charakteristische der Menschengattung [ist]... dass die Natur den Keim der Zwietracht in sie gelegt und gewollt hat, dass ihre eigene Vernunft aus dieser diejenige Eintracht, wenigstens die beständige Annäherung zu derselben herausbringe" [A, VII, 322]. In describing his moral ideal, he writes about "die Welt als ein schönes moralisches Ganzes in ihrer ganzen Vollkommenheit" [MS, VI, 458], "die Einhelligkeit mit allen Menschen (ja aller endlichen vernünftigen Wesen)" [R, VI, 96], "[d]ie erhabene, nie völlig erreichbare Idee eines ethischen gemeinen Wesens" [R, VI, 100], "[e]in ethisches gemeines Wesen unter der göttlichen moralischen Gesetzgebung " [R, VI, 101] and "das menschliche Geschlecht im Ganzen seiner Vereinigung" [SF, VII, 87]. The motive of moving from conflict to unity is given particular attention in Saner's interpretation of Kant: "Kant's work is ... framed in the polarity of conflict and unity, and in the pursuit of whatever unity can be established" [1973, 303].

einem System wohlgesinnter Menschen" [R, VI, 97–8; see also: A, VII, 333][57]. That is, only if we enter into a civil society, in which the freedom of each is protected by external laws, and, furthermore, commit to shared moral principles, can we realize the perfect rational ordering of our interactions demanded by reason[58].

Given reason's demand for systematic unity and the notion that reason's needs ground duties, Kant holds that we have a duty to enter into an ethical community with other rational beings [R, VI, 97]. That is, in order for us to satisfy the demands of our reason, we have to coordinate not only our external actions through the submission to shared positive external laws in a civil society, but also the principles on the basis of which we decide on these actions. This duty to enter into an ethical community with others is in some aspects similar to, but in others different from, our duty to enter into a civil society. The two duties are similar in that in both cases the realization of the object of our duty depends on the cooperation of others. They are different, however, in that—as membership in a political communion only requires abidance by external laws and given that individuals can be forced to make their actions conform to these laws—individuals can and should, Kant thinks, be *forced* to enter into

---

[57] Kant insists that we have only fully managed to exit from the ethical state of nature if all human beings are part of this ethical community, i.e. if the wills of all persons have adopted shared moral laws as their determining grounds. Yovel notes that "the creation of such a rational system may be seen as a collective conversion, corresponding to the conversion or 'revolution' that takes place in the individual personality when it overcomes the 'original evil' that it had chosen and adopts a moral disposition" [1989, 110]. Like the exit from the juridical state of nature discussed in the previous section, the exit from the ethical state of nature is only complete if all individuals have been integrated into the newly established structures. Unlike in the juridical case, however, where Kant advocated not a single super-state, but the establishment of a federation of states as the most realistic solution to the problem of inter-state conflict, all individuals are to be part of the same ethical community: "[W]eil die Tugendpflichten das ganze menschliche Geschlecht angehen, so ist der Begriff eines ethischen gemeinen Wesens immer auf das Ideal eines ganzen aller Menschen bezogen, und darin unterscheidet es sich von dem eines politischen" [R, VI, 96; see also: Wood, 1999, 315]. Kant calls the attitude of the individual who works towards establishing a moral community with all rational beings a "cosmopolitan disposition" ("weltbürgerliche Gesinnung" [MS, VI, 473]).

[58] This point is overlooked by Nyholm, who writes: "By subjecting ourselves to [moral] principles, we leave the ethical state of nature behind and enter into a state of virtue in which we are fully responsible for our conduct" [2012, 15n]. To exit from the ethical state of nature, it is not sufficient that an individual act on moral principles. Rather, to achieve such an exit he must coordinate the moral principles he acts on with his fellow human beings. (On this point, note the key quote in [R, VI, 97–8] highlighted in the text below.) Furthermore, according to Kant we are always "responsible for our conduct" (insofar as we have moral personality, i.e. are noumenally free). This moral responsibility is, contrary to Nyholm's assertion, not dependent on our "subjecting ourselves to moral principles".

civil society [MS, VI, 312]. There is, however, no way to coerce them to adopt certain ends [MS, VI, 381; see also: R, VI, 95]—or to make certain shared principles the determining ground of their willing. Thus, the duty to enter into an ethical community with others, Kant holds, is unenforceable. It depends, for its fulfillment, on the free cooperation of all [R, VI, 96], based on their insight that such cooperation is a requirement of the proper use of their own rational faculties.

The highest good as a social conception of the good life

We are now in a position to appreciate the essential social dimension of Kant's conception of the highest good as the best possible state of affairs in the empirical world. As we have seen in Chapter 7, this notion is best understood as the combination of the most complete happiness with the highest degree of moral perfection. Our discussion in this chapter highlights how both these elements of the highest good—the pursuit of our happiness and our moral mission—are dependent for their realization on our interaction with others. Achieving the highest degree of happiness (i.e. perfection in the use of our technical-practical reason) requires that we generate the conditions necessary for us to make effective and secure use of our external freedom (i.e. our ability to pursue our projects without being hindered by others). As we have seen, Kant argues that such an effective use of our freedom is possible only in the context of a civil society, governed by laws subjecting all individuals to the same restrictions on their external freedom. The most complete use of our external freedom requires that freedom be restricted in order to ensure that it does not undermine itself. The freest man, for Kant, is not the unrestrained hermit, but the citizen of the coercive state.

Furthermore, to achieve moral perfection it is not sufficient for us unilaterally to develop a good will. Rather, morality—concerned with satisfying the essential interests of pure practical reason—demands that we achieve a fully unified use of our rational faculties in their practical application, which, in addition to developing a good will, requires that the wills of all rational beings are joined in systematic unity (i.e. enter into a condition in which they are coordinated through their adoption of shared moral principles)[59]. In this sense, the highest good for Kant is a collective good ("gemeinschaftliches Gut" [R, VI, 97]).

---

[59] On the interpretation here presented of Kant's moral philosophy, founding the realm of ends is an essential part of realizing the highest good. Rawls seems to disagree with this view, asserting that the "idea of the realm of ends (as found in the Groundwork) and the idea of the highest good (as found in the second Critique) are distinct conceptions with different implications for

Consequently, Yovel is right when he identifies the highest good as the second stage of Kant's moral theory [1989, 32]. The first stage—presented in *Grundlegung*—is concerned merely with the formal quality of our will (i.e. making the moral law the highest determining ground of our will). In his discussion in *Grundlegung*, Kant emphasizes that the consequences of our actions are not morally relevant [GMS, IV, 416; see also: KpV, V, 45–6]. All that counts, at this first stage, is that we choose our maxims on the basis of their having universal form. In this sense, the notion of duty is not linked to the material content of our maxims (i.e. what they are aiming to achieve in the world), but their formal quality. At the second stage, however, Kant's moral theory is concerned with the consequences of our actions: we are to bring about a certain state of affairs in the empirical world, namely the highest good, i.e. the condition that combines the greatest happiness with the highest moral perfection [R, VI, 6n].

A further important difference between the first and the second stage of Kant's moral theory is the shift from a focus on the individual to one on the community. In ensuring the proper moral quality of my actions at the first stage (concerned with the moral quality of my will), I am perfectly self-sufficient: all I need to do in order to fulfill my duty is to have the right moral attitude. Consequently, doing my duty is completely in my power[60]. In helping to realize the highest good, on the other hand, I have to coordinate my efforts with those of my fellow human beings. This is a duty that I cannot fulfill by myself, but which by its nature can only be completed as a collective effort [R, VI, 97–98]. While other Kantian duties are private, in the sense that all they require of us depends on our own effort, the duty to promote the highest good has a distinct social component.

Kant's view" [2000, 311]. In the subsequent discussion Rawls is less than clear about his grounds for holding this view. The most likely explanation is that he does so because "I do not believe… that the content of the moral law… enjoins that in a realm of ends people are to act to as to make happiness strictly proportional to virtue" [2000, 313]. This suggests that it is Rawls' acceptance of the juridical conception of the highest good (as discussed in note 21 in Chapter 7 above) that leads him to believe that there are significant differences between the notions of the realm of ends and that of the highest good. However, as we have discussed, there are good reasons for rejecting the juridical conception of the highest good. Once we do so, there appear to be no good reasons to doubt that the notion of the realm of ends is a central component of Kant's notion of the highest good.

60 "Diese formale Beschaffenheit meiner Handlungen (Unterordnung derselben unter das Prinzip der Allgemeingültigkeit), worin allein ihr innerer moralischer Wert besteht, ist gänzlich in unserer Gewalt; und ich kann von der Möglichkeit, oder Unausführbarkeit der Zwecke, die mir jenem Gesetze gemäß zu befördern obliegen, gar wohl abstrahieren (weil in ihnen nur der äußere Wert meiner Handlungen besteht), als von etwas, welches nie völlig in meiner Gewalt ist, um nur auf das zu sehen, was meines Tuns ist" [KU, V, 471].

Hence, Beck is mistaken in claiming that the duty to promote the highest good does not add anything to the demand to make the moral law the highest determining ground of our will [1960, 244–5][61]. He overlooks precisely the difference between the first and the second stage of Kant's moral theory: the difference between a moral effort that is individualistic and focused merely on the moral quality of my will—and one that is focused on bringing about a certain state of affairs in the empirical world and which requires, for its realization, the coordination of our efforts with those of all other human beings. The point about the duty to promote the highest good—i.e. the second stage of Kant's moral project—is to unite ourselves with others, rather than following our individual ethical project.

Before concluding our discussion, we should note that Kant's conception of the good life in its social dimension links the two contrasting ideals of independence and inter-dependence. On the juridical level, as members of a civil society we are protected from the attempts of others to force their goals and ends onto us. We alone are responsible for the projects we spend our lives pursuing. No other individual—and no government—is to interfere with this right of ours to set and pursue our own ends (as long as doing so is consistent with the right to equal external freedom of all other individuals) [TP, VIII, 298]. Yet, we only enjoy these rights because of our agreeing with our fellow citizens on shared external laws that protect these rights and that can be coercively enforced against us. On the moral level, we guide our lives on the basis of moral laws that are an expression of the essential needs of our proper self, i.e. our reason. Yet, at the same time, these laws lead us to abstract from our own idiosyncratic interests and goals, based on that which is private about ourselves (our desires)—and make that which is shared (the objectively valid moral law) the main determinant of our actions. As a consequence, the interests and ends of others become important reference points in our deliberation on the right course of action [GMS,

---

[61] Here is Beck's argument, which we have already encountered in Chapter 7: "[S]uppose I do all in my power—which is all any moral decree can demand of me—to promote the highest good, what am I to do? Simply act out of respect for the law, which I already knew. I can do absolutely nothing else toward apportioning happiness in according with desert. It is not my task; my task is to realize the one condition of the summum bonum which is within my power; it is seriously misleading to say that there is a command to seek the highest good which is different from the command to fulfill the requirements of duty" [1960, 244–5]. This passage shows that Beck's rejection of a duty to promote the highest good is based on his acceptance of the juridical conception of the highest good, which we have argued in the previous chapter should be rejected.

IV, 434; see also KpV, V, 87][62]. Thus, Kant's vision of the good human life—and its expression on both the juridical and ethical level—are marked by both the independence and the interdependence of rational beings in their interaction with one another[63].

Conclusion

Kant highlights three important social aspects of our moral mission to make full and proper use of our reason. First, we require social interaction for the development of our talents—and, in particular, the correct use of our rational faculties. Secondly, we have to enter into a society governed by shared external laws to be able to make secure and effective use of our technical-practical reason in the pursuit of our ends. Thirdly, satisfying our reason's interest in the systematic unity among the wills of all rational beings requires that we determine our wills on the basis of shared moral principles, i.e. enter a realm of ends. Thus, we require lawful interaction with others to realize both elements of the highest good—the greatest happiness as well as the greatest moral perfection of all. This makes the highest good an essentially social vision of the good human life.

---

62 "Paradoxerweise sind meine Zwecke und Handlungen genau dann am wahrhaftigsten meine eigenen, wenn sie unter der Einschränkung einer möglichen gegenseitigen Beziehung—einer Art Freundschaft—mit jedermann ausgewählt sind" [Korsgaard, 2004, 219].
63 Kant gives expression this dialectic between interdependence and distance in *Metaphysik der Sitten:* "Vermöge des Prinzips der Wechselliebe sind sie angewiesen sich einander beständig zu nähern, durch das der Achtung, die sie einander schuldig sind, sich im Abstande von einander zu erhalten; und sollte eine dieser großen sittlichen Kräfte sinken, 'so würde dann das Nichts (der Immoralität) mit aufgesperrtem Schlund der (moralischen) Wesen ganzes Reich wie einen Tropfen Wasser trinken' (wenn ich mich hier der Worte Hallers, nur in einer anderen Beziehung, bedienen darf)" [MS, VI, 449].

10 Conclusion

This work has highlighted the central—but often overlooked—role played by the notion of the interests of reason in Kant's practical philosophy. I have argued that only by taking seriously the notion that Kantian autonomy involves reason guiding itself on the basis of its own essential interests can we make sense of Kant's fact-of-reason argument (the foundation of his practical thought), his theory of value and his notion of the highest good as the best possible state of affairs in the empirical world.

The account of Kant's practical philosophy emerging from our discussion is the following: Kant conceives of human beings as finite rational beings—that is, as hybrids endowed both with physical bodies and self-reflective thought. The faculty of self-reflective thought—reason—has, Kant holds, not merely an instrumental use (serving as a tool to satisfy whatever independent interests we happen to have), but has itself essential interests. The most important of these is the interest in imposing systematic unity on our knowledge (in its theoretical application) and our actions (in its practical application).

As hybrid beings, we are consequently confronted by two distinct sets of interests: on the one hand, our rational interests, and, on the other, the sensuous interests we have as physical beings in the satisfaction of our sensuous desires. Kant holds that the interests we have as physical beings are contingent and idiosyncratic—while the interests of our reason are necessary and shared. That is, whether or not we have a certain sensuous desire is a contingent matter, with desires varying across individuals according to their idiosyncratic physical make-up. Yet, we all share in the interests of reason as the condition for the possibility of the complete use of our rational faculties. In this sense, our rational interests are necessary (i.e. required conditions for the proper use of our rational faculties) and objective (shared by all rational beings).

Building on this distinction, Kant holds that there is a hierarchy between the two sets of interests. Insofar as we are physical beings, we exist passively as mere appearances in a world governed by natural necessity, while as rational beings we conceive of ourselves as fully active and autonomous wills. Consequently, Kant holds, we have to regard our moral personality, our existence qua transcendentally free wills, as our "proper self" (*eigentliches Selbst*)—and the interests of our reason as our proper interests (while our sensuous interests are merely the interests we have as phenomena).

This notion of a hierarchy between the two sets of interests is formalized in Kant's theory of value. According to that theory, value is not a natural property, but one that only appears in the world from the perspective of conscious thought. More specifically, our will (our faculty of desire insofar as it is guided by our conscious thought) projects value onto the world by choosing certain objects as its ends, based on our interests. In parallel with the two types of interest facing our will, there are two types of goods: goods that have merely subjective (or relative) value, linked to our contingent subjective interests as sensuous beings— and goods that have objective value, satisfying our necessary rational interests.

Hence, for something to be objectively good is for it to satisfy our rational interests. A state of affairs that is completely good from an objective point of view is one in which the interests of our reason are completely satisfied. Kant calls this completely good state of affairs the "highest good". However, given that it is our practical reason that chooses our subjective ends (by incorporating them into our maxims), a state of affairs cannot be regarded as completely good (i.e. as one in which the interests of our reason are fully satisfied) if our practical reason's attempts to achieve its subjective ends are frustrated. Hence, we have to regard the realization of our subjective ends (i.e. our happiness) as being part of the highest good—yet, crucially, only insofar as the principles of our will in pursuing our subjective ends are consistent with the interests of our reason (that is, insofar as we have made the moral law the highest determining ground of our will, i.e. have developed a good will). We can express this (slightly complicated) thought by saying that our happiness is not only a subjective good, but also a conditional-objective good (i.e. a required part of the highest good), conditional on the moral quality of our will. In this sense, we can then distinguish the unconditional-objective good (the satisfaction of the essential interests of our reason) and the conditional-objective good (our happiness, provided that we have developed a good will).

With this distinction in place, we can conceive of the state of affairs that is completely good from an objective point of view (the highest good) as the state of affairs in which all rational beings have achieved the unconditional-objective good and the conditional-objective good. However, this ideal conception of the highest good is a mere idea, i.e. something we can never have any experience of (principally, because we can never be certain whether we have succeeded in developing a good will). Kant contrasts this ideal vision of a completely good state of affairs with the best existence that we are actually capable of as finite rational beings—namely, one marked by the constant struggle to overcome the obstacles posed by our sensuous desires and the fragility of our own fledgling rational faculties in our attempt to realize the highest good in the empirical world. Kant emphasizes that our moral mission of realizing the highest good in the world of our experience is not one we face as individuals, but is rather a collective task: it requires us to enter into an ethical community with other human beings, adopting shared principles of willing and thus achieving systematic unity among our naturally uncoordinated wills. In this sense, the highest good is an essentially social vision of the good human life.

Bibliography

Works by Kant

Works by Immanuel Kant are cited with reference to the *Akademieausgabe*—with the exception of the Lecture on Ethics (*Eine Vorlesung Kants über Ethik*), transcribed by Paul Menzer, which does not appear in the *Akademieausgabe*. The references to texts in the *Akademieausgabe* comprise, first, the abbreviation of the work in question, secondly, the number of the relevant volume of the *Akademieausgabe*, and, thirdly, the page number. References to *Eine Vorlesung über Ethik* are marked with an "E" for ethics, followed by the year in which Menzer published the lecture (1924) and the relevant page number. References to Kant's handwritten reflections are marked with an "R", followed by the number of the reflection in question, the volume of the *Akademieausgabe* and the page number. Where the texts are quoted in the German original, I have corrected the idiosyncrasies in Kant's spelling to make the quotes easier to read. All translations of Kant's texts into English are my own.

III	KrV	Kritik der reinen Vernunft, Zweite Auflage	1787
IV	KrV	Kritik der reinen Vernunft, Erste Auflage	1781
IV	GMS	Grundlegung zur Metaphysik der Sitten (referred to in the text as Grundlegung)	1785
V	KpV	Kritik der praktischen Vernunft	1788
V	KU	Kritik der Urteilskraft	1790
VI	R	Religion innerhalb der Grenzen der bloßen Vernunft (Religion)	1793
VI	MS	Metaphysik der Sitten	1798
VII	SF	Der Streit der Fakultäten	1798
VII	A	Anthropologie in pragmatischer Hinsicht	1798
VIII	IAG	Idee zu einer allgemeinen Geschichte in weltbürgerlicher Absicht	1784
VIII	WA	Beantwortung der Frage: Was ist Aufklärung?	1784
VIII	MAM	Mutmaßlicher Anfang der Menschengeschichte	1786
VIII	SDO	Was heißt: Sich im Denken orientieren?	1786
VIII	TP	Über den Gemeinspruch	1793
VIII	ED	Das Ende aller Dinge	1794
VIII	EF	Zum Ewigen Frieden	1795
VIII	VT	Von einem neuerdings erhobenen vornehmen Ton in der Philosophie	1796
IX	L	Logik	1800
	E	Eine Vorlesung Kants über Ethik	

Secondary literature

Allison, H., Kant's Transcendental Idealism: An Interpretation and Defense, Yale University Press, 1983
Allison, H., Kant's Theory of Freedom, Cambridge University Press, 1990
Allison, H., Idealism and Freedom, Cambridge University Press, 1996
Ameriks, K., Kant and the Fate of Autonomy, Cambridge University Press, 2000
Ameriks, K., Interpreting Kant's Critiques, Oxford University Press, 2005
Ameriks, K. & Sturma D. (eds.), Kants Ethik, mentis Verlag, 2004
Arendt, H., Lectures on Kant's Political Philosophy, University of Chicago Press, 1992
Beck, L. W., A Commentary on Kant's Critique of Practical Reason, The University of Chicago Press, 1960
Beck, L. W., "The Fact of Reason: An Essay on Justification in Ethics", in his: Studies in the Philosophy of Kant, The Bobbs-Merrill Company, 1965
Beiner, R. & Booth, W., Kant & Political Philosophy, Yale University Press, 1993
Bittner, R., "Maximen", in: Funke, G, ed., Akten der 4. Internationalen Kant-Kongresses, de Gruyter, 1974
Brandt, R., Die Bestimmung des Menschen bei Kant, Felix Meiner Verlag, 2007
Denis, L., (ed.), Kant's Metaphysics of Morals. A Critical Guide, Cambridge University Press, 2010
Dodson, K. E., "Autonomy and Authority in Kant's Rechtslehre", Political Theory, Vol. 25, No. 1, 1997
Engstrom, S., "The Triebfeder of pure practical reason", Reath, A. & Timmerman, J., eds., Kant's Critique of Practical Reason. A Critical Guide. Cambridge University Press, 2010
Formosa, P., "Is Kant a Moral Constructivist or a Moral Realist?", European Journal of Philosophy 21, 2013
Frierson, P., Freedom and Anthropology in Kant's Moral Philosophy, Cambridge University Press, 2003
Guyer, P., Kant on Freedom, Law and Happiness, Cambridge University Press, 2000
Guyer, P., "Moral feelings in the Metaphysics of Morals", Denis, L., ed., Kant's Metaphysics of Morals. A Critical Guide, Cambridge University Press, 2010
Henrich, D., "Der Begriff der sittlichen Einsicht und Kants Lehre vom Faktum der Vernunft", in: Prauss, G., ed., Kant—Zur Deutung seiner Theorie von Erkennen und Handeln, Kiepenheuer & Wisch, 1973
Henrich, D., "Die Deduktion des Sittengesetzes", in: Schwan, A., ed., Denken im Schatten des Nihilismus, Wissenschaftliche Buchgesellschaft, 1975
Herman, B., "Jenseits der Deontologie", in: Ameriks, K.& Sturma D., eds., Kants Ethik, mentis Verlag, 2004
Hill, R. K., Nietzsche's Critiques, the Kantian Foundations of his Thought, Oxford University Press, 2003
Hills, A., "Kantian Value Realism", Ratio 21, 2008
Hinsch, W., Erfahrung und Selbstbewusstsein, Felix Meiner Verlag, 1986
Höffe, O. (ed.), Grundlegung zur Metaphysik der Sitten, Ein kooperativer Kommentar, Vittorio Klostermann, 1989
Höffe, O. (ed.), Zum Ewigen Frieden, Akademie Verlag, 2004
Höffe, O., Königliche Völker, Suhrkamp, 2001
Höffe, O., Kant, Akademie Verlag, 2007

Kemp Smith, N., A Commentary to Kant's Critique of Pure Reason, Palgrave Macmillan, 2003
Kersting, W., Wohlgeordnete Freiheit, Suhrkamp, 1993
Keynes, J. M., The General Theory of Employment, Interest and Money, BN Publishing, 2008
Kittmann, S., Kant und Nietzsche, Darstellung und Vergleich ihrer Ethik und Moral, Peter Lang, 1984
Kleingeld, P., "Moral Consciousness and the 'Fact of Reason'", in: Reath, A. & Timmermann, J. (eds.), Kant's Critique of Practical Reason, Cambridge University Press, 2010
Köhl, H. Kants Gesinnungsethik, de Gruyter, 1990
Korsgaard, C., Creating the Kingdom of Ends, Cambridge University Press, 1996
Korsgaard, C.,"Die Konstruktion des Reichs der Zwecke", in: Ameriks, K.& Sturma D., eds., Kants Ethik, mentis Verlag, 2004
Korsgaard, C., "The Activity of Reason", Presidential Address delivered before the One Hundredth Fifth Annual Eastern Division Meeting of the American Philosophical Association, 2008
Łuków, P., "The Fact of Reason: Kant's Passage to Ordinary Moral Knowledge", Kant-Studien 84, 1993
Meerbote, R., "Wille and Willkür in Kant's Theory of Action", in Gram, M., ed. Interpreting Kant, University of Iowa Press, 1982
Menzer, P., Eine Vorlesung Kants über Ethik, Heise, 1924
Nyholm, S., "On the Universal Law and the Humanity Formulas", doctoral dissertation at the University of Michigan, 2012
O'Connell, E., "Happiness Proportioned to Virtue: Kant and the Highest Good", Kantian Review 17, 2012
O'Neill, O., Constructions of Reason, Cambridge University Press, 1989
O'Neill, O.,"Kantische Gerechtigkeit und Kantianische Gerechtigkeit", in: Ameriks, K.& Sturma D., eds., Kants Ethik, mentis Verlag, 2004
Paton, H., J., The Categorical Imperative, University of Pennsylvania Press, 1948
Pogge, T., "The Categorical Imperative", in: Höffe, O. (ed.), Grundlegung zur Metaphysik der Sitten, Ein kooperativer Kommentar, Vittorio Klostermann, 2000
Prauss, G., Kant über Freiheit als Autonomie, Klostermann, 1982
Quine, W. V., "Two Dogmas of Empiricism", in his: From a Logical Point of View, Harvard University Press, 1953
Rawls, J., "The Basic Structure as Subject", American Philosophical Quarterly, Vol. 14, No. 2, 1977
Rawls, J., Lectures on the History of Moral Philosophy, Harvard University Press, 2000
Rawls, J.,"Themen der Kantischen Moralphilosophie", in: Ameriks, K.& Sturma D., eds, Kants Ethik, mentis Verlag, 2004
Reath, A., "Formal Principles and the Form of a Law", in: Reath, A. & Timmermann, J. (eds.), Kant's Critique of Practical Reason, Cambridge University Press, 2010
Reath, A., "Two Conceptions of the Highest Good in Kant", Journal of the History of Philosophy 26, 1988
Reath, A. & Timmerman, J. (eds.), Kant's Critique of Practical Reason. A Critical Guide. Cambridge University Press, 2010
Ricken, F., "Homo noumenon und homo phaenomenon", in: Höffe, O. (ed.), Grundlegung zur Metaphysik der Sitten, Ein kooperativer Kommentar, Vittorio Klostermann, 2000
Rosen, A., Kant's Theory of Justice, Cornell University Press, 1991

Sala, G., Kants "Kritik der Praktischen Vernunft". Ein Kommentar, Wissenschaftliche Buchgesellschaft. 2004
Saner, H., Kant's Political Thought. Its Origins and Development, University of Chicago Press, 1967
Schneewind, J.B., The Invention of Autonomy, Cambridge University Press, 1998
Schönecker, D. & Wood, A., Immanuel Kant: 'Grundlegung zur Metaphysik der Sitten', Schöningh, 2004
Schönecker, D., "Kant's Moral Intuitionism: The Fact of Reason and Moral Predispositions", Kant Studies Online (http://www.kantstudiesonline.net), 2013
Schopenhauer, A., Die Welt als Wille und Vorstellung, accessible at: http://www.zeno.org/Philosophie/M/Schopenhauer,+Arthur/Die+Welt+als+Wille+und+Vorstellung, 2013
Shell, S., The Rights of Reason, University of Toronto Press, 1980
Simmel, G., "Kant und Nietzsche", in: Simmel Gesamtausgabe, Band 10, Suhrkamp, 1995
Timmermann, J., Sittengesetz und Freiheit. Untersuchungen zu Immanuel Kants Theorie des freien Willens, de Gruyter, 2003
Timmermann, J., "Reversal or retreat? Kant's deductions of freedom and morality", in: Reath, A. & Timmerman, J., eds., Kant's Critique of Practical Reason. A Critical Guide, Cambridge University Press, 2010
Vaihinger, H., Die Philosophie des Als Ob, VDM Verlag, 2007
Wicks, R., Kant on Judgment, Routledge, 2007
Williams, H., Kant's Critique of Hobbes, University of Wales Press, 2003
Willaschek, M., "The primacy of practical reason and the idea of a practical postulate"; in: Reath, A. & Timmerman, J., eds., Kant's Critique of Practical Reason. A Critical Guide. Cambridge University Press, 2010
Wood, A., Kant's Ethical Thought, Cambridge University Press, 1999
Wood, A., "The Final Form of Kant's Practical Philosophy", in: Timmons, M., ed., Essays on Kant's Moral Philosophy, Cambridge University Press, 2000
Wood, A., "Kant and the Problem of Human Nature", accessible at: http://www.stanford.edu/~allenw/recentpapers.htm, 2003
Yovel, Y., Kant and the Philosophy of History, Princeton University Press, 1989

Subject index

Achtung, *see* respect
action   2, 4, 6–9, 14, 18–23, 26, 30, 33, 44, 46, 49, 53–55, 58f., 64–67, 69, 71–75, 77–81, 85, 87, 98f., 101–123, 125–144, 147, 151, 159–161, 163, 170, 173, 179, 183–185, 189, 192, 204–207, 210, 212f., 216–218, 220, 224, 229, 232, 237, 240, 246f., 249–253, 255–258
affect 79, 101, 117f., 161, 168, 185
animality (Tierheit)   139, 143–145, 149f., 159, 178f., 204–208, 225
Anlage, *see* predisposition
Anschauung, *see* intuition
anthropology   6f., 103, 109, 144, 205, 209, 214, 216, 232, 261
antinomy   165, 182, 214
– antinomy of the faculty of judgment   165
– antinomy of practical reason   182
Antrieb, *see* impulse
a posteriori   45
appearance (Erscheinung) 7, 10, 12f., 17, 19, 21, 29, 32, 75, 77f., 80, 93, 167
apperception   7, 30, 73, 95, 120
appreciative reading of Kant's conception of morality, *see* morality
a priori   3, 11f., 15, 19, 27–32, 34–36, 38, 42–45, 47f., 51, 54–57, 60f., 78f., 83, 87–89, 91, 94f., 98, 106, 114f., 122, 154, 183, 189, 218, 224, 229, 232, 234, 237, 243
Aufklärung, *see* enlightenment
autonomy   46, 59, 61, 77, 99, 115, 118, 120, 145, 153, 183f., 227, 245, 251, 258

Begehrungsvermögen, *see* desire
Begierde, *see* desire
Bestimmungsgrund des Willens, *see* determining ground of the will

category   10f., 30–32, 34f., 38, 40, 42, 54, 79, 95, 154, 165, 218
– deduction of categories 34f., 42, 54, 79, 154

causality   6, 10, 17, 21f., 26, 31f., 35, 44, 58, 60, 71, 78–80, 84, 91–94, 102, 107, 112, 119, 122, 163–166, 174, 204, 222
– law-governed causality   32
– law of causality   17, 20, 32, 57
– mechanical causality 102, 107, 163
– teleological causality   102, 107, 163–165, 174
cause   2, 6, 9f., 13, 21f., 26, 31, 39f., 53, 65, 78, 101f., 109, 113f., 163, 168, 190, 193, 199, 215, 243
– first uncaused cause   65
– teleological cause   163f.
– unconditional cause   39f.
character   6f., 32, 36, 64, 69, 76f., 81, 83, 92, 111, 117, 129, 131f., 138–140, 145, 160, 176, 192, 218, 221, 231, 236
– formation of the character   218
– intelligible character 129
citizenship   242f.
– active citizenship 243
– passive citizenship 233, 242f.
civil equality   242
civilization   210, 223, 225f.
civil personality   243
civil society   236, 239, 241–251, 253f., 256
coercion   244–246, 250
– inner coercion (innere Nötigung, Selbstzwang)   215, 221
cognition   7, 9f., 19f., 28, 33, 36f., 54–56, 61, 66, 101, 104, 109, 111, 172, 198, 209, 214
common sense (Gemeinsinn, sensus communis)   231, 234
completeness   13f., 21f., 24, 39, 63, 65, 157, 190
concept   2, 9–11, 16, 18, 26–30, 33, 35–39, 42–44, 49–53, 68, 86, 91–93, 96, 98, 103, 123, 165, 167, 195
– logical possibility of concepts 16, 18f., 22–24, 35f., 67, 123, 197, 200f.
– real possibility of concepts 16, 18, 22–26, 35f., 49, 51, 53, 67–70, 79, 84, 87, 122f., 194f.

– regulative use of concepts   37
conscience   103, 113, 139, 214, 224, 229, 233
consciousness   11, 24, 33 f., 68, 83, 86, 88–90, 94 f., 99, 113, 143, 150, 172, 207, 209, 235, 250
constitution (Verfassung)   242–247
constructivist reading of Kant's conception of morality, *see* morality
contradiction (Widerspruch)   8, 13, 16, 18, 22 f., 41, 46, 49, 51, 53, 59, 62 f., 80, 90, 93, 97, 99, 110, 114, 138, 153, 155 f., 156, 170, 174, 185 f., 189, 196, 200, 214, 217, 224, 229, 239, 244, 252
cultivation   210, 223, 225 f.
culture   66, 139, 144, 210–212, 223, 235, 242

deduction   34 f., 38 f., 54, 68 f., 79 f., 82, 84, 89 f., 95, 97, 99, 123 f.
– deduction of categories, *see* categories
– deduction of transcendental freedom, *see* freedom
– deduction of ideas, *see* idea
– deduction of the moral law, *see* moral law
– strong form of deduction 79, 82, 95
– transcendental deduction   34 f., 37, 42, 154
– weak form of deduction 79, 82, 89
desire (Begierde)   4, 7, 13, 15, 20, 47, 55–59, 65, 69, 77 f., 80, 85, 91, 98, 101–105, 107–109, 111–114, 116–118, 121 f., 126, 138, 140–143, 146–150, 154, 159, 173, 177–180, 182, 193, 198, 204–208, 212, 214–218, 220 f., 223, 228, 235 f., 256, 258 f.
– faculty of desire (Begehrungsvermögen) 58, 75, 80, 101–104, 109, 114, 116, 125, 127 f., 147 f., 157, 171, 259
determining ground of the will (Bestimmungsgrund des Willens)   3, 15, 21, 47, 58, 85, 104, 107, 114, 117, 125–127, 132, 166
– highest determining ground 120, 160, 168, 175, 198, 220, 255, 256, 259
– objective determining ground   3, 125–127, 134

– subjective determining ground 3, 125–128, 131, 136 f., 142
dignity (Würde)   6 f., 10, 16, 19, 24, 29, 45–47, 57, 59, 64, 66, 69, 71, 75, 82, 85–87, 92, 103, 134, 137, 144–146, 152–154, 159–162, 169, 171 f., 213, 217, 219, 222, 224, 228, 230–232, 234, 257
Ding an sich, *see* thing in itself
discursive   9 f., 16, 30, 37, 46
dogmatism   50, 83, 95 f.
duty (Pflicht)   39, 64, 66, 78 f., 96 f., 112 f., 127 f., 131–135, 137–139, 144, 149, 151, 156, 159, 162, 178, 181, 183, 186–188, 191–194, 198, 203, 211, 213, 216 f., 221, 224, 228 f., 232 f., 238–240, 248 f., 253–256
– duty to enter civil society   248 f., 253
– duty to enter the ethical community   253 f.
– duty to realize the highest good   1, 187 f., 194, 196, 200

education   139, 232 f.
effectiveness   123, 238 f., 248 f.
eigentliches Selbst, *see* self
end (Zweck)   4 f., 12–14, 34, 45, 51, 65 f., 69, 74, 80–83, 92, 103 f., 106–108, 117 f., 120, 122–124, 126–128, 132, 134–136 f., 139, 143–181, 185, 187, 190–193, 204 f., 207, 210–212, 217–219, 222 f., 227, 233, 237–239, 242, 248 f., 251 f., 254–257, 259, 261
– end in itself (Zweck an sich selbst)   92, 120, 145 f, 149, 152, 155–160, 162 f., 172 f., 187, 211, 249–251.
– end of reason, *see* reason
– final end (Endzweck)   82, 157, 159, 163, 168–172, 174, 186, 192, 200–202, 223, 225
– natural end (Naturzweck) 163–165
– objective end 148, 150–152, 156
– realm of ends (Reich der Zwecke)   65, 187, 251 f., 254 f., 257
– subjective end   4, 126, 150 f., 179 f., 182, 212 f., 259
– ultimate end (letzter Zweck)   223
Endzweck, *see* final end

Subject index

enlightenment (Aufklärung) 4, 204, 209 f., 219 f., 223, 226, 232, 236, 261
epistemic apparatus 2, 17 f., 28, 36, 52, 166
epistemology 56, 76, 108, 165
ethical community 160, 210, 226 f., 249 f., 253 f., 259
evil 63, 85, 110, 116–118, 129, 131, 134, 137, 139, 149, 151, 156, 181, 186, 193, 206–208, 214 f., 217, 222, 235, 241 f., 250 f., 253

fact of reason, *see* reason
faculty 1 f., 9, 11–14, 24, 32, 34, 39, 51, 55 f., 58, 60, 65 f., 88, 94, 98, 105, 107, 115 f., 123, 144, 158 f., 164–167, 179, 205, 213, 231, 258
– faculty of desire, *see* desire
– higher faculties 20, 32, 55, 109
– lower faculties 19 f.
feeling 7, 20, 54 f., 78, 101 f., 108 f., 112–116, 125, 127, 161–163, 178, 187, 235
– moral feeling 78, 112–114, 126, 147, 161
finite rational being 2, 13, 69, 101, 103, 149, 154, 173, 175, 191–193, 198, 204, 207, 215, 232, 242, 249, 252, 258 f.
freedom 3, 8, 15 f., 18, 20–22, 35, 58–60, 64, 69–73, 75 f., 80, 83 f., 86 f., 91–93, 97–99, 105–107, 109, 112, 118–121, 140, 145, 149 f., 153–155, 158, 171, 179, 189, 197, 205 f., 211, 215, 227, 234–237, 239–249, 253 f.
– comparative freedom, *see* psychological freedom
– deduction of transcendental freedom 69–71, 82, 89, 97, 124,
– external freedom 3, 120, 161, 227, 236–245, 248 f., 251, 254, 256
– freedom of judgment 8, 15 f., 18–20, 22 f., 25, 71, 73 f.
– logical possibility of transcendental freedom 22–24
– moral freedom 3, 119–121, 236
– negative freedom 3, 21, 103, 105 f., 108, 118 f., 143, 145, 150, 206, 236
– paradox of freedom 241 f., 246 f.
– psychological freedom 105, 119, 145, 150

– real possibility of transcendental freedom 22–26, 51, 53, 68, 84, 87, 101
– transcendental freedom 2 f., 8, 15 f., 18, 20–24, 26, 37, 40, 43 f., 51, 53, 69–71, 74 f., 78, 87, 90–92, 96–99, 101, 105 f., 118–121, 124, 143, 145 f., 150, 153, 156, 189, 207, 236
– wild freedom 240, 242, 246 f.

Gemeinsinn, *see* common sense
Geschicklichkeit, *see* skill
Gesinnung, *see* highest maxim
Glückseligkeit, *see* happiness
God 4, 37, 39–41, 61, 115, 164, 167, 172, 175, 184 f., 193–197, 199–202, 213, 222
– moral proof for the existence of God 172, 194 f., 197, 199, 201 f., 222
– objective reality of the idea of God 185, 194–197, 199–201, 203
good 1, 3 f., 50, 53, 57, 89, 112, 115–117, 127 f., 130 f., 135 f., 138 f., 141, 146–153, 155, 157 f., 160, 169 f., 173, 175 f., 178–183, 185, 190–192, 194, 198, 200, 202, 204, 207 f., 210, 212 f., 215–217, 229, 231 f., 235 f., 242, 250 f., 255, 259
– conditional-objective good 150, 152, 178, 180–182, 191, 259
– objective good 4, 148–153, 155, 179–182, 191, 194, 202, 259
– subjective good 146–148, 152, 173, 176, 178–180, 191, 194, 259
– supreme good 157
– unconditional-objective good 146, 152–157, 160, 173, 181 f., 194, 259
good life 4 f., 204, 210, 219, 226, 256
– social conception of the good life 5, 227, 254, 260
Grounding Thesis 65 f., 191
Grundsatz, *see* principle

happiness (Glückseligkeit) 1, 4, 15, 47, 64, 67, 91, 108, 122, 132, 146 f., 151 f., 158, 175–184, 186–194, 196 f., 199–202, 210 f., 213, 219–221, 223 f., 226 f., 245, 248, 251, 254–257, 259
heteronomy 73, 118, 184, 205, 213

highest good (höchstes Gut) 1f., 4f., 137, 157, 160, 169f., 174–177, 180–194, 196–204, 210–212, 217, 222–224, 226f., 254–260
– juridical conception of the highest good 1, 175–177, 180, 182–191, 193f., 196f., 199–203, 255f.
– maximal conception of the highest good 2, 4, 175–177, 182f., 186f., 190–194, 197, 199, 201–203
highest maxim, see maxim
höchstes Gut, see highest good
höchste Maxime, see maxim
humanity (Menschheit) 4, 66, 113, 139, 143–145, 149f., 155, 158f., 161f., 173, 178f., 204–207, 209, 211, 217, 219f., 224, 231, 235, 237, 243

idea 2, 8, 12–14, 17, 19, 26, 33, 36–42, 44f., 47–49, 51f., 57, 61, 66f., 69–78, 80, 86f., 90–94, 110f., 114f., 121f., 128–130, 132, 137f., 142, 145, 147, 158, 161, 163, 165–171, 177, 179, 183f., 190, 194–197, 199–202, 208, 211f., 219, 221, 230f., 233f., 240, 243, 245, 247, 252, 254, 259, 261
– deduction of ideas 38f.
immortality of the soul 37, 184, 197–199, 208, 225
identy of all rational beings 154f., 252
imperative 38, 59, 63f., 78, 87, 94, 99, 122, 130, 149, 151, 183, 192, 207f., 239, 248
– categorical imperative 54, 59, 65, 69, 72, 76f., 112f., 122, 124, 130f., 151, 159, 192
– hypothetical imperative 122–124
impulse (Antrieb) 57, 101–103, 109, 140, 142, 216, 234, 235
incentive (Triebfeder) 3, 39 58, 66, 78, 81, 87, 104, 108, 112–116, 118, 125–127, 132, 134f., 138–140, 142, 144–146, 179, 193, 208, 212, 220, 223, 241, 250
inclination (Neigung) 13f., 47, 55–57, 59, 65, 69, 77f., 81, 85, 101, 105, 108, 111, 114–118, 121, 126, 145, 152, 161, 177–179, 193, 208f., 212, 214–219, 221, 228, 230, 233–235, 240
Incorporation Thesis 104f., 140

innate right 236f., 239, 241, 243
innere Nötigung, see coercion
instinct 159, 179, 204–206, 208, 223, 240
interest 1–3, 5, 12–15, 18, 21, 24, 26, 37, 41f., 44–49, 54, 56, 59–61, 63–67, 69, 75–79, 84–88, 97f., 101, 107f., 111f., 115, 118, 123, 138, 142–144, 147, 149–155, 157, 161, 164, 167, 170, 172–175, 182, 184, 188–192, 196, 205, 212, 214f., 217, 219, 221, 223, 225f., 229f., 232, 238–240, 244, 248–252, 254, 256–259
– interest of reason, see reason
– moral interest 60f.
– practical interest 42, 44, 49–51, 76, 87, 93, 96, 189
internalization 102, 104, 111f., 119
intuition (Anschauung) 9f., 17, 29–31, 33f., 36–38., 42–44, 57, 73, 83, 88, 92, 94f., 136, 154, 195, 218
– intellectual intuition 19
– intuition of our senses 10f. 16, 36, 42, 108f.
intuitionism 37, 94

judgment 2, 8f., 11, 16, 26–31, 33f., 36f., 40, 44–47, 49, 51, 70, 75f., 86, 90, 93, 96, 105, 112, 165f., 174, 189f., 228, 230f.
– analytic judgment 27
– a posteriori judgment 27
– a priori judgment 27f.
– determining faculty of judgment 166, 222
– logical possibility of our freedom of judgment 18f., 22, 24
– real possibility of our freedom of judgment 23
– reflective faculty of judgment 166, 222
– synthetic a priori judgment 27f., 31, 34, 36
– synthetic judgment 27, 36

knowledge 2, 10–14, 36–39, 43, 48–51, 54f., 66, 77, 96, 103f., 109, 114, 129, 164f., 167, 172, 187, 195, 210f., 258
– doctrine of practical knowledge 3, 44–48, 49–51, 53, 70, 75f., 84, 90, 92f., 95f., 188f., 195

- practical knowledge   2f., 26, 42–51, 53, 70, 72, 75f., 84, 86f., 90, 92f., 95f., 98f., 188f., 195–198, 202, 225
- theoretical knowledge   42f., 48–50, 55, 75, 107, 189, 195

law   5, 9, 12, 15, 19, 21, 32, 39–41, 48, 53, 56–60, 63–65, 69, 73–75, 78–81, 85–87, 93f., 97–99, 103, 113, 115, 117–120, 122, 125f., 130–132, 135f., 141, 145, 154, 157, 162, 165–167, 169, 173, 179, 186, 190, 192, 200, 205f., 212f., 215–218, 222, 227, 229, 231, 236f., 240–251, 253–257
- a priori law   52, 54–56, 60, 86f., 237f.
- law, moral, *see* moral law
- law of freedom   58–60, 72, 76, 79, 98, 250
- law of nature   2, 6, 16, 19, 32, 51, 56–58, 60, 64, 77f., 96f., 108, 163, 165, 167, 184, 188f., 193, 197, 202, 224
- natural external law   237–239
- positive external law   237, 239, 244, 253
Legalität, *see* legality
legality (Legalität)   131f., 142, 151, 181, 250
Leidenschaft, *see* passion
Lust, *see* pleasure

maxim   15, 40f., 54f., 57, 63f., 74, 78, 80f., 84, 103–113, 116–125, 127–142, 144, 156, 160, 162, 164f., 168, 175, 179–182, 192, 207f., 212, 217f., 220f., 229, 231f., 234, 237, 247, 251, 255, 259
- agnosticism about maxims   129–132
- descriptive account of maxims   139, 141
- first-order maxim   4, 110f., 129f., 133, 137
- highest maxim (höchste Maxime, Gesinnung)   109–112, 115–118, 120f., 125–127, 129–138, 140, 142, 151, 153, 173, 176, 179, 181, 195, 198, 212f., 215f., 221, 253
- maxim of reason, *see* reason
- normative account of maxims   119, 139–141
Menschheit, *see* humanity
metaphysics   43, 48, 50, 58, 66, 87, 106, 113, 139, 144, 163, 167, 171, 179, 195, 197f., 200, 213, 237, 244, 257, 261

misology   209
moral   3f., 14f., 46, 49, 54, 56, 59, 61f., 64, 66f., 72–74, 78, 80–86, 89, 94f., 98f., 110–117, 121, 124–127, 129–134, 136–141, 143–147, 150f., 156f., 159–161, 169, 171f., 175f., 180f., 183f., 186–190, 192–195, 197, 199–203, 207, 210, 212, 215–218, 221f., 224f., 227, 229, 233, 236, 239, 249, 251–257, 259
- moral certainty   225
- moral command   54
- moral consciousness   86, 143, 150, 172, 207
- moral demand   3, 69, 85, 94, 99, 114f., 118, 147, 172, 206, 221, 229, 250
- moral feeling, *see* feeling
- moral experience   54, 124, 146
- moral interest, *see* interest
- moral skeptic, *see* skeptic
Moralität, *see* morality
morality (Moralität, Sittlichkeit)   1, 45, 49, 50, 53f., 58, 60f., 63, 65, 67f., 78, 81, 85, 87, 89, 99, 115, 117, 131f., 143–145, 150f., 158, 160, 167, 176, 179f., 183f., 189f., 192f., 210, 212f., 215f., 221, 229, 232, 244, 249f., 254
- appreciative reading of Kant's conception of morality   61f.
- constructivist reading of Kant's conception of morality   61–63
moralization   210–213, 216–221, 223, 225f.
moral law   3, 15, 19, 24, 37, 44, 47, 51, 53–61, 63–69, 71–73, 75, 78–99, 101, 106, 108, 111–121, 125–131, 133f., 133f., 141–144, 146, 148f., 151–153, 155f., 159f., 162, 168f., 170f., 173, 175, 181, 183–185, 187, 193–195, 198, 202, 207f., 212f., 215–218, 220f., 223, 229, 239, 252f., 255f., 259
- deduction of the moral law 68, 80–84, 89f., 95, 97
- objective validity of moral law   3, 67, 99, 229
- real possibility of the moral law   67, 69, 79

nature   2, 4, 6, 9f., 12–14, 16, 18, 20–22, 24, 26, 29f., 32f., 38, 47, 53, 55, 61f.,

64–66, 72 f., 81, 85, 91 f., 96, 98, 101, 103, 105, 107–111, 114, 116, 119, 125 f., 133, 138 f., 142–146, 149, 154 f., 157–159, 161, 164–167, 170–173, 175 f., 178–180, 183, 193, 198–200, 203–205, 207, 209, 212–215, 222–226, 228–230, 232 f., 235, 238, 240 f., 248, 252, 255
- cunning of nature   222–225
- physical nature (Sinnlichkeit)   6, 10, 15, 17, 51, 57, 66, 73, 75 f., 79, 88, 104, 106, 112, 114, 116, 118, 134, 143 f., 162, 173, 179, 204 f., 208, 216, 223, 230

Naturzweck, *see* natural end

necessity   2 f., 6, 12 f., 15, 18–20, 26–29, 32, 34–36, 45, 48, 53–58, 65 f., 72, 85, 87–89, 102, 106, 114, 124, 195, 208, 242
- natural necessity   2, 6–8, 15 f., 18–24, 44, 53, 55, 76, 79, 99, 101, 109, 111, 119, 142, 144, 150, 189, 258

Neigung, *see* inclination

noumenal   3, 16, 18 f., 22, 24, 52, 56–60, 66, 73 f., 76 f., 79, 86 f., 92, 99, 110 f., 118 f., 130, 137 f., 145, 147 f., 153 f., 172, 199, 215, 220 f., 226, 239, 245, 252
- noumenal existence 3, 19 f., 23, 55, 60, 75–77, 79, 82, 87, 92, 98, 146, 171, 189

noumenon   17, 138, 152

objective good, *see* good
objective validity of the moral law, *see* moral law
objective value, *see* value
obligation   66, 149, 191, 237, 239, 242
original contract   245, 247

passion (Leidenschaft)   117–119, 235
perfection (Vollkommenheit)   13, 103, 152, 177, 195, 198, 210, 216, 223, 226, 232, 236, 247, 252, 254
- moral perfection   177, 198 f., 216, 227, 249, 252, 254 f., 257

personality   4, 59, 112, 120, 143–146, 149 f., 152–162, 168–170, 172–174, 192, 204, 207, 217, 229, 243, 253
- moral personality   119–121, 154, 229, 236, 239, 250, 253, 258

Pflicht, *see* duty
phenomenal   16, 18 f., 22, 77, 86, 215
- phenomenal world   18, 86
philosophy   14, 22, 38, 50 f., 61 f., 64, 69, 80, 83 f., 91, 94 f., 120, 123, 129–131, 157, 160, 166, 172, 176, 183, 199, 219, 225, 227, 229, 233, 249, 251, 254, 261
- practical philosophy   1, 6, 24, 26, 44, 51, 53, 93, 107, 112, 119 f., 124, 208, 211, 258
- theoretical philosophy   1, 26, 56, 93, 106, 109, 124, 202

physical impulse, *see* impulse
physical nature, *see* nature

pleasure (Lust) 78 f., 101, 108 f., 112–115, 125, 147, 180, 206

possibility   3, 16, 18 f., 23, 25 f., 28 f., 34, 37, 42, 51–56, 58 f., 63–66, 69, 78 f., 81 f., 86–89, 91, 96, 98 f., 106, 108, 110 f., 114–116, 120, 123 f., 129, 132, 138 f., 142, 150, 152, 154–157, 163, 165, 170, 174, 176, 180, 184 f., 188 f., 193, 195–199, 213, 222, 224 f., 230 f., 233, 244, 250, 258
- logical possibility   16, 19, 23, 35 f., 81, 123, 197, 200 f.
- possibility of experience   31, 33–35, 44, 52, 57, 154
- real possibility   16, 18, 22–25, 35 f., 49 f., 53, 70, 122 f., 194 f.

postulate 39, 45, 48, 84, 110, 137, 196–199
practical data   43, 47–49, 87, 92, 106
practical love   251
practical point of view   48, 70 f., 79, 86, 90 f., 106, 109, 143
predisposition (Anlage)   134, 139, 143 f., 146, 204, 216, 224, 234, 235, 242
- moral predisposition 113, 134, 229, 250
principle (Grundsatz)   6, 8, 11–16, 24, 31 f., 34, 41 f., 46 f., 49, 53–56, 59–63, 65 f., 71–73, 80, 82 f., 86, 89, 91, 98 f., 103, 105, 109, 111, 115–120, 125–129, 131–134, 137–139, 141 f., 146, 148, 151, 154, 161, 165–167, 176, 180 f., 189, 192, 205, 214, 216–218, 222, 230, 232–235, 237, 240, 245, 250–255, 257, 259
- moral principle   5, 61–63, 251–254, 257
- principle of adjudication   53 f., 115, 128

Subject index — **271**

– principle of execution   53 f., 69, 115
– regulative principle   37 – 41
progress   138 f., 192, 198 f., 206, 209, 222, 224 f.
proper self, *see* self
publicity   231

quid facti   35, 53, 68, 97
quid juris   35, 53, 68, 96, 98

rational faith   45, 48, 50, 84, 93, 198
rationality   12, 62, 122 f., 160, 220, 231, 233
reality   10, 16 f., 20, 23, 33, 36 f., 40 f., 43, 48 – 50, 70, 90, 96, 98, 164 f., 167, 172, 184, 187 – 189, 194, 196, 202 f., 211, 222, 246 f.
– empirical reality   23, 33, 41, 43, 164, 188, 196
– noumenal reality   86
– objective reality   3 f., 21 f., 24, 26, 40, 48 f., 51, 53, 68 f., 75, 86, 90 – 93, 96, 98, 101, 106, 124, 143, 145, 147, 167, 172, 189, 195 – 197, 199 – 202, 208, 222
realm of ends, *see* end
reason   1 – 3, 5 – 9, 11 – 16, 18 – 21, 23 f., 26, 31 – 33, 37 – 51, 54, 56 – 63, 65 – 68, 70 – 99, 101, 103, 105 – 118, 120 – 128, 131 f., 135 – 138, 141 – 155, 157, 159, 161 – 167, 169 – 174, 176 – 195, 197 – 201, 204 – 210, 213 – 226, 228 – 233, 235, 237 – 241, 244 – 246, 248 – 253, 255 – 259, 261
– broad meaning of reason 7, 19, 144
– critique of reason   41, 49, 213, 229, 240
– end of reason   12 f., 15
– fact of reason 1, 3, 24, 68, 79, 83 – 85, 87, 89 – 91, 93 f., 97, 106, 114, 118, 120, 124, 144 f., 150, 172, 229, 239, 258
– formal-logical use of reason   11
– hypothetical use of reason   11, 108
– idea of reason, *see* idea
– instrumental use of reason   108
– interest of reason   1 – 4, 13 – 15, 23 f., 26, 47 – 49, 51, 56, 60 – 63, 65 – 67, 84, 98, 103, 112, 121, 123, 125 – 127, 131, 138, 148 f., 153, 155, 157, 160, 164, 167 – 170, 172 – 175, 178, 181, 185, 190 f., 203 f., 207, 212 – 214, 217, 220, 237 f., 249, 258

– maxim of reason   39, 103
– moral-practical reason   4, 81, 143 f., 179, 192, 204, 210, 212, 217, 221, 226, 250
– narrow meaning of reason   7, 144,
– need of reason   13, 21, 47
– practical reason   44 – 46, 49 f., 55 f., 61, 63 – 65, 73 f., 79, 84, 90, 107 – 110, 113, 118, 123, 127, 134, 146, 169, 171, 173, 178 f., 182, 197, 214 f., 221, 229, 252, 259
– public use of reason   230
– pure practical reason   3, 24, 55 – 58, 60, 85 f., 98, 138, 154, 173, 210, 254
– real use of reason   11
– reason as teleological 14, 123,
– social aspect of reason   233
– technical-practical reason   4 f., 81, 107 f., 112, 121, 124, 143 f., 178 – 180, 192, 204, 210 – 212, 217, 223, 226 f., 236, 239, 247 – 250, 254, 257
– unity of reason   14, 46 f., 63, 96
receptivity   103 f.
Reciprocity Thesis   59 f., 69, 71 f., 75, 87
reflective distance   9, 105, 107, 112, 204 – 206
Regel, *see* rule
Reich der Zwecke, *see* end
representation (Vorstellung) 7 – 10, 16 – 18, 30 – 33, 38, 55, 81, 88, 101 – 104, 107 f., 112, 116, 119, 125, 127 f., 135, 138, 144, 147, 149, 163, 166, 234
respect (Achtung)   113 – 117, 142, 156, 161 – 163, 186, 256
right   161 f., 173, 179, 220, 222, 236 – 239, 241, 243 – 245, 248 f., 250, 256
rule (Regel)   9 – 12, 15, 22, 27, 29 f., 32, 39 f., 42, 46, 54 f., 58, 61 – 64, 74, 85, 87, 99, 103 – 105, 108 f., 116, 118, 124 f., 129 f., 135 f., 140 – 142, 165 f., 183 – 185, 205, 211, 213 – 215, 223, 226, 228 – 230, 232, 240 – 243, 247, 249

Selbsttätigkeit, *see* spontaneity
Selbstzufriedenheit   147, 221
Selbstzwang, *see* inner coercion
self   2, 7 f., 14, 24, 41 f., 46, 55, 60 f., 63, 67 f., 72, 75, 77, 79, 85, 87, 90, 92, 95, 99, 102 – 105, 107, 109 – 111, 113, 119 f.,

127, 129–131, 137f., 141f., 144, 151, 153, 155, 174, 179, 189, 205–207, 214f., 217, 219–221, 223, 225, 228–230, 232, 234–237, 239, 245, 250, 252, 255, 258
- empirical self   67, 77, 99, 245
- higher self   79, 221
- proper self (eigentliches Selbst) 60, 76f., 79, 92, 112, 117, 121, 154, 174, 220, 256, 258
self-consciousness   7, 33
self-discipline   41, 118, 121, 208–216, 219f., 226, 233f.
self-love   15, 111, 116–118, 121, 126, 128, 131, 134f., 138, 141f., 146, 151, 176, 181, 235
self-realization   171, 174, 199, 220, 223
self-reflective thought   2, 7, 46, 55, 109, 142f., 258
sense   1, 4, 7, 9–15, 17, 19f., 24, 26, 28–31, 36–38, 41, 43f., 46, 49f., 52, 54, 61, 68–72, 74, 80–82, 84, 86f., 89f., 92f., 96, 102–104, 106–112, 114f., 117–121, 129–131, 136, 138, 140, 143–150, 152, 154–156, 160f., 164f., 167, 170, 174f., 178, 180f., 184, 186, 188, 191f., 195, 201, 204, 206–208, 210f., 216, 218–220, 222, 229, 232f., 236–241, 243f., 248, 254f., 258–260
- sense-experience   10, 88, 172
sinnliche Anschauung, see intuition of our senses
Sinnlichkeit, see nature
Sittlichkeit, see morality
skeptic, skepticism   3, 85
skill (Geschicklichkeit)   122, 140, 210, 238, 242
social life   210, 227, 234, 236
society   5, 227f., 234f., 242, 244, 249f., 257
space   9, 16–18, 29–32, 35, 43, 50, 76, 84, 88–90, 92f., 95f., 146, 150, 152, 180
spontaneity (Selbsttätigkeit)   2, 8–11, 18–20, 24, 31–33, 41, 55, 62, 74, 76f., 79, 82, 103–105, 109, 114, 120, 147, 218f., 229f.

state of nature   64, 222, 225, 240f., 244, 246–248, 250f., 253
- ethical state of nature   64, 250f., 253
- juridical state of nature   240f., 244, 246–248

teleology   163–174, 195, 199, 201f., 222
teleological causality, see causality
theology   40, 183
- rational theology   40
thing in itself (Ding an sich)   13, 16f., 19, 61, 77f.
time   6, 16f., 20, 23f., 29–32, 35, 46, 56, 61f., 76, 82–84, 88–90, 95, 110, 115, 124, 130, 138, 141, 146, 148, 168, 182, 190, 193, 197, 204, 212, 216, 218, 228, 247, 256
transcendental freedom, see freedom
transcendental idealism   16, 18f., 23, 25f., 30, 41, 51, 70, 73, 77, 84, 90, 93, 96
transcendental illusion   40, 230
Triebfeder, see incentive
truth   2, 26–30, 34, 36, 40f., 45–47, 49, 62f., 70, 72, 86, 93, 96, 113, 133, 187–189, 196f., 201, 225, 228
- a priori truth   27–30, 34, 36, 52, 94
- geometrical truth   29f.
- necessary truth   28f., 34, 36

unconditional value, see value
understanding (Verstand)   1, 6–12, 16f., 19, 23, 28–33, 36–39, 42, 44, 51f., 54–58, 61, 63f., 68, 73, 78, 86, 94f., 98f., 101, 104, 106–109, 125, 130, 132, 140, 166f., 178, 188, 194, 196, 200, 208f., 214, 218, 226, 228, 230–234, 244, 251
ungesellige Geselligkeit, see unsocial sociability
unity   9f., 12–14, 29, 32, 35, 39f., 46f., 63, 96, 103, 108, 120, 164, 167, 179, 206, 218, 240, 245, 249, 251f.
- systematic unity   2f., 5, 11, 13f., 24, 38, 46, 63–65, 97, 131, 155, 157, 164, 167, 172, 185, 190, 229, 247, 251–254, 257f., 260
univeralizability test   130f.
universality   54–56, 124, 217, 231

universalizability 130 f., 136
unsocial sociability (ungesellige Geselligkeit) 234

validity 15, 34, 48, 53 f., 60, 62, 68 – 71, 73, 75, 79 – 83, 85 – 87, 89, 91, 93, 96, 98 f., 122, 144, 154, 167, 184 f., 194, 237, 239
– objective validity 3, 26, 34 f., 44, 47 – 49, 67, 74, 87, 91, 96, 99, 123, 229
value 2, 4, 26, 47, 49, 57, 61 f., 65, 77, 81, 86, 93 f., 105, 128, 132 f., 135, 143, 146, 148 – 163, 168 – 174, 179 – 182, 187, 189 – 191, 194, 197, 203, 213, 216, 219, 222, 225, 235, 255, 258 f.
– conditional-objective value, *see* conditional-objective good
– moral value 4, 127 f., 131, 133 – 138, 142, 184
– objective value 65, 149 – 157, 159 – 161, 163, 168, 170, 173 f., 178, 180 f., 190, 259
– subjective value 148, 152, 159, 178
– theory of value 65, 143, 146, 150, 169, 172, 174, 179, 182, 190 f., 194, 203, 258,
– unconditional-objective value, *see* unconditional-objective good
– unconditional value 4, 65, 151 – 158, 160, 178, 181
Verfassung, *see* constitution
Verstand, *see* value
virtue 1, 4, 55, 61, 110, 148, 153, 158, 160, 171, 175 – 178, 180 – 184, 186 – 188, 190, 193 f., 196, 198 f., 202, 215 f., 221, 224, 233, 237 – 239, 243, 250, 253, 255

Vollkommenheit, *see* perfection
Vorstellung, *see* representation

Widerspruch, *see* contradiction
will 1 – 11, 13, 15, 17 – 19, 21 f., 24 – 26, 28 f., 31, 34, 36 – 39, 42 – 44, 49 – 51, 53 – 61, 63 – 77, 79 – 82, 84 – 86, 89, 91 f., 97 – 99, 101 – 104, 107 – 109, 112 – 138, 140 – 143, 145 – 155, 157 f., 160 f., 164, 166, 169 – 183, 185 – 187, 191 – 194, 198 – 201, 204 – 218, 220 – 222, 224 – 227, 234 – 239, 241, 243 – 260
– determining ground of the will, *see* determining ground
– good will 4, 112, 120 f., 151 – 154, 156 f., 159 f., 168 – 170, 173, 175 – 178, 180 – 182, 187 – 191, 193, 197 f., 200 – 202, 207 f., 210, 216, 221, 226, 252, 254, 259
– holy will 149, 198 f., 207, f., 216, 220
– pure will 3, 56, 58, 66, 99, 216
– sensuously affected will 66, 198, 216, 220
– transcendentally free will 3 f., 58 – 60, 69, 101, 119, 140, 154, 161, 171 f., 180, 258
Willkür 7, 45, 58, 81, 87, 103 – 108, 110, 117 – 119, 125 f., 140, 144 f., 208, 212, 232, 236, 243, 252
worldview 1, 11, 16, 21 f., 35, 38, 40 f., 46 f., 53, 87, 89, 91, 93, 95, 97, 111, 166, 189, 194 f., 199
Würde, *see* dignity

Zweck, *see* end

Index of names

Allison, H. 4, 7–9, 11, 18 f., 31 f., 58 f., 61, 68, 70, 73, 84 f., 88, 99, 104 f., 110 f., 113, 115, 127, 130 f., 133, 135 f., 143, 145, 147, 177, 198, 211, 215, 218, 220 f., 251
Ameriks, K. 24, 61, 83, 92, 95, 97, 215
Arendt, H. 63, 231
Aristotle 63, 111

Beck, J. S. 32
Beck, L. W. 1, 4, 11, 16, 32, 35, 38, 40, 46–48, 54, 56, 58 f., 65, 67, 83–85, 89, 94, 102, 105 f., 108 f., 112–115, 119, 126, 140, 146, 149, 156, 175 f., 178, 182 f., 185–187, 196, 198 f., 218, 256
Brandt, R. 14, 30, 64, 88, 94 f., 115, 154, 173, 195, 211, 223 f., 228, 233, 243, 250

Descartes, R. 38, 41, 102
Dodson, K. E. 249

Engstrom, S. 117

Fichte, J. G. 94
Formosa, P. 151, 178
Frierson, P. 4, 84, 133

Goldmann, L. 225
Guyer, P. 4, 14, 16, 59, 63, 113, 120, 130, 145, 155, 158, 160, 177–179, 184, 192, 198, 211, 237, 244, 246, 249, 251

Haller, A. 257
Henrich, D. 8, 23, 59, 63, 68, 79, 81 f., 89, 97, 99, 115
Herder, J. G. 219
Herman, B. 149, 151
Hill, R. K. 33, 222
Hinsch, W. 27, 30, 34 f., 88
Hobbes, T. 64, 240, 248
Höffe, O. 63
Hume, D. 26, 28, 34, 85, 105, 111
Hutcheson, F. 100, 115

Kemp Smith, N. 7, 11, 31, 33 f., 38, 40, 86, 88 f., 150, 172, 233
Keynes, J. M. 231
Kleingeld, P. 84
Köhl, H. 129, 141
Korsgaard, C. 4, 8, 83, 105, 111, 131, 146, 155, 157 f., 171, 185, 257

Leibniz, G. W. 10, 34, 105, 111, 182 f.
Locke, J. 38, 248

Marx, K. 206
Mendelssohn, M. 224

Newton, I. 64, 243
Nietzsche, F. 85, 220
Nyholm, S. 253

O'Connell, E. 176
O'Neill, O. 4, 15, 62, 81, 103, 105, 108, 112, 115, 129, 131, 136, 141, 209, 228, 234, 245

Paton, H. J. 72
Plato 8
Pogge, T. 63
Prauss, G. 19, 83, 88, 105, 121, 156, 172, 177

Quine, W. V. 27, 29

Rawls, J. 24, 55, 61 f., 83, 90, 93, 145 f., 177 f., 183 f., 187, 190, 192, 254 f.
Reath, A. 176 f., 181, 190
Ricken, F. 120
Rosen, A. 99, 130, 145, 158, 177 f., 228, 231, 239, 241–245, 247, 249
Rousseau, J.-J. 59, 206, 225, 233, 235, 246

Sala, G. 106, 109, 117
Saner, H. 64 f., 240, 242 f., 252
Schiller, F. 221
Schlegel, F. 64
Schönecker, D. 77, 113, 115, 153, 159, 161

Schopenhauer, A. 166
Shell, S. 38, 173, 243, 245, 247 f.
Socrates 11, 63
Sturma, D. 24

Timmermann, J. 56, 136, 141

Vaihinger, H. 96

Wicks, R. 172
Willaschek, M. 46 f., 49
Williams, H. 228, 233, 242, 245
Wittgenstein, L. 50 f.

Wizenmann, T. 47
Wolff, C. 8
Wood, A. 4, 36, 63, 77, 84, 101 f., 108, 112, 114 f., 119, 121 f., 127 f., 140, 143, 145, 147, 149, 153, 155, 157–161, 164, 170, 178, 206, 210 f., 219, 223, 227 f., 231 f., 235 f., 242, 244, 249, 251, 253

Yovel, Y. 4, 6, 8, 12, 14, 45, 48 f., 62, 88, 103, 105, 110, 161, 163, 165 f., 170 f., 176 f., 179 f., 182, 185, 187, 192, 197–199, 205 f., 209, 213, 222–225, 229, 233, 235, 249 f., 252 f., 255

www.ingramcontent.com/pod-product-compliance
Lightning Source LLC
Chambersburg PA
CBHW050856160426
43194CB00011B/2177